DEEP PLAY

The purpose of the ladders is to convey the searchers to the niches. Those whom these entice no longer climb simply to get clear of the ground.

Samuel Beckett

PAUL PRITCHARD

Deep Play

A CLIMBER'S ODYSSEY FROM
LLANBERIS TO THE BIG WALLS

FOREWORD BY JOHN MIDDENDORF
ILLUSTRATIONS BY ANDY PARKIN

BÂTON WICKS · LONDON
THE MOUNTAINEERS · SEATTLE
1997

Deep Play is published simultaneously in Britain and America in 1997 by
Bâton Wicks Publications, London and The Mountaineers , Seattle.
© Paul Pritchard 1997.

All trade enquiries in Great Britain, Europe and the Commonwealth (except Canada) to
Bâton Wicks Publications, c/o Cordee, 3a De Montfort Street, Leicester LE1 7HD.

All trade enquiries in the U.S.A. and Canada to
The Mountaineers • Books, 1001 SW Klickitat Way, Suite 201, Seattle, WA 98134.

British Library Cataloguing in Publication Data
ISBN 1-898573-14-X   A catalogue record of this book is available in the British Library.

United States Library of Congress Catalog Data
ISBN 0-89886-565-4   A catalog record of this book is available at the Library of Congress.

Printed and bound in Great Britain by Hartnolls Ltd, Bodmin.

AUTHOR'S ACKNOWLEDGEMENTS Firstly I would like to thank Maggie Body, my editor, for helping me turn
something I wasn't so happy about into something I was. I am also indebted to John Middendorf for honouring
me with his Foreword and to Andy Parkin for his wonderfully enigmatic drawings which embellish the text.
Then I must thank Harold Wooley for teaching me how to climb and ruining my academic career. I am deeply
indebted to Gill Kent for having so much faith in my writing for so long. Thanks too to Gwion Hughes, George
Smith, Noel Craine, Jim Perrin and all my other mates for their reading and criticism and Greg Rimmer for his
work with my manuscript. The photographic spreads have been strengthened by the contributions of Tony Kay,
Bill Hatcher, Iwan Jones, Simon Yates, Ben Wintringham, Ken Wilson, Sean Smith and Alun Hughes to whom
I owe thanks. A thank you also to: the MEF and the BMC without whose financial help some of our trips might
not have happened; Ben Lyon for his continued support for my pie in the sky schemes; Glenn Robbins for saving
my life and Olly Saunders for finding us; Nick Kekus for saving it again and Robert Hester and Nick Burring for
coping so well on that awful day; Lochaber and Valley Rescue Teams and the Holyhead lifeboat crew for doing
their jobs so faultlessly; all my friends I have lived and climbed with and who have given me the raw material to
write about in this book. I would also like to show my gratitude to my parents for letting me be what I wanted
to be. Finally, thank you Celia for the love, the laughs, the tears, the support – for sharing the adventure. Cheers
Ed, Philip and Teo. My book is dedicated to those times.

Contents

COLOUR PHOTOS PLUS CLIFF DIAGRAMS IN THE TEXT

*All pictures by the author (or in the author's collection – taken on his camera
by his rope companion) unless otherwise credited*

LLANBERIS SLATE

Raped by Affection. *Tony Kay*; I Ran the Bath. *Tony Kay*;
Rainbow of Recalcitrance. *Iwan Jones*.

ANGLESEY SEA CLIFFS

Super Calabrese. *Ben Wintringham*; The Red Walls. *Ken Wilson*;
Enchanted Broccoli Garden. *Tony Kay – Pritchard collection*;
The Unrideable Donkey – two photos. *Tony Kay – Pritchard collection*.

SRON ULLADALE

The Scoop: Pritchard leads Pitch 1. *Alun Hughes*;
Pritchard and Dawes below the cliff. *Alun Hughes*;
Dawes on the Flying Groove pitch; Dawes on the final difficult pitch.
(Note: The first two pictures were taken at the time of the Knuckle Sandwich ascent.)

CENTRAL TOWER OF PAINE

The first ascent of El Regalo de Mwono: On the snow-covered slab apron. *Sean Smith*;
Above the Portaledge Camp. *Sean Smith*; The East and North-East Faces of the
Central Tower; The second aid pitch on the Great Scoop:
Jumaring up the Great Scoop. *Sean Smith*; Yates abseiling in a snowstorm;
Yates on the pitch below the Coffin. *Sean Smith*; Pritchard at the Portaledge camp;
Yates on the upper cracks. *Noel Craine*; Pritchard on the final aid pitch. *Sean Smith*.
Pritchard and Smith after a visit to Puerto Natales.

MT ASGARD, BAFFIN ISLAND

Hypoborea: The western flank of the Asgard tops; Yates, Pritchard and Craine in
the Boulder Camp; Craine free-climbing on the Great Flake;
Quinlan and Tosas on the first difficult aid section; Craine in the Portaledge Camp;
Quinlan leading the first corner pitch. Pitch 10 with Craine belaying;
Quinlan jumaring; The climbers on the summit; Abseiling down the face.

TRANGO TOWER

The Slovene Route from the Shoulder. *Bill Hatcher*; A group photograph;
The Trango Towers plastered with snow; Wainwright leads one of the
upper corners. Wainwright and Pritchard on the summit.

Foreword

by JOHN MIDDENDORF

Shortly after Paul Pritchard extended the honour to me of writing the foreword for his book, I had the opportunity to catch up with him for a climb of The Old Man of Hoy, a five-hundred foot sandstone stack on the sea cliffs of the Orkney Islands, a climb which for me has been a lifelong ambition. In fine Scottish weather, a drenching rain and fierce wind, we crouched on tiny stances far off the deck and chatted about the state of affairs. "Bit of a job lately," he told me of his most recent employment. "Been rappelling down a nuclear processing plant, sweeping out the dust in dark, deep chambers. Haven't felt well since the work ended." Paul is a natural story teller and always has an interesting tale, generally told in understated terms. We discussed different climbs around the world that we've mutually appreciated, and watched the sea waves pound on the rocky pedestal below us. It was good fun on the Old Man with Paul, terrified as I was after months at a desk, climbing the exposed, wet, and overhanging 5.8 and 5.10 crack pitches. We reached the summit toward dusk and shared the airy perch with dozens of calm puffins, who showed us their dance on the rims of the stack with magnificent hummingbird-like flight in the stiff ocean winds. I reflected on Paul's book and on the emotive side of climbing, and how an essay of such moments is a treat for the times when we are bound to the reality of terra firma, towards which we soon began to descend.

Although I had never before climbed with him, I was nevertheless not surprised when I noticed Paul's calm nerve on the stone. He belongs to an imaginative and talented group of individuals who I have had the pleasure to meet all over the world; people who share little in terms of cultural backgrounds, yet who have a common bond in their eclectic pursuit of a particular aspect of climbing. It is a group of folks who have honed a bold climbing style and who share an interest in the same thin strips of rock rearing up the most magnificent and giant rock walls on our planet. It is people who, in Paul's own words, share the experience of "the wind and the waiting" in the mountains. It is interesting how climbers with diverse languages, meeting perhaps in the Mountain Room Bar in Yosemite or maybe in a remote campsite on a tributary of the Baltoro Glacier, will discuss in detail each feature of a particular unclimbed line on a mountain which is thousands of miles away. The discussions share a common thread: a desire to find a wild place where climbing is the most intense and pure.

Paul's own realisations of such desire are on some of the world's biggest rock faces: Meru, the Central Tower of Paine, El Capitan, Mt Asgard. He captures the common essence of these climbs in stories of his adventures of bold climbs, long climbs, cold climbs, and insane climbs. In fine British tradition of pushing the limits of human endeavour on difficult rock routes in the mountains, Paul's climbs add to a rich history of British climbing which includes the original ascent of Trango Tower in 1976 by Martin Boysen, Mo Anthoine, Joe Brown and Malcolm Howells, the alpine-style push up the Golden Pillar of Spantik in 1987 by Mick Fowler and Victor Saunders, and the bold foray on Cave Man on the Cuerno de Paine by Twid Turner and Louise Thomas in 1993. Many of these climbers cut their teeth on the cliffs of North Wales and wild sea cliffs of Gogarth on routes of unmatched on-sight first ascent standards, and later took their bold techniques into the mountains.

The routes at Gogarth have always fascinated me – many times in my twenty-five years of climbing, I have seen the fear in climbers' eyes while talking about their hands-on experience with Gogarth routes. Preserved from the modern trend of grid-bolting due to the general rejection of bolts on the sea cliffs (an attitude enhanced possibly from the fact that any bolts would corrode instantly in the saline sea air) and safe from the current view that regards difficulty solely by its number, Gogarth has been the arena of several generations of the world's boldest routes. Paul's route Super Calabrese on the Red Wall, which he climbed in 1986, represents the extreme of ground-up climbing. The Gogarth guide says of the Red Wall, "This superb orange wall gives open climbing of a serious and often precarious nature. None of the routes should be treated without respect, the situation contributing its fair share of intimidation."

In the story Lost in the Broccoli Garden, Paul reflects after a Gogarth pitch, "I wasn't experiencing the anticipated satisfaction of completing such a frightening pitch. It was numbness." The guidebook lists the route with the notation, "a contender for the poorest belay on Gogarth". He explains the delicate experience of finding oneself in a crazy location, dependent only on one's mettle and driven by adrenaline, and finding the body and mind take over for the climb.

Paul Pritchard's tales are not only of the extreme intensity of bold routes, but also of the essential nature of the lifestyle. The book begins with "Fire Starter" a background of his childhood and the political and social atmosphere in which he grew up. The stories give insight to the motives of climbing extraordinary climbs, and tell of Paul and his mates as youths getting into the vertical in a world without limits, rife with lawlessness and little regard for personal safety, and with an immutable code of retaining the purest climbing style. He tells of a life of irreverence and a tad of decadence, that seeks the experience of utter dependence on craftiness and motivation. These stories link the common theme of the spirit's search for a purity of desire.

Deep Play is a collection of reflections on people and places, and of stories of deaths of close friends, and the experience of a brush with mortality. The author's sensitivity in seeing the true nature of his friends is captured spot-on with tales of other climbers: José Pepe Chaverri, Silvo Karo, Philip Lloyd, Teo Plaza, and others. The book is an analysis of a climber's mind, with the full realm of emotion. It's about sharing with new friends, and climbing new things and being in new places, on adventures where climbing the mountain is only half of the experience.

It is a rare and inspiring thing that such tales of intensity, joy, and suffering have been put onto paper, rather than the usual event of the magic being lost via a rough translation from mind to paper, or mere lack of documentation before the essence leaves the consciousness. Thank you, Paul, for reminding us about that magic, and congratulations for your finest timeless testpiece yet.

JOHN MIDDENDORF
San Francisco, 1997

[9]

Playing the System

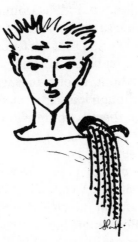

I AM DEFINITELY a climber who writes. I've always written about what I've done and how I felt about myself and those I went with. I have come home from trips with battered books full of scribblings, half of it illegible, self-indulgent babble. At home I have mulled things over, added reflection to the gut reaction of my diaries, and somehow ended up with finished pieces. But the rock has always come first.

Illness on return from trips has allowed me the time to create and smashed bones have also been kind to me, holding me back from my normal unquestioning frenzy of activity and forcing me to sit and think. Indeed I would not have found the time to put these writings together had I not suffered a broken back in Scotland. I used to be so single-minded. Girlfriends and great things I could have done were left behind as I kept searching for the perfect climb. Then, after I fell at Gogarth and momentarily died, I had so many questions to ask the night. I couldn't make any sense of it all and I began writing as an exorcism. At first I thought that moment of drowning felt too good and this terrified me but, as I wrote, I began to make some twisted sense of it all.

Most importantly, the trauma of the events which are documented in this book have helped me to grow and have taught me valuable very personal lessons. Falling at Gogarth revealed to me my position within humankind; as unimportant as anyone else. That insight allows me to treat all others as equal to myself more readily. There I also learned that death can be painless, yes, but more than that, utterly sublime. This simple knowledge has helped me reconcile the sad thoughts of friends who have died in pain, Ed and Philip and Teo, though it also revealed to me that death really was the end and that there is no time to waste in this short term that we have.

Joe Tasker and Menlove Edwards are two people who have inspired me to put pen to paper, Tasker for his honesty and Edwards for his sensitivity. I will never forget being shocked, as I first read *Savage Arena*, at the vivid description of the arguments which Tasker and Boardman had on their ascents, arguments which many climbers would try to hide for fear of causing offence and embarrassment. And the admission of the fact that their motivations often came from the less admirable corners of their psyche. What can I say about Edwards? Only that, for me, he transforms his insight into nature and the society around him onto paper better than any climber I know of. Nothing or no one seemed able to disguise anything from him. I admit to wanting to emulate their traits but, I hope, I keep my own style.

This is not a simple autobiography. I have tried to give a whole image of the existence and psyche of a climber from my generation, for I do not see myself as so unique within it, though of course 'A Game One Climber Played' and other moments in the book are very personal to me. This is why some of the chapters appear altered from what has been published in magazines. A magazine that readers dip into, not knowing what kind of excitement they are looking for, and so only happening across a piece of your life, is not the place for such intimate subjects, In a book, on the other hand, readers must go out and find, already knowing that they want to learn about you or read what you have to say.

The rock climber who learns his craft and then makes the transition to the mountains is less common now than in previous eras and so my stories of trips aren't perhaps so typical of my genre. But there are a number of us who, even though we might not have experienced it first hand, have roots in the past, have a great respect for the old pioneers and the evolution of our climbing lives would seem to mirror theirs to some extent.

My generation of climbers, the ones who began making their impact in the eighties, had their own peculiarities that set them apart from other generations. These differences were a result of social circumstances in the UK at the time. We had time on our hands and an opportunity to forfeit the worker's life and just go climbing. Some called us selfish. It was a world which produced a crop of British climbers in the early to mid-eighties who showed the world how it was done. I wouldn't be so bold as to rank myself alongside eighties sport climbers – Myles, Moon, or others who were of that new 'leisure class' – but in my own way I feel I've given something to climbing in Britain. I have threaded lines up mountains and sea cliffs and shown others where to go. It wasn't all selfish on my part; I have created steep, mind-testing challenges for climbers to stretch themselves out on. Asgard's velvet smooth wall, Paine's mile-long knife-blade crack, Meru's shark fin I needed to try. They were only imaginable for me after a decade of living for the rock every day, blowing off everything else. My need to get stronger, to use all my time struggling towards my dreams, even though I had no private wealth, is what some found disagreeable.

There was a letter sent in to an American climbing magazine once deriding me for "lacking in character" because I indulged my passion "at the expense of the British tax-payer by claiming the munificent British Dole". There are many of this opinion when it comes to judging the out of work. I would like a little room to explain the system I grew up in. I would like to give those people a portrait of the Lancashire of my youth.

In '79, after Callaghan lost, it could be said that the blanket attitude of the young began to change. By '83 there were 4,000,000 men and women unemployed, workers' morale was sinking. Companies won contracts by paying their workers less money for longer hours. The dismantling of the heavy industries and the move toward communications and finance sucked the life out of the industrial areas. This led to a widespread loss of respect for the Conservatives in my home, a northern mill town, which still endures today. To the north of Manchester the miners' strike brought communities to tears, as the collieries of Brackley, Ashtons Field and Hulton stood silent. But, for us youngsters, this was now the land of opportunity, the government told us anything could be ours. We were free to gamble, but if we failed, we would be at the bottom of the heap. When it came time to leave school most of my friends either signed on as unemployed or went on government job creation schemes. The ones that signed on had free time to develop sometimes obscure skills that seemed at first to have no use to the community. Later this would be seen not to be the case as, throughout the country, champion runners and cyclists and famous painters and writers emerged.

At Hulton some of our neighbours went through the picket lines to work because their families needed food. They compromised principles, though they agreed with the strikers' cause. Moral decay had been forced. Nationally this went even further as armaments became one of the biggest industries of the UK, our most marketable product, and who the buyer was didn't matter. How do climbers fit into this you may wonder? Out of the ashes of this social, economic and moral turmoil the full time climber rose like some scruffy, bedraggled phoenix to push the boundaries of what was possible on our crags, quarries and sea cliffs.

There had already been full-timers for a while then. Bancroft, a gritstone cult hero, was probably the original dole climber back in '77, followed by such masters as Allen and Fawcett who gave so much to us younger climbers. When I stood at the bottom of Beau Geste or Master's Edge I could see them moving just as I wanted to move. I wondered if I could ever be like them. Many then could still use university as an excuse to climb. Grants were good and it gave lots of free time, and a chance for MacIntyre and Rouse to become such great mountaineers. Later, as grants decreased, students even had to work their summer holidays (as they still do) and the university life became less appealing to the dedicated climber.

As the young athletes strove to ascend wilder and wilder rock climbs the endeavour became more time-consuming. They had to train long and hard to develop the power needed to create these masterpieces. These climbers paid little thought to the politicans in Westminster, who were inadvertently creating an environment most suitable for the serious climber – with so many unemployed it was easy to sign on. How could they prove you weren't actively seeking work if there wasn't any work to be found? And it became easy to justify too; you could go out to the sea cliffs self-righteous in the knowledge that another was working and feeding his family as a result of your sacrifice! We did look for work, me and my friends, but we were not going to go into a factory after the freedom we had tasted. That no jobs were ever offered to us by the job centre, as was the system, only reflected the economic circumstances of the country, especially in the rural areas of Wales. So why should I not use my time to go climbing? It now seems ironic that my passion contributed to the transformation of the gigantic Dinorwig slate quarries, the scar left after the community was near fatally wounded by its closure. Together we unemployed bums created, from what was once a thriving place of work, and then a vast, silent ugly space, a place of leisure for the weekend climber. And it was hard, dangerous graft, let me tell you, the clearing of loose rock and the drilling, just like the quarrymen had once done. Harder than any desk job I used to think.

But the dole handout or the government climbing grant, as we called it, paid very little. For my first two years as a full-timer, living in the Stoney Middleton wood shed or in caves around the Peak, I received eighteen pounds a week. I had to buy and sell, borrow and steal to get a rack and feed myself. We lived in the dust on a diet of cold beans and white bread. They banned us from the pub because we didn't spend enough and they thought we would give the other customers our flu. It was a gamble climbing on the dole, to deprive yourself of all those potential luxuries for the sake of pushing up the grades. Most of my old school mates had cars and girlfriends by then. And what if you didn't make it? What would you do in ten years time if you got injured and you had no education or trade to fall back on? I still wonder. But I don't regret forfeiting the career and the consumer durables.

Some of the route names of those days celebrated the unprecedented situation in which climbing found itself, which couldn't have come about in a more healthy economic state. Doleman, Dole Technician, Dolite, Long Live Rock and Dole. One of the ardent Stoney dossers, Dirty Derek, said he'd vote Tory again to ensure he'd get another four years of Giros! But the dossers have gone now. Their generation only really lasted a decade. A climber on the dole is scum in the eyes of many now. New rules have made it tough to stay signed on for any length of time and to be a traveller, like many US climbers, is not an accepted way to live. They put barriers up in Britain and signs, NO OVERNIGHT PARKING. Now many climbers aspire to wealth and sponsorship and a sporty car as an escape from the trap of conformism. They want to attain what their heros have attained. But neither type, not the doley nor the new professional ever escapes. They both play the system.

It is acceptable to be a student, to study philosophy or art, and you can receive a meagre grant, but to filter out a little money to create great lines up cliffs is, in the eyes of some, morally wrong. It doesn't quite adhere to the system which we manufactured. What does appear ironic now is that those unemployed, who appeared of no use to the community, having perfected their craft, were seen on the pages of magazines and in advertisements. They were transformed into heroes who helped to sell the equipment the manufacturers were producing and so, inadvertently, became an indispensable part of the system they thought they had dropped out of.

To live the life we chose we rode on the wealth of others, just like the explorers of old and these, surely, must command all our respect. Shipton, Tilman, even Darwin made their journeys of discovery using the riches of the empire – from exploitation of conquered lands. They were of the original leisure class which will always be with us. They have been around for ever, almost. The working-class climbers slowly came on the scene from the thirties to the fifties. They were hard men who gained fame on the outcrops near their city homes. After the war there were enough jobs for everyone and their ascents could be made in a day or two at the weekend. As the boom babies grew up job opportunities diminished and the seventies brought the new leisure class, rebels with a rock hard cause. And now, are we heading back to the beginning? You can climb Everest if you have enough cash. Or perhaps you would prefer Antarctica or Irian Jaya? It was said in the eighties that at either end of the economic spectrum there was a leisure class. Through unemployment the poor had the time to have their adventures, albeit on a smaller scale, on the rock outcrops close to their homes. Now, in the nineties, this may still be true but the opportunities open to the lower leisure class would seem to be restricted somewhat when compared to how it was a decade ago.

As the economy of our island grows again and more restrictions are put on our welfare state the unemployed climber is becoming a thing of the past. Now you'll see less and less of our type. I knew some real characters dossing on that Peak District garage forecourt we called The Land of the Midnight Sun. They lived for the rock and material gain never really entered their heads. I think when we opened the door for the new professionals some of those characters slipped out the back.

Crack

Fire-Starter

I WAS BORN on top of the quarry. It was the best place to mess about a kid could ever want. I never had to go to my mates' houses to play, 'cos they would always come here if I said let's go in the quarry. It was a glowing green hole in the moors. It was my Grand Canyon, my Amazon, my centre of the earth and my one million years BC. I had seen Tyrannosaurus fighting with Stegosaurus, flying saucers with deathrays, and even a ghost – a yellow custardy thing. That ghost gave me such bad dreams that I shat in my bed when it drifted across our best room towards me.

If you leaned out of our bathroom window, the cliff went sheer down to the scrappers' yard and me and my mates used to push bits of our garden wall over the edge so the rocks would land and crash on the pile of dead cars and corrugated tin below. We'd count one ... two ... three ... f ... always a little too fast. But then the scrapper would come up and him and my old man would shout at each other. Another good one was to stand and pee over the edge and see if you could see it reach the bottom by leaning out more and more, but you had to have good balance for that. There was one tree that tilted out right over the drop and we would climb it, up into the thin top branches and look straight down a hundred feet. We could get the whole tree moving like mad if a few of us started swaying. We even made a death swing out over the cliff, but that disappeared one day.

In the dry summer I sometimes nicked a box of Swan Vestas, we always had matches on us, and we would set the grass on fire on top of the cliff. It always got out of control really fast. We tried to put them out, the fires, but we all secretly wanted the whole moor to burn 'cos when it got too big we'd all laugh and betcha whether the fire engines would come or not. When we heard the sirens we'd all get dead excited and run off, but not too far, so we could hide behind a wall and see the fire brigade beating at the grass. But once we got caught after we'd burnt a derelict hospital down and the pig said the arsonist always returns to the scene of the crime. Me, Lloydy and Cooksy were bricking it but they couldn't prove anything. It's just it was the same ones who caught us after we'd tied the elastic across the road and it had twanged their aerial, so they were suspicious.

But down inside the quarry it was all shady and cool and we would get goose bumps as we sat and chewed the white roots of the couch grass which tasted of summer. Heather tickled the backs of our grass-stained legs and we sprinted off, with our hands and feet, up ledgy rocks. To the top of Cleveland's Edge we would go, a thin finger of rock miles high sticking out into the quarry, only three feet wide at the end. We would play tig on it, and if you didn't stand right on the end you were a big girl's blouse. But the ramp up the front was the best dare. We knew a kid had fallen off the top and died but that didn't stop us. The whole gang of us would swarm up, sometimes standing on each other's shoulders to reach the next shelf. In summer the rocks were dusty, but in winter they were green and slippy – and you'd always have soaked keks before you got to the bottom, from the long grass and heather. Once, trying to get onto a ledge that all the others were on, with the rocks all sloping the wrong way, they started lobbing matches at me. I shouted, "Quit it. Quit it!" and after we got on top I hated them. I got my own back another day though, when I set a plastic bag on fire and dropped zippers, that's what we called the dripping plastic, on Sucks' kid brother while he was stuck on a ledge. He hadn't done anything to me but he was the easiest to pick on – even Sucks kicked him in all the time.

My dad used to tell me stories of when he was in the army. Of Egypt, the Pyramids and Petra. Down in the quarry the towers of rock became great sitting Ramases and Sphinx, the mill-wheels spare parts for Egyptian chariots. The slag heaps became burial mounds which I excavated in search of treasure and mummified bodies. I had my tool kit in a canvas satchel, with trowels and brushes for clearing the dirt off potential precious objects, and a ball of string. During one excavation, at the entrance of a definite burial chamber, we found a stack of nude books which we all gathered round, pointing at the pictures and giggling confusedly. We hid them and came back most evenings for kind of club meetings, but when we came back one day someone had nicked them.

My old man didn't like me going to school. He said I would learn more walking on the moors with him. He never really went to school when he was a kid and he said he was better for it. So we'd go off in the early morning with the shotguns along the edge of the hole, shooting at whatever we saw. Besides rabbits, hares and pigeons, we shot blackbirds, peewits, geese and even, once, a fox. We ate everything but the fox tasted horrible. The worst time was when he went mad at me 'cos I looked inside the barrel of the shotgun when it was loaded. "What the bloodyellfire," he shouted, pulling the 12-bore out of my hands. Once, on top of Cleveland's Edge we saw a family of owls, a mother and three babies. We just sat and watched them. We didn't want to shoot them. They were the best things I'd ever seen. After that I got really into watching the birds and didn't want to shoot them any more. A bit later I remember crying when he shot a kestrel. I held it in my hand and it was so soft and still warm. Its blood trickled down my hand.

It was the same kestrel whose eggs I once nicked when me and my brother still had our big collection. It took us ages to work out

how to get to the nest. We'd known where it was for ages, miles up
the cliff, but only a stupid get would climb down there. But then
we nicked some bailing twine from Locker's barn and I was
lowered over the edge. It was all grass and loose rocks and the
twine dug into my kidneys. At the nest I was mesmerised, the eggs
were so perfect. I put them both in separate pockets and scrambled
back up with the gang pulling from above. Later we made pinprick
holes in each end of the eggs and blew them into a saucer. Then
we proudly set them in their right place in the collection, in their
bed of sawdust between the thrush egg and the crow's egg.

In the winter-time we lived in Spain. It was great 'cos it meant
that I didn't have to go to school. I laughed about all the others
back at home in school and here was our Dave and Trace and me
doing what we wanted every day, playing on the beach or fishing
or adventuring. We lived eleven storeys up in some apartments,
right above the cemetery. Sometimes we'd be having our dinner
and there'd be a funeral going on down below. Once me and our
Dave went exploring in there and saw these dirty hunchbacked
men digging up all the graves. There were coffins and piles of
bones everywhere. We started to go nearer for a closer look but
this grave-digger saw us and picked up a skull and ran at us with
it. We started legging it and my heart was beating dead fast and
then this skull came bouncing past me. We told our mum and she
told us not to go in there again.

Me and our Dave used to fight a lot but he was six years older
than me so I always got paggered. But he tormented me so much
that I'd get my own back on him by stealing his spends. He got
really angry with me once 'cos I had told on him for drawing
pictures of people with no clothes on and when mum and dad
went out he picked me up and dangled me by the ankles over the
balcony. I stopped shouting and wriggling and just went quiet as
I stared down for hundreds of feet. He dragged me back over but I
didn't cry, I just looked at him, and he said that if I told I would get it.

Back home we had pigs and hens and rabbits, too, and my
dad showed us how to slaughter them. My sister wouldn't get
involved, but me and our Dave loved it. We killed the rabbits by
chopping them on the back of the neck but they didn't always die

straight away. The hens were easier, you just twisted their necks and sometimes they would run around with their heads flopping around. Once a year we had to kill our pigs and to save money my dad didn't take them to the slaughter-house. One Sunday morning, dead early, we went up to the pen. The farmer had told dad that if you draw a line with a magic marker between the pig's ears and eyes and hit it spot on with a pick-axe, the thing will die in a second. So my dad crept up to it and whacked the pick into its head, but it went mad and started screaming. It tore the axe out of his hand and ran about the pen. Its howling was like a baby. It was horrible. My dad picked me up and ran out of the pen with me and told me to get the gun. He was worried 'cos he said the bloody neighbours might call the bloody police. I ran like mad back up the steps with the 12-bore and the cartridges. Pinky, that's the name our Trace gave the pig, was still screeching and the axe handle was waving around in the air. My dad loaded the gun, aimed it and fired. He's a good shot, my dad. Pinky shut up straight away and fell on its face and my dad was pleased 'cos he'd shot it right in the heart. We tied a rope around its head and lifted it into a bath for cutting up. As me and our Dave pulled on the rope, dad chopped at Pinky's neck with his Bowie knife and we went flying backwards as its head came off. Our Trace didn't like eating bacon for breakfast after that.

Most of Bolton's joyriders dumped their night's fun in the quarry, too, and we would always be first there to strip off all the useful scrap. Even the windscreens and seats we got for our dens, but we never found a suitcase of dosh in the boot. If they hadn't already been burnt we would set them on fire and run off to hide nearby and watch the black smoke rising. Running through the quarry I cut my knee open on glass. It didn't hurt, but I still cried. The blood tasted of metal. Suddenly I hated the quarry and wanted my mum to wash the cut. Back home in the cool cave of our dining room it took a while for my eyes to get used to the darkness. She put a sticking plaster on my cleaned up knee, ruffled my hair, and got back to top and tailing gooseberries. I limped back out into the heat, proud of my wound, to eat slugs and horse muck for 10p dares off my mates.

We found a brand new shiny rope on the floor behind Cleveland's, and some other stuff, but we just took the rope and sneaked off up our secret path. We made a massive death slide in Bluebell forest which should have been ace but the stupid rope stretched and you hit the ground.

I always saw climbers on the walls. They were just part of the quarry, up there for ages, not moving and shouting signals to each other. It was then that I found out how to make petrol bombs and I loved throwing them off the top of the cliff. There was one time I did something really daft and threw one down at a bunch of climbers. The milk bottle smashed on the cliff face and fire showered down on them. They started pointing and shouting and I ran for it with my heart beating dead fast.

We went back with the stretchy rope and tied it to the top of the cliff face. Then we threw the rest off and went round to the bottom. We swarmed up the rope one at a time. trying to be like the climbers, but it cut into our hands. Then one of the climbers came over with a proper helmet on and everything and said he'd take us up a route. We weren't sure what a route was but he tied the rope around our waists with a proper climber's knot and showed us how to use the cracks and that with our hands and feet. It was loads easier than trying to grab the rope.

❄

We had to leave the big old house when mum and dad split up and go into a flat on the main road in town, above a hairdressers. But I still wagged off school and went up over the moors to the quarry. I took new mates with me though. I'd lost touch with my old ones. Cooksy had moved to another town and Lloydy had killed himself joyriding. He got drunk on cider and nicked a car and when the pigs came after him he hit a tree going dead fast. I can't drive. We'd take cider and drink it as fast as we could and lie in the warm heather 'till late, our mothers wondering where we were. Three days a week the gun club would come to the quarry. Grown Lancashire men dressed as American cops, shades and bomber jackets. They'd chew gum and shoot automatic pistols at cardboard cutouts of people. When they stopped to change cartridges we'd shout "Waaaaankeeeeers" ... and leg it.

We saw a man chasing a woman around the slag heaps and we crawled over to the edge. They lay down behind Cleveland's Edge, amidst the tin cans and whirlpools of crisp packets, and she pulled up her skirt. We watched them doing it for a while, biting our collars to stop the giggles, but shy too, in front of each other, with longing. Then Judd shouted something and we rolled on our backs laughing so much that we couldn't breathe. I saw our house at the end of the quarry with strangers in the garden, and stopped smiling. We walked back along Scout Road, the lovers' lane from where you can see the whole of Manchester, Jodrell Bank space telescope and right across to the Snowdon mountains, where we played spot the used johnny, and where we once saw a car rocking to and fro with a pair of bare feet at the window. I didn't want to go back there. I went to town instead 'cos that's where my new mates hung out. We did loads of shoplifting. We'd nick anything for a laugh and sometimes have to run out of Woolys or somewhere being chased by security, and we'd turn our jackets inside out and our hats around as a disguise. We moved on to half bottles of Bells and hung around the town centre, drunk. We acted like stupid buggers when we were drunk. "When all the lights are flashin' we're goin' Paki bashin'" a bunch of skins were singing. They were old lads, maybe eighteen. I shouted something to them, I don't remember what, and they ran over and swiped me round the head with a bike chain. When I went down they all put the boot in and I woke up in some woods, bruised and all covered in dry blood. I told my mum I'd fallen out of a tree. She always pretended to believe me.

I didn't like the secondary school. I'd never really been to school that much before 'cos we always lived in Spain in the winter and my mum would teach me the stuff I needed to know. The white kids called me Paki because of my tanned skin. They were just jealous. But I did have my mates and we'd wag off together and go and play space invaders or go robbing. So I don't know why I jumped down the stairs. I just looked down the well, four storeys from Mr Wooley's Physics lab, like a spiral tunnel, and slid over. I didn't want to kill myself – more like I did it to live, to prove I could do it. I knew I could do anything and I'd jumped off loads of things for dares. But that wasn't for a dare. Something gripped me as I stared over the edge. Something drew me over and I knew I wouldn't hurt myself. A teacher saw me as I was clambering over the rail and moved to stop me, so I just let go and dropped. I saw his face recede into the distance. The banisters echoed as I bounced between them and my hands ripped as I clutched at them. I remember seeing Wingnut on my way past and trying to shout to him, but my breath was taken. I remember hitting a big grey radiator down in the pool changing area and seeing the red floor tiles for a second, but nothing else. I woke up in hospital. At first I couldn't move. My body was rigid and aching. I trembled. My hands were all torn and bandaged, like after I'd jumped I'd regretted it and was trying to stop myself. I think I do that a lot, throw myself into things and then wish I hadn't. It's hard to believe I didn't break anything and I was back at the school in a few days, but I kept having these breakdowns where I'd start crying and shaking. But everyone wanted to be my mate then and they even put metal studs on all the banisters in the school, like a special memorial to me.

I wasn't good at games and when we had to go on cross-country I'd always throw up, or we'd sneak off to Judd's house, which was on the circuit, and smoke a fag. We got caned for that when they caught us. But then they had this new scheme where we could go rock climbing with Mr Wooley instead of getting killed trying to play rugby. I thought it was great. I hadn't been up to the quarry for ages and every week we did a different climb from the guidebook. I wanted to do every climb in that book, each with its own name and grade, either jamming or chimneying or laybacking. Some of the lads hated it, getting scared and dirty and the midges and everything, but I wanted it to go on loads longer. I loved the taste of that dust from the rock, just like when I was a kid, and I knew these holes like the back of my hand. Now I was sitting on ledges that I could never get to before.

I went and bought a pair of proper rock boots and started traversing around the walls after school. Sometimes I met climbers who would take me up a route on Cleveland's Edge, the climbers called it The Prow, and sometimes I brought my sleeping bag and kipped on top of the crag. I went and looked over the garden wall of our old house, I had to, and they had pulled up the fruit bushes and chopped down the orchard to make a lawn. The giant oak I swung in with my farm mates had been chopped down, and one of those new estates had been built. It made me feel hollow inside, but it was easier to let go of now that they had made it ugly and all the nooks and crannies of adventure had been demolished.

❄

On a summer's day, just before they sent me on the Youth Training Scheme, I was sat in the familiar heather, picking hardened chalk from behind my fingernails with a piece of grass, when I noticed a thin man bobbing along the top of the crag with a sack on his back. He stopped, peered over the edge and then climbed down a smooth overhanging face. I flicked through the guidebook and stopped at the right page: The Grader, E3! I didn't know this sort of climber existed. I saw him another time, with some friends, climbing up and down a leaning wall again and again, with the sack on like last time. I kept my distance, like I was scared of these superclimbers, but they called me over and explained to me that they were training and the bag was full of rocks. John, Tony and Monksy said if I did the same I'd get better, too. That was it. I quit the scheme after fighting with the care-taker of the technical college I was at. He broke my nose with his broom handle. I spent all my time in the quarry, traversing there and back and trying all the problems the superclimbers had shown me. Before long I was going up and down The Grader, too, with my other dole mate, Phil, and a bag of rocks.

At sixteen I was in the Black Dog with the hard guys, nursing tired, bloody hands and supping bitter. Monksy was telling a story of when they were all bouldering, years ago mind, and some kid lobbed a petrol bomb over the crag, right at them. They didn't find him but if they had, they would have given him a right good hiding.

[29]

2

Rubble Merchants, Slateheads and Others

Wales, 1987

CIGARETTE BUTTS, crumpled beer cans, the Captain's been on the sofa for weeks. The carpet's still damp under stocking feet since the pipes burst in the winter. No gas, no fifties for the leccy meter, no window in the front door, hardly any food in the cupboard and no one's washed up for a month. But there's thirty bottles of spirits in the kitchen. Sell some of them and we'll have some dosh. It's daft having all those bottles of evidence in here though. The house is dark and smells of sweat and breath and mould. A muffled cough comes from upstairs. I creep up there for the bog. The door to Carlos's room is lying on the floor. That's it, I remember, Gwion kicked it in last night to make him go and sort Karen out who had put a bottle through the front door window and was making a scene in the street. The broken glass crunches under my All Stars as I step outside. The sun's been up for ages and pricks hot needles into my eyes. Spring's doing its thing now and the Snowdon railway whistles good morning. Its sulphur smell catches my nose. I'm uneasy on my feet down the steep hill of Rallt Goch. I spit as I turn into Goodman Street and ruffle my hair. That wakes me up a bit. The kids in the park slide and swing with their young mums. There's the Professor. He makes me shiver as he stops and watches the children through the mesh fence. All those things you hear are only rumour though. You've not to forget that around here.

I grind the gravel of the pavement under my shoes. It feels real – more real than anything that happened last night. In Pete's Eats the tea's too hot for my lips. I hunch quietly and watch the others through the steam. There's the Fly, bent over his plate. He's called that because he sometimes throws his food up and then eats it again. But I don't think he'll do that this morning. The Lobster looks as though he's had a long night. I try and avoid the Lobster, all red and shiny, short in his long robbing coat. He'll get anything for you, dead cheap. Give him your order in the café and he comes back half an hour later with the goods. Pulled two ice axes out yesterday and dropped them on the table. They say he's the most well endowed man in the village. I rub my eyes and try and push the hideous image out of my mind. The juke box is playing Jimmi Hendrix too loud and the smell of burnt liver makes me gag.

"Number twelve. Fried egg and beans."

"Yeah, that's me."

Women, aged before they should have, sag at the next table and push Embassy Regals into their mouths, tired of it all. Their husbands are in the betting office. They'll meet up at the chippy and chatter in a high pitch Creole of Welsh and English. Dafydd Chips, the second biggest boy in the village, will scoop their deep fried offerings into newspaper packets for them to rush home with up the steep side of Llanber'. Meeta comes in. Looking happy, she snaps her tobacco tin down on the table top. I have to hang on her words at this hour to decode her Swiss accent and she entrances me with tales of Bolivian jails and Indian mystics. I gaze outside and imagine distant places.

Rain is spitting onto the glass now. Looks like another slate day.

[32]

The slate's best when it's showery, it dries in minutes. It's where it's all been happening of late, why I came here. I saw a picture of a moustachioed, muscley guy manteling these tiny edges, trying to put both feet next to his hands, grinding his nose into the purple rock, and not a runner in sight. Now I'm living with him, Carlos they call him because of his Spanish waiter looks, and Gwion. They're letting me doss there till I find a place of my own. No luck yet though, and I've been there six months. We did have an ace place before but we got kicked out after we got caught with a pin in the meter.

I asked Carlos about the photo and he told me he'd fallen off just after it was shot and went sixty foot. When I got here the slate scene was already big. The days when the mysterious Rainbow Slab was spoken about in hushed voices, a top secret location, were near since gone. The falls you could take off the hard slate routes were already legendary and I wanted to take one. I didn't have to wait long before I was emulating Redhead and Carlos by falling eighty feet off a new route I was trying, drunk on the Rainbow. When I came to a stop, four feet off the ground with my nine ripped nuts stacked on the rope at my waist and Gwion higher up the crag than I was, I was content, and later bruised. I need to buy some chalk.

The sky is sagging and dark now and the village seems to be resonating at a low frequency. The Lard (the biggest boy in the village)'s new van is throbbing to house tunes and he's sat inside his shell suit on double yellows, menacing. Last week he knocked Manic Ben over, right there in the street, in front of everyone. I don't return his stare. I must take care not to tread in dog shit on the pavement. There's Tatan on the other side of the street, "Hi, Tat." He looks ghastly. The other week on the way back from a day trip to Dublin, lashed up, the lads ripped his clothes off him and threw them overboard into the Irish Sea. He's always the brunt of their jokes, but they love him really. When he showed up at customs starkers, and the officials had to kit him out with a too small pair of nylon football shorts, they all had a good laugh. Climbers in yellow and pink tights and ripped jumpers are in the street, some live here, some are visiting. They pace around like

[33]

peacocks, too colourful for a dark Welsh village. The old quarry men don't know what to make of them. The young locals react against them. I got pushed around in the street after hours a couple of times, but Gwion's a good man to know. He's a local himself, one of the few who hasn't gone the other way and doesn't want anything to do with the mountains. He's our mediator. He let the guys know I was OK and now I can drink a pint with the same blokes who hated me before. Outsiders aren't always accepted here, especially big-time climbers with inflated egos. I've become the same, wary of newcomers, safe in our group.

Some try too hard to be accepted. One guy, the Weird Head we called him, who appeared for a while, said he'd base jumped the Troll Wall. He just wanted to fit in, that was all. When Bobby confronted him and told him that we knew he hadn't, he broke down and sobbed. There's a lot of crazy people here, people who can't sit still. The place is like a magnet, and for some there's this perceived pressure to be crazy too. The ones that try too hard don't seem to last long, they disappear. This old slate mining village has many good people. It just seems unavoidable that it should make winners and losers.

There's a distant brass band and a voice from a tannoy. It's carnival day. I'll run up the hill and wake the guys and head across to Vivian or up to The Lost World maybe. "Yahoo, guys. Who wants to climb?" Gwion's psyched. Carlos isn't moving – he's turned nocturnal, stays in his room all day reading horror stories. Gwion apologises for hitting me last night (I was only trying to stop him from slashing his wrists on the broken glass) and then we're back out on the street. The carnival floats by, children in outfits with paint all over them looking self-conscious and, at the head of it all, this year's carnival queen. Graham Sis they call him, a fat man, very effeminate in his long red halter-neck. He drifts by waving in his lipstick, his dream come true. The village is heaving now and we hurry across the fields toward the big holes.

In the quarry they're all there; new routes going up all the time. Things getting repeated and talked about. The Captain's having a tormegamite experience on something loose as hell, sweeping as he goes. The Dawes is trying a horizontal double dyno with his

[34]

tongue sticking out the side of his mouth. There's JR creeping up the rock, thinking about genitalia. Nicky is psyching up for her ninety foot leap into the steel black water of the pool and Skeletor is wrapping his vast ape index around the purple rock. The Giant Redwood is on a rope, trundling blocks to uncover a modern classic. Harms the Stickman prances up the Rainbow looking unhealthy (how can he do this on his diet of chip butties and Newcastle Brown?). The Horn pops in and flexes his tattooed biceps on Colossus Wall. Moose is soloing like a maniac 'cos his girlfriend's left him and Bobby's bouncing around like a thing on a spring. And there's the Tick, recording all these antics through the lens and turning them into history. Uncle Alan watches from the bridge and reminisces about the thirties, when he was blasting and pulling the slate out of there. He warns us of the dangers, the giant rock falls, but he's glad to see the quarry alive again. It's why Llanberis exists and why it had prospered for a hundred years, until the sixties, when it shut down and all the men had to look elsewhere. That's why, now, so many shops are boarded up around here. But this is a real village, with real struggles, not tarted up, making concessions for the tourists.

There'll be teams out on the island today, it'll be baking out there. I feel like I'm missing out teetering around in this man-made scar, and for a moment I want to be above the sea, brushing lichen off crimps with my finger tips, searching for ways through uncharted territory, studied by seals. But you can't be two places at once and it could be worse. I could have a job. Big G and the Waddy will be out there with car inner-tube knee pads on, barring their way across some incomprehensible ceiling with sea-reflected sunshine dancing on their backs in a dark cavern. Pengo and Manuel could be taking a trip to the moon on the Yellow Wall and the Crook will have invented new jargon with which to describe an obscure nook or cranny which will be the scene of an even more obscurely named new route. Tombs the mathematician could be with him. "No money, no job, no girlfriend. Might as well be dead," he had said. Ben and Marion will still be on Red Walls, moving in and out of the quartz, smooth and solid after all these years. And there'll be Craig, making his name in a splash of colour as the sun sinks into a receding tide. Up in the mountains Cloggy is turning gold and Mr Dixon will be up there doing his own thing on the cathedral of rock.

So as hands tire and blood sugar levels drop in the twilight, the climbers home back to Llanberis, to eat badly and rush for last orders. In the Padarn they're all drinking – the farmers, the girls from the chemist and the Co-op, the hairdressers and the builders, the walkers and the climbers. That builder I've seen doing one-arm pull-ups on a door frame at a party and laughing at the supposed climbers who couldn't get near it. And there's big Tommy forcing his weight against the bar, as if trying to stop it toppling over, as he sinks his pints. Gabwt's standing on a chair shouting *"Hash for cash"* with his Nunchakas in his hands, terrifying those who don't know him, as merrymakers sneak out to the Broccoli Garden for some extra stimulation. That's Dewi playing pool. He killed the vicar with the end of a snapped off pool cue that looked very much like the one he's holding now. Once he was beating Bobby at a game when Bobby remarked without thinking, "Bloodyhell, Dewi, you're a killer with a pool cue!" We all stepped back and waited for the explosion, but he mustn't have heard 'cos he just missed the black and sat down. Those climbers over there are standing cool and not talking about routes and moves, even though they want to. I ask Johnny for the numbers on some route or other up the Pass. "Three, five, two, eight, one," he says and makes me feel about this small. But me, Carlos and Gwion are buzzing. We downed a load of our spirits before coming in 'cos we haven't any cash to buy drinks. Those Giros only seem to last a day or so and then you're skint for a fortnight until you post your next slip in. Tonight's dinner was a rotting cauliflower that we got from the Co-op for 10p, boiled up with five strands of pasta and a stock cube which we found in the bottom of the cupboard. We called it cauliflower surprise. But Carlos has usually got some scam or petty crime worked out to keep us in food and other stuff. Never mind. Tonight people will be queueing to buy vodka and gin and tomorrow we can eat full sets in Pete's. As last orders is screamed out Kenny the Turk erupts in a fury and starts spinning a cast iron table around his head. The crowd sweeps backwards in a wave and tries to paste itself to the nicotine-stained walls of the room. The guy who has fallen out of his wheel-chair in the crush pulls out a baseball bat and lashes out at anybody who tries to help him. For a moment things are completely out of control until Ash the barman, five ten and thin as a rake, gets in there and calms the Middle-Eastern stand-up comic's temper. Just another night in the Pad really.

Out in the street drunks mumble to themselves, dossers look for dosses and the partiers want to know where 'the scene' is. So it's off to some terraced house under an orange street lamp to try and prolong the day, wishing sleep would never have to come. The house is throbbing with the beat and those inside are giggling and dancing and you can tell, by the look in their eyes, that some people will be up all night. But if you eat those 'shrooms you won't get to Gogarth tomorrow, you'll sit around and waste your day away. Next to some hot knives on the stove we swap our stories of bricking it miles out, or talk of the moves on some slate horror and how you should try it like this or like that next time. But some of the others are bored by your keenness and wish you would shut up and you suddenly feel self-conscious as the herbs take effect. You realise you've overdone it and are incapable of speech, and the girl you've wanted to work up the courage to ask is talking with that other guy. So you leave for home without saying your goodnights, tripping over your own feet as you head down the hill. In the dark house you get into your pit, lie on your back and drift off, your head swimming, dreaming about tomorrow.

3

Lost in the Broccoli Garden

It was a vile day and the gigantic breakers from the Irish sea were surging halfway up the 400-foot wall, drenching the cliff top with spray. I came away with vivid impressions of dripping, disintegrating granite set at a thought-provoking angle.

Tom Patey commenting on Gogarth's Red Walls, *Climbers' Club Journal*, 1966

IT WAS IN 1986 that the hard climbers returned to Gogarth, and in that year an insular band of the young and not-so young subjected the 'Mother of all rock' to a bombardment of frightening and characterful new routes. That same year my intense relationship with the Red Walls began.

There are two Red Walls, a left one and a right one. High, vertiginous, wedge-shaped sheets of ancient quartzite, separated by a knife-edge promontory. The oldest rock in Britain some say. The right-hand wall became public property in 1966 when its first ascent went out on television, live. The show was called *Cliffhangers* and involved the likes of Joe Brown, Ian McNaught-Davis, Royal Robbins and Tom Patey. This wall is a contorted and sensuously confusing place to be. Parallel shallow dykes of sandy, horned grovelling nearly always lead the climber into a cul-de-sac and the shape of the wall is perspectively deceiving, luring you over the edge when you stop at the tourist viewpoint.

The left-hand wall is different. A crimson headboard to the sea bed. From a distance the upper two-thirds appear featureless and ill at ease atop the lower third, a warped and undercut wave of a soft grey chalky substance. To be on the wall is to be on a vertical desert of pocketed rock, and as a desert, seething with hidden life. Sea slaters and springtails disperse in all directions from behind the odd loose hold and the face is also host to some huge spiders (likened to my prematurely aged digits). Rare flora also abounds; round comfortable cushions of green cling to the wall which is also one of the few haunts of the Mad Sea Broccoli.

I'd only been to Gogarth once before, when I'd waltzed up Positron, stopping occasionally to gaze into the exposure. I'd laughed and shook my head in disbelief all the way. Then, looking for an enjoyable climb to finish the day on, Gwion [Hughes] and I rapped into the Red Walls for the first time. After being puked on by an ugly ball of fluff, we crouched at the bottom of the route Mein Kampf. Uninspiringly, the first pitch looked quite horrific, but looks can be deceiving. They weren't. It was a loose and awful climb to the belay ledge and then it was my turn to puke through a mixture of the smell and the terror. We escaped up the wall's namesake and vowed never to return. That night in the Padarn, over calming beers, one of the older guys revealed to us that Mein Kampf hadn't been repeated after seven years. So that was it, we were back there the next day, climbing a little direct variation too. For me it was love at second sight.

When sprawled out in comfort on the belay ledge of Left-Hand Red Wall it's hard to miss the hanging flake of Schittlegruber*. I was gobsmacked to learn that no one had climbed that flake so I rapped in and inspected it. I found an overhanging scoop with

* A pun on Schicklgruber – Hitler's family name.

only a meagre scattering of holds leading up to the jagged shield of the flake. The scoop looked hard and difficult to protect and, once again, looks weren't deceiving. The climb [with N. Harms] went OK, I was taking well to this type of climbing, and the line came to be one of the classic hard routes of the island. It was repeated quickly, for Gogarth, by Yorkshire men Dave Green and Clive Davis who likened it to Gordale Scar's Mossdale Trip, a famous tottering pile of limestone. I wondered whether this was complimentary or not.

The wall drew me further in, to the central sweep right of the Heart of Gold. Rappeling down and discovering continuous lines of pockets and seams, it was like unwrapping a surprise parcel. And once I'd torn it open it was just the gift I'd been waiting for. In 280 feet I managed to find one peg placement, a poor downward-pointing knife-blade, which would have to serve as a belay. With Moose [M. Thomas] I descended to the foot of the route. I set off on a tramline of sandy pockets in the grey wave. The first protection came after fifty feet of overhanging pocket-picking, taking care not to snap off the brittle edges. It was a briefcase-sized block detached on five sides and attached on its smallest end. Once looped it had to be laybacked and manteled. The bloated bodies of the Monster Alien Spiders wait for prey at the roof. I pull by and gain a foot-cramping rest on a hanging porcelain slab a little higher. I arrange a clutch of shallow protection in the blind seams in front of my face and begin what looks like three bodylengths of wicked dink-pulling. I gained height in convulsions. Classical music I'd heard in some car advertisement droned through my brain. I stopped being scared and, after an age of schizophrenic debate, I convinced myself that I could not fall off. I then began to look at myself rather than the rock. It was as though my body climbed while I gazed on ... Peg. Stop. A threadbare stance in the middle of this Broccoli Garden.

I wasn't experiencing the anticipated satisfaction of completing such a frightening pitch. It was the numbness. And it was also that I was hanging on a tied off knife-blade with one small foot-hold. There were some tiny slots that would take RPs, there and here, but I'd used all four off mine on the pitch below. "Please don't fall off, Moose," I shouted down, but not too loudly so as not to worry him about the state of the belay. He didn't come off and we filled every imagined nut placement optimism could provide. Expecting the next pitch to be OK, I tried to send the Moose up it, but every time an RP popped out of the belay and we dropped another heart-stopping inch, our nervous disorders got worse. After a valiant attempt he refused. I led up and, quivering, pulled off the boulder problem, a slap for a tiny edge a bodylength above a nut in a wobbly block. I flopped over the rim trounced, with the buzz of an arsonist (I remembered the burning moors). Sitting on top and trying to calm down with ice-creams, we wondered if the runners or the belay would have held what would have been a long free fall. I attempted to question why I went for those moves when I could have backed off, reversed down, but no one answered. (Did I ever pause to ponder as the hospital curtains turned to yellow?)

A murky September day. The sea mist, the diffused flashing of the South Stack lighthouse. The distant subterranean boom of the North Stack foghorn. A melancholy mood. The dull lapping of the waves reverberates around the huge Gothic archway at the very base of the wall. Having just failed an on-sight attempt on the shale corner at the back of the arch, which we dubbed Television Set Groove, I passed two limp rope-ends to Johnny [Dawes]. Silently he tied in and set off up the actual arête of the arch. I dodged the falling blocks for over an hour. To us the impact of the rocks made loud crashes but the fog would eat up any sound we made, swallow our cries for help. Did anyone know we were down here? Then a large part of the arête came off and I instinctively locked off the brake plate, waiting for the exploding gear placements. He screamed and began to fall, I saw it, but then he caught hold of the rock again and continued upwards, up the grey wave. After swinging around a short roof and pulling off more quartz rockery blocks, Johnny found a Friend belay in a wide crack. The crack went up to an apex and then back down to the lip of a giant roof further to the right. I struggled up the arête and approached the belay.

Johnny stared at me with an expressionless face. Something was wrong. It took a while to place it, and then I sniffed. It was the smell, the smell of fresh soil coming from inside the crack. We looked at each other still in silence. The crack formed one side of a bus-sized block which had recently slipped. The block was the roof. It wasn't supported from below, only from above by, perhaps, some kind of vacuum suction. Johnny's only belay was constructed of three shifting Friends in the crack. With hardly a word I set off on the next unprotected traverse pitch. I edged sideways with loose spikes for my hands and dinnerplates for my feet, right on the lip, which kept snapping off. I glanced back at Johnny, just a loop of slack rope between us. If I fell would the centrifugal force be enough to bring the stance down? My head begins to swim with fear so I concentrate on the mosaic of bubbles and ridges just beyond the end of my nose and keep on blindly feeling to my right. Eight feet from the corner now where the promontory meets the wall and the loneliness begins to shake me. Boom, flash, boom, flash go the other inhabitants of Gogarth. The fulmars and guillemots seem strangely quiet. After a seeming eternity on one small muscle-cramping foothold, Gwion and Trevor appeared on the ramp. They broke the cathedral-like atmosphere with their chatting and laughter and this cheered me across to the last jump move into the corner. One, two, three ... No, I can't. Yes, you can. I can't. *You can.* An internal pantomime raged in my head. One, two, three ...Yes, gotcha! I clung onto the grass tufts of the slabby side of the promontory. It was all over. Come to Mother, we like to think, stood as a monument to on-sight climbing for five more months, before the roof collapsed of its own accord.

The next month I was back again, this time with Trevor [Hodgson]. I stole a fine direct on the second pitch of Heart of Gold and followed 'Carlos', as he was then known, up a short, hard direct start to Cannibal. But these were only to be fillers in before a new episode began.

In my search for unclimbed rock I began to visualise an almost imperceptible line between Heart of Gold and The Enchanted Broccoli Garden. It was a line marked by its lack of flakes, cracks and corners and would follow small edges and pockets from one tiny seam to the next. The first pitch had a small roof to be surmounted and the holds were hidden under wet tufts of grass. I climbed, ice axe in hand, cleaning as I traversed the initial overhang. Two king spiders watched me place a peg. This time they made me feel good. I took a fall whilst leaping across the overhang. The peg moves but holds. The thought crosses my mind that the spiders have smiled and granted me one fall. Next time up brings the Heart of Gold stance, once rumoured to be iffy but now recognised as bombproof in comparison with its neighbour. Nick, my partner for the day, refused to follow me so we left. Four months later an exceptionally bitter January day found Gwion and me sliding back down to the belay to attempt the next two pitches. Pudding and debauchery weighed heavily on my stomach and conscience, as I contemplated the accumulation of Christmas calories. The middle pitch only took a few minutes because there was no gear to slow me down, just clip the belay and go for the layback. And there I was again at the dreaded Broccoli Belay. Silently, I sighed with relief when Gwion shouted over that he was bailing out.

It seemed to be becoming increasingly difficult to find rope-holders for my escapades, so I jumped at the chance when Bob Drury offered his services. It was the last day of January and on the first day of February the seasonal bird ban came into effect. The rock had trickles of water but it had to be today or not at all. We slid over the edge from a world of coach tours and ice-creams back into the tilted desert. Two opposite universes separated by a right-angle. At the hanging stance Bob was intent on clipping into the abseil rope but I threw it well out of his reach. I began to regret my decision as I repeatedly almost came off whilst attempting to rock over onto a slimy nipple. Three times I contrived to scrape back down barn-door laybacks to the minimal sanctuary of the Broccoli Belay and re-psych. I squeaked the inside edge of my left boot and climbed up to the nipple on my outside edge. That gave me just enough stick and I rocked over; the only consolation a Rock One in soft red rock. The face above is steep and carpeted. I brush the hairy lichen from the rock with my hand and it floats into my eye. There is no more protection. I begin to shake, then I go beyond shaking and once again my mind enters that realm of depersonalisation. I move away from the rock and come

[44]

Grading Note: *British E grades (sub-dividing and extending the old Extremely Severe grade) encompass climbs with a technical grade of 5b/5.10 or harder. They denote a composite of the challenge, protection and technical difficulty of normal rock climbs – E9 presently being given to the hardest and most committing climbs. The E system, though used for sport climbs, has little relevance to them as sport climbs are essentially safe.*
British technical grades correlate roughly with American technical grades as follows: 4c/5.7, 5a/5.8, 5b/5.9, 5b,5c/5.10, 6a/5.11, 6b,6c/ 5.12. British numerical grades bear no relationship to French rock and sport grades which grew out of alpinism – French technical 6 being about British 5a/b.

Left-Hand Red Wall, South Stack, Anglesey.

This 100m wall backs a deep zawn (inlet) flanked by two supporting buttresses. Lacking obvious natural lines the wall remained untouched (except for three routes) during the earlier stages of South Stack development. Thereafter, as standards of protection, ability and confidence rose, it was steadily developed. The compact rock offers only sparse natural protection yet, apart from the odd piton, the use of fixed protection has been carefully avoided. Because of this, fine, challenging climbs were discovered by each generation of activists and Red Wall Left is now seen as one of Britain's key cliffs for demanding rock (i.e not 'sport') climbs.

0	**Vena Cava**
1	**Auricle** 1967 HVS/4c Joe Brown, Brian Fuller, (Mo Anthoine).
2	**Alligator** 1978 E1 Al Evans, Paul Williams, Jim Moran, Ben Wintringham.
3	**Cannibal** 1978 E4/5c Jim Moran, Al Evans, Paul Williams, Ben Wintringham
4	**Schittlegruber** 1986 E6/6b 1986 Paul Prichard, Nick Harms.
5	**Left-Hand Red Wall** 1967/76 (FFA) E3/5c Joe Brown, Pete Crew (AL,2pts); Henry Barber and party (free).
6	**Mein Kampf** 1979 E5/6a Jim Moran, Dave Cuthbertson, Paul Williams, P. Aubrey.
7	**Heart of Gold** 1978 E5/6a Mick Fowler, (Stevie Haston), Phill Thomas.
8	**The Super Calabrese** 1987 E8/6b Paul Pritchard, Bob Drury.
9	**Enchanted Broccoli Garden** 1986 E7/6b Paul Pritchard, Mike Thomas.
10	**Pagan** 1973 E4/5c Pat Littlejohn, Andy Houghton.

11	**Deygo** 1968/73 (FFA) E3/5c Tom Proctor, Geoff Birtles (5pts); Ron Fawcett, J. Heseltine (free).
12	**Come to Mother** 1986 E7/6a Johnny Dawes, Paul Pritchard.
13	**Infidel** 1978/78(FFA) E3/5c Ben Wintringham, Joe Brown, Marion Wintringham (2pts); Gordon Tinnings and party (free).
14	**Anarchist** 1978 E1/5b Ben Wintringham, Jim Moran.
15	**Salem** 1987 E4/6a Paul Pritchard, Pete Johnstone.
16	**Outside the Asylum** 1988 E5/6a Paul Pritchard, Pete Johnstone
17	**Ramilina** 1991 E6 Mike Turner, Louise Thomas.
18	**Howl the Trowel** 1991 E7 Mike Turner, Louise Thomas.
19	**Yarding Lard** 1996 E6 Mike Turner, Steve Hartland.
20	**Care in the Community** 1995 E5 Glenda Huxter, Howard Jones
21	**Ceefax** 1986 HVS Paul Pritchard, Paul Barbier.
22	**Horn of Plenty** 1986 HVS Paul Pritchard, Gwion Hughes (solo)

Notes: The author's climbs marked with dotted lines; AL – alternate leads; FFA – first free ascents. Arrows show principal abseil descent points. Main climbs only are shown – variations and girdles are not marked. The main stances are marked ●

back with a crash at the end of all the difficulties, retching, about to puke. Sitting on top of this Super Calabrese, watching the clouds billowing out on the Irish Sea and, beyond, the Wicklow Mountains silhouetted by the setting sun, which then begins to play a trick on us and lifts the mountains so that they are floating on shimering stilts, I am numb and unaware of what I have done. It never really attained a relevance.

I climbed some more routes on the Red Walls, but the big lines had gone. There is something sad about a cliff becoming worked out – for me it's a sign to move on. But there were still a couple of blanks in the guidebook that I wanted to fill. At last I found a keen partner in Pete Johnstone and we took residence in South Stack bogs in the winter of '88. Over a couple of freezing days we climbed Outside the Asylum, because we were alone in an insane world, and Salem, named after a famous Welsh painting depicting worldly vanity – a woman comes into chapel late so that the congregation will notice her new shawl, and in the folds of the shawl is the face of the Devil. The folds and contortions of the rock reminded me of that shawl.

I don't often go back there now, but I do remember a daydream – of becoming entangled in one of those viscid webs, cocooned, to be excised as a Monster Alien Spider, to face my existence, shuffling silently, watching and soloing on that red wall.

4

A Piece of Driftwood

DO YOU WANT TO KNOW why I didn't think about you on all those other climbs? When really I should have been laughing and joking about all the good times there were. Berating you for being such a fool. Or even wishing that we could still be huddled by the dirty fireplace, under a blanket, in that freezing house we shared through that winter. Rock 3 Terrace. I think we'll have to go back a little way. To a starting point, if you like. Perhaps I should begin with our first Scottish winter trip.

We hacked it up to Ambleside in your very knackered Mini to get Fluff. Do you remember? I could never drive and you always cursed me. After a night at the Charlotte Mason disco, in that barn, where we didn't cop off 'cos we were too scruffy and drunk, we switched to Fluff's knackered Ford Fiesta and hit the M6. We slept, the three of us, sat up in our seats like crash test dummies, fermenting in our pits, with snow settling on the windscreen. Next morning in the posh Aviemore café they frowned at us and wouldn't give us a top-up of hot water. Not the right kind of clientele. So we set off late to the Northern Corries and you led a route, which one I don't recall, that neither Fluff nor I could follow. You held us both on the rope and took the piss, as you liked to do. We maintained that it was only because you'd hacked off all the ice but, really, we knew.

Then we headed west, to Meaghaidh – remind me where we slept. Smith's Gully was a breeze. You barely paused to put a screw in, you were always so confidant (Fluff thought too confidant), and you moaned about the party in front holding us up. Luckily, if you recall we didn't have a map and compass, the skies were clear and we slid like lunatics down toward the car park. Slotted back into the Fiesta, we boated round bends toward Glen Coe. On Raven's Direct you did it again, teetering up slabs on millimetre spikes of metal, almost doing the splits in the verglassed chimney on the top pitch. I felt like I was learning from you – but wait a minute, we were beginners together. I didn't reveal my impression. I took the piss out of you, too. But you didn't like that and you'd snap at me. When you came back and I'd drunk a bottle of your beer you got angry and didn't know how to react. After sulking and making me feel like I didn't care, you made me pay for it, and ever since I got the feeling you thought I didn't respect you. I did. We did. But if we'd shown it, you might have got big-headed. As it was you went for things as if tomorrow might not arrive, trying to prove to the world that you could do it. And afterwards trying to remain modest. Sometimes not even telling what you'd done. But you knew we'd find out. You might disagree, but anyway, do you remember what we climbed next? We soloed all those gullies on Aonach Dubh, but they were too easy and we got bored like only young blind men do. So we stopped below the summit and built a snow fertility symbol big enough to be seen from the Clachaig. Well, it made us laugh. You were the rudest person I ever knew.

On the Ben we did Point Five and The Curtain 'cos we'd seen them in *Cold Climbs*. It didn't matter if the ice was good or bad, you just went for it, and so did I. Well, compared to rock climbing these ice axe handles were like jugs. We didn't think about what kind of crud the picks were stuck in. And hell! we could hang on

[48]

all day. Sliding down Number Five Gully they scowled at us as we flew past roped together and screaming. I came to a stop and you slid into me crampons first and made my leg bleed.

Driving back home, I don't need reminding. Between Glasgow and Carlisle, going fast, surrounded by thundering, spraying lorries, 'I've Got the Power' playing loud on the stereo combating the noise from the engine. And the windscreen blows out. We had no cash or any way of fixing it so we just kept going. It was night-time and blizzarding on the motorway and we got into our sleeping bags, Fluff with his feet poking out the bottom to work the pedals. And we had to wear mittens, balaclavas, and shades to keep the stinging snow out of our eyes. I don't know what the hitchhiker must have thought with his thumb out below the street lamp as we, like the PLO without a cause, imprinted against the windows, waved through the front of the car and shouted "No room, mate." We had to turn the music up even louder trying to get a ton out of the Fiesta pelting over Dunmail Raise. And when the doors sprang open we fell out into the street, unable to stand, we were so chilled. But we were pleased with ourselves. And now I'm glad that I made that trip with you.

And then, less hazy in our memory, there was Eigg. Mid-summer. We went to free the Sgurr, and to be fair you did lead a scary pitch (and I took another fall, flying with that block which squashed my thumb), but we soon gave up and decided to regress. We went mad like children. You showed off your public school athleticism in the inter-island soccer match, we laughed, drunk, as we rowed around in circles, on millpond morning water in our 'borrowed' rowing boat. You danced the fling with schoolgirls at the village hall ceilidh. The sun seemed to shine all night and we stripped and swam at 4 am – the night those islanders turned up on a tractor loaded with ale and we carried on, scared that it all might end soon. But the one picture that I keep with me, a photo in my mental pocket, is of you coming back across the little sandy bay pulling that trunk of silver driftwood behind you in a washed-up pram, coming out of the sun like a perfect recollection. We sat at a dining table made of sand and ate the finest food from the island post office. That driftwood, just like a wild horse's head,

[49]

which you went to such lengths to hump across the island and onto the boat home, is now in George's house. He's the keeper and he cherishes it. And when any of us goes round there, we touch it and it transports us to Eigg and a time when we lost our heads.

✳

Dingle, Ireland. George, Glenn and me were sat in Tom Long's bar when the phone rang, drinking Irish coffee.

"Its for you, Paul," says Liam, and I walk over.

"Hello ... Hi, Zoe ... What d'you mean?" I shook. "OK, I'll tell the others."

The room had changed when I looked up, grown bigger and the angles were wrong. She'd just told me you were dead. Soloing on Snowdon. I told the others and Liam poured us three stiff ones. And three more. Then Liam had the idea to take us out in his boat, to see the dolphin. He said that dolphins had been used as a kind of therapy for ill or sad people, and when it surfaced right by us and looked at us, the moment felt important. There was this creature, free in all this space. Like you now, maybe.

We danced all night like we were dancing for you and we laughed uncontrollably as we carried Glenn, me at his hands and George at his feet along the harbour in the morning sun. We leaned against a flagpole and joked about you, called you the lighthouse; Ed Stone – Eddy Stone Automatic – the lights flash but nobody's home. You'd have got grumpy if we'd said that to your face.

I didn't think about you because of a whole confusion of reasons. Little disagreements left unsaid, you being in on some of my most cherished memories (I fell in love on Eigg). But – the painful but – in you I saw mirrored some of my recklessness, and others'. It's what gets you up things, past those moments of pinpoint contact. Isn't it?

On the Big Stone

"IT'LL NEVER GO. Yer don't stand a cat in 'ell's chance," said the old-timer and Johnny and I ignored him, as we sat in Pete's looking at the photos of The Scoop in *Hard Rock*. Much to Johnny's bewilderment I'd never done a route in *Hard Rock*, so I was psyched up. Ken Wilson's photos looked terrifying, Doug Scott with EBs and jeans on, looking gripped with the rope being blown out horizontally behind him, and the big colour photo of the giant tilted corners in the evening sunlight with the climbers looking like tiny stick people under those black overhangs. And the words didn't add to the optimism – particularly the bit about "overhanging bands of loose schist". I had spent my Giro and had no money. Pete had just given me a chip butty out of pity but I was depressed. I wanted to go but knew that I wouldn't be able to make it. Johnny said he was bored with us lot never having enough cash and offered to pay for me. So I grinned and with no time for negativity we jumped in the van and headed for Scotland.

We got as far as Llandudno when I realised that in my eagerness, I had omitted to bring my rucksack.

The ride went quickly as driving with the Dawes always does. Up the M6 we motored with The B52's playing loud and the windscreen-wipers working hard to maintain some kind of visibility through the torrential rain. In Glasgow we tried to get our friend Face into the van and sweep him off to the outer isles but he was having none of it. He had just got a job at the Hoover factory and couldn't risk getting sacked. He refused to take us to his local Motherwell pub 'cos he said that if Johnny opened his mouth with his posh southern accent we'd be beaten up straight away. Along Loch Lomond the Dawes actually got 'the Hovis' (as the silly, top-heavy van was affectionately known) onto two wheels as he went for a drastic overtaking manoeuvre. I think I upset him a little when, never having driven myself and failing to grasp the concept of road danger, I didn't get at all fazed. At Fort William we stopped to buy provisions – three big cabbages, a bottle of cold pressed olive oil, a bottle of white wine vinegar, a sack of petit pois and a packet of panty pads (excellent for sticking onto the rock and soaking up trickles onto the crux smear). We also bought Moskill, Repel, Attack and Jungle Formula. We couldn't fail. Before we left I rolled up a malt loaf into a big turd shape and laid it out on the aisle floor. It gave us a laugh watching the shoppers disgustedly steering their trolleys around the offending dollop. It was even funnier to see their faces as Johnny stooped down, picked it up and munched it.

I hadn't visited Skye since my mother brought me there as a small child but I remembered the shapes of the Red Cuillin, like velvet cushions, and the way the patches of light shifted across them west to east. And I remembered her smoking cigarettes and I being shocked (she never did that) to keep the midges away. I couldn't remember anything else, though. We gave a ride to an enormous musical hitchhiker, all the way from Canada, on her way to play at the Skye folk festival. We had to help her squeeze in through the side door and the Hovis listed badly all the way to Portree. As he drove, Johnny would glance at me occasionally and grin with a lurid expression on his face.

Waiting at the outpost of Uig for the Tarbert ferry, I managed to squirt a jet of Jungle Formula into my eye. The warning label said keep away from plastics and skin and my eye felt as though it were melting. Passers-by stopped and pointed at the scrawny youth moaning and trying to drown himself in a muddy puddle in the street whilst Johnny guffawed with sympathy. On the boat, and now nearing our objective, the rains began again but this was beginning to feel like a real adventure, the likes of which I had never been on. At Tarbert we cowered in doorways, hiding from the rain. The sky was so dark it felt like dusk, though it was only midday. After some enquiries we found a man, Big John Macleod, who would take us on his tractor to the start of the walk-in at Amhuinnsuidhe Castle. With our huge bags we rattled slowly along a bleak lochside, past a deserted whaling station and the most remote schoolhouse in Britain. We climbed down from the trailer dripping wet and shivering and handed Big John a tenner. Johnny and I struggled to glance sideways at each other through the horizontal rain when he informed us dourly that it was "clearing up". Sadly, on a later trip when we tried to hire Big John again we were told that he had succumbed to the 'island fever' and had taken a shotgun on himself.

During a lull in the tempest we began our walk-in. After what seemed like hours of sprinting and collapsing with a large ruck-sack on back and front and large cabbages in our hands (very good training) we reached a dam and, wrapping ourselves up in the tent fly, bivvied exhausted. We were awakened by rain on our cocoon. I poked my head out into the morning and to my horror discovered that it was a rain of midges and not just rain. We panicked which is the best thing to do in a midge attack and, shouldering our four packs, ran away. To help keep the rain off we made cabbage-leaf hats which one could munch when hunger took hold and, after a few hours of stumbling around, we (kind of) saw it.

The bottom half of the mighty Strone* looked like the underside of some great beer gut. A steep rock-strewn hillside led up to the cliff and where the two met there was a wide band of loose-

* Strone Ulladale, recently renamed Sron Ulladale by the O.S.

looking shale. Water poured out of the cloud that kept the secrets of the upper part of the mountain. The waterfalls exploded into spray hundreds of feet in front of the overhanging wall. It was falling from the lip of the face and seemed to clarify the distorted perspective that the cliff presented. I tottered into the valley with the hillside on my back.

After pitching our tent in what was to become the biggest water puddle in the surrounding area, excited, we raced up to attempt the first pitch before it went dark. The rock was quite unsound and the ancient Rurp for protection disconcerting. Johnny led and after some trouble clambered onto a small ledge belay. It had been hard and more than a little dangerous but we had made a start on a climb we had been dreaming of for a long time. Down below our unhygenic lifestyle and diet of salad and sheep shit wasn't doing much to keep our recently acquired streaming colds at bay. Then the midge paranoia began and we stayed awake half the night exterminating each invader as it forced its way through the tent zip. When the morning came the space between the inner and outer tent was thick with the evil little buggers. We were prisoners. To make our escape we first drenched ourselves in Jungle Formula, though we knew that they went crazy for the stuff (they like to lick it off before biting you), then we lit yards of mosquito coils and, quickly opening and shutting the airlock, hurled the pieces into the bell. After a while we could pull our stockings over our heads and make a run for it.

After forcing down a pan of glutinous gruel we headed back up the hillside to continue our adventure. The day was clearer and I shivered as I tilted my head back to see the whole height of the crag. It was easier to face away from the rock and look up at the face out above my head. Corners staggered up the overhang, slashes on a sheet of dark material. Could they be linked? Higher on the face one corner was soaking wet and water drizzled out of the bottom of it and we felt it like pinpricks, wet on our faces. I knew we'd never get up that. The next couple of pitches went more steadily, a short technical groove and a long beautiful corner. The rock was immaculate and we could find no placements for our ice screws which we had brought for the schist. We shouted and waved at two men fishing on Loch Ulladale, the only others we were to see that week. On returning to our dining cave that evening we were warmed to find two trout lying there. "Bugger vegetarianism, pass me the penknife."

With the ropes now fixed up to the huge wet corner we had hit an impasse. The way on looked downright offensive. There was so much slime oozing out of the cracks that it wasn't even worth trying. The only feasible alternative was a ridiculous-looking forty-foot groove/roof thing running out over the glen. I spent the day hanging in slings while Johnny aided and cleaned the first pitch of our alternative free route. Eventually, that tedious but necessary job done, we could slide back down for more cold salad. The next day Johnny's enthusiasm got him up the pitch quickly after some sequence difficulties at the start. The flying groove pitch got us to a lovely sofa of a belay ledge back on The Scoop – to where Doug Scott pendulumed on the first ascent. I wasted the rest of the day trying to follow the original line up a technical arête and over desperate bulges, the loch below my heels. That feeling grabbed me again. That same feeling as when I first went to the Verdon at sixteen. The space, the updraught, the freedom. This is why I go climbing. It's easy to lose sight when you get fuelled by ambition. With the updraught came the sound of ruffling feathers and the golden eagle was below my heels now. Like I could have stepped off onto its back and ridden away. I climbed to below that infamous bolt and came down. "It might go, but not this week."

Before zipping off down the, by now, very spacy abseils we scoped out the possibility of a traverse left from where we could perhaps get back up and right. Again we had no choice. Being just a couple of rock rats, we struggled with our jumars on the fixed lines and all the while the midges followed us up the cliff. We even took to climbing with burning mosquito coils tucked in our hats. They say that things as small as midges aren't capable of conscious thought. But these! They made secret plans of torment. There was method in their torture. It rained continuously but the Strone, overhanging more than a whole rope-length, kept us dry and always gave us new hope when our free passage was barred.

[55]

The leftwards traverse was a joy. A useless peg under a loose block led to strenuous slapping across a sloping shelf and a hanging blade belay. Johnny swung through and took us up an easier face pitch to a stance below the final capping roof. Oh dear, we sighed, it looked blank and impossible. But to the right the overhang was stepped with a slanting wall running through it. There appeared to be no protection but there was a smattering of pinches and small edges. It was my lead but I backed off after placing a titanium angle in a hole. In a situation like this, lonely and homesick and faced with a terrifying lead, Johnny could be counted on to dispense with caution and just be downright irresponsible. It would be quicker if he led and, not being too proud to realise this, I handed over the rope-ends. The mood had now become very sombre and few directions were vocalised as Johnny lurched across the overhang, pinching and struggling to keep his feet in contact with the lichenous rock. On the lip, pumping, he fiddled a slider into a little slot and slowly, quietly sat on it. The last gear, the angle, was at the back of the roof. As he fiddled with the gear on his harness the slider shifted. "Aaaah, don't rip, don't rip." Then, as he was futily trying to place a blade in a blank seam, the piece stripped and Johnny plummeted. He disappeared under a band of overhangs and began a long pendulum. I held the ropes tight and watched with horror as they slid along the sharp lip, spraying a cloud of nylon fluff into the air. As one rope snapped, the blade tinkled on the rocks 700 feet below. Johnny prusiked up and, silent and worried, we did the space abseil and tried to get our heads together.

After a solemn discussion we both agreed things were getting a little out of hand. Johnny was shaken up and felt unsure about going back up. All this fear to be stopped ten feet from easy ground. We had to come up with a plan. We were halfway through our last cabbage and our head colds were intensifying.

Early next day Johnny ran up to the top of the crag and began rappeling, with me below shouting directions – "Left a bit, right a bit." A brief peek was all he needed to see he was only a couple of moves from easy ground, so off we jumared excitedly, dropping all the fixed line behind us. Committed now, Johnny began the pitch,

Sron Ulladale (Scoop Face), Harris, Outer Hebrides.
Free routes – dotted, remaining 'un-freed' sections of original aid routes – dashed.
● – stances on the author's routes. AL – alternate leads; VL – varied leads.

1 **Moskill Grooves** 1989 Ben Moon, Johnny Dawes, Paul Pritchard (VL) E6, 6b

2 **The Scoop** 1987 Johnny Dawes, Paul Pritchard (AL) E6, 6b, (originally E7)

2a **The Scoop** 1969 (the remaining aided section of the original route) Doug Scott, Jeff Upton, Guy Lee, Mick Terry. A3/HVS 1 bolt.

3 **KnuckleSandwich** 1987 JohnnyDawes, Paul Pritchard (AL) E7, 6c

3a **Knucklehead** 1977 (the remaining aided section) Paul Lloyd, Terry King. A4

4 **The Nose** 1972 Doug Scott, Guy Lee, Dennis Hennek. A5/HVS (the dotted section indicates part freed in 1994 by Johnny Dawes at E7, 6b)

5 **The Chisel** (Gloaming Finish) 1989 Crispin Waddy, Drury, John Biddle 1989; Waddy, George Smith (AL) E7, 6b

6 **Sidewinder** 1971 (general line – now eaten into by several of the new free routes though large sections originally went free). Doug Scott, Guy Lee A5/HVS

went for the run-out and wobbled up to the last Scoop belay. We both whooped with delight. I led through up to the last easy pitch on perfect gabbro and we had a summit roll-up with the last of our tobacco. After the descent we buried lots of our equipment under rocks as we began enthusiastically making plans for our return, when we would attempt the other unbelievable lines (on return we never managed to find our cache). We ran down to Amhuinn-suidhe where we gorged on food from the remote post office that was ten years past its sell-by date and used the phone at the grand castle to call up Big John for a rescue. In the castle the gillies and watchers told us about Gerrard Poncho, the Belgian business tycoon, who 'owned' Strone Ulladale and charged £200 per bullet to shoot a mighty stag. In my pride I thought "He doesn't own the Strone right now. We do. And the eagles."

When we wrote up our free ascent of the Scoop in the Nevisport book we postscripted it 'On-sight', which it was, apart from the last ten feet. We felt we had tried so hard for that climb that we were entitled to forget about our little indiscretion.

6

Bhagirathi Diary

It is better to waste one's youth than to do nothing with it at all.

Georges Courtline

July 10
Walked into Bob's new office this morning to find him peering
through the curtains, spying on those in Pete's Eats across the
street. He likes to know what's happening, who's about. When he
senses my presence he swings round on his swivel chair and
lowers his shades. "Hey, Aardvark." This is his 'affectionate'
nickname for me. "We've had more arrivals." Bob jumped up and
beckoned me to the giant mound of boxes dominating one side of
the office. "Soya Dessert, ten cases! We won't have to buy food for
ages." Bob has sent a draft letter to every food, equipment and
cosmetic company in the country and the swag has been rolling
in for days now: five cases of mushroom pâté, mountains of
chocolate, muesli, noodles, a case of Golden Virginia tobacco,

hundreds of tins. Things seem to be getting out of hand. Last week I even got to visit a peanut butter factory. Watching it all oozing out of that giant sphincter made me feel sickly and I had second thoughts about walking out with twelve gallons of the stuff.

July 15

The portaledges we've been making with Hugh Banner are coming on. We hired a local machinist to make the tent which looks like a wendy house with a plastic window in it. A £100 voucher came from the co-op to help us with our trip which we promptly cashed in for hard liquor at Leo's supermarket.

July 20

Had a fund-raising slide show at the Heights which went a bit crazy. Some of the speakers got too drunk to work the projector or even to communicate with the audience. First prize in the raffle was Johnny's Skoda which we had to push down to the pub. At least it tempted lots of folk to come, the fact that first prize was a car. The first winner didn't want it after she saw it and neither did the second. It must have been the spray can graffiti all over it that put them off. We pulled out loads of tickets before we found someone who would tow it away. We had to give some of the straighter members of the audience their money back. One said it was the worst slide show she had ever seen but the hard core seemed to like it.

July 30

Got our cheque off the MEF for £800. I'm made up as I wasn't sure how well I'd done at the interview. I was wierded out, there at the RGS with all those faces looking at me, and when Hinkes asked me if I'd ever worn crampons before I wanted to say "Course I've frigging well worn crampons before," but I just had to play it cool and say yes. We'll show 'em.

August 8

Thirty tubs of pear and apple spread arrived. We've been busy on Joe Brown's sewing machine making holsters. I bragged to Joe about the Golden Virginia sponsorship and he just told me to "Give that up for a start. It's a mug's game."

August 12
Portaledge trouble. And only thirteen days to go. Bob went on the radio in the garden of the station and pretended to be on the summit of Snowdon. Johnny's obsessed with synergy and wants to make a ledge that will turn into a sledge or a glider. Climbing's falling by the wayside as we speed around the country collecting stuff.

August 16
Got pulled and fined on our way to get jabs at the Tropical Medicine Centre in Liverpool for doing ninety in a fifty. Bob's not happy as he's been banned for years anyway for under-age driving. The Heights want us to move the Skoda out of their car park.

August 18
A week to go and the damned portaledges still won't work right. Once you put the thing together it won't come apart again. Our expert engineers at HB are doing a great job though.

August 23
Packing turned into a Soya Dessert fight on the banks of the Menai Straits and we practised with our new Charlet Mosers on a telegraph pole in the garden. Getting up the pole was easy but getting down again was a bit trickier and resulted in some dangerous falls with brand new sharp spikes flailing around.

August 25
Last night is too much of a blur to remember. We overslept. Outside Bob's house this morning there were bodies everywhere, under cars, in the fields and on the side of the road. Like an invasion of colourful giant slugs. We piled into the Dwarf's van and got to Manchester late. Even after extensive repacking and jiggery pokery – I had my pockets loaded with pitons, screws and other potentially dangerous weapons – our bags were still too heavy and the man wanted a grand in excess baggage. We

became incensed: "But we're the official Bhagirathi 3 expedition, supported by the BMC. Surely we can arrange something?" We did. The guy let us on and even allowed me to empty my pockets of iron into the hold. As we ran for the plane the passport controller thought we were a rock band; Dawes has a bald head with a single plait coming out of his forehead, I've got my usual Mohawk and Joe and Bobby are in bright clothes, shades and jewellery and are swaggering around like a pair of rock stars. Sat in Moscow airport now waiting for our delayed Aeroflot plane to Tashkent. Just saw the airport cops beat up a black guy for daring to complain about this gross food.

In the air now. What a take off. The whole thing shook violently and the baggage compartments sprang open, jettisoning the luggage onto the heads of the passengers. Someone started to scream and was reprimanded by one of the burly hostesses. Just been drinking vodka at the back with a team of Siberian workers who kept trying to force mouldy sausage on me.

August 27
Delhi. What is going on? This place is completely barmy. When you get off the plane it's like walking into a steam room. We almost collided with an elephant that had strayed onto the dual carriageway on the taxi ride into town. In a traffic jam a woman came over and held her baby to the window. It had a hole in its stomach showing its intestine. I didn't have any money to give and didn't know what to do. I wanted to take them to hospital but we don't know how this place works. It smells really bad here, there's flies everywhere and people with limbs missing. But there's colour, too, and action to make cities back home seem like big brother is watching us. I'm going out walking.

August 28
Went walking last night with Bobby, just soaking the place up, and ended up in these tiny pitch dark streets around Payer Ganj. We heard groans and piles of rags would shuffle about in the dirt, but it wasn't worrying. In some downtown area in Britain we would have certainly been mugged. Today we met Simon and the

[62]

rest of the team and they took us to a 'café' for lunch. Well, it was a corrugated shack stood on top of an open sewer. The cook was filthy, with a running nose and smoking a *bedi* and he cleaned our plates with a brown rag that also served as his handkerchief. Simon smiled, he was obviously trying to psych us out. But it didn't work. We tucked into the *dahl* and *roti* and, in the sweltering heat, washed it all down with dusty glasses of tap water. Johnny complained that his glass was dirty and much to all our mirth the cook wiped it clean with his snot rag. Later we drank copious amounts of fruit juice with crushed ice at a street stall. I had read somewhere that ice was dangerous but Simon assured us it was OK. We also met our liaison officer who is a truly repulsive man. Hermunt is short and fat and his teeth are rotten and yellow and he chews betel nut constantly and spits the dark contents of his mouth to the side of the dining table. At dinner tonight he boasted about his caste and seemed angered when I was not impressed that he was a Brahmin. He snapped his fingers at the waiters and also shouted at them if they happened to bring the wrong dish out.

One other ridiculous event of the day involved Johnny. We were all hanging out in our hotel room, trying to cool down, and Dawes appears with these three Sikhs. He tells us that they've told him his future and his past and that it's changed his life. He said all he had to do was write his mother's name on a piece of paper, making sure the Sikhs who where all around him couldn't see, then hide it in his pocket, and they were capable of telling him his mother's name. Then they told him he would marry an air hostess. He was so impressed he gave them seventy quid which we worked out to be about six months' wages for a Delhi cab driver. We took the piss out of him mercilessly and joked that he might fall in love with one of the Aeroflot women. Johnny actually had the last laugh though as tonight Bob and I went our separate ways to buy some of the fabled Indian *charas* and each came back with match boxes full of incense!

August 30
Hired our own bus, loaded it up and headed for the Himalaya. We'd only been going a few hours when in the dark we came to a

halt. Up ahead there was a crowd shouting and flames in the road. It looked like there was a body on fire but it was hard to see, and none of us was going to investigate. It turned out that some kids were pouring petrol over each other and torching themselves. Hermunt explained that they were unhappy because the government had, in an attempt at equal rights for all castes, given a large percentage of professional and civil service jobs to the lowest castes. The students who had studied long and hard were now out of jobs and this was their demonstration. I am amazed at the strength of their feeling. Students at home might do some banner-waving, but this is on another level. I've got so much to learn here.

August 31
Uttarkashi. Met our agents who are going to organise our cooks and porters. It's a pretty shifty outfit. Mr Buddi is small and weasely with piercing dark red eyes and the first thing he did when we got in his office was roll a joint under the desk with one hand. He insisted we all smoked some of it before doing business and then slowly turned to look at us all in turn and grinned. Occasionally he ordered the boy out to buy ten cups of hideously sweet tea. Bobby and Johnny could not control themselves and began giggling. Then came in Mr Rana, the brother of Mr Buddi. He was short and muscular and looked hard as nails and his eyes were even redder and darker. Bob and Johnny had to turn away and hide their faces, they had lost the plot. When we got to our hotel we tried to pack all our equipment into twenty-five-kilo porter-loads but we ended up just sitting and staring at the floor. I tried to sleep but I couldn't and I kept looking at the curtain for what seemed like hours as it appeared to dance before me.

September 1
Got on the bus bound for Gangotri. At first it was OK but as we climbed into the Gangotri Gorge our driver got progressively more stoned. On the mud road we were dangerously close to the edge many times and we could look down a thousand feet to the wrecks of other buses. We took comfort in the fact that Mr Rana

wasn't driving, as he was swigging back the whisky also. After a tea stop we climbed back aboard and, to our horror, we found Mr Rana sat behind the wheel. He offered me the bottle and put his foot down. We lurched wildly round corners on the road cut out of a scree slope as he played chicken with the oncoming vehicles. He kept grinning at us and gesturing for us to roll one up as we sped along. We all partook just so there would be less for him but at each *chai* stop he seemed to find more. At one stop Mr Rana introduced us to a friend of his. The man was tall and evil-looking and was draped in gold jewellery. He wore the smartest clothes and showed us his gold teeth with a sly smile. We shook hands. Keeping his eyes on us, Mr Rana nodded towards him and then looked sternly at us. "Smuggler," he said, breaking into a grin. Johnny looked interested and asked him just what did he smuggle. But the man only grunted and stared at us. Bobby was busy across the road reaping wild marijuana which grows everywhere.

We booked into a medieval hotel with stone beds and no windows and after unloading all our kit went to explore the village. This is the last settlement on one of the most famous pilgrimages in the world, to the source of the Ganges. There are naked men with long dreadlocks huddled under boulders, women selling *pujas*, flowers and things for throwing into the raging brown river and hundreds of well dressed Indian pilgrims furiously eating *dahlbhat* with their fingers in the tiny dirty cafés. There are monks and yogis and colour everywhere. In the temple the pilgrims queue to kiss the stone *linga*, Shiva's penis, in the morning cold. Bobby and Johnny are both complaining of feeling ill.

September 2
Didn't get much sleep last night as Bob and Johnny kept crashing into each other in their desperate attempts to beat each other to the bog. All night they were puking and shitting. On the walk today Johnny shat in his new tie-dye trousers and a New Zealander had to carry his bag as we were all too tight to help out. We have hired loads of porters and they have come from Nepal to work their off season. They are a good bunch. Saw Bhagirathi 3

today and it's hard to believe that we'll be on it soon. I feel funny from the altitude already.

September 3
I feel lousy. I'm in an ashram at Bhojbasa and I've been sick all night. The others have all gone but Johnny's stayed with me. I'm itching too, like there's fleas in this bed. I'll be better tomorrow.

September 4
Still feel queasy but have to escape the food at this place. Will start walking soon.

September 9
God, I feel dreadful. I'm back in bleeding Bhojbasa. It's a bit of a long story and only now do I feel well enough to write it down; Johnny and I left this place a day after the others, thinking we'd be up at base camp in no time. Neither of us has ever been this high before, even base camp is higher than Mont Blanc. We passed Gamuk, the source of the Ganges, where it comes spewing out from beneath the Gangotri Glacier and had a last *chai* stop with the *babas*. Then we climbed up onto the glacier and traversed the left side, like we were told to do. We moved dead slow 'cos neither of us was feeling brilliant. We walked all day over endless rubble heaps until we had finished all our water. It started to go dark and the camp was nowhere in sight, so we had to admit it, we were lost. Johnny searched for water and prepared for us to bivvy, whilst I nursed a blinding headache. We had a few sips with gravel in it and went to sleep in the rocks. I had a pretty bad night and in the morning we realised that we had gone too low and that the camp should be just above us. I felt dreadful as we scrambled up a giant scree slope and then I saw Uttar Singh, our young cook, above us. He came running down, smiling, and helped Johnny with his bag! At camp Bob and Joe were relaxing in the sun. I had a brew with them and crawled straight into my tent.

I guess it must have been a couple of days later when Joe came into my tent and forced me to get up. He told me he wanted to do some tests. I had been puking and moaning endlessly. I crawled out before the panel of Bobby, Johnny and Joe, who had in his hands a copy of *Medicine for Mountaineers*. How many fingers am I holding up? they asked me. How many hands are you holding up? I asked them. Walk heel to toe for us, they said. And I fell over. They whispered amongst themselves and flicked through the pages of their book and then they casually informed me that I had cerebral oedema. If you don't get down straight away you'll die, they said. But I can't walk, said I. I'll carry you, offered Johnny. And that was it, back to the hell hole of Bhojbasa. It was going to be a long piggy-back for the Dawes, but as we descended I felt better all the time and after a few hours I was able to support myself. He stayed for a couple of days but then went back up to the others. I've been hanging out for a few days longer, eating *dahl* and gravel soup in the black hole and listening to the Butthole Surfers in my room. I occasionally go outside and sit by the Ganga and just stare up at the mountains. I've been to America and Mexico before, but here I feel a long way from home. Everything feels way out of my control. I'll be back on track tomorrow.

September 11
Walked up to BC alone and felt OK. Johnny was there on his own as Joe and Bob had decided to switch to the Scottish route. He seemed a bit dejected that the team had split so early on, but the guys, who are back down from their carry now, didn't know when I'd be better. JD and I will have a look at freeing the Spanish route.

There is a tense atmosphere up here. Joe says he's not that happy climbing with people who've never been mountaineering before and that's why he wants to go just with Bob on the easier route. Shivling is incredible in the moonlight. There are more stars here than I've ever seen – it's so clear, so high and no smog.

September 12
Load-carrying today along the mudflats, past leopard prints, and up a heinous hill we called the Triple Cromlecher. We dumped fifteen days' food under a huge boulder below the West Face. I'm glad we've decided not to try it. It looks possible but I got scared

[67]

just looking at it. The wall consists of an El Capitan of freezing granite topped with a thousand feet of disintegrating shale. When the sun came round and started to loosen things up you could hear the rocks spinning through the air for ages before they hit the base. Back here at BC Bobby and Johnny had an argument over a game of chess. I couldn't understand the waste of breath. And later Johnny and Joe had an argument about onions. The team seems a bit stressed. Maybe it's Uttar Singh's badly tuned radio which transmits an incessant din from the confines of his tent. At dawn, when the woeful wailing starts up, it is greeted by groans and shouts from the other tents. In the end Bob burgled the poor lad's batteries.

September 14
More load-carrying. When we got back up to our cache we found all our food had been eaten and we don't know by what. Perhaps it's blue bears or leopards. It's spooky up there. Johnny had to make his own rucksack for load-hauling today as he'd left his sack up at the cache the first time up. When he tried to use one of the others' sacks it resulted in a real barny. I hate all this conflict and I don't know what the hell's going on in everyone's heads. Things would be a lot easier if everybody calmed down. Guess we'll have to carry more food up.

September 16
Snow. Tent. Killed a fly. Perhaps I'll die.

September 18
Cleared up. All going up for an attempt. Bleak atmosphere.

September 22
Back at BC. Didn't do very well. My arm is knackered. When we got to our cache more of our food had gone, this time from zipped up bags. But we saw the critters – choughs. Choughs that can unzip bags! We slept out on a rock and got snowed on. It was freezing. Had a dreadful breakfast of porridge and set off too late for the wall. As we waded up the snow slope the rocks already

started falling from above. We did a few pitches on granite and were close to the tower on the Spanish Pillar when we heard a loud whirring. A rock came from nowhere to hit me in the arm and knock me down the slope. My ice axe shot off like a boomerang. At the time I thought it might be broken but I got some movement out of it. Must be just badly bruised. So that was our big Himalayan adventure over. We kicked our bags off and struggled down after them. Then we spent the whole night scrambling over moraines and traversing scree slopes which were like sand-dunes, no mean feat with one arm. Johnny was a real help. Got to camp at dawn. Bob and Joe had come down also. They had got higher than us but were stopped when Bob developed a suspected hernia whilst dragging their inordinately large haulbag. He seems to be OK now though, just a little groin strain. Guess we didn't 'show 'em'.

September 30
Joe left straight away, keen to escape from a bunch of young incompetents I suppose. Got a lot to learn about mountains. Bob left soon after, to meet his girlfriend and tour the south, and Johnny headed back to university at Norwich. Uttar Singh returned to Uttarkashi also. I came over to the others' camp below Shivling. Andy's been painting lots of pictures of Bhagirathi, it looks wild from over here. My arm's no better yet. Looking forward to our tour of the south and good food and tropical heat.

October 6
Helped carry stuff up to Shivling for Andy and Sean and saw an awesome unclimbed tower of rock on Meru's East Face. One day I'd like to come back to that. Freezing cold now that winter is coming.

October 10
The boys did Shivling. Said it was very cold and they've got frost nip as souvenirs. It was way below zero here at base camp, so God knows what it was like up there. This is the coolest place I've ever been and I reckon I'm keen to keep trying these mountains. But for now, *get me out of here.*

Outside the Asylum

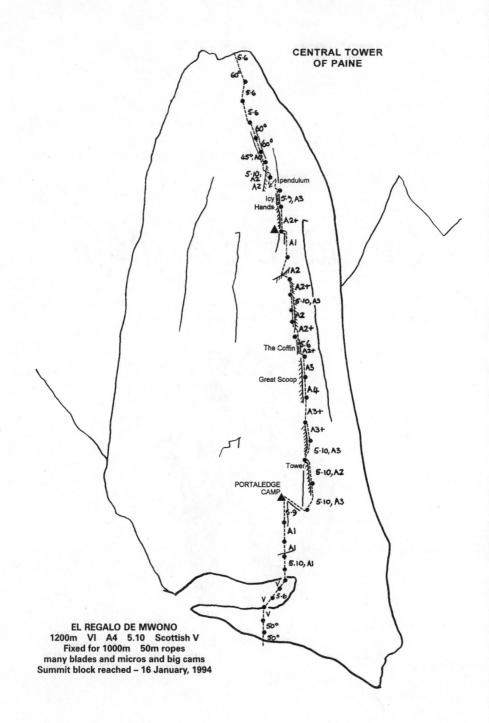

CENTRAL TOWER OF PAINE

5·6
60°
5·6
5·6
60°
60°
45°, A0
5·10, A2 — pendulum
A2
Icy — 5·9, A3
Hands
A2+
A1
A2
A2+
5·10, A3
A2
A2+
The Coffin — 5·6
A2+
A3
Great Scoop — A4
A3+
A3+
5·10, A3
Tower — 5·10, A2
PORTALEDGE
CAMP — 5·10, A3
5·9
A1
A1
5·10, A1
V
V — 5·6
V
50°
50°

EL REGALO DE MWONO
1200m   VI   A4   5.10   Scottish V
Fixed for 1000m   50m ropes
many blades and micros and big cams
Summit block reached – 16 January, 1994

Central Tower of Paine:
El Regalo de Mwono

Imagination could scarcely paint a scene where humans have less
authority. The elemental forces prevail. In this desolation the wider
powers of nature despise control; as if to say "We are sovereign".
Here mankind does not look like the lord at all.

Charles Darwin, Patagonia, 1834

A VERTICAL SHEET without horizons. Two dimensions. Up.
Down.

Slide jumar up as far as it will go. Inhale. Weight foot loop. Pull
with right arm. Stand up straight. Exhale. Clink. Sit down in
harness. Gasp. Look up. No nearer. Slide jumar. Inhale. Weight
foot. Pull. Stand. Exhale. Clink. Sit. Gasp. Slide. Weight. Pull.
Stand. Clink. Sit. Gasp. Slide. Weight. Pull. Stand. Clink. Sit. Gasp.
Slide. Clunk ... Fraction point. A peg. Weight. Exhale. Stand.
Clink. Sit. Gasp. Darkness. Moving points of light. Remove top
jumar. Place above peg. Slide. Weight. Remove chest-jumar. Pull.

Stand. Replace above peg. Sit. Gasp. Repeat. Headtorch? No. Moon. Slide. Weight. Pull. Stand. Clink. Sit. Gasp. Fear. Perpetuating other thoughts. Family? Why didn't I? Slide. Weight. Pull. Stand. Clink. Sit. Gasp. Why did he shout at me? Said he thought I was hypothermic. Hate. Sweat. Prickles. Slide. Weight. Pull. Stand. Clink. Sit. Gasp. Repeat. Why doesn't she want me? What more can I do to convince her? Wild swings of conviction. Should I have gone to be a gold miner in Sierra Madre? The west coast of Ireland? No. Look up. No nearer. Breathe. Above laughter. Chatting. Not alone. Warmth. Food. Space. Still. A cavernous room. Spinning. Spiralling inside. Thud thud thud. Giggling. Slide. Weight. Pull. Stand. Clink. Sit. Gasp. Space. Nil comprehension. Emotion. Ever-changing. Sadness. Love. Anger. A hundred questions. Why? Slide. Weight. Pull. Stand. Clink. Sit. Gasp. Pain. In hand. In shoulders. In arse. Sack pulling backwards. Gasp. Again. Sleep. Ambivalence. *Snap. Foos.* Guts rising. Screaming. Intensifying. Gasp ... Awake. Inhale. Exhale. Repeat. Slide. Weight. Pull. Stand. Clink. Sit. Gasp. Repeat. Again. Lamp light. A rock crystal reflecting. A mirror. Repeat. Repeat.

My jumar hits a fraction point. A peg in the corner that I am in and I am shocked back into the night. It's 2 am and we have been sliding up this line of ropes since the previous afternoon. The headlamp beam forms a mirror upon the wall. In this mirror I see the past, the present and appalling visions of the very near future. Below the rope fades limp into the darkness. Above it disappears, taut as a hawser, into the constellations of the southern night sky. Way below Sean follows. I know he's thinking about the state of the fixed line. In this dark it's impossible to see how much more damage our violent and unshakable companion, the wind, has made to our frail cords in the past five days of storm.

❋

Five weeks earlier we had arrived in Chile joyful and unsuspecting, and with some glaring omissions in our badly packed equipment. Rattling down the country allowed time for our excitement to grow. Noel Craine and I were like the kids let loose, whilst Simon Yates and Sean Smith were the old hands at this world travel game. Hanneke seemed the most relaxed of us all. A Dutch woman, living in London, she had seen a fund-raising slide show of mine in the Heights, the Llanberis meeting place. Having always wanted to trek about Patagonia, Hanneke asked if she could come with us in the capacity of Sherpa, at which she was one of the stronger members of the team and very quickly became one of the gang. We went third-class on a train full of farmers lugging their crops from Santiago to Puerto Montt. Lucky as always, I found a canvas tent, which would be my home for a few months, left by the Boy Scouts under a seat.

We laughed and joked as the lush countryside floated by our window, until the train ground to a halt and we were faced with an ugly scene. Although we were only moving at twenty-five miles per hour, a *campesino* had stumbled onto the track right ahead of us and got under the wheels, somewhere in the Central Valley. Everyone got off the train to look as the drivers dragged out the badly mangled corpse. We were shocked by the reactions of our fellow travellers, "*Un boracho,*" they said, a drunk. Youths began break dancing with ghettoblasters, a real party scene ensued and oldsters started passing around the *maté*, a potent stimulant drink made from herbs. It was only one year since Pinochet had been ousted and we wondered whether the people had been desensitised to death or just plain learned to live with it, and were now beginning to celebrate life again.

On the sixty-hour bus journey south across the Pampa, staring out of a dust-smeared window at the flat brown scrubland, it was easy to see how Southern Patagonia had become known as the uttermost part of the earth. Somewhere south of this monotony, over the horizon of this lens of barren soil, so level that in all directions you can make out the curvature of the world, so that it becomes simple to picture yourself on a great big ball, somewhere down there lay white and gold towers that even the most cloud-headed imagination could never dream up.

In Punta Arenas we tried to avoid sailors who wanted to drink with us. We were flattered to pose for photos and sign autographs for young women who didn't see many blond-haired guys on the

Magellan Strait. "One kiss!" they shouted to us and we were happy to oblige. We drove past millions of burnt tree stumps, the legacy of the beef industry, *en route* to Puerto Natales where we did our supermarket dash and bought $700-worth of food and pots and pans. Noel bought a football, keen that we should keep fit playing soccer at camp. During our first game, and much to the gauchos' mirth, the ball punctured on a yucca plant.

When we arrived below the mountains we relaxed and partied with an American team who had been successful on the South Face of the Torre Centrale, and they gave us advice on big walling there. Eric, a huge, leglessly drunk wall veteran, told us to get up there and kick butt. We also partied with a local horseman who was to help us carry our kit to a camp high up in the beech forests. Pepe, a second-generation Croatian, and his family lived in tents in this grey and blue wilderness and, as they said themselves, had no use for the law. A man of great wisdom and few teeth, Pepe was to become our teacher in the customs and politics of Chile. He had seen many teams of climbers come and go. "Not many guys leave this place having made a summit," he had said as the carafe of wine diminished. Later in the evening he spoke of the other days, of how Patagonia, or Magellanes, had held out longest. But of how eventually the regime took hold. "The soldiers stood on my head and cut my hair with a knife. You were not allowed to grow your hair."

Walking behind Pepe's horses, Noel and I raced to turn each spur to see what would confront us next in the mysterious beech forest of the Vallee Ascensio. Black woodpeckers flocked on a bush and a pair of condors arced lines about the summit of Paine Chico. "It's like a zoo," pointed Noel when he saw a family of guanacos trotting by. The team thought it highly amusing to knickname me Nandu after the rhea-type birds which ran about the place. "Yeah, very funny, Simon."

At Campamento Torres we found two deserted cabins. Inside were fireplaces, black with years of use, well made botched furniture and plaques commemorating the great climbs, carved in their image with all the names scorched in below with red hot wire. In a side room off one of the cabins I found an oven

[76]

made from a large square tin encased in stones and by its side a skillfully carved pizza shovel. There was even a wooden telephone which some homesick climber had lovingly whittled out, during some eternal infernal storm, to make a dream call home. I stocked the shelves of our new home, whilst Noel sorted out the wall gear with the impatience of a child – the weather was sunny and calm and we knew, from all we had heard, that it couldn't last. We each put up our tents about the tranquil microcosm under the forest canopy. The wind could blow all it wanted outside but in here it would be calm. Our retreat. We came to know it very well.

Three days after getting off the bus we loitered below the gigantic pepper pot of the Central Tower of Paine. I hadn't seen anything like this in my life, so overhanging for so far. It was like some kind of optical illusion, like it shouldn't be standing, like it should be falling on us. I stumbled backwards, off balance. The other three had all done big routes before. I was the only one who hadn't done this kind of thing. What if I let them them down? I was glad they trusted me. Noel and I were the best of friends and I knew he would always support me and help me through if I made a mess of things. I soaked up information and techniques from Simon and Sean. To me they were old hands, they seemed to know it all. They showed us how to make a snow cave and how to read the clouds, though the clouds didn't behave as they should. All four of us were indecisive and nervous and argued about where to climb. The other face, on the west of the mountain, was only half the height of the face we were looking at but it took the full brunt of the wind. I wanted to go for the biggest face. I have always thought big and gone for the most daring option and many times I have failed, but that's just the way it goes. The failures I have experienced far outshine the mediocre events of my life. After many hours of deliberation we stumbled upon a decision. The West Face was too far to walk and the East Face had *the* line.

We were the only climbers in the park. As we ferried our gear through wind and snow storms up the long talus slopes, we dined and slept in our own private forest. We now knew where we

[77]

wanted to go. The steepest, smoothest and highest part of the East Face was split by a crack, but thin, too thin for fingers, for more than a kilometre. We were in awe but all agreed, over the sickly feeling this view caused, that we had to attempt this most aesthetic of lines.

Just as they had all told us, the weather was diabolical. At home that Patagonian veteran Rab Carrington shook his head and raised his eyebrows when I excitedly told him where we were off to. "What the hell d'ye want to go there for, lad?" he enquired. "It'll just piss down for two months!" We spent our first week burrowing up the initial 300-metre apron which was buried deep beneath unstable powder snow. Under the snow we sometimes found bolts and much later, when the snow cleared, we counted sixty on rock slabs of a VS standard. We were dismayed. Who would want to do such a thing? The snow made easy pitches difficult and insecure, and spindrift and wind-blown ice ensured that all time on the wall was very uncomfortable. It was slowly becoming obvious; we had come on holiday by mistake.

We clambered onto a sloping snowy ledge just below where the face got really steep and set up a multi-storey portaledge camp. We had been warned against using ledges in Patagonia due to the fierce winds. Indeed, a past expedition to the South Tower was aborted when a large chunk of ice fell right onto a portaledge camp, breaking an occupant's leg. But we were much too lazy to walk continually up and down the valley and, besides, the over-hangingness of the wall seemed to offer some protection. In fact, we hardly ever saw rockfall on this face and the huge pieces of ice seemed to fall horizontally with the south-westerly jetstream.

Simon pulled onto the ledge and scowled at me. "Don't just sit there, do something." I couldn't believe my ears. Who did he think he was. I had been leading all day and had set up this whole portaledge camp with Noel. Now I was taking a breather for a minute or two and he just arrives and tells me to get a move on! I felt like hitting him or telling him at least I could do hard rock climbs, but I just kept quiet and held a grudge for most of that climb on the Central Tower of Paine. I couldn't work it out. Back home in the pub he was always so relaxed and on our India tour he was easy-going when he asked me if I was into doing a big trip.

Andy Cave introduced me to him at the bar in a Harrogate hotel. I'd never been real mountaineering and I became transfixed that evening by his stories of faraway places; of Mark Miller getting beaten up by the taxi drivers in Rawalpindi because he'd spent his fare on a carpet, or the stories of tropical illness which Simon has had his share of (hepatitis, twice, or the mystery illness which, even after taking colon core samples, the doctors could never diagnose), or the many dealings on the streets of Delhi with Indian con artists. I could smell the sweet hot air, though I'd never been there. This man interested me. Now on our first big wall together I started thinking I didn't know him at all. I didn't want to climb with him. What if he turned on me again? For the next few days I stayed partnered with Noel.

I never confronted him about that incident by the portaledges until recently when he asked me if I could give him a few impressions of the climb for the book he was writing. I told him how I felt at the time and he replied saying he thought I was hypothermic and he was worried about me. What I mistook for a needless attack was in fact Simon showing his care for me!

I remember, a couple of years ago, climbing on a big loose and vegetated sea cliff on the Lleyn peninsula, I asked Simon why he wandered around the world so and his answer made me reconsider my own plans to keep on travelling the globe. "Hey, I'm trying to move a lot less now," he said, looking searchingly out over the Irish Sea. "I'm only doing three or four trips a year now. I used to be on the move much more but that was because I was lost. It was something to do, there was nothing else for me. It became consumerism, like anything else, a list of places to be ticked off, and the experiences became flatter and flatter. I was searching for myself I guess." Then he turned and looked at me knowingly: "You'll do the same. You'll want to step out of the fast lane and find out where you are. You'll want a base and some stability." That was the first time I found myself resenting him and his arrogance. How could he possibly know what I want? At the time I felt like I was being lectured, told to settle down. But later,

[79]

for me, layed up with injury and illness, some of what he said, not all, rang true.

The sloping ledge was the high point for a Spanish team from Murcia who had made two expeditions to get there. Three years earlier they had abandoned nine haulbags full of gear which we had seen from below and which did play some part in our choice of route. As we rummaged in the bags we felt some twinges of guilt but these were easily cast aside as we did have the backing of the powers that be: the park rangers had enquired if we would be able to get that rubbish down off the mountain. They had been eyeing it up for years and were wondering what kind of flash clothing they might get out of it. But bootymania soon turned to disappointment as we unpacked our vertical salvage. Inside the bags were mostly very bizarre items, including a barrel with hundreds of rotting batteries, huge flags with company logos on, a transistor radio and fluorescent strip lights. What was going on? We thought with this much gear it's no wonder they got no higher.

After a fitful night's sleep in our portavillage, comprised of a double and two single ledges, Noel and I set to work on the hundred-metre spire above the camp. Although too overhanging to hold snow, there was much ice in the cracks. Noel took the first of numerous falls when he unzipped a string of bashies on an aid pitch and dived ten metres. He accused me of dropping him, which I did, but I denied it vehemently. Well, I was cold and daydreaming to relieve the boredom ... And I did stop him, eventually. I ended that bout of activity by climbing an icefall in my flimsy rock slippers which froze my feet, so I packed them away not to be seen again.

The following day, while Simon and Sean worked hauling, the two 'crag rats' set about the Great Scoop, the formidable central feature of the line. Once again Noel tried to make swifter progress in slippers, but the intense cold forced him to lower off halfway up a pitch and don double boots. I then led on up a rotten choked up chimney. Halfway now and I was equalised on two tied off Lost Arrows, trying to arrange a blade. I heard the snapping of a hawser under tension, then more, and more. I knew what was happening, I'd been there before about thirty minutes ago, falling from the same spot. I bounced off the same ledge and landed on Noel again. He was disgruntled but still managing to smile, even though his belay was of the same wobbly pins as my placements. He seemed more upset that I had landed on him as he was rolling up his last tobacco. In time I reached another hanging stance on this great shield without the slightest foothold, a full rope-length above the last. I gobbed and it floated upwards like a spider's web on the breeze. If I followed that strange urge, the one that everybody gets when they look over the side of the Eiffel Tower, and untied, I wouldn't touch rock all the way to the glacier.

Christmas passed in an up and down succession of accelerating storms and retreats on ice-encrusted ropes. Weathering one forty-hour tempest in our constricted nylon tomb was to prove a particularly good insight into human relations when confronted by fear and poor personal hygiene. Through the maelstrom Noel shouted quotes from his book of quantum physics whilst I made long cigarettes from its pages. As we pondered Schrödinger's cat, the ledge began to fly like a kite and the seams of the tent began to split. Cooking in there was a dangerous procedure and used up valuable oxygen. Condensation poured down the walls and created a kind of soup under our sleeping mats. It was infinitely preferable to be the cook than the one who went outside to collect the snow. Noel passed two pots of snow in and perched on the end of the ledge desperately trying to relieve his inertia-induced constipation. I shouted at him to hurry as the spindrift was blowing in, and in his haste he fell off into the whiteout, stopped only after two metres by his slack tether. "Lord, I'm not cut out to be a big wall climber," he grumbled, and I giggled and shook my head as he hauled himself back into the ledge.

Then a day dawned calm and wondrous and two carbon-monoxide-poisoned figures jumared laboriously back to their high point. Noel began a huge overhanging corner with a stack of loose filing cabinets neatly slotted into the top of it. I was belaying directly below, in the path of any keyed in blocks he chose to unlock. To pass the blocks Noel first had to expand them with a pin, a delicate manoeuvre, and then aid up on micro nuts – I had nowhere to run. He would say to himself "I'm weightless. I have no mass." Using that meditation even the most dreadful Rurp placement could be forced into offering some support. Two days of worry, daydreams, fear and mind games were consumed by that pitch. I ran out another pitch up a smooth overhanging shield and arrived at the base of the Coffin, one of the few features we had seen from the ground. Again it was getting late and we could see Sean and Simon starting the long jumar 600 metres or so below. It was time to switch shifts.

For three more days the corner went on through snow storms and past false horizons. Everyone was growing weary and the twenty-four-hour attention to knots, karabiners and each other's safety was becoming hard to sustain. Everyone had his close calls checked by his partner. But the view over the ridges into the surrounding valleys got better by the day; a little like climbing the oak in the back yard until you can see into the next-door garden.

Sean added to the collected air-miles when he stripped his gear out of an iced up chimney leading up to what was to become our top bivvy. The ground was so steep that it was an air-fall without danger. As the two 'mountaineers' prepared to spend the night up high, Noel and I rested at the portaledge camp, waiting nervously for a midnight start on the ropes. As we dossed and discussed relativity, we were startled by a twanging on the fixed ropes a few feet below our bed. This was weird because, aside from our friendly condors, we hadn't seen a soul in this valley for over a month. We heard heavy breathing and then saw a pair of gloves. Then we laughed when the face of our American friend, Steve Hayward, popped up with a cheesy grin. He'd jumared 350 metres to come and have a big wall party. We salivated as he unloaded wine, beer, chocolate, bean burritos, real cigarettes and mail from our base camp manager and coach, Hanneke.

The middle of the next morning we rejoined the other half of the team, careful not to boast too openly of our gluttony. We huddled together on a piss-stained snowy ledge a thousand metres above the glacier, with Simon leapfrogging bashies up a thin seam way above. We were pitifully low on 'biners and he had nowhere near enough to clip every piece. At last, forty metres out, Simon found a good Friend placement and weighted it confidently. *A scream ...* With our heads flung back we saw his soaring buzzard form silhouetted against the grey frothing atmosphere. He bounced and somersaulted down the corner and hit a ledge just above our heads. He made a long whine with an occasional splutter. We attempted to lower him but the ropes had become fast in the crack. We glanced at each other, terrible thoughts flashing through our minds. A serious injury here, so far from help, could turn into a right epic. He came round and answered our worried pleas with, "The rope's stuck, I might have a broken arm. Give me a minute to sort this mess out." As he had fallen the rope had become sandwiched in a thin crack which made it impossible for us to lower him to us right away. He acted hard, Simon has survived some terrible ordeals in his past, and soon he had got himself down to the ledge. He rolled the arm at the shoulder and it seemed OK but he was shaking. He apologised for cocking up and, in that bad situation, I found respect for him and my grudge disappeared.

Noel re-led the pitch, throwing caution through the window (in Paine the wind is too strong), and I swung through into a vice of an overhanging chimney. Massive hands of water ice grew out of the granite at bizarre angles and I wriggled in the fingers like Fay Wray in the grasp of King Kong. I pulled myself free and it was like coming up for air – there was the summit block and lesser angled ground. We were euphoric. Screaming and yelping I sent Noel up the next pitch, a hidden crack which took a big swing to find. In darkness we fixed our haul line and lead rope and slid down to the bivvy with tidings of great joy. Dinner was cold porridge and rehydration salts.

The day dawned strangely; it was too warm and very windy. Water was dripping onto us. I stood up and my sleeping mat blew away and circumnavigated the summit block like some unpiloted flying carpet. We didn't pay too much attention to the ominous signs but within an hour a full thaw was upon us. We began by jumaring through a waterfall in the icy hands chimney. The nylon gardening jackets we had found in Noel's parents' garden shed had worked surprisingly well up until this point but were no match for this torrent of melting ice. Simon bravely led half a pitch but retreated, bitterly cold and in pain from the previous day's plummet. Sean, who had decided to go for the top in his canvas hiking shoes, now had frozen feet. Added to the fact that we had no food or gas, this fuelled our decision to bail out. We slid down a kilometre of wet, deteriorating rope, but our hearts slid further. Once on the ground there is an odd mixture of emotions. We didn't really want to go back up there, but we mouthed the words that we would. Did we try as hard as we could have done? Should we have moved faster on earlier days? All questions with no answers. We decided to escape.

We abandoned our base camp in the beech forest and ran the three hours to the roadhead, just making the last bus. Three more hours and we reached the fishing village of Puerto Natales. It was a depraved team of hill-billies that hit town. Starvation stares from behind scruffy beards and inane gruntings passing as language worried restaurant staff, who timidly placed endless plates of salmon in front of the savages, fearful of losing their hands. After a night in the bar, Sean and I visited the Mylodon Disco, a sound mountaineering decision. Reality became an obscure concept. A short while earlier we had been three pitches below the top of Torre Centrale, with all its sickly heights and violent winds. Now we were jumping to throbbing music below spinning lights of all colours. Velvet mylodons on the walls, senoritas, fluorescent liquids. Again I found myself screaming. We staggered out into the dawn and some local women helped us gain entry into another bar, though this one was obviously quite exclusive as it had no sign up and the door was locked. After a coded knock the door was answered by a blurred figure. Our friends ran away, I assume because they didn't want to be associated with us, but we gained entry. I remember a very spartan living room with crates of alcohol. I remember ordering beer and Sean collapsing. After rifling through Sean's pockets I had to admit to the blurred man that we couldn't pay, so I was forced to drag Sean back into the street. I wasted some time trying to pull him down the pavement but Sean Smith is a big man. There was only one course of action – I had to abandon him.

When I eventually located the hotel I found the others having breakfast. I was in a drunken panic and quite emotional. "You've got to come quickly. I've abandoned Sean." They ushered me out of the dining room because, they said, I was creating a scene and accompanied me to where I'd left him. When we reached the spot there was no sign of Sean, only a pile of vomit. Oh well! Sean's a big boy now. He could look after himself. When Sean did show up in the middle of the day he described how he had woken in a strange room and how he must have been carried in by the house-owner with whom he could not converse at all. That was just one in many instances of great Chilean hospitality that I have witnessed. And so, sated, we headed back to our mountain.

Noel was becoming increasingly agitated and we were not quite sure why. It soon came out that he had told his Oxford University bosses that he was going on a short holiday to Chile. He wanted to get back to his laboratory as quickly as possible. I stole his passport in an attempt to get him to stay but he played his trump card and pulled out a second passport. Damn! We were sad to see him go. He had done more than his share of the graft and he deserved another crack. True though, the near future looked bleak.

It had been a stressful time for all of us. The seemingly endless problems which the tower and the weather had put in our way made the relations between the team progressively more tense as time had gone on. For Simon it seemed an especially stressful period. Later he revealed that he had agreed to come on the trip almost out of habit, though truthfully he felt as though he had been on the move for too many years. What else could he have done, though? This was all he had ever done – gone from one trip to the next, around the world on some frantic whirligig of tropical cities, walk-ins and mountains. He had always ploughed forwards, blinkered, not wanting to look to either side for fear of seeing ... a home ... a woman ... some stability ... a bit of cash for a change, all the things he had previously seen as a trap, a part of the rat race. Maybe there was something in it; to live like other people and not like some perpetual wandering freak. After his fall and our frightening retreat in a furious storm he also chose not to go back up there. The state of the fixed ropes worried him and there was too much to live for now his decision had been made. Fair enough, I thought. There's no honour in dying, only image enhancement.

✳

When my ascender hit the fraction point in the corner, I wearily removed the top clamp and replaced it on the rope above the peg. I raised my left leg in its foot loop and slid the clamp upward. With an effort I took my weight on one leg, unclipped the chest-clamp, stood up and replaced it above the peg. And so on and so forth.

At 9 am Sean and I were together at the top of the ropes. The wind blew hard making shattering cracks, the likes of which we had never heard before, as the gusts exploded through the gendarmes above. At this moment the sky was blue. We had left our cabin in the forest a day earlier at 3.30 pm. We had been moving continuously ever since. Over a few hours I led another long pitch with free bits, edging in plastic boots. I was tired of all this now and felt strangely detatched as I took risks above my gear. I was thinking about my father and his night club singing routines and how he liked to play the showman. But now I was the showman, as I took a large air-fall from a roof when I stripped a nut from a rock-ice sandwich. I had to wrestle with myself for control of my mind. There was no place for emotion here, only room for non-judgmental corrections and an awareness that an accident could have catastrophic consequences. Since the thaw the mountain had refrozen and the cracks had become choked in hard water ice. This made getting protection in time-consuming as every placement had to be chipped out. At the end of the pitch I arrived at a snowfield and above I could see old fixed ropes leading up toward the summit, not far away. This time, with the euphoria was a weary relief. But now it was certain. Just below, condors contoured the wall, shadows flitting from corner to face. Sean led through and after some mixed gullies and frozen frayed lines we wallowed onto the top. A different view! After twenty-one days on the wall we could at last look west. Lago Paine, La Fortaleza, El Escudo. The Fortress and the Shield. They appeared

[86]

as hurriedly as they disappeared while the clouds shunted past with a fast-forward velocity. We were unable to stand and our eyes watered, from the wind rather than with tears of joy.

On the first abseil the ropes got stuck in some jumble of boulders so Sean had to reclimb the top pitch to release them. That wasted a lot of time and we didn't land on our top bivvy ledge until midnight. I immediately fell into slumber, whilst Sean kept waking me up with brews to rehydrate us. With the daylight came our early morning alarmstorm. The wind blew vertically, which made the already desperate task of cleaning a kilometre of rope, and dismantling a camp with only two people, even more desperate. Our ropes spiralled and twisted above us in the updraft, searching for crevices and flakes to hook onto and forcing us several times to cut them. In my haste I raced ahead a couple of pitches to a ledge and waited for Sean, but he didn't show up. After an age I leaned out and spotted him fighting with the ropes up in the foaming cloud. I shouted but my voice was ripped away from me. I could only wait. After an hour Sean slid to my side and went crazy. "I needed you up there and you just buggered off," he bawled in my face. "You were supposed to take the loose ends of the rope down to stop them blowing away. They fucked off round the corner and got stuck in a crack. It took me ages to free them." I apologised and felt ashamed. I had rushed things and put Sean at risk. Down to the base I tried extra hard to please, doing more than my fair share of the work. But we were focussed now on getting back to warmth and safety as we rappeled over the ice-coated rocks of the lower slabs. We descended the glacier in the night, front-pointing on twenty degree ice to avoid being swept away by the wind. And when we crept back into the forest in the early hours we didn't wake the others. In the morning Hanneke and Simon came into my tent and told me they were happy for us. I got tearful and went back to sleep. Celebrations didn't commence until a few days later.

Down in the meadow we were relaxing with Pepe and his family when we heard news of the imminent arrival of a Murcian expedition. There could only be one and they had probably already seen their clothes being modelled by the park rangers. We

[87]

prepared for the confrontation by hiding when they arrived. Sean and I hid in a bush and watched the Murcians unpacking their two jeep-loads of gear and setting up camp. We began to get worried when they started to practise Kung Fu. What had they got in mind for us? The inevitable happened round at Pepe's shack one night and the four unhappy Spaniards came out of the darkness. It started with hand-shakes but soon degenerated into a shouting match. After informing us that their leader was so upset that he had had to go to hospital because his stomach ulcer was flaring up, they then demanded to look in our tents. Sean wasn't having any of this and, seemingly growing in the firelight, barred their way. What he wanted to know was why they used sixty bolts on the first 300 metres of easy slabs. A small scuffle broke out but no one was really willing to attack Tres Platos, the name by which the local gauchos knew Sean in respect of the inordinate amounts of food he could put away. We had nothing to give the Murcians. The few bits and bobs of clothing had been distributed among the gauchos and the rangers. The Spaniards left, hating us. Sean and I felt terribly guilty and left our ropes for the climbers, although they did seem to have arrived very well equipped. That was the last we saw of them, though we did hear that they went straight back home without attempting anything.

We named our climb El Regalo de Mwono, which means The Gift of Mwono, after the Tehuelche god who lives amongst those frozen steeples. The Tehuelche are gone now, wiped out by the settlers, many of them hunted down like animals. They chose never to set foot in the mountains for fear of inflaming the wrath of Mwono* but I knew that one of them, perhaps a young agile, dirty lad, dressed in a guanaco skin, would not have been able to suppress his curiosity and will have ventured forth and explored and hunted below the great cliffs. Though I doubt whether he will have considered climbing them. The gift was the climb, not the booty which caused so much bad feeling, and we felt honoured to be granted such a gift.

---

* Mwono is misspelt as Mwoma in many journals and on the plaque in the Torres Hut.

4 El Regalo de Mwono 1991/92 Paul Pritchard and Sean Smith, with Noel Craine and Simon Yates and (support) Hanneke Steenmetz. 5b (5.10), A2–3 (one pitch of A4) British with Dutch support. ● Portledge and bivouac camps, x high point on first attempt

5 North-East Face (South African Route) 1973/74 Michael Scott and Richard Smithers with Paul Fatti, Roger Fuggle, Mervyn Prior and Art McGarr. A2, A3 and A4 with some free 5.8.

6 Una Fina Linea de Locura 1993/94 Diego Lura, Ramiro Calvo and Teo Plaza with Peter Garber, then (a week later) Nicholas Benedetti, Philip Lloyd and Lura. French 6b and A3. Argentine, with American and South African support.

Routes on the East Face (above) and North-East Face (right) of the Central Tower of Paine, Chile

1 The Whale of the Winds 1990/91 José Carlos Tamayo, Jon Lazkano, Eric Brand, Steve Heywood and Sebastian de la Cruz VI 5.10b/c, A2. Spanish/American/Argentine.

2 Via Magico Est 1987 Maurizio Giarolli, Elio Orlandi and Ermanno Salvaterra UIAA 7, A3. Italian.

3 Riders in the Storm 1990/91 Kurt Albert, Wolfgang Güllich, Bernd Arnold, Norbert Bätz and Peter Dietrich. 5.12d, A3. German. (The leading team aid-climbed preparing the route for a following free-climbing team.)

[89]

Paine North Tower:
El Caballo de Diablo

"PAUL ... PAUL ... Wake up. It's 3.30."

"Huh. Waaah?"

"It's 3.30. The stars are out and the pressure's still pretty high."

At that moment nothing matters. The whole world could go to hell. I wasn't bothered about climbing the North Tower of Paine anyway. My dream! There was somebody there I knew from back in Wales. Come back! Now see what he's made me do. I've lost the thread of my dream – if I look around every pebble-dashed corner, up and down the dark Welsh street, I might be able to find it again, under the orange cone of a street lamp in the mizzle. No. Gone.

"The Italians have already set off. Here, have some porridge."

The Italians! High pressure! The North Tower! My eyes sprang open and I wriggled out of my oily pit on the soil floor of the cabin. I looked at the altimeter, smiled, and forced cooling, pasty porridge down me with urgency, gagging.

"Don't they teach you how to make porridge in South Africa, Phil?"

Our footfalls upset a dark, cavernous forest and the rebounding stillness upsets me. It wasn't normal. A third day of high pressure and no wind. I had grown used to the wind and its rhythms and the creaking of the forest. Now in the stillness I could hear whispers, whispers of conspiracy. I stepped up my pace to keep up with Phil. Yesterday we had relaxed in the sun on the edge of the forest, by the river where we could get a good view of the towers. A hot, calm day and we were too tired to go to our peak of ambition. The day before that we had climbed Planet Earth to Pisco Control, a silly name for what might one day become a classic climb on Paine Chico. We climbed that apron on friction and then hand cracks through leaning corners up the tower above, all free, and topped out at 10 pm. The next morning, with our fingernails lifting from the dehydration, we couldn't get out of our pits. But today we had a dream. An unclimbed peak – just like Bonington and Whillans in '63, and again, twenty-nine years later, we were racing with Italians for the first ascent. But the Italians were an entertaining, noisy, laughing bunch whom we could never begrudge getting to the top first.

I struggled to keep up with Phil, a hard glob of porridge in my throat and my halogen pond of light bobbing, making shadows dodge behind trees or silently edge backwards. The Japanese camp was deserted. The cabins that the woodworking mountaineers had built whilst sitting out month-long storms were now like a ghost town on a spaghetti western movie set. I moved like an engine, too fast for my lungs, up the gully bed. The trees shrank until only knee-high and the world of towers opened out in the half-light. Only five or six of the shiniest stars still sparkled above Fortaleza and Escudo.

Phil stepped up the pace and I sweated. I couldn't curse him – like I couldn't envy him. His strength, his blond Viking looks, his educated conversation should have been all a pale, scrawny, uneducated Brit would want to be. But he was too big-hearted to inflame envy. And, of course, to be jealous of anything would be to make a mockery of this place we were in. Anyway, the deal was that he'd carry the heavier sack and I'd show him how it was done on the hard free pitches. You see, he'd seen my name in the magazines and was under the impression that I was some superstar free climber. And, what made it worse, I didn't try to side-step this compliment. I stood fast and preened my fame feathers. My free climbing renown, however misguidedly represented by the press, was my dutch courage to tell confident anecdotes to, and teach techniques (from the safety of our cabin) to this, to me then, near perfect man. Over the weeks of waiting, for the rain to stop falling and the forest canopy to quieten down, I would feed him tales of dynos and long run-outs above RPs at Gogarth or other loose and overhanging British crags. Through the successive waves of storm there seemed little chance that I would have to prove my mettle – though I wanted to. And now we were panting with hot, wet backs and brows toward a pillar which draped down from its virgin summit like a princess's gown dragging on a boulder-strewn floor.

The Italians were above us in the snow gully and they had made good steps for us. Hanging back always pays. But they also had a head start on the wall – another Italian team had already attempted a line and had left ropes fixed on the face. I dragged my legs ever upwards, lagging further always behind Philip and I came across a tangled mound of wood with shreds of canvas skin hanging from its skeleton. I rooted around and found the words 'Paine Hilton' painted on what must have been a door – it was the original Whillans Box tent I had stumbled across almost three decades after its construction. As I collapsed at the base of the pillar our friends were already jumaring. We had chosen a route to the right, not the easiest way up but we thought the most beautiful – an enormous, bottom-heavy hourglass, it seemed now, of worm-holed and wind-finished granite, beginning as a slab and becoming overhanging 600 metres above.

To go extra fast we carried nothing except a litre of water, a small bag of dried fruit and our jackets in a small sack which the second would carry. We left our plastic boots at the base and set off sprinting. The deathly cold of the rock seeped into our hands and they too died, became brittle, so the skin would tear off the backs of white knuckles in gritty finger cracks. We arrive at a squeeze coffin, an empty iron maiden, leaning over us, nearly horizontal. The rope-ends are passed to me. I set off shaking with cold bones and, maybe, the fear of having to prove myself. But good gear appeared in the recess and, as I back and kneed out towards La Fortaleza, I mellowed and grinned, and hot joy poured to my guts. We both had that feeling as we climbed, the one that comes with those alpine starts, that you are still wrapped in your early morning dream. Not fully awake but a lifetime away from being asleep, feeling as though you know where the next hold or jam is without bothering to look up. We shouted across to Fabio, Mario and Danny. They were at the top of the ropes and had begun a nailing pitch. We were level now. The sun rolled out from behind the Central Tower and massaged our faces with its prickly radiation. We sat on a square ledge and nibbled stony dried peaches. Elephant-bum cracks and tower-block corners fell rapidly behind us and we moved well together. We could hear, but were blind to, the explosions of rock as El Escudo shed some shale over the edge of its table top, in a penny-pushing arcade game, at the other end of our arena. Over here, right now, our mountain seemed harmless, in a lighter shade of silence.

Then came a wall, the crux for sure, sheer and split by a thin crack. I moved towards it on edges, sandpaper-rough, and slotted my fingers, bony, into its positive locks. I keyed in a good hex just in time for the first strong breath to come, like a sigh, off the icecap, rustling nylon and flicking tapes. El Hielo Sur, as they call it here in Magellanes, exhales after holding its breath for three days. You expect it to come some time, it's just that now we had another contender in our race for the summit. I moved as quickly as my body, waking up to the strains of the day, would allow, placing my left slipper on the uptight edge of the crack and my right crushed into crystalline dishes which offered more stick, like squashing a beetle, than the steep wall around. My fingers slipped and skin ripped. Thick dark blood bubbled up on my chalky hand and I sucked at the iron taste. I knew I couldn't fall and I milked the crack for all it was worth, like some demented maid grappling with uncontrollable udders. Phil's shouts of encouragement echoed around the walls (or in my head) and I whooped out loud when I

[93]

grabbed big jug holds. I got safe, hanging, and looked out west. Clouds poured like a mad scientist's experiment over the brims of our giant neighbours. But it couldn't be far now. We had to see how near we could push it. That shallow shame would always be there in the recesses of our minds if we bailed out now and the Italians climbed on. We egyptianed up wafer corners amidst ice-cream cornets for a few more comfortable lengths and arrived at a sundae ridge. We waded in our slippers, hugging the back of the mountain in defiance of the wind, which blew up the skirts of our jackets, up towards our summit ...

A flash of red, and some gagged shouts. The team from Trento had just squeezed onto the top a couple of minutes before us. Oh well, *es la vida!* We hugged, shook and tried to smoke. Later, the photos made it look like we were gurning; the wind didn't show up on celluloid, only our struggles against it.

"Just like Bonington. A new tower!" shouted Fabio, happy in the storm.

They invited Philip and me to share their descent. It wasn't far down to the fixed lines, six rappels perhaps. We slinged a block, and with four ropes we dropped faster than the SAS, over roofs and down flat walls in the ventilation shaft updraught. At the lines we felt safe and began to clean them down, so the route would be left, unlike so many other Patagonian walls, free from never rotting threads, tempting future climbers to miss out the crux pitch and trust to unseen threadbare edges ... Then the ropes were snagged by some unseen hand. The Italian trio were below us in the funnel-webbed corner. "Give it a good pull," I said, in what became the conclusion of the urgency with which we had started and spent our day. The way we led our lives.

One tug on this bell rope was all it took to peel away our good fortune and ring in the bad. The rope loosed and fell and in a baffled moment a house-brick rock followed. We pasted ourselves into the wall and screamed impotently *"Piedra!"* First Fabio took it on his head, then Mario clutched his leg and swung around silently. For a long moment all went still. It's funny how catastrophes don't always seem so catastrophic at the time. No flashing lights or flares shooting off, no screams of terror or fountains of blood –

just an image, like a newspaper photo of an earthquake or some-thing. You can choose to glance past it, move on to the crossword. It has all the impact you choose to attach to it. The two spinning in the wind could have been having a cheery chat or taking the piss out of us for, as so often happens, nearly wiping them out. But with rationale,the moment accelerated into urgency. No time for guilt just yet, we slid down to them as fast as friction would permit. Fabio giggled in his hysteresis and held up his broken helmet for our inspection. Mario moaned as we lowered him 300 metres. He was a big guy, mild-mannered and strong.

At the foot of the wall it was raining. Danny and Fabio, whose head, astonishingly, was not marked, eased off Mario's plastic boot to Italian cries of pain. Philip and I watched with sickly stomachs as the lower leg swung around wherever the boot did, like a second knee. Once the plastic shell was off and the bloody sock peeled back, Philip sighed to see the tibia thrusting up out of the front of his shin. When the leg was nudged a thick lump of dark blood would glop out and slither down his calf. He shook. We all did our bit; one put the emergency tent up, thoughtfully packed by Danny, others dressed the wound and splinted the leg with ski poles, and Fabio ran down to call a helicopter rescue. That would take him six hours if he kept moving. Philip, his chores done, held his head in his hands. I watched him silently torture himself with his very own herculean earth of guilt at what he had done.

But it was only your hand that pulled the rope down, Philip. I was the one who said to give it a good tug. I was the impatient one. And didn't Mario tell us he knew the risks that mountains offered, after all he'd climbed all over Paine. I just wish you were around to receive a postcard from him, cranking in Peru or on the Marmolada or the Cirque of the Unclimbables. I just wish you were here so we could go together and visit those mad Italians on their own mountains.

We slid down the slushy gully later to bring food and dry clothes up the following day. Philip was swifter than I and so I was alone again in the dark forest. Now the voices of the wood devils were clearer and I halted to hear what they were saying. *Troubletroubletrouble* the river muttered incessantly, and from the tree tops the leaves whispered *death ... death* in rustly gusts. I

[95]

cracked ribcage twigs and trod on skull boulders. From the mountains I could hear stranded climbers wailing from eternity. I had heard it all before in this magic forest but tonight it made my spine hunch up in protective spasms.

It should have been the sleep of the just but Philip couldn't calm himself. He had broken a man's leg and so now would not rest (only silently score patterns in the dark earth of the hut floor) to purge the guilt he felt. We abandoned our cosy cabin, with log fire and refried beans, before dawn and (I begrudgingly) returned through the cloud base. Midday we turned up with sleeping bags, mats, gas and nice food. Mario was loitering within his tent. In his own place with sticky drops of morphine. Danny's good humour was leaching into the wet snow. We waited ... Like long-suffering statues in a blustering, wet winter town centre, we stared out blankly into a prematurely induced twilight. Someone points out a useless fact.

"Can you hear that!"

"What?"

"Helicopter."

"Nah. It's a rock."

Boom. And a giant rumble comes from over by the Torre Centrale.

"It's a rock."

Minutes turn to hours turn to days turn to weeks turn to hours again in a didgeridoo wind of hypnosis.

Again. A pulse – to a different beat – very faint at first but getting nearer. Then like a flower-burst of hope over the ridge opposite a chopper surfaced, a tiny thing. The little black insect slalomed around the gusts as we shouted with clenched fists, thumping invisible tables – "*Yes*" and "*Yes*", and encouraged Mario. The hovering bubble with the one big compound eye rocked violently, and once dropped like God had cut its string. It struggled to free itself of the fat cherubs' great puffs for a little longer and then, to our dismay, turned and fled. We pricked our ears and scanned the milky sky, searching for a sign, like four unholy prophets waiting for a door to open in the clouds through which might stampede the Devil's horses to our salvation.

[96]

HE SLATE BOOM North Wales climbing was revitalized by the developments in the Llanberis slate
uarries in the early eighties. Many of the routes had long run-outs with marginal protection, calling for
reat skill, coolness and tenacity. There followed comparably bold forays on the Anglesey sea cliffs and
Sron Ulladale and the greater ranges. The photos illustrate three of the finest slate climbs: Rainbow
f Recalcitrance (E6, 6b) on Rainbow Slab *(above right)*; the author making the critical moves to reach
e bolt and sling on Raped by Affection, E7, 6c *(top left)* and leading the first ascent of I Ran the Bath
(E7, 6c) – Nick Harms belaying *(left). Photos: Iwan Jones (above right) and Tony Kay*

THE ANGLESEY SEA CLIFFS

The slate boom was matched by an equally intense period of new-routeing on the North Wales sea cliffs, most notably on the Left-Hand Red Wall of South Stack (*left*) and in Wen Zawn of Craig Gogarth (*right*).

South Stack's Red Walls (*lower left*) had been comprehensively developed, except for the blankest headwall in the Left-Hand Zawn. Here Pritchard's leads of Enchanted Broccoli Garden E7, 6b (first ascent view – *near left*) and the very serious The Super Calabrese E8, 6b, (*far left* – a repeat showing the author leading the critical second pitch with Andy Popp belaying) marked a distinct rise in wall standards in the area. *Photos: (far left top) Ben Winteringham, (bottom) Ken Wilson.*

On the overhanging back wall of Wen Zawn the Dawes/Smith creation Conan the Librarian (E6, 6b) captured the headlines in 1986. Paul Pritchard and Nick Dixon then added The Unrideable Donkey (E7, 6b) to the left of Conan (*above and left* – with Pritchard on Pitch 1). Later Pritchard nearly died here when he fell to the zawn bed from Games Climbers Play.

SRON ULLADALE'S (name recently changed from Strone by the O.S.) 200-metre overhanging end wall was first breached by Doug Scott's three aid climbs in 1969, 1971 and 1972. Paul Pritchard and Johnny Dawes forced the first free climb up the face in 1987 (E7, 6b – based on the original line of The Scoop) and later added Knuckle Sandwich (E7, 6c) and, with Ben Moon, Moskill Grooves (E6, 6b). These climbs triggered a full scale assault on the cliff with fourteen major new routes pioneered since (many Crispin Waddy and his friends), making it now a contender as the main venue for very hard on-sight traditional (i.e. not bolted) climbing in Europe and, possibly, the world.

enes during the 1987 first free ascents of
e Scoop – the original route (1969) on
e face:

ove: Johnny Dawes and Paul Pritchard
joy a midge-free moment below the
f. The overhanging Scoop section is on
e left. *Left, below and right:* Pritchard
ding the first pitch (6b) and Dawes on
e Flying Groove (6b) pitch and the
tical 8th pitch (6b). *Photos (left and
ove): Alun Hughes.*

CENTRAL TOWER OF PAINE Paul Pritchard, Noel Craine, Sean Smith and Simon Yates added a fifth climb on the East/North-East flank (*far right*) in 1991/92. These cliffs were first climbed in 1974 by the obvious diedre-line in the sunlit area. Three lines were then added to the face to the left (topo, p.72). The British team took a line up the right of the shadowy face, based on an impending diedre (the Great Scoop), followed by a chimney (the Coffin). Above these, at the 29th pitch, deteriorating conditions, plus food and fuel shortages forced a retreat from the face. Five days later, Smith and Pritchard, after a night of jumaring, pushed the route to the summit block. The pair managed to remove the bulk of the fixed equipment during their descent. *Above:* On the slab apron below the face – pointlessly equipped with over sixty bolts by Spanish climbers during an earlier attempt. *Right.* Craine and Pritchard at work on the face above the Portaledge Camp placed at the foot of the main tower. *Photos: (above and near right) Sean Smith*

The Great Scoop proved the hardest part of the Paine climb. It had two long pitches, the first led by Pritchard, with a major fall, the second (seen here) by Craine. "It had a stack of loose filing cabinets slotted into the top of it. I was belayed directly below, in the path of any keyed blocks he chose to unlock. To pass the blocks Noel first had to expand them with a pin, a delicate manoeuvre, and then aid up on micronuts. I had nowhere to run. He would say to himself, 'I'm weightless. I have no mass.' Using that meditation, even the most dreadful Rurp placement could be forced into offering some support."

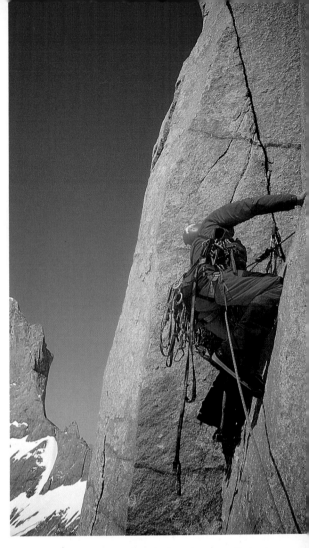

ove: Jumaring up the Great Scoop.
ht: Simon Yates climbing up to the foot
he Coffin pitch using a crack in the wall
he approach groove (5.6, A2+). *Photos:*
n Smith.

Left and below: At the Portaledge Camp at Christmas –
Yates abseiling, Pritchard in camp. The climbing involved
exploiting the short spells of good weather between the
regular Patagonian storms, all from this rugged but
serviceable hanging campsite. *Photo: (left) Sean Smith*

PAINE (cont.) High on the face a pendulum gained a crack system which led to less steep terrain a few pitches below the summit. At this critical point (*above*) a major thaw soon had the rocks streaming with meltwater, forcing a return to the valley. After a morale-boosting session in the fleshpots of Puerto Natales Pritchard and Smith felt 'rejuvenated' enough to return (*right*) to the mountain, jumar 1000m to the high point, and tackle the final difficulties (*below*). After ten hours of climbing (including a fall) they finally gained the summit area but, with time pressing, did not climb the final icy 7m obelisk. *Photos: Noel Craine (top) and Sean Smith.*

T ASGARD (Baffin Island) is a magnet to ...ern flank (above). In 1994 Simon Yates, ...ul Pritchard, Noel Craine (*inset – l to r*), Steve ...uinlan and Keith Jones set up a boulder/ ...owhole camp on the glacier below North ...ak's West Face (main picture – left profile).

MT ASGARD (cont.) The plan w
to tackle the West Face without t
use of bolts. But whereas the Pai
Towers are riven with vertic
cracks, the Baffin walls are ic
eroded and blanker. Americans w
had attempted the Asgard wa
believed that any future route wou
require bolting, or at least rivetin
to link features and make progres

Bad weather extended t
schedule and Jones and Yates we
compelled to leave for home. Luck
the Spaniard Jordi Tosas was able
team up with big-wall expert Quinl
to make up the foursome.

The line chosen had the m
linking features, starting with
obvious series of flakes which le
towards a corner system in the cent
of the face. A long free pitch, ther
section of aid, was followed by
pendulum to gain the Great Fla
which Craine climbed free at 5.
(*lower right inset*). On the wall abo
(*right* – Quinlan belayed by Tosa
vague seams and incipient featur
(blank sections turned by pendulur
or riveted), led to the central corn
where a Portaledge camp was sit
(*upper right inset*).

In the corner the aid difficulti
unexpectedly increased (*left* – Quin
lan leading) with brittle rock a
shallow seams, climbed with coppe
heads and birdbeaks, giving two A
pitches. A pendulum gave access
Pitch 10 – A2/A3 cracks (*below*), whi
led to a skyhook and rivet traverse
gain access to the diorite vein.

MT ASGARD (cont.)
After eleven days – climbing in the arctic light, non-stop, day and night, *(top:* Quinlan starting a night shift) – the final seven pitches (5.8–5.10) brought all four climbers to the summit. (*l–r:* Tosas, Craine, Pritchard, Quinlan). They had kept the drilling (all by hand) to 36 rivets and 10 bolts. There followed a 16-abseil descent de-equipping the route of the fixed

TRANGO TOWER Craine and Pritchard (part of an 8-person group) targeted a new route on the North Face in 1995 but, early on, Craine was injured in a crevasse fall. Pritchard teamed with Adam Wainwright (on his first Himalayan season) to try the Slovene Route (5.10, A2 or 5.12b). After one attempt (to five pitches above the Shoulder) bad weather forced a retreat. *Left:* The upper tower from the Shoulder – the route takes the central apron to overhanging corners. *Photo: Bill Hatcher. Below:* The team – *l to r* (back) Geraldine Westrup, Noel Craine, Kate Phillips, Adam Wainwright, Andy Cave, Capt. Jamal Mohammed; (front) Celia Bull, Donna Claridge, Ali Hussein Abadi, Paul Pritchard and Ismael Bondo.

TRANGO TOWER (cont.) A week of storms left the peaks encrusted with snow and ice (*above –* t Slovene Route takes the left edge of the Tower). At the earliest moment they left the shoulder for a rap lightweight summit push, only to find that every crack was choked with ice (*below –* Wainwright power up one of the upper corners). The lightweight tactics gave problems with just one pair of rock shoes, o pair of boots, one axe and no crampons – between two. On the third day, in deteriorating conditio with Pritchard having been hit by an ice block and showing signs of altitude sickness, Wainwright to over all leading and at 6.30 the pair summited (*inset*) during a fierce wind. With all stances 'equipped took just two hours of urgent abseiling to regain the Shoulder!

You can hear it again. Rotor blades. This time coming from below. There it is, just above the glacier's bad complexion. Barely moving and wagging its tail. But it turns tail and deserts us. The wind punches us in mockery, left hook, upper cut. Below the belt. There would be no helicopter rescue – so we made our own plans. I picked my way down the thousand-metre snow gully, which was now a series of waterfalls, to guide up any rescuers, whilst Philip and Danny prepared to lower Mario. Back in the trees, the mosses and bark were electrified with colour, I sank up to my ankles in the shagpile floor.

I arrived at the cabin to find the Chilean army grazing through our supplies, leaning on their guns, all in fatigues and jack boots. They had come to help with the rescue and, initially, I was grateful. In my tent snored another soldier, clutching his rifle, just in case. I shook hands with Fabio who chattered, with wild eyes in a too fast mix of Castillano and his own tongue, about the roller-coaster helicopter ride he had survived. He had a mission in those eyes and was gone – followed by Dad's Army. I tried to keep the same pace but my plastics turned to concretes and I dry heaved. It was like someone had pulled the plug on my record – I ground into the ground and couldn't play anymore. I curled up and snoozed in a four-poster gully bed, pulling a leaf quilt around me. Just a few minutes. Just a few ...

"Heh, huevon. Que pasa?"

I jump out of my dream, angry to have to leave Celia in that same orange lit, murky Welsh street. I was being shaken by Capitan Mainwaring and a group of journalists with big lenses who wondered if I was dead, they said. I guess I did look a sight. I don't bother to brush myself off, or explain my behaviour, before I regain my zombie strut in the tedious gully, followed by an excitable herd. I joined a growing team of helpers and spectators camped out at the base of the melting snow couloir. Fabio, Phil and Danny were lowering and sliding a green chrysalis, helped by other worker ants, Paula and Flavia, Italian partners. The Chilean army refused to go on the snow in their Doc Marten boots (which made the rescue much simpler), preferring to direct operations from below and throw the packing from our food around the moraine. I clambered up to my friends, sheepish for having been gone so long, though I had lost days somewhere. Phil turned and smiled briefly, but I didn't think he really noticed me in his strain of thought. I made myself useful by rolling a fag and sticking it in the pupa's mouth. It smiled back at me in a drunken sort of way. But it shouted out when we man- and woman-handled it down greasy crags, slipping and bumping. Fabio, who was close as a brother to Mario, took the rope at the head of his bound and bagged friend and dragged him through the snow, taking on himself as much weight as all us others would give. Like Gulliver and the Lilliputian ships, but he had a face full of agony. Mario was then passed onto the moraine shoreline from the ocean of snowy danger, into the hands of our fatigued lifeguards. Our corpse in a carpet suddenly became weightless as our testosterone-fueled friends eagerly proved their worth to us, passing him around like an antique Russian doll and marching off in a scrum, with a song, along the rubble ridge. Phil and I backed off while the others answered a hundred stupid questions, and the action was snapped that would be frozen on the front pages of tomorrow's nationals. But these badly shod paparazzi were an OK bunch, just a little out of their depth up here. But weren't we, also, doing a little more than mere paddling?

The Japanese camp welcomed us with open branches and spotlights from the beech leaf canopy. Tea was already brewing. The river played xylophone rhythms now and chatter and laughter competed with the mantra of the wind. Mummified Mario's ceremonious unwrapping was observed by an audience of faces all squeezed in. Flashguns flashed, questions were fired and notes were scribbled. Phil and I sat by the water, leant against an old mossy beech. He tossed pebbles into a green pool, occasionally glanced back at the throng.

"But it *was* a good route, Phil."

"Eh, it was." He threw another pebble with more force.

"What shall we call it?"

"El Caballo de Diablo." Slow, deliberate and well pronounced. A little girl we knew called Columba, Pepe the horsepacker's daughter, had shown us a Devil's coach horse one day and told us what it was called here in Chile.

"Sounds good." I meant it but perhaps, in my exhausted state, didn't show it. We both understood. To our ears the familiar wind metamorphosed into the throb-throb of the little insect chopper and down it settled on the shingle beach, blowing on our faces. I got a lump in my throat. We all held Mario's hand before they slotted him into the black bubble to fly him off to Punta Arenas, eighty miles away. The insect lifted off and the trees leaned to let it through. They swayed back in to prevent a long goodbye and the sound was soon stolen back by the wind. We were left to mill around. It was late February and, for us, the end of the climbing season.

The Italians returned home to their jobs and tight families. Philip and I went to Argentina for more adventures before I went my own way on my nine-month wander of South America. Mario got an infection in his break but recovered within a year, so he could continue his work as a Dolomite ranger.

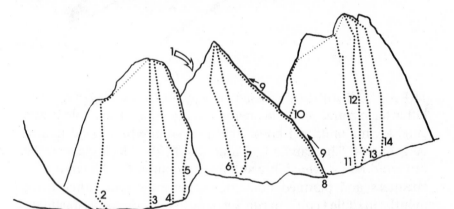

The North Tower (left and centre summits) and Central Tower of Paine (right) – North West Faces (Based on topos and reports in the American Alpine Journal with some changes).

1 East Face (Kaweskars) 1993 Anthoine Cayrol, Francois Bernard with Tierry Petitjean, Laurent Fabre, Hubert Giot.
2 Armas y Rosas 1993 Lorenzo Ortiz, Jose Chaverri.
3 Adrenalina Vertical 1992 Mario Manica, Fabio Leoni, Danny Zampiccoli.
4 Suetra para Mañana 1992 Carlo Besane, Nobert Riva, Mauricio Garota, Manuela Panzeri, Umberto Villota.
5 South Buttress (El Caballo de Diablo) 1992 Paul Pritchard, Philip Lloyd.
6 Capachín Tórtola 1993 Ramiro Calvo, Diego Luro, Teo Plaza.

7 Ultima Esperanza 1992 Michel Piola, Vincent Sprüngli.
8 Corn Wall 1993 Paul Pritchard, Celia Bull, Leigh McGinley.
9 Via Bich (Monzino Route) 1958 Jean Bich, Pierino Presson, Camillo Pelissier, Leonardo Carrel. (from Col)
10 Central Tower, Original Route 1963 Chris Bonington, Don Whillans with, in support, John Streetly, Vic Bray, Barrie Page, Ian Clough, Derek Walker. (from Col)
11 Kanterarikez 1991 Jon Lazkano, Kiki de Pablos plus, in support, Guillermo Banales.
12 Wild, Wild West 1990 Scott Cosgrove, Jay Smith.
13 Via Defrancesco / Manica / Stedile 1987 Fabrizio Defrancesco, Mario Manica, Fabio Stedile. 1987
14 Via de las Mamas 1992 (line on AAJ diagram but details not recorded).

Just Passing Through

THE *MATÉ* GOURD was passed my way again. I sucked it dry, the bitter taste convulsing the opening to my gullet. I was told it was good for me and, as I knew, the taste of anything good had to be acquired. The candle had a double in the black glass of the hut window. I shivered. It was a freezing night. Los Chicos played chequers and planned new routes for tomorrow. After three months in Chile I could hardly recognise their tongue as Castilian. The sound of *Metallica* came from the kitchen. They played their heavy metal all the time and they grew their hair long and wore leathers and beads. Here, somewhere in Argentina, a small pocket of teenagers mirrored other pockets of climbing subculture in the UK or America. They were living for the day and for the rock. And on the rock they were already experts, tutored by their, at twenty-one, elder statesman Sebastian de la Cruz. Sebas, spindly, nervous yet driven to the point of obsession, of Swiss descent, had climbed the giants of Patagonia at sixteen and los Chicos had followed, climbing Cerro Torre, Fitz Roy and Torre Centrale sometimes by new routes. I was impressed by their ability and drive. It's more difficult to give it all up for climbing in this country. There is no welfare state and, with the Catholic church, religious values are stronger than in Britain. Las Chicas are stretching on the wooden floor in the candle light. They're into metal and rock too but seem a little less inclined to give up their career options totally. Gaby and Marcella study in nearby Bariloche and Fera works in the ski area in winter, teaching and guiding. Las Chicas and los Chicos seem to do everything together; climb together, eat together, party together and sleep together. They chatter incessantly and make plans for their next day.

I was dizzy. I needed air. *"Buenas Noches, Chicos y Chicas."* I stumbled out of the *refugio* door into a night which was a long way from home. Frost pinpricked the exposed and unexpecting flesh of my face. It pinpricked the skin of the sky too and stark light shone in through the holes. This night was strangely two-dimensional. Scores of spires were silhouetted against starlight and crowded around like Klu Klux hoods. I liked *maté*. To look down on the lake was as to look up at the sky, creating the illusion of being suspended in the centre of a giant ball, dark, matt, but with millions of tiny holes. I buried my head in my pit and began to dream on the shore of the lake.

An almighty explosion.

I jumped bolt upright in shock. So did Phil.

"What was that?"

"I don't know. A meteorite perhaps."

"Yeah, right. G'night."

"G'night."

We awoke with the sun. The Klu Klux hoods were now bright shadowless spires. Five condors wheeled above the highest one, el Torre Principale. Over breakfast we pondered the mysteries of the night and decided that the next evening we would take more *maté*.

We shouldered our packs and went exploring. The mountains were further away than they appeared. We gazed at the panorama from above the forest canopy for these dwarf beech grew only to our nipples. Bluey chinchillas ran up and down the vertical walls. We arrived at the base of the Pyramidal and touched the rock. It was warm and rough to the touch. Unclimbed cracks were lined up side by side.

"Wow! This must be what it was like in Yosemite in the fifties."

The *vias normales* had perfect lines but new rock was the essence of climbing for us; throwing loose holds over the shoulder, feeling the exposed grains crush like sugar on footholds, no chalk ahead to show the way and no idea, apart from a contract which the eye has with the body, of whether you are capable of getting up a thing or not. I uncoiled the rope at the bottom of a hand crack which snaked up the wall and flared through a roof. The rock was deep red liver. The crack went, just, but intolerant. It meted out its punishment like Wackford Squeers, so that's what we named it. I had the bloody hands to prove it. From the summit we looked across to the Chilean Lake District and its volcanos; Osorno and Villarica, floating on a plate of cloud. On the Argentine side was Tronador, the Thunderer, that later claimed Teo's life in an unfair avalanche. Out east shimmered the brown Pampa and, nearer, the resort of San Carlos de Bariloche fitted snugly between the Andes and Lago Nahuel Huapi like some South American Inter-laken. The tourists down there would be buying their ski passes and eating famous chocolate. Nazi war criminals who had escaped Europe after the war used to live there. Perhaps some still do. Nearer again los Chicos and las Chicas could be seen and heard laughing and ascending other spires. I felt then that Frey was another special place. A place where climbers lived who cared for it, and knew it well enough to say that the yellow rock was more brittle than the red, or that there are hidden holds inside that crack, or that the number of condors is on the up, that the boulder in the next valley gives good shelter, or at what time exactly does the sun shine on that face of the mountain. Simple shared knowledge. That which we have of our home rocks. And, for all their magnificence, this particular specialness is lacking in the more remote mountains of the Himalaya or amongst the Patagonian giants. Very few climbers live through all four seasons in those places.

"*Las Malvinas son Argentinas. Las Malvinas son Argentinas.*"

[102]

That night the army arrived, a hundred of them with horses. They made a lot of noise and crapped a lot. I became the butt of all their Malvinas jokes and agreed, we shouldn't have sunk the *Belgrano*. But I came out on top after selling most of my gear to them. With that cash I could head on to Brazil and Bolivia. They had come to lay their yearly siege on Torre Principale and for days a khaki ant line was lashed to the tower which buckled under their enthusiasm and jollity. With the *maté* the nights became more feverish and the dreams more intense.

It was getting late in the season and a cold wind blew in from the icecap. Climbers were migrating. Phil, my transient South African friend, to the Atacama Desert and los Chicos, after evading national service, to Peru. Ramiro was the only one who had to have his dreads cut off and join up. They sat around the radio and listened to the lottery of numbers, each with their own army number, which they had been recently posted, clenched in their fists. "*Siete, dos, cinco, tres*" the officer's voice had said over the air waves and Ram's head dropped with his friends' hands on his shoulder. He wouldn't get to Alpamayo and Huascaran now. I took to soloing for a while.

In the shade it was cold but, if I turned to the sun, I felt its warm hand on my cheek. The 180-metre Torre Principale stood stark white above me. I was the only climber in the whole of Frey that day. I took my clothes off, it felt like the right thing to do, and put my boots on. Goose flesh prickled up on my body and I started to climb fast to keep warm. The first couple of pitches were easy but on the exposed off width of the third pitch the wind picked up. Though my genitals had shrunk dramatically, I couldn't help scraping them on the edge of the crack. Higher, a more sheltered steep corner began with a boulder problem which was luckily above a ledge. This led more easily up to the notch between the twin summits. I huddled up and shivered in the shade of that notch until I could linger no more. I tiptoed onto the summit block which leaned over a dark void and I crimped and edged, pecking at holds like a chaffinch toward where there was no more rock. The condors were near. This was their country. Now they were below me as they spiralled the tower. Their giant wings against the wind made the sound of an aircraft or sometimes, and not without surprise, the whoosh of a falling rock. As I climbed higher the rock fell away before me and I broke into a sort of vertical sprint. I manteled onto the top feeling like a chimpanzee, stooped, with my arms swinging low. I surveyed the now familiar world below and sensed something had come to an end. I opened the heavy summit tin and, after signing my name in the book and reading the soldiers' comments, I began to wonder how I was going to get down.

10

The Doctor and the Witch

THE DIMENSIONS of the room grow alternately larger then smaller. I can still remember my name, though I don't care to. Faces I think I know, faces I don't, come and peer over the edge of some invisible rim every minute or every age, I don't know. The bed is wet under my backside. I'm so hot I'm burning up. I itch. I want to sit up and ask these people what is going on.

"*Se parece peor, no.*"

"*Si. Vamos a buscar un doctor.*"

"*Es un buen idea pero hay unas brujas afuera en la calle.*"

What are these people talking about? Where am I? Hold on. I remember. It's becoming clearer.

I'm fighting through dense undergrowth. It's very hot and sticky. The wall isn't getting any nearer. Rat and Iñaki are up ahead and I am following with Kiko. Early morning and so hot already. This jungle climbing freaks me out, since getting stung by giant black bees in Rio.

Every insect makes me flinch. They say there're hundreds of kinds of poisonous insects in the Amazon. There must be spiders all over these trees just waiting to drop on us. Big hairy tarantulas and black widows.

"Hola, Paul. Hemos traido una Bruja. Te va a mejorarse."
What are they saying. Translate. They've brought ... a witch ... who will make me better. They have set a paraffin stove up by the bed and are boiling water. The old woman pulls some dead plants from her colourful bag and stuffs them into the pan.
"Aqui, bebe."
A witch! I've seen them out in the street, lined up selling llama foetuses and coca leaves. What's she giving me. No. I don't want it.
"Bebe, bebe!"
She's making me drink from the cup. Ahhh, it's revolting. GET THAT STUFF AWAY FROM ME. I nearly puke again but I've nothing left to give. The big woman with the bowler hat on disappears and I'm ...

At the base of the wall now. We think we've found the start of the route. Salinas has a big North Face, twenty pitches they say. There's no cracks anywhere to be seen, all face, dead run-out apparently. Kiko and I go first. I lead in a still heat. It's easy to start with, just scrambling. Then it gets steeper and I have to think. I've brought some nuts but there's no place to slot them. The cloud forest opens out below us as we climb above the canopy. Kiko begins singing and I join in. We whoop and whistle at our friends below.

I'm on my hands and knees in a corridor. I think I wanted the bathroom, or have I already been? It was that dog, I know it. I was camping below Condoriri and that dreadlocked dog came and licked my pans in the night. For days previously I had shat by the same rock and every morning I would find my shit had been eaten. It was that dog, I know it. That dog gave it me. If I see it again I'll shove its balls down its throat, the dirty hound. I've got to get myself cleaned up. Got to get myself back to bed. I stagger into my room. My bed has a large brown stain on it. Outside the window I can hear the witches touting their wares and there's a brass band approaching. I pull off the sheet, throw it under the bed and climb back in. I want to go ...

"Mum, I was just attacked by a group of boys. They shot at me with air rifles and chased me." I lied to her again and she took me out driving, looking for the yobs who would dare to threaten me. We drove up and down the lanes in our blue Datsun, scouring the countryside. It made me feel happier. Did you know that I lied to get attention? You were good to us, but with the family breaking up you had to work hard to build a new life for us. At the time I thought that you just had no time for us. She looks at me kindly and says I know.

But it's so hot here, and my head is pounding. Sweat is stinging my eyes.

The rock is steeper now and hot to the touch. There's never any gear, just a rusty old bolt every half rope-length that the local Brazilians had drilled. The pockets in the granite slope and my hands are sweaty. Watch me, Kiko, watch me. There are evil cactus and giant yucca growing out of the rock. If I fall I'll be impaled on these evil things. My fingers begin to slip. I don't want it to end like this. I want to ...

Get better. To carry on with my South American adventure.

Who's this?

"Soy el doctor, Paul. Tu amigos mi dicen que no te sientes bien."

Damn right I don't feel well. He's asking me question after question and it's all blending into one. I wish someone would speak sweet English to me. He is going in and out of focus and talking with others. NO I DON'T WANT TO GO TO HOSPITAL. *No mi voy al hospital.* Get me in there and I'll never come out. He's pulled out a big syringe and is squirting liquid from the end of it. So cold. It's so cold. He's putting the needle in my arm now. I don't feel anything. Just the cold. I need to get to ...

The top of the wall is a long way above and the clouds have come swirling all around us. This mist is wet and freezing cold. Should have brought more clothes than just this shirt. We are forced into a long

*leftwards traverse now by an overhang above our heads. There is no
protection in sight. Our friend Sergiño, the capsicum farmer, who
pointed us at this mountain, said this was the most difficult passage,
5.12b. That's a hard grade for these conditions. I cast a worried glance
toward Kiko, my Argentinian friend . He's happy seconding the whole
wall. He hasn't done anything like this before and I told him it would be
una riesa, a laugh. I'm twelve metres away from him now and I can
only just see him through this cloud. I have to fingertip mantelshelf
these tiny edges. These Brazilians are psychos. I try once, pushing
down with my fingertips, my back arched, wanting to put my right foot
where my hand is. I waver. On the fence. My fingers begin to buckle and
my feet skate back down to their little refuge. I stare into the rock and
flex my knuckles. This time. I dig my nails behind the tiny edges, as if
to prise them from the rock, and bounce my torso up and to the right,
using only the rock's friction for my feet. Again I start to totter,
metronoming back and forth, but now I push harder, stabbing the wall
with my toes, arse out, Sniffing the rock. I don't think I can ...*

He's still here, the doctor. Or has he come again? His syringe is
out again and it is gigantic, towering above me. He shakes his
head and says that all us gringos take too much of the white
powder.

"*Demasiado polvo blanco, senor.*"

I just stare and ... Aaaw! And then I can't ...

Make the move. It's my first VS. My skinny arms are tired and
I'm holding my hex 9, the drilled-out one which I bought off PK.
Trog is belaying me and he's stood miles away from the bottom of
the crag. Why is this called the John Henry quarry? Who was he
anyway? I make one last lunge, aiming for nothing in particular,
and then I am falling. I clutch my new hex to my chest and I
wonder if my original Moac will hold. Trog runs even further
away from the wall to take in the slack and I land, bent kneed on
the taut rope. I slide toward him, upside down, then I flip off and
hit the heather. Behind the knee of my hairless leg there is a large
wound. I can see the tendons like white strings and I begin to
blubber, just like when I would run to my mum as a kid. Trog
starts laughing. Guess I'm still a kid.

Shaking. I can't control the shaking.

Get your foot on. Stand up.

Rayo and Unai have left me some boiled rice before they went to do Llimani. I can't face it. Why have they left me? Such a long way from home. Home. Is that the derelict industrial wastes to the north of Manchester, where my blood is, or a sofa in Llanberis, where my friends and my rocks are? The dereliction is home. Can't get away from that. That's where I would go crying to my mother. But you're too old for that. The walls of the dark room have moved away and it's light and exhilarating and ...

I push with my leg and push with my hand on my knee. I rise in shudders and jabs, shaking in the updraft and then I am stood straight, on the tiny edge. I know I've done it. It looks easier ahead. I continue shuffling and still no gear. "You'll love this, Kiko." He comes across with a backrope from the others, laughing at me. It's getting late, the sun is low. If we move it we can top out before it gets dark. We need to top out if we want to ...

Get better. I just want to be better so I can carry on to Peru. If I can sell the rest of my climbing gear there, I can buy a ticket out of this place and hang out with my old friends again, see my family (this time I will visit them more often, let them know how I feel). I can hear Unai and his girlfriend having sex on the other side of this flimsy wall. It goes on and on and I stare at the flakes of paint on the ceiling, making shadows in the white light of the street lamp. I hear my Basque room-mates groan, "If he drank less maybe he would be able to come and give us all some peace." I curl up with more stomach cramps, my ten second warning ...

The witch. It's the witch again. I don't want her in here. No more of your potions. You tried to poison me.

"*Tranquilo. Tranquilo. Vamos a ver tu futuro.*"

She wants to tell me my future. She's lit her stove again and she's melting lead in a pan. Now the lead is molten she pours it on the floor. She is sat on her haunches looking at me grinning from her big head. *"Kamisiraki,"* I say, my only Quecha word. *"Gualiki,"* she replies. The lead is set and she peels it up and lifts it in the air. She studies the frozen molten shapes, tracing them with her finger, and holds my wrist. She speaks.

"Te vas a mejorar, Y te vas a llegar a tu hogar algun dia pronto."

I will be better. I will get home soon. Thanks, witch. *Gracias, gracias ...*

We are below a chimney and the sun is burning again. I wipe the sweat from my forehead with my T-shirt. I move into the coolness of the shadows and bridge and back and foot easily upwards, though some gear would be nice. The clouds come swiftly back again, swirling hands fingering my passage. They take Kiko and the whole world away from me and I move as fast as I can to outrun their grasp. Into the light again. And back into chilly fog. I can hear something. Morena la de los ojos azules No. That's not right.

"La reina de las mujeres."

I can hear a serenade. And laughter. It's the Basques on the balcony. They're inside now taking lines and going on about some sleazy club they're off to in the centre of La Paz. *Cuidado*, guys. Watch out for *sucia policia*. The cops are bad news here. They took Kiko's passport off him the other day and said he couldn't have it back unless he gave them fifty bucks. The lad had no choice. The military are crazy, too ... I am walking along minding my own business. A mumbling has started in the street. *El Terror, El Terror* they whisper. The mumbling has turned into shouts and people begin to panic. Street traders hurriedly pack up their jewellery and start to run. I just stand here and wait like an idiot. Then I hear the engine and into the street rumbles a yellow armoured vehicle and on its flank, in black, is painted EL TERROR. The soldier on top opens fire with his water cannon and sprays anyone who comes into the monster's way. I cower in a doorway and feel appalled at this mindless intimidation. I want to go home now.

The angle is easier now. We can see the top and we are cruising.

I feel more alive today. The guys are back off the mountains and I ate some more rice. Hope I can hold it down.

Look, I've found a metal tin. There's a scruffy little book. Let's sign our names in it. Ours are the first non-Brazilian names in here. Across the cloud forest we can see false horizons, one dome of granite after another stretching past the horizon. Our sun is setting and back-lighting them.

Night-time. They are all bladdered and loudly asleep. Something's changed. I feel OK. No more possessed by that heinous virus. God, I'm hungry. I want cornflakes, cheese on toast and beans, dough-nuts and custard slices. But first I need to shower the past ten days from me.

I hate rappeling in this darkness. I can never find the belays. The air has become heavy and moist and cold. Ten raps they said but I can only just see a metre in this fog. We have hit a terrace of spiky plants and it's my turn to go first. I slime over the edge and begin to descend. I have tied a knot in the end of my double ropes. When I reach the end of them I am still on a smooth wall. I swing back and forth in the whiteness of my headtorch beam, expecting to find a ledge but there's nothing. I am carrying Rat's rope, so I tie that on and rap again. Another fifty metres and still nothing. Guess this is the wrong spot. In this cold it doesn't seem very important to me. I just wish I had some prusik loops. I tie my shoe-laces onto the rope and begin to struggle upwards. It is boring and difficult. I tie the climbing rope to my harness at intervals so that if my shoe-laces snap I won't die. It's an hour or so later and I slump back onto the ledge. Iñaki has gone completely silent and is shaking violently. I question him but he won't answer. This is annoying me. Rat is the only other that has climbed anything big before so the two of us hold a conference, in English so the other two can't listen. "God knows what's down there, Rat. It could have been three metres to the ground or a hundred. I feel wasted now."
"Let me take over, Paul. You look after Iñaki." Rat disappears down a different route and I don't know what to do with our hypothermic friend. We huddle together and shake in our T-shirts. Then there's a

shout. *Very faint but we just hear it. "Come On Down Venga." I send the others and follow them to a ledge with a worn tree. This is the one, look, it's been abbed on before. Now there is more hope the boys buck up and in a couple more rope-lengths we hit the deck.*

There must be a path here somewhere but I think we lost it long ago. There's no point in backtracking. We'll just have to keep crashing downwards over small cliffs and through spiky bushes. Bet this place is crawling with spiders and snakes at night. What's that? Eyes! No, glow worms I think. Get me out of here, They have coral snakes, you know. The most dangerous snakes in the world. Dead in seconds and this place could be crawling with them.

I can breath again. We are out of the undergrowth and into a pasture. Look there's the hut. I look up at the sky. The stars are out now. "Hijo de puta," says Iñaki. "Vamos a Bolivia." I couldn't agree more. Let's get to La Paz where there's warm beds and bars and parties. I've had it with these walls.

A Game One Climber Played

I AM LYING in long grass, naked, I think, foetal. Warm. It's so pleasantly warm. I can hear distant cries. Children playing? I am adrift, going further and further toward slumber. I don't see but I feel I am surrounded by tall hedges. Insects buzz. Darkness begins to creep over me – my eyes are shut but I can feel it. Still warmth and a smiling comfort. Someone takes my hand – she must be knelt by me. I don't open my eyes, nothing need be physically gestured.

Then the hand slips inevitably away and I am left in a cavernous night with all the contentedness of a young child dozing in the afternoon. This is it, the most beautiful part of all my life. Utterly final.

"*Paul.*" A distant voice calls out.

"*Paul, wake up.*" Nearer now.

"WAKE UP."

Leave me alone. Let me sleep. Let me go.

"Come on, Paul, WAKE UP." My body is being shaken violently. In anger now I turn to scold my disturber. "Why don't you just ..."

... LIGHT – My eyes open. Someone has just thrown an electrical appliance into my wet dream and 240 volts are put through me. A blur. It's too bright for me to see. I want to ask questions (*Where am I? What the hell is going on?*) But it's impossible. I am just a single painful thought in a space of white noise. Then somewhere, below me and my thought, a body, I think related to me, attempts to breathe. An implosion of sharp points. The body convulses and is thrown onto its side. Lines, horizontal, vertical, diagonal. Beginning to focus. And colours, too. I gain some comprehension of what I am. *And colour!* A jet of red pisses out of my mouth and then a deafening sigh. Convulsions follow. More red water. Enormous gasps. Daggers are screwed further into my chest. *My chest!*

"Paul, you're in Wen Zawn and you've just ripped all your gear. You hit these rocks and then you went in the water. This is Glenn."

The words swim around in my head looking for a place to attach themselves. They settle in all the wrong places, though anagramatically they make some sense ... Glenn Zawn ... Hit the sea rocks ... "You've been wedged under water for about ten minutes. I pulled you out feet first." Glenn ... Gogarth ... "Glenn," I shout but no sound comes. Again I try to inhale the white noise but my throat will not allow it. Something stabs and twists. This is it. You've done it now. You've punctured your lungs for sure. Sleep ... Sleep. *Yeah go on, go to sleep and you'll die, you pathetic shit.* Is that me or someone else being cruel? I sob uncontrollably. My eyes focus now on Glenn. He's trying to solo up the wall of the Zawn. My whole body feels broken. Is it spread over all these rocks. "Don't leave me, Glenn." Still nothing comes out. Like a dolphin I dive in and out of a sea of unconsciousness. I want to continue my sleep, but my slumber is intruded upon.

"Paul, wake up – I'm your doctor and I just want to put this tube up your nose. Swallow as I push it in."

The sky, the sea, the walls of the zawn are stark white and ugly.

[114]

The whole world is ugly. The pieces of my life are shaken through a sieve and the finer particles settle around me. My family, my friends, the woman I love. My body shudders in waves. I'm falling again but I can never tell if it's for the last time.

"Paul, it's raining outside. Let's stay warm under the covers. Let's stay in bed."

Am I this sad for them or for me? What a profound welling up of all the unfinished stories. The potential fairytale endings or the emotional farewells. From my right temple blood wicks across my wet face. It's still raining. My shoulders feel like they're in pieces. With each tiny gulp of air I inhale more panic. I want oxygen. Another time I slip into blackness.

"Paul, wake up – the stars are out, the weather's clear. We could be at the base of the Torre by 8.30."

Pain in back, in pelvis, in both ankles.

Glenn has dressed me in his clothes, but still I have gone beyond the shivers. From time to time the rigidity falls from me as though I am soaked in a hot bath. Then again distant voices laugh and shout. I strain but they don't come nearer. My imaginary saviours drift away. I am held.

"Paul, wake up." Glenn is slapping me about my face. "Don't sleep, it's dangerous." Now he's holding up a piece of frayed wire. "Look, you snapped a bloody wire. And the tide's coming in pretty fast." The bag of bones rattles on the hard, spiky floor. The tide could come in, night could fall, a storm could blow in from the west. I could slip out of my own back door and never return. It's not a problem for the bones. But it is a problem for Glenn. I hear him shouting. He informs me that five hours have passed.

My eyes hinge open. Above, the walls of the zawn are like the ribcage of some giant animal seen from the inside. The clouds are bent. For a fabulous moment my view becomes the cupola of Madrid's church of San Antonio, a circular sweep of Goya's colourful people against dull grey and green. The saint performs his miracle as the murderer slinks off into the crowd. The livid corpse I don't see. Over the railing San Antonio beckons to us down here. He waves. I feel important, at the centre of his miracle. They all wave.

"Paul, they're here. The rescue team."

Rescue? Ah! The cliff top. Adrenaline-fuelled ambivalence gives way to momentary excitedness, and more gulping for air. I hear the throbbing pulse of a helicopter and out beyond the neck there is a red boat which says RNLI. A dinghy speeds in and out clamber men without faces. As they lash me to a stretcher one of them asks me, "What's wrong? You've done way harder things in this zawn." I laugh. They are good at their job. I get panicky as I'm nonchalantly passed around inches above a clawing swell, all strapped up. Little gulps. Small gulps.

I am clipped into cables, winched up, swung around, lowered down, winched up again and pulled into a hovering yellow helicopter. The noise worries me. A mask is planted over my nose and mouth, a tap is turned and with a hiss my anxieties dissipate. The men grow faces. I shut my eyes ... *A sloping shelf running with water. I can't swing my feet back onto the rock. I can't hold on any longer.* I try to move up but I am strapped down. I slump back and relax. My body and the day begin to fit together.

I had wanted to reacquaint myself with the intricacies of climbing in Wen Zawn before attempting the big new line again up the back wall. It is wild rock down there. Unpredictable, untamable for some. You have to take time to build up a relationship where you and the rock can trust each other. I had been here many times, scared myself and forged partnerships. Conan with Dave Green, The Unridable Donkey with Nick Dixon, Rubble (the softest route in the world) with Leigh McGinley. 'An easy day,' on the direct start to Games Climbers Play, I had said to Glenn. It went near the line of my project and we would have a good view across. We rappeled in to the foot of the zawn and Glenn got a belay about fifteen feet up above the lapping waves. Drizzle steadily fell. The moves began scary and awkward. I had to climb down twice before I could arrange some protection in clay/rock mix. I started to move up, confidently, with all the inflated ego of a seasoned Gogarth climber about to plod up an easy Extreme. A couple more small wires, tips laybacking, then dripping hand cracks through steps of roofs. I was tiring but I knew how far I could go after I had hit the lactic acid wall. The belay was right there. Chalk was turning to mud in the cracks. I hung in there, pumping heavily and my forearms burned. I threw in a couple of extra Friends in case I should fall. "Jeez, Glenn, this is strenuous for E4!"

In the flared crack, fisting to the cuffs, I was faced with a choice; continue with deadmeat hands for six more feet and step across to the ledge, or move right now and grab hold of the same ledge. The decision had to be made in less than a second. I swung right from the crack and grabbed the ledge with my right hand. Water began to make little rivers down to my armpit. My feet cut loose into space, so I repositioned them on greasy smears and brought my left hand over. My error became apparent – the ledge was smooth and moist and sloped toward me alarmingly. I tried to mantel. No. Again. No. One more time. Utterly pumped I hung like a rag doll for a few timeless seconds contemplating the inevitable.

Without shouting to Glenn I throw myself off the rock to avoid falling badly. I am not too worried as I've got plenty of gear in, but I begin to accelerate. The horrid notion flashes across my mind that the cams haven't held and I brace myself for a longer fall. In the confusion I feel myself slow down imperceptibly and almost begin to relax. Then I continue to accelerate again. Instinctively, like other animals, I prepare to land on my feet. Ten pieces of gear explode from the rock. I land atop a sharp ridge sticking up out of the zawn floor and my right ankle crushes with the impact. In the same blurred moment I rocket head first into a narrow cleft of flushing sea water and stop.

And then I am lying in long grass, naked, I think.

12

Adrift

A BARE ROOM. A cell within a cell within a cell. Solitary confine-
ment at a high angle. Under the interrogation lamp. Trickling salty
sweat. Blinded by the light. Ball and chained by my rack of iron. I
contemplate the pendulum from where I am. Riveted to the spot –
on a ladder of rusty dots. Halfway up a clown's face, bending over
us. With orange skin and black streaks where his mascara has run.
Yes, he gets crazy and cries, but now he's laughing. The victims of
his slapstick humour hold on, not getting the joke, getting nervy.
Whilst the crowd below roars with laughter.

❋

One, two, go.
No.
One, two, three, go.
One, two, three, shit.

One, two, go.

Again.

One, two, three, *no.*

One, two, three, yes, yes, c'mon, shit, no.

"Steeeeeve."

"Whaaaat?"

"I'm level with a spike. 'Bout twenty-five feet away. Trying to lasso it."

"Okaaay."

One, two ... No.

Two, three ... No.

What's wrong with the thing.

One, one, go. Why do I bother ...

"Paauul."

"*Wot?*"

"What's taking so long?"

"It's not easy, Steve, believe me."

One, two, three, no.

This time. One, two, yes. Ahaah. Yes.

"Got it, Steve."

"Niiice work."

Tie in to the lasso rope.

"Now lower me."

Come on, calm down, You can't hurt yourself yet.

I'm scared.

You're scared of failing in front of him. That's what it is.

But what about all these ropes and knots? I'm confused.

Concentrate on your job, man.

Swooosh.

The peregrine again.

Just climb the rope and prepare the spike for the pendulum, will you.

OK, the sling's on but the spike's a bit rounded now that I look a bit closer.

It'll do fine. You're just bottling.

"OK, Steve. Lower us, will you."

Why do I use 'us'? It implies that there's more than one of me.

"That'll do."

Perhaps there is.

There's only one of you. Now think about this swing ... You don't need to check your knot, you checked it ten minutes ago!

"OK. Hold me there. I'll get a swing going."

(From the meadow a wall-watcher sees a tiny dot, like a money spider, swinging left and right, left and right in a draft a little higher than some white bags).

There's an edge, an edge.

No, can't reach.

(The swinger's arc decreases and stops).

"I'll have to come down some more, Steve."

(The watcher's eye is still on the lens as the dot swings further and further. The watcher feels giddy just looking. The dot bounces out as well as across).

The edge – go on.

No.

One more.

One, two, three, jump ... One, two.

One, two, jump ... One, *yurs*!

(The dot stops at the end of its swing. Like an executive toy disobeying gravity).

OK, more edges. Free climb but keep the tension.

Sweat. Grains of granite the size of boulders.

"Keep the tension."

Can't go any further, I'll take a pisser. I'm level with the spike. It's miles away.

Get a hook on.

Fuck, fuck the hooks. Where the fuck're the hooks?

On your left, idiot.

Found them. *But the ledge slants.* If he gives me slack my body weight will be pulling straight down and the hook'll roll off.

Use two hooks in opposition then.

Facts like billboards.

That kinda works ... *Phoooo.*

Calm down. Calm down.

There's nothing here, I gotta drill.

If you drill it won't be A5.
I can't climb A5. I can't cope.
Thudthudthud.
My heart sounds like the hammer.
Very observant. Come on you've got a long way to go.
He knows I'm drilling.
He would, too. What makes him so high and mighty?
Bangbangbang.
The hammer's become a limp fish.
At last.
Finally.
"OK, Steve. I gotta bolt in."
"Good one. Howzit look above?"
"More hooking then a ramp thing."
Hear that?
"Hear that?"
The girls
"The girls."
*They've laid out their colourful clothes on the grass and their shouts
harry to your fear.*
"'Honeeeeee, wee loave youuu.'"
Do you think they heard?
"Yeeeeeaaaah."
They heard.
I want her. Couldn't they rap in to us or something?
OK, hooking, hooking. Yes. Stand up. And another.
"This is awesome, Steve. A1 hooks!"
Just hope I've drilled the bolt OK.
Or you're on for some granite rash.
Get lost.
The bolt's a way below now.
Smack a blade in then.
Steady. Or you'll rock your hook off.
How's that?
Vury Naaace Meesta Preeetchard.
I need a drink.
I need a fag.

"Just taking a break, Steve."

God, my feet hurt.

La la. La la la la la la. La la la la la la. La la la la la la.

But, I feel mad.

You're a long way from home, Sonny Jim.

"I'm going to start nailing up this ramp, but the placements are really shallow."

"I'll staay awaake."

Dingdindgingding.

That sounds OK.

Clip in.

Stand up.

Huh! Oh God, it moved.

Care ... ful.

No sudden moves.

You're OK.

Another blade.

Dingdingdunk.

Not so good.

Watch you don't pull it out.

It points downwards, so if I lean out on it I can create a mechanical key.

Dunkdunkdunk.

Now my heart sounds like a peg being placed.

Another bad one.

This land is your land this land is my land.

Mmmmmm – a flared Friend slot.

Not so good. Only two cams.

Weight it.

From da da mountains to New York Island.

Dead easy.

This land was made for you and ...

Snap.

Fuck.

Hold on.

What's happened?

The Friend's ripped.

[122]

Come on. Crimp like a bastard.
Gotta get the Friend.
Hook it with your foot.
It's slid away.
What to do now?
"Haaaaah."
Get moving.
Slap one on for that edge.
But that's moving further away from the pegs.
The pegs are shit.
Yeah, go on. And again. Side-pulls. Smear.
Wish-had-rock-shoes.
Heelhook. Brush the lichen off. Hang in. Dig the soil out of that
hole. Pull that root out. Go on. Get a nut in.
P-u-m-p-i-n-g.
Tap it in with your hammer.
Clip in.
Carefully.
Yes.
Another piece. A good pin.
Dingdingdingdingdingdingding. Ding ding.
Safer now. It's OK. I'm here. I'm here.
"Paaauuul."
"Yeah."
"Howsitgoing?"
"OK, Steve. Had a frightener but I'm back on track now. AAA111
to the beeeelay."

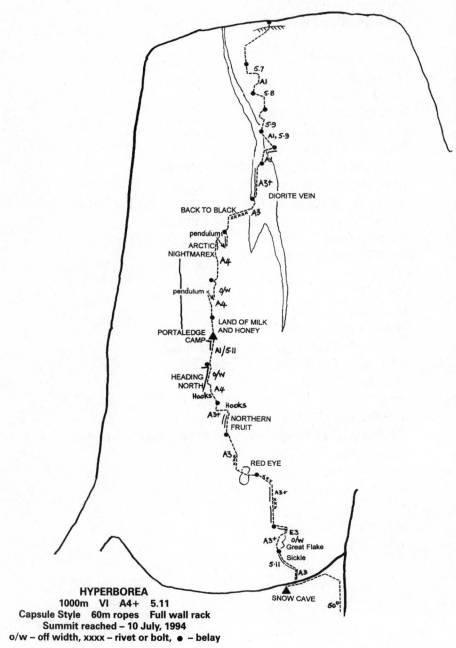

MT ASGARD

5.7
A1
5.8

5.9
A1, 5.9
A4
A3+
DIORITE VEIN

BACK TO BLACK   A3
pendulum
ARCTIC
NIGHTMARE
A4

pendulum x | o/w
A4
LAND OF MILK
AND HONEY
PORTALEDGE
CAMP
A1/5.11

HEADING | o/w
NORTH   A4
Hooks
Hooks
A3+ | NORTHERN
FRUIT

A3
RED EYE

A3+

E3
o/w
A3+ | Great Flake
Sickle
5.11 | A3
SNOW CAVE
50°

HYPERBOREA
1000m   VI   A4+   5.11
Capsule Style   60m ropes   Full wall rack
Summit reached – 10 July, 1994
o/w – off width, xxxx – rivet or bolt, ● – belay

13

Hyperborea

TO THE NORTH of the Arctic, beyond the tundra, beyond the vast sheets of ice, even beyond the pole is a land more wonderful than a mortal's most fanciful dream. A magical land where trees bear fruit throughout the four seasons and wheat is harvested in loaves. The land of unicorns, the abode of the gods – Odin, Tyr, Thor and Loki – known to the Norse as Asgard. The ancient Greeks called this place Hyperborea – beyond the north wind – and their boldest navigators went in search of a perfect life without toil or hunger. They never found their Hyperborea but this is the story of how we found ours.

At Denver Airport Steve and I sipped coffee and reminisced about the technicalities of our recent new route, Adrift, on El Capitan in Yosemite. The last call for boarding went by unheard during discussions about the UK Cowboy Lasso pitch and the Big Island Bivouac. And as Steve led up to the Illusion Chain our plane was thundering down the runway. After a firm telling off by the woman at the gate, we laughed at how we were so often untogether everywhere but on steep dangerous rocks, and blagged our way onto the next flight.

We had planned to try the Asgard Wall a year before. Plans rolled along haphazardly; many useless items were packed and crucial ones forgotten. As if by accident the team eventually camped together on the windswept, boulderstrewn fjord shore of Pangnirtung. We met local Innuit people and got briefed at the park headquarters on how to behave if we got attacked by a polar bear. Apparently we had to run around the bear as quick as we could as they were incredibly fast at sprint starts but slow at turning. It was a desolate place. The people used to camp on the land throughout the year but in the early sixties the Canadian government undertook a huge programme to offer prefabricated housing to all Baffin's people here on the shores of the fiords. The loss of their traditions has created a generation gap and a new problem – unemployment and all its associated ills. In the supermarket the solvents were kept in a reinforced cage and to buy white gas we had to get a special permit from the police and take it to a sealed bunker where it was stored. Alcohol is banned, too.

Right up to the last day Simon Yates and Keith Jones had been working hard building portaledges at the Lyon Equipment factory in Dent and the day before Noel heard he had become Doctor Craine, zoologist. Just one week before I had been Steve's apprentice in modern hard aid on the vast sheet of El Capitan's East Face. And now, after years of picking up Doug Scott's *Big Wall Climbing* and gazing at that photo, we were taking a skidoo ride across the sea ice toward Asgard. Ipeelee, our driver, sped across the ice and towed the five of us on two trailers behind. Often we would come across cracks with dark water in them and Ipeelee would either drive around them or, if they were too long, turn around, take a run up and bounce across them. But we trusted him and, anyway, we were too in awe of the landscape that we were passing. The rolling hills had turned into giant granite slabs on either side of the fjord and, up ahead, snow-capped golden spires.

We had packed 1200 pounds of lentils and bigwall gear and this had to be moved thirty miles from the fjord head to the base of the wall on the Turner Glacier. There are no porters in the Arctic, so you either carry everything yourself or use a helicopter, which we resisted. However many plans we made of how all this gear was going to be shifted, the bags themselves seemed to decide when they would arrive at the wall. Dreams of hand cracks and stemming corners had overshadowed the reality of the workload. The idea of getting two people cracking on the wall almost immediately while the others ferried loads seemed a little naive. Food was rationed from day one and our loads never weighed less than eighty pounds.

As we crossed the Arctic Circle for the fifth time in three days I heard Noel comment, "Lord, every time I see those geese I feel less and less like a vegetarian." After the ninth day of load-carrying, our designs to trap the Arctic hare and geese had become elaborate in the extreme. The solitude was profound. Apart from a lone Catalan, who had come to attempt a solo of Mount Friga, we were the only people to have made footprints in the Auyuittuq National Park this year. Auyuittuq – 'the land that never melts'; the name was apt. None of us had ever known such cold. As we skied up the frozen rivers of the flat-bottomed Weasel valley we wondered how on earth we could climb in such temperatures. It was obvious, we had come too early and the land needed time to warm up.

Ferocious storms came on a whim from whichever horizon they cared to as we skied up the Caribou Glacier and became stormbound at the col. After 130 miles hideous load-carrying we decided that never had an expedition reached such depths before the mountain had even been seen. The food fantasies. The girlfriend fantasies. Warm beds, coal fires and steam pudding. We spent two days at the Caribou Col as deep snow drifted around our tents. It was a welcome rest from the constant grind.

On the morning of the thirteenth day the sun came out and we peered down the slope which led to the Turner Glacier and the face we had come to climb. It was in dangerous condition but with so little food what could we do? We couldn't wait any longer and were desperate to see our line. Taking one of those risks that are accompanied by a silent prayer, we rappeled off the portaledge poles, lowering haulbags. The slope lay quiet and let us be. Roped together and dragging a haulbag apiece, we slithered down the glacier and our wall of dreams slowly turned to meet us. What we saw was both awesome and sickening. Huge patches of rime ice coated the face which was still very much in the shade at 5 pm. The ice slope leading up to it was loaded and we all doubted silently whether, even if we got up the slope, it would be possible to take our hands out of our gloves to do technical aid work.

We set up camp and checked out the mountain, each impatiently awaiting his turn to look through the telescope. Panning upwards from the glacier the magnified arc traced a route: snow – scree – snow – buttress – ice – bergschrund – utterly blank granite. Working left and right the circular eye revealed only two cracks leaving the 'schrund on the whole face. This was disheartening but it made the choice simple. On the left a chimney led to the top of a pillar but above the wall blanked out. Further right a sickle-shape flake reached up to more flakes which died in mirror smooth rock. These disjointed features lured the imagination into believing that there was a way to reach the snaking corner halfway up the wall. The corner looked about five pitches long and above it a black vein of diorite led all the way to the decapitated summit. From previous experience of diorite we knew it would be loose but that loose, fractured diorite is climbable and blank granite isn't – without drilling.

Pinned down for thirty hours in another hoolie we made a pretty good guess at how many minute squares of ripstop nylon made up the inside of my tent. The next day dawned – I use this term loosely as there is no night during the Arctic midsummer – sunny and freezing and we attempted to wade waist-deep in snow up the lower slope. Breaststroke worked but it felt like a suicide attempt and we ran away sharpish. Back at camp Noel strolled to his tent and reached for the zipper. But it wasn't there. And neither was the tent. Luckily the tent's prints were all over the slope and we easily tracked it down a mile away. Steve shook his head in dismay at these displays of British incompetence. That night Keith make the soundest mountaineering decision of the day and broke the rationing. A noble *dahl*, fit for a glass case, as Tilman would say, was followed by pears, apricots, chocolate buttons, peanuts and caramel wafers covered in custard.

The following day was pivotal. Keith and I again attempted to fix ropes on the bottom slope but, instead of improving, the slope had gotten worse. Ten-inch slabs broke off in six-foot pieces which pushed me backwards as I tried to lead the traverse, It was futile. The snow needed a week or two and a good thaw to either slide or consolidate but, by now, Keith and Simon only had a fortnight left. Bad planning on the catering front meant we hadn't allowed for the huge appetites worked up load-carrying. We were already low on food.

The excruciating decision was made to walk the fifty miles home. We would shop and rest and stomp back in racked, ready and raring to go for another blast. And so, with our plan sorted, the pressure dropped 800 feet and we were pinned down in a blizzard for two more days. We met Jordi, our Catalan friend, on the descent. The reality of soloing a wall on Baffin had hit him like Thor's hammer, Mjöllnir, and he had decided to bag it. Noel, Steve and I glanced sideways at each other, cogs clicking in our heads. Wouldn't it be useful to have an extreme bigwall soloist on the team? "Hey, you come with us. Yes? *Ven con nosotros.*" He was delighted and joined us in the forced march to town.

After a very painful eating experience, and a farewell to Simon and Keith, we shopped and took a boat back up the now rapidly melting fjord. The boat couldn't make it all the way through the drift ice but the walk was easier with lighter packs and after three days of carbo-loading and power-lounging, we got pinned down by ferocious weather halfway to Asgard, but began to see a pattern of two days bad then one day reasonable emerging. We walked at night on the glacier.

Jordi's haulbag full of rope and hardware had been swept away in an avalanche. He was upset but *"Es la vida."* From the base of Friga we looked across to the hourglass figure of the Scott/Hennek/Braithwaite/Nunn route on the East Face of Asgard, glowing gold in the 2 am sun. This must be one of the greatest rock climbs in the world. Forty pitches all free at HVS (that's what Doug said, but Braithwaite reckoned more like E3!) and arcing a line with the purity of the Nose of El Cap. "Why are we struggling with this pie-in-the-sky wall when we could have done numerous routes alpine-style already?" These thoughts cannot be entertained seriously.

We got back to our ditch which we referred to as base camp at 6 am after twenty-eight days of shuttling loads. We now had thirteen days of food with which to attempt a big wall. Chances were slim but we work for the means and never look to an end. With no time to waste, Steve and Jordi went straight up and, finding the slope in much better condition, fixed nearly to the wall. Noel and I went up later and got a rope on the last section. The fixed lines would make it feasible for us to hump our vast amount of kit up the seventy degree ice slope to the start of the route.

At the top of the slope we discovered the perfect advance camp to work from. The glacier-polished face arose, continually over-hung, out of a huge bergschrund banked with snow. This proved to be an effective catchment area for all the dropped gear. The outer lip of the bergschrund was thick and high and a good, safe spot for a cave. It would shield us from the wind and exposure and the constant reminders of where we were. I like to hide away in the evening, go home for a few hours. Then we touched rock. It felt like a symbolic moment after thirty days of labour and the agonies of migration. We joked about planting our Survival International flag right here.

I eagerly racked up, tied in and surveyed the start of the route. It was hard aid right off the ground. The first placement was a poor micronut high up, so I taped one on the end of a ski pole and, at full stretch, fiddled it in. Earlier the team had all agreed that there should be no falls on the route, as the consequence of an injury here could be disastrous. I swarmed up to the nut and fiddled for a few minutes, trying to place a Lost Arrow. Then the nut ripped and I landed flat on my back. After the hysterical laughter had died down I finished the pitch with the help of Noel's shoulder and a few skyhooks to bypass a three-piece suite of loose blocks. Noel moved swiftly up the next sickle pitch in one long fluid layback. This was why we were here, to climb rocks, not carry ninety-pound rucksacks up a downward-moving escalator. We fixed and came down.

With July came another terrible storm. This place was beginning to make Patagonia look like a holiday spot. But the weather cleared and the pitches crept by slowly. Beforehand we had decided on a no-drilling-on-Asgard policy but Steve, veteran of fifteen El Cap routes and new lines on Hooker and Black Canyon's Chasm Wall, knew better. Middendorf, one of the world's greatest wall climbers, had studied the face and commented, "Eighty holes at least." To the Americans, riveting blank rock is acceptable and I had become accustomed to linking features on otherwise blank walls during my Yosemite trip. On El Capitan most routes use up to 200 holes. The features themselves are good sport and if you want to climb them you have to get to them somehow. This was a new way of thinking to Noel but on the fourth pitch, as the rock blanked out, he was not upset when we pulled out the Californian riveting kit and made four holes to get from one flake to the next.

We began working in shifts. One pair would push the route higher, while the other two slept. After fifteen hours or so the teams would switch. Using this system, it was possible to climb around the clock. Our 200-foot ropes meant we could really stretch the pitches and we would, overall, waste much less time building belays.

On the fifth, red-eye pitch, Noel was learning how to drill a rivet ladder, engulfed in the swirling mist. Time nudged forward, sometimes stopping altogether as I lay in the portaledge drifting into unconsciousness and, occasionally, jerked back into semi-reality to feed rope out through the Gri-Gri. I took my boots off and rubbed my feet. Time jumped ahead a little. The bombardment of ice particles continued unabated, the odd fat rogue hitting me square on as I huddled under the fly sheet. And, suddenly, for the first time, I became aware of where I was. Not in India or on the Central Tower or on Zodiac. I was on the West Face of Mount Asgard on Baffin Island in the Arctic. I threw back the fly and looked out across a marvellous panorama of ice, rock and mist in the alpenglow of midnight. It struck me that this moment was the culmination of all that had passed in my life.

There were no shortcuts to arrive at this belay and even a minute's change on the compass could have led me a long way from here. Feed more rope out and light a cigarette. What if I had never met Mo Anthoine and he hadn't invited me on the Gangotri trip which got me started mountaineering? What if I had never met Noel or Steve? What if I'd parapleged myself when I fell at Gogarth last year? This lack of order makes me feel wonderfully insecure.

Time stops again until Noel shouts down, tapping home another shaky rivet into soft flaky rock, "I'll never confuse riveting with sport-climb bolting ever again." I shout up words of encouragement. One of the four or five insincere phrases pulled out of one's helmet during periods of intense boredom: "You're doing great," "Go for it," "Yeah," or "Nice one." While drilling the final rivet a shard of quartz shoots out of the hole and buries itself in Noel's eyeball. We fixed the rope pulled up from the ice slope and rapped back to the cave.

Noel's eye swelled up and we couldn't get the piece of rock out. He was in pain and we discussed him bailing out. We knew there was a doctor with a German team fifteen miles away in the Weasel Valley but Noel would need a guide and that would mean the end of the trip for all of us. There was too much work for two people. We laughed about his karmic price for debauching the rock but it was no joke. He might not lose his eye but the frailty of our plan was reinforced. Noel soon recovered but that piece of Asgard will forever be in his eye.

I belayed Steve on the double groove pitch. Easy nutting up the first groove led to a pendulum for a massive expanding flake. At the top of this the rock looked utterly blank. As Steve arrived at the dreaded blank section whoops of joy drifted down. At this point a knife-blade crack cheese-wires Asgard. We could follow it leftward and get toward the base of the main corner. After ten tied-off blade moves Steve headed up diagonally on circle heads and hooks and found a little foot ledge to belay on. What remained to the corner was a full pitch across loose flakes with big ledge-out potential. It was my turn to lead again.

'Heading North' was a sustained stretch of intense concentration and dubious mental games. It took the whole array of Rurps, beaks, heads and hooks to cross from one expanding dinner plate to the next and, finally, with monumental rope drag, I slumped onto a fine ledge at the base of the easy looking corner. In my dehydrated and fatigued state I was convinced we had pulled off the hardest part of the route. I couldn't have been more mistaken. Happy, I rapped off for a rest and left Jordi to belay Noel. He tried to free climb the first corner pitch but after a strong attempt reverted back to nailing. As Steve and I started the long rope climb back up for our next stint I felt a shiver and glanced up to see a black speck against the blue sky. The speck grew and I shouted to Steve, *"Rock."* All I could do, stuck on a rope as I was, was to watch the rock as it spiralled for a thousand feet, sailing toward me. It'll never hit me I thought, one person on such a massive expanse of wall. Never. But it kept coming, and then I heard it, like a buzzing sound. In the last seconds I knew it was going to hit me and I tensed my whole body and prepared for the flash that I assumed would come with death. I heard the impact, a deafening crack and then it hit me … But I was OK. It didn't even hurt. The rock the size of a house brick had landed on a small ledge about a foot above me, almost stopped dead and the rolled onto me with no force at all. Steve and I shouted up the wall in unison, "Stuuupid bastaaards," and from above came a meek, "Sorreee."

Later, in the warmth of our three-roomed ice house, Noel and I discussed the tactics employed on many free wall expeditions. We could have aided the pitch, left the gear in place and redpointed it at our convenience. As with the rest of the route, we could have chosen to free whichever pitch we felt like along the line of fixed rope. We had looked at Proboscis in The Cirque of the Unclimbables and were saddened to hear of its rap-bolting by two American friends. And the retro-bolting of the Pan-American route on El Gran Trono Blanco and walls in Yosemite.We decided that the essence of wall climbing was to get from the bottom to the top as efficiently as possible which, in the mountains, means as quickly as possible. But speed does not go hand in hand with redpointing. Most of Yosemite's big walls have taken the best part of a year to free. Free cruising is definitely less time-consuming than aid climbing but not necessarily more enjoyable. We didn't want to go back down and free lower pitches. We were looking upwards only and, besides, the hard aid opened up new doors of fear and excitement. Once the pins were in place we could have freed the first pitch at 5.12c. We would have got kudos of a hard free rating on a big wall but felt this would have made a mockery out of Asgard.

So with six days' food left it was imperative we should free what we could, dog what we couldn't and nail the impossible. Big wall free climbing does have an exciting future, though. The Salathe Wall of El Capitan and the Slovene route on Nameless Tower will get on-sight ascents but, to date, have any of these big wall media events truly been freed? (Since writing this Lynn Hill has made a fantastic one-day ascent of the Nose on El Capitan). I must admit it wasn't a big issue for us.

We felt like the only people in the Arctic but presently four dots appeared on the glacier below. They left their haulbags at Asgard's feet and returned the next day with more loads. We knew they had come to try the wall but we had to bury any intrusion we felt. After all, this was one of the most sought-after unclimbed walls in the world. Perhaps it was the German team who we met on our shopping trip to Pangnirtung. They had with them a Hilti power drill and a twenty-kilo car battery. They wanted to make a route "that everyone could enjoy". We despaired at the thought of the noise pollution on our wall and future queues of climbers with only a rack of quickdraws. But use of the Hilti seems almost standard practice now. In 1992, whilst on the Central Tower of Paine, we happened upon machine-drilled bolts on easy ground just two pitches from the top on the German route.

The dots grew until they became full-sized Swiss climbers who had arrived to try our line. They were not too put out, though. It's a big face with lots of room. They would try further left. Steve set off on the eighth monster pitch, a snaking openbook only just split by a fragile knife-blade fissure. The fissure disappeared after fifteen bodylengths and reappeared four bodylengths to the right at a gross, loose, fat crack. Again the cold and boredom of my belay duty produced a transcendental state.The hours pass, falling with the avalanches which crash down the slabs of Loki opposite. It is night-time and the sun, weak yellow disc that it is, warms my face if I look square into it and shut my eyes. It coasts along the western horizon throughout the night rolling up and down the profiles of the mountain ridges and casting long shadows to the north, then east and south by morning. Now and again the ice falls.A small chip floats by and warns that we are in for a barrage. Slightly bigger pieces follow and then some very big chunks. Bugger transcendental states, now's the time to get cracking to avoid being taken out. As the ice blocks spin through the air they make the fearful whirr of aboriginal instruments that warn of their approach. The Innuit have a word for this kind of fear in the face of unpredictable violence, such as having to cross thin sea ice. The word is *kappia*.

Steve made the top of the first crack and, again, had to place two rivets from which he could make a pendulum into the fat crack. I feel here that, for the British reader at least, I should outline the distinction between riveting and bolting, for they are two very different things. Both require the drilling of a hole but rivets – being only a half inch long by a quarter inch diameter threaded nut – are body weight pieces for upward movement only. They cannot be considered as protection should one fall. After five or six hours Steve had built another fabulously exposed belay on blank overhanging rock. As I cleaned the pitch the portaledge flew up the face like a giant black bird and at 3 am I led off up the last rope-length in the open corner. Miles of brittle dinnerplating placements led to a disgusting diorite band about seventy foot thick. The diorite had the consistency of stale cake and would not be subdued by nailing. Only very silent nutting, *kappia* again, would get us through this delicate section which we named the Arctic Nightmare.

After twelve long body weight moves I found myself equalised on an RP2 and an RP3 behind a creaking cupboard door. Above was no place for a nut, so I tapped in an Arrow. Standing up in my aider I began to scrape a Walnut placement in the cake high above me. I heard a faint sound like the sounds you can hear when trying not to wake sleeping friends. The audible sound of taking the foil top off a milk bottle or turning a door handle. The Arrow slowly turns its hand from nine o'clock to twelve and the side of the crack falls off. The peg lands in my lap at the precise moment my right boot contacts a tiny edge and my fingers grasp the cupboard door. The door stays shut and I timidly weight the RPs. After some deep breaths and vivid pictures of home, friends and the future, I shout down for the bolt kit. In this soft muck even a bolt did not fill me with the warmth of security but it sufficed to finish the pitch.

At midday, after twenty hours of work, we slid down and switched with Noel and Jordi. They attempted the next pitch but became lost in a sea of dead calm rock. After some sleep Steve and I began work hauling a camp up the wall. It had taken six hours to climb the ropes to our highpoint, so we decided it was time to live on the wall. We had been putting this off as long as possible because our home-made portaledges – made out of a Lyon Equipment display for hanging clothes on – kept breaking whenever we sat on them, even at ground level. Keith and Simon had tested them for a few minutes, bouncing up and down in the factory. We also hauled food for five days, sleeping gear and a plastic barrel full of water. After the first night on the wall Noel and I christened our ledge the Potato Chip because of the pronounced twist it took on whenever we lay in it. The whole night would be spent fighting to stay in the thing.

In the morning we were woken by the throbbing sound of helicopter blades. It was the Californians, Brad Jarrett and Chris Breemer. We had met in Yosemite and wished each other luck. The helicopter settled them right below the mountain and within seconds had flown away, leaving them shocked on the glacier. We screamed to each other as Americans do and I pondered on what different memories we would each have of the approach, fantastic aerial views against a month of grind. I wouldn't trade places. I went up with Noel and finished what he and Jordi had started the day before. Our big wall soloist, who was going to lead all the hard pitches for us, was having a considerable amount of trouble even on the easiest pitches. In Spain he had led A5 but here he was finding A2 difficult. But he was good company and we were glad for his sake that he was with us and not trying to solo Friga.

This pitch was the key, linking the snaking corner to the diorite vein which led to the summit, and was sorted with hooks and heads and six rivets in blank rock. On the last move of the pitch I placed a fish hook and stood up to peruse the belay situation. The hook ripped straight through the soft rock and I was left hanging from my arms more petrified than the rock. After shouting repeatedly to Noel – after six hours your belayer can often be asleep – I let go and took the whipper. A blade held and I climbed to the belay with more caution.

On the raps back to the ledges we held a hanging conference with the other two and decided that Noel and I would get four or five hours' shut-eye and come back up. From now on we would go alpine-style to the summit. The weather had been gorgeous for a day or two and we were all aware that every good day was a day nearer the impending storm. Everything was going to plan. This just doesn't happen mountain climbing. After filling our faces with mash potato and Parmesan and trying to force down Noel's attempt at baking a coffee and walnut cake, a valiant effort in a portaledge, we rested a little and clamped back onto the lines. Steve's pitch was hard and soft but went steadily and above, after eleven 200-foot pitches, the rock stopped being overhanging. We raced up the rope and congregated on a snowy ledge.

From here we could look straight down Charlie Porter's line. It is the only line on this side of the mountain, a superb corner prising open the south-west edge of the North summit. Porter was first to climb many of Yosemite's hard classics in the seventies and his presence there was a driving force in raising the standards of the day. The Shield and Mescalito and his solo of Zodiac were milestones in big walling but the crowds got too much for Porter and he went north in '79 in search of total solitude. He found it on Asgard in the form of an epic and painful adventure. Utterly alone he climbed the corner during two weeks of rain. When he got back down to earth he had to cut his boots from his swollen feet and crawl the thirty miles to the fjord-head. There he met some

Innuit who gave him Coca-Cola! Soon after completing this magnificent climb Porter gave up big walling and holed up in Chile to work on an Aqua Culture project.

The sun blazed and we climbed as fast as a party of four could. Some mixed pitches and some free pitches on superb granite fell behind us. All the time the top was in sight. On Asgard there is no tedium of one false summit after another, you just slap the top and mantelshelf! I led a slow aid pitch and belayed twenty feet below the rim to give Noel the thrill of topping out first. We had to be very controlled and precise here as we were all getting extremely tired. Noel led up and free climbed through the summit overhang. By the time we had all jugged up it was 10 pm and the sun was shining low and bright from the west. It was an emotional time and after the hand-shakes and hugs we each wandered off on our own about the flat white field above the Arctic. To at last look east was special. Ranks of unclimbed Thors and Asgards marched deep into the distance. Out west the Penny Icecap shimmered in the haze. Noel shed a tear as Steve took photos in all directions.

Jordi spotted his avalanched haulbag at the base of Friga and I took my first shit in three days. As I squatted, I giggled at how lucky we were. If the bad weather had continued just a day or two longer we would have used all our food and run out of time, but the window opened and let us in.

After a couple of hours on top and a good feed we carefully rapped back down the seven pitches to our fixed rope and cleaned that down to our ledge camp. We arrived at 3 am; for Steve and Jordi it had been thirty-six hours of non-stop work. We had no trouble collapsing into a twelve-hour coma.When we awoke the weather was showing signs of change. A mackerel sky was shunting in from the west. So with battered, throbbing hands we began rappeling and lowering our kit down the face and staggered in one push all the way to base camp. The glacier had become horrifically soft and even on skis we sank to our knees.

After sleeping some and striking camp we shouted good luck to the other climbers and waddled out under hundred-pound sacks down the Turner Glacier. Black clouds boiled and poured over Loki. We tried to hurry but the storm had no trouble catching us.

We were secretly glad that the other climbers were now experiencing some real Baffin weather. It would have been too much if our Californian friends had, after flying in by helicopter, got weeks of Mediterranean sunshine. The long walk out is a blur. We fell repeatedly under our loads

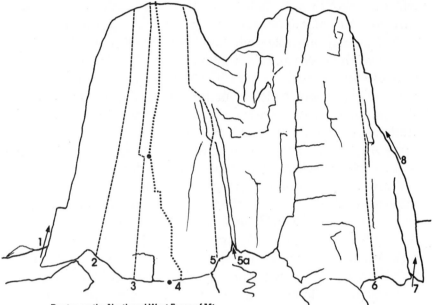

Routes on the North and West Faces of Mt Asgard, Baffin Island

Hd – Bolts or rivets placed by hand drills.
Pd – Power drills used.
US Big Wall grades employed where known.

1 Valkyrie 1994 Chris Breemer and Brad Jarrett (with helicopter approach). VI, A4+.

2 Inukshuk 1995 Denis Burdet, Cedric Choffat, Pierre Robert and Jean Michel Zweiacker. VI, A3+, 5.10+. (Hd) Swiss.

3 Nunavut 1996 Txus Lizarraga, Miguel Berazaluce, Raul Malero, Natxo Barriuso (helicopter approach). VI, A3, 5.8. Spanish.

4 Hyperborea 1994 Noel Craine, Paul Pritchard, Steve Quinlan and Jordi Tosas with (earlier) Keith Jones and Simon Yates. 16 days A4, 5.11, 37 rivets/10 bolts (Hd). Anglo/American/Spanish.

5 Porter Route 1976 Charlie Porter (completed solo) with Rick Sylvester and Shary McVoy (for the first two thirds of the climb). One bolt (Hd). American. **5a** The dihedral line initially tried by this team following the earlier attempt by the Scott party.

6 South Face Direct 1988 Earl Redfern, John Barbella and two others. American.

7 South Edge from West Flank 1988 Mario Manica, Fabio Leoni, Leonardi Luca and Fabrizio Defrancesco. Alpine-style in 27 hours. (The upper part of this may follow the Lee/Koch/Wood Route). Italian.

8 South Ridge 1971 Guy Lee, Rob Wood, and Phil Koch. Alpine-style. Anglo/American.

and I had the hallucinations I had known before that come at the end of an epic climb. The electric colours of the lichens and mosses made me stand, sway and stare but the feeling of an invisible presence and the voices were disturbing.

We met kind people who gave us morsels of food and at 10.30 one evening we met a small boat at the fjord-head and were whisked away toward civilisation. Noah and Joaby gave us tea, cake and cigarettes and we could only laugh as our boat stuck fast in drift ice only one mile from town. But we got in and that night were given real beds and fresh salmon. The people of Pangnirtung were celebrating because they had just caught their first beluga whale of the season. We joined in the jollity and entered the Innuit Olympics. After a long battle I won the stick jumping contest, as young mothers looked on with their babies in the hoods of their sealskin coats. And they all roared with laughter as Noel managed to whip himself on the backside with a twelve-foot bull-whip.

I can't remember on which long belay session it was, but I can recall the cold creeping onto the portaledge, numbing my feet, my legs and cradling my mind with torpor. I had drifted back to our desert trip only a couple of months before. Standing Rock, Shiprock, Monster Tower. We had climbed loads of towers and doing that allowed us to study the desert, from a distance, from up close and, unique to climbers and aviators, from above. The desert, the tundra and the ice of the poles may be the only places on earth where, at a glance, there seems to be nothing. But if you search closely the wealth of the land becomes apparent. There are vast forests but Arctic willow is only three inches high. The animals are so well camouflaged that they are difficult to detect even up close. Everything needs intense study, including the rock and especially if you are aid climbing. Examining the skin of the rock and trying to puncture it, not wholly unlike a sheep tick.

The history of the land is part of its wealth. The people who have moved upon it, the creatures that have evolved to live there, the angle of light that has pulled the same shadows from the boulders and pinnacles for thousands of years. During my cold meditations I too felt a part of the land and, by leaving our invisible mark, maybe we will always be a part of it.

14

A Survivor's Affair

I HAD ARRIVED in Aragon and it was with a nervousness I felt I knew well that I punched in the six figures. Why was I calling him? I needed to talk but I didn't know if he would want to.

I had met Pepé twice before. The first time, in Madrid Airport, I had noticed the expedition T-shirts and, like a spy, edged nearer to see where they were heading. Luckily the T-shirts weren't heading to Cerro Torre's East Face (where we were) but to La Catedrál. The next encounter was on a narrow trail by the side of Paine's Lago Nordenskold. He and Lorenzo Ortiz approached and babbled, their eyes staring somewhere above and behind us. They were escaping the mountains after completing a new climb, Cristal de Roca, on La Catedrál's East Face. Two months of precarious aiding, balancing around on a 3000-foot wall and jumaring fraying lines in awful winds would be enough to give any one of us the 2000-yard stare. So now, as the phone rang, he was a stranger to me but I felt as though I knew him. We shared something more than just the common bond of climbing or even the closer bond of Patagonian climbing, the shared experience of the wind and the waiting.

The telephone rang. Would he feel the same way? Beads of sweat broke out on the palms of my hands.

"*Hola, Pepé. Esta Paul Pritchard aqui. Estoy en Riglos y quiero verte,*" I spoke in faltering Castillano.

Do you remember his big lumbering way, his utter motivation, his daftness and his smile? How nothing was ever taken seriously, how generosity wasn't a word in his vocabulary – whatever was his was common? How anyone would struggle to keep up with him on an approach? Philip said that on Torre Centrale he'd never seen a lead like it – out there on a vertical wall crimping tiny edges with the spindrift burying his knuckles. And ... ? And have they found him yet?

"Yes, Riglos is wonderful." I hadn't said what I'd wanted to but I hoped there would be time. "See you tomorrow."

Pepé's full name is José Chaverri. He arrived at Riglos with his partner Xavier at 6 pm and, as they were off to the eastern fjords of Baffin Island in a week's time and he hadn't climbed all year because he had to work for the money to pay for such an expensive trip, he was keen to climb. So without hanging around (and in true Spanish style) they set off up the thousand-foot overhanging face of El Pison. Darkness saw them on the summit without headtorches – so we all went to bed, as they made the long rappel descent, safe in the knowledge that, although slightly unorthodox, they could look after themselves. The next day I was off the ground and we didn't talk. Well just once. "I don't know if they've found him either." Sometimes the will to climb is paramount. Almost anything can be delayed. This is understood, indeed expected, amongst climbers.

Sat in a darkened room the hypnotic click-click of the projector beckons us into Pepé's memories as they are cast onto the wall. He first shows his slides of the Kurtyka/Loretan and then the Slovene route on Trango Tower. Astonishingly, he climbed both of these routes in one trip, though for him these memories seem a little tainted.

"Too much fixed rope. On the Kurtyka dangerous snow means we don't stand right on summit and on the Slovene we forget our headlamps and get benighted only thirty metres below."

He seems almost more lackadaisical than a British climber but wears his inner drive on the outside. As he smokes perhaps his fortieth cheap cigarette of the day he informs us in dislocated English, "For make expedition the physical is not so importante. It is the motivation."

This talk of motivation and the click of the projector onto Patagonia makes my reason for coming here surface again. He had been mentioned now and again over the last few days but the mutual ice was hard to break. Teo – perhaps it's better if they don't find him. The memories flash onto the wall, each one punctuated by stark white light. Motivaciones Mixtos on Cerro Standhardt was their big new route together. Photos of golden granite glistening with trickles of water, front-pointing up ice-choked cracks. Immense, weird mushrooms of snow. For Pepé it was a departure from the siege tactics used on Trango and Catedrál. Eight times they walked up the miles of glacier and began the route, each time to be thwarted by storms. Teo's unwavering motivation and fine sense of the ridiculous ensured that going home was definitely not an option. Then, at last, after climbing the lower pitches for the God-knows-how-many'th time, they found themselves swinging past each other in the sunshine. In the ultimate lightweight style they carried no sleeping bags or stove, only a small bag of food and a spare jacket each.

A thick cloud of smoke is illuminated in the cone of light between the projector and the dangerously thawing ice formations of the headwall. After a long hard day where, to pay for the good weather they were receiving, the pair had to struggle through rapidly deteriorating snow conditions, they found a bivouac site below the headwall. Their clothing had become soaked after climbing through the meltwater and Teo had dropped the food bag. When light came again they warmed themselves up to another day of heat and decomposure of the mountain. There was only one thing to do and that was to continue. The 200-metre headwall was mixed free and aid on rock running with water

[143]

amidst a barrage of ice blocks and always under the shadow of the grotesque and unstable summit mushroom. Like ostriches they minimised the risk by building belays under small overhangs. As the slides took us higher I pondered over the results of chance meetings between certain individuals and the dynamics which lead to such ludicrous schemes being undertaken. If fate plays no part, as scientists will have us believe, then chance is the most wondrous thing in our world.

On the final pitch as Teo aided on axes around the last over-hang a few more molecules turned back to water. A fridge-size block of ice plunged down the wall and landed in Teo's lap, ripping every notch in his daisy chain, crushing his hands and tearing the muscles and tendons in the whole of one leg. With Teo's backing, Pepé made him safe and completed the pitch onto the summit snow. Then, metre by metre, the descent became a slow misery. Teo couldn't open a karabiner or shout directions and, occasionally, he would lose consciousness. No more slides appeared now. They had planned on rappeling the route down to the ramp of the original route, where they had bivouacked, and then descend, more or less on foot, the original route. As Teo could not walk, Pepé decided they would rappel straight down.

They had brought a very meagre amount of equipment for their lightweight ascent and were slowly using it all up on the endless rappels. Into the night they slithered. At the end of every rope-length into unknown territory Pepé built a belay with whatever kit they had left. Sometimes it would be one peg, in one inch. Twice the ropes got stuck and Pepé had to jumar up on unattached lines to free them. He placed their very last piton for their very last rappel and they collapsed to sleep out on the glacier. Pepé came round to find they were in a dangerous situation. Teo needed to get to hospital, he was hypothermic and his leg had swollen badly, though only twenty-one years old, he was already showing the mental skills necessary to be a survivor. Together they stumbled and crawled in the early morning light across the glacier to the Norwegian bivouac boulder where they had stashed food and sleeping bags. Ermanno Salvatera, the Italian Patagonia expert had been watching their progress through the telescope from the Bridwell camp and, realising they were moving slower than was normal, had raced up to the bivouac to offer assistance. Soon they were in a helicopter heading for Calafate. That was in '94.

Pepé then talked about the local people who live in El Chalten, a desolate outpost at the foot of the mountains and, from the warmth and tone of his voice, his love for everything about Patagonia became evident.

"The rescue cost $1500 and we had no money. The people of El Chalten each put $100 to help Teo. He was well liked there."

An exhalation of sadness fell through the darkness, like the room had sighed and, momentarily illuminated in the stark whiteness, Pepé seemed more than his twenty-six years.

I drifted off to the Andean climbs I had made with Teo. The new rock climbs on La Pyramida above Bariloche. I could see him again on the end of a long loop of rope superimposed on the blue. Was Blood, Snot and Farts the best route name we could come up with? There were no such epics, though, and I felt jealous: I wanted to share the real intensity, too. But those pangs were dispersed as Pepé spoke.

"It was not as *un compañero de climbing* but as a life friend that I loved Teo. He is like a brother."

At first, when I felt the nervousness, I had no idea what we would talk about over Teo. I just guessed they would be important things. Big words that would make some sense of it all. In reality the words came out flat. The same words I had heard in a thousand movies. But later I found that if I didn't try so hard and just sat back and listened to Pepé's stories, that was enough. It is in those tales, shared and exaggerated, that our dead friends live on. Click.

"It was in '91 when I made Cerro Torre and Poincenot, and then Fitz Roy with Teo. He only had seventeen years then."

The last slide was of a very large and very blurred limestone buttress in the Aragon Pyrenees.

"And this is where we will go and climb."

The alarm sounded at 5 am. I crawled out of bed hungover and cursing the fact that we had only had dinner five hours ago, but this is the way Pepé and his friends always seem to behave. It had transpired the night before that we were to attempt the third ascent of the 350-metre Pillar de Sobarbe on La Peña Montañesa which had taken three days to climb on the first ascent. During the evening Pepé had tried to contact Lorenzo (who had made the second ascent) to get an over-the-phone topo. He failed, so we would go with no idea of what might happen. After a high-speed slog up the scree slope in the darkness I was nearly vomiting and sweating heavily. We reached the foot of the route at dawn and I was shocked, as the buttress took shape, to discover that it was like 1200 feet of Stoney Middleton!

The pitches fell by and the rock was horribly loose – but these guys thought it was solid. This I couldn't understand and felt embarrassed after boasting about the intricacies of loose Gogarth climbing.

"The route is too good, no?"

They had another way of climbing to me. They just seemed to go all out for every pitch, on or off like they were sport climbing next to bolts. The long layback up the creaking flake made me nervous but they didn't understand my protestations. They went ahead and reefed on the loosest rock. A griffon vulture passed close and then rode away mimicking the drone of an unseen jet plane.

"*Aaargh!*"

I am awakened out of my enchantment by a loud deep scream. I look up for a second to see the blue sky above darkened by falling blocks. One of the blocks Pepé stops, but the others come thundering all around me before taking to space for the eight pitches below us.

"*Hijo de puta*," he groaned and rolled his obviously paining shoulder before finishing off the pitch.

At the next belay we had a couple of hours to kill whilst Xavier led a long nailing and hooking pitch. Again the conversation turns to plans and past exploits. A couple of months before Pepé, with his friend Danial Ascaso (another Baffin partner), had made the first one-day ascent of the Torre Marbore in winter. This 400-metre mixed climb at Gavarnie, the jewel of the Pyrenees, is perhaps the hardest of its kind in Spain. The space below us seeps into the wall for a while as Pepé enthuses about the technicalities of free climbing steep snow-covered rock in plastic boots. He tells me of his Peru trip in '89 when he did the Ferrari route on Alpamayo and Huascaran, and of how he soloed Vallunarraqu and climbed Quitarraju's North Face. I inhale information for next year. We even touch upon the secret Peruvian granite big wall, and we laugh. It seems there are a few wall climbers around the world all with their imaginations churning over the same handful of lines on the earth's most aesthetic points.

Pepé is also eager to talk about the Aragon way of life. He displays a love of his land and a pride in his culture which gives me a sadness. It has all but disappeared in the industrial North of England, my home. But here also it would seem to be doomed eventually. One by one as the old shepherds die there are few youngsters who want to take their place. The ancient fiestas, mountain people tying chickens on the ends of poles or throwing goats to their deaths from the tops of tall towers, are less each decade. But the mountaintop monasteries appear strong and impenetrable and the legacy of the Moorish occupation cannot be taken from the land. As a mountain guide in the Aragon Pyrenees Pepé is expected to know about his territory and he enjoys learning more.

On the free-hanging prusik the void floods back out of the wall and becomes a sea of dizziness under my foot loops. As we climb higher the rock improves, as does, I feel, my friendship with these Spanish strangers. The last pitch goes to Pepé, skyhooking up pockets on top of the world, and we top out to catch the sun setting behind the snowy Pyrenees.

Despite the rush to get down in the fading light I made a moment of silence for myself to picture his big lumbering way and just to say, "Cheers, Teo."

Teo Plaza. An avalanche came and took him away on the side of Mount Tronador. Even though they haven't found him yet – he is still under the snow close to his home in Bariloche, Argentina – he is still curbing the future of his friends lives and affecting the dynamics of those 'chance' meetings. Plans will be hatched.

Making Castles in the Sand

HERE I GO AGAIN. I lurched forward and fumbled with the zipper. I fought my way out through the tent door and launched vomit over the edge to watch it begin its thousand-foot spiral into the moonlight. Adam didn't stir. This was my first night at the shoulder camp (5600m) and I felt wretched. I slumped back, delirious, and felt icy water travel down my gullet. Lonely in the silence, I began to mull over the lessons I had learned so far on this trip and the lessons I was about to learn. I took out my notebook and scribbled:

1 ... on dealing with power crazed officials ...
The 45-degree heat in Rawalpindi lent an intense and surreal feel to the whole business of dealing with the authorities. Todd Skinner and his team, also heading for Trango, had had their appointment with the Ministry of Tourism just a little while before us and they came out with horror stories. Due to the secretary

loosing an important piece of paper the team had been forced to stay in the city for days longer than planned. When Todd commented on how hot the day was the head of the mountaineering division asked him if he knew how hot was the bomb that was dropped on Hiroshima? "7000 degrees. And do you know what happens to the body at that temperature? Eyes explode, skin melts, everybody dead!" With this in mind we entered uneasily into the office. But our briefing went a little differently. We were allowed to go quickly but only after an anti-American rant. Then he thumped his fist on the desk and disclosed that he didn't just respect Britain, no, he loved it. We praised our luck and ran away to our hotel.

2 ... on dealing with irritating reporters ...
Again that damned reporter was waiting for us at the hotel. He wrote for a Pakistani national and hung around us for days. All he wanted to know about was 8000ers and how many had died on them. When he asked us about our climbing credentials we told him that Geraldine [?] had made the first ascent of Lockwoods Chimney and that Adam had done a speed ascent of Mousetrap in two hours! He went away happy with his story and we headed for the mountains.

3 ... on putting your life in the hands of others ...
Driving the Braldu Gorge had more than a few moments of terror. What was described as the new road to Askole turned out to be little more than a footpath hairpinning its way across mud slides and deep canyons. We lost one jeep, because of an insane driver, luckily before we got to the really terrifying bit. The top-heavy jeeps skidded to a stop before a 200-yard scree chute. The porters dismounted, said some prayers and ran for it, stopping occasionally to dig out the road whilst being bombarded by falling rocks of all sizes. We joined in and afterwards the drivers put their feet down and went for it with the raging Braldu river a long way below. The key was to sit on the very top of the jeep (to ensure a quick escape) and to maintain complete faith in the inshallah factor.

4 ... on the eradication of dangerous creatures ...
Andy [?] regaled us with the time when, up on the nearby Biafo
Glacier, his team was plagued by a bear. It chewed all the cans,
including gas canisters, and had to be fought off with fire. It was
one of the last Himalayan brown bears in the area and over lunch
Usup, a porter, told us proudly of how he had shot it dead. "Always
eating trekker food and making trouble." Before all these trekkers
and expeditions the Balti people had no real reason to go into the
bears' habitat. But then came the tourists to create a bear
problem. Andy and I looked at each other in disbelief.

5 ... on local beliefs ...
Many of the porters prostrate themselves toward Mecca and pray
before undertaking anything they feel may be dangerous, such as
passing before a loose hillside or climbing a gully. Watching a lone
porter above the vastness of the Baltoro Glacier meditating in
such a place of grandeur was a powerful scene which I will find
hard to forget. I could equate with that need for a few moments'
tranquillity. Myself, agnostic at this time, can still respect the
healing of such a ritual. It made me want to construct my own.

6 ... on heroes and role models ...
On seeing Trango for the first time, thirteen years of sometimes
hilarious, sometimes frightening stories and daydreams solidified.
In '83, when I was struggling with VS's in the Lancashire quarries,
two of my teachers in the arts of climbing and revelry, Ian
Lonsdale and Dai Lampard, headed off to make the second ascent
of a remote tower. We were all fired up by their enthusiasm. The
guys got to within a couple of pitches of the top but then had
to retreat in a storm after Lonsdale got his head stuck in a fat
crack. Sometime after, I moved to North Wales, where I met Mo
Anthoine who introduced me to mountaineering. He was on the
first ascent of Trango with Boysen, Brown and Howells. That was
in '76. Again the stories stuck with me; the rock fall in Tin Can
Alley, Boysen getting his knee stuck and having to hack at it with
a sharpened piton. Trango had become a subconscious ambition.
And now, stood like a matchstick amidst these minarets, I felt as

though I was in a house of God – the Gothic shapes and those echoes. You didn't want to make a sound. And over there, that one is even called the Cathedral, perhaps Gaudi's Sagrada Familia but on an incomprehensible scale. Until we made out the blue dot of Greg Child's abandoned portaledge on the Minamura route, that is. Then the whole place didn't shrink but grew larger in our perception. The famous Pole Voytek Kurtyka made a great climb up there too. Ever since my initiation into the mountains I had always looked to these two climbers for inspiration. And what was Kurtyka's comment after he had made it, with Erhard Loretan, to Trango's summit? That it took a greater physical effort than any of the 8000-metre peaks he had ascended. An imagin-ary voice with a Polish accent repeated the words in my mind, again and again, as I strained my neck to gaze up at the rock.

7 ... on choosing a suitable approach to the mountain ...
We made a base camp on the Dunge Glacier. After twelve days load-carrying in the Gullies of Hell, where we climbed only at night, like vampires, avoiding the hazards which day brings, we had a visit from some of our American friends. They happened to let slip that there was absolutely no snow on the Trango Glacier side of the mountain. We sighed. With most of our kit a thousand metres up in the gully we decided to stick with it. The women's team and Adam and Andy were trying to approach the Slovene route on the South Face and Noel [Craine] and I were heading for a new line on the North Face. After almost two weeks of frying by day in our Gemini and gasping by night under pig loads of wall gear we were almost at the rock wall. Noel felt he needed some rest as the sun came up, but I thought I would continue with my load higher up the couloir. He told me to be safe and I assured him that I would be as I plodded off feeling angry that he was not strong enough to come with me. The ground was easy at first above our perched little camp on an exposed ridge above the Dunge Glacier. After a couple of hundred metres the ice became steeper and my bag of ironmongery was weighing me down. I wanted to turn back, but I'd got the bugger so high! I know, I would leave it hanging on an ice screw and collect it tonight. Towards the end of

the day it stormed and we sat out the night in our claustrophobic tent. I irritated Noel with my ability to sleep for long periods of time, as if mocking his insomnia. Avalanches raked our gully but we were safe on our little ridge. I began to worry about my bag of crucial gear up on the avalanche slope and my worries were founded when the next day on our way to the col we couldn't find it anywhere. What an idiot I had been, abandoning equipment in such an exposed place. I was amazed that Noel did not even begin to chastise me and felt guilty at my response the day before when he said he needed a rest.

We roped up and climbed in pitches up unstable snow and reached the Col Curran in the dark and, after tying our ropes together and making a long rappel, retreated to our little camp. At 5.30 am we awoke to rain and wind and decided to run away to base camp and *dahl*. It should have been a simple descent but we had a little mishap. As I front-pointed down the slope for 500 metres Noel didn't emerge into the gully. I heard Kevin Starr of the American North Face expedition, who were up on their ledges, shouting. "Are you OK? Do you need help?" What was going on? I didn't understand. As I climbed back up the slope Noel's head appeared and moaned. It continued to rain and, as Noel crawled and slithered slowly towards me, he was hit by a slush avalanche. He dug in both his axes and screamed as I looked on useless. The river of slush cascaded over him and, credit to Noel's grip and determination, didn't sweep him away. Eventually the torrent abated enough for Noel to escape out of his rut and begin crawling over to me.

When we met he just spluttered, "Crevasse. Ribs."

"Don't say anything else, Noel. Let's just get you to camp." I felt terribly guilty – I should have stayed closer to him in such a dangerous place but hindsight doesn't appreciate the cold wet urge to hurry off that morning. We had no ropes with us, so I fielded him as he struggled down the steeper ice pitches. From his chest came a disturbing gurgling sound and I tried vainly to hurry him as heavy wet avalanches slid down the sides of the gully. Noel put a brave face on though, and after many hours we stumbled into camp. The whole team laughed when they saw

Noel's familiar bedraggled form, they had no inkling of what had happened that morning. Noel burst into tears with the relief of the stress and our friends became more concerned. Donna, our expedition veterinary surgeon, checked him out by asking him to stand on all fours (the stance of most of her other patients) while she moved her stethoscope over his back and that was the end of the trip for him. Three broken ribs and a punctured lung. Andy, who with Adam had already fixed to the shoulder at 5600 metres, escorted Noel out of the mountains and home safely. So with only two of us left and my wall rack (including forty-seven cams and fifty RPs) lost in an avalanche we decided to go around to the right side of the mountain.

8 ... on building sand castles ...
Chasing these granite spires around the world, which is what I've been doing for the last five years, can be a frustrating business. A little like building sand castles – like the ones we built as children at the sea's edge. The tallest castles are very delicate structures and, like our best planned schemes, can topple before us. Sometimes you succeed and build a perfect castle but in time the tide always turns and your castle melts. Then it is time to build another.

9 ... on dealing with military liaison officers ...
"I will come with you on this mountain."
  "Sorry, Captain Jamal, but you have not the experience."
  "If a woman of forty-three can climb Trango then so can I."
  Geraldine looked dismayed and shook her head. Captain Jamal had begun the trip as quite a friendly young man. We even bridged the cultural gap briefly and got him raving on the glacier. A full moon night, blowing his whistle and grooving to Left Field and Primal Scream. But as soon as even the more absurd rules were slightly bent his humour evaporated. Growing up in the Thatcher age some of us had come to distrust and often view the military with contempt and now we had to work with a soldier. Jamal found our liberal views and apparent lack of cohesiveness as difficult to cope with as we found his fatigues. That is not to say

that he didn't have our respect and friendship but there was always a wall up which our concepts could never climb and meet on top. Ali and Ismail, our cooks, were good guys. They had turned our base camp into a garden with windmills and flowers and they always kept us happy with fine food when the storms lasted a little too long. We had to ask Captain Jamal to stop his reprimands and ordering them around. As the trip progressed our irritation intensified so much that his physical appearance began to change before us. He slowly transformed from a handsome boy into a bullfrog. To be fair, it must have been hard for him – his first time in the mountains, with strangers and for so long. But a little later something happened that was to make our captain even less approachable.

10 ... on the extraction of bodies from lakes ...
Mr Saki had tried to swim across the lake at the American base camp on the moraines of the Trango Glacier. He was their assistant cook and it was the eighteen-year-old's first time in the mountains. Out in the middle he had succumbed to cold and sank. He came up and shouted but everyone on the bank thought he was shouting for joy and waved back. When he went down again one of the Spanish expedition jumped in and tried to get to him but was repulsed by the freezing water. Three weeks later we had moved around to the American camp, from where the approach gully was wonderfully safe. One morning, when we emerged from our tents, we noticed that Mr Saki had surfaced so the LOs set about building a raft out of thermorests with which to go and fetch him in. They worked with childlike enthusiasm, like they were glad to have something 'manly' to do. Adnan, the Americans' LO, being a major, gave the orders while Captain Jamal obeyed, along with the cooks. When the raft was completed and the grim job in hand was imminent the awful thing happened – Major Adnan pulled rank and ordered Jamal to go out there and lasso the corpse. We sat down and groaned. As Jamal tried again and again to paddle out the wind changed direction and Mr Saki turned around and headed out toward the centre of the lake. Jamal paddled frantically turning round and round and then

capsized. The Japanese expedition were capturing all the action on the three video cameras. Jamal was dragged in on our hundred-metre static rope and the LOs scratched their heads. As one of the women had suggested earlier, they then decided to use the blue barrels as extra ballast. Out Jamal went again, paddling with a snow shovel and with Adnan shouting in an excited voice, "Left a bit "and "Right a little", as if it were not obvious where the poor lad was floating. I remember a man in Llanberis lake who used to float up for just long enough to allow his rescuers to get near him and then, irritatingly, sink again to come up a few days later. Thankfully, Mr Saki stayed afloat long enough for Jamal to lasso and pull him in. With this ridiculous scene in our heads, and trying not to believe in bad omens, Adam and I set off up Tin Can Alley.

11 ... on choosing optimum bad conditions ...
We decided to go very light. Perhaps too light. We took one pair of plastic boots between us and one pair of rock shoes, one titanium ice axe and one pair of crampons. For a rack we had two sets of nuts and two sets of Friends, supplemented with huge Camalots. We had no pitons and no bivvy bags. Every item not absolutely essential was discarded. Todd and his team had very kindly let us jumar their ropes to the shoulder Adam had already climbed to. Here I spent the night vomiting and hating Adam for sleeping. For two days we took our time fixing four pitches above the shoulder, getting off on the feeling of climbing – something you don't do much of on trips of this kind. We were on an apron of glittering orange granite. In cherub-bum cracks sculpted by the ice and finished off by the hands of the wind. As Adam led us up a verglassed off-width on tipped out Camalot 5s, we fixed our ropes and, as the sun dogs and high cirrus had prophesied, in came the next storm. Down we fled. After an age of playing Nintendo at base camp we were getting desperate. All we wanted was to get this thing over and done with. The women had run out of time now and were about to leave and we wanted the same. Captain Jamal said he couldn't permit the team to split up but they had careers to rush back to and Adam and I were staying as long as it took.

"This is no way to conduct an expedition, Mr Paul. Things were going so well and now everything has fallen apart."

The glittering orange was fading crimson in the back of my mind. I was in danger of losing the magic amidst all this bad feeling. But as one day dawned the storm clouds had scattered and the altimeter told us to go. We waded through fresh snow and jumared up icefalls to again sleep at the shoulder. The Americans were looking weary. They'd been on this ledge for thirty days without going down. We packed two days of potato powder and stuffing mix and minimal clothing and jumared to our highpoint. As the sun came onto the wall we realised our unavoidable fate. Ice began to crash down the wall all around us, chandeliers falling in slow motion, and easy looking cracks were choked with foot-thick water ice. The sky was still hazy and we knew we only had a small window. It was now or not at all. Progress was unbearably slow, like climbing hard Scottish mixed pitches with one toffee hammer. After our two days we were still 300 metres from the summit and very low on food. Adam made a terrible dinner of undissolved dried potato and my face was blooded after being hit by ice. We slept at the 'good bivvy' marked on the topo above a dark void. The third day dawned and illuminated eerie clouds. The wind had changed to a northerly, which we hadn't seen before, and the temperature steadily dropped. I started to have some trouble breathing and my lungs began to rattle – I just thought I was a bit chesty. I led my hardest pitch of the route, an overhanging icefall with lots of sculpting. The weather continued to deteriorate and this snail-pace was frustrating.

12 ... on choosing an able partner ...

Adam had never been proper mountaineering before and he found moments of this trip quite harrowing. This storm he found particularly worrying and he had suggested that maybe we should retreat. We perched on a ledge and had a brief conference. I was having increasing difficulty getting air in but was loathe to bail out this close.

"If you can lead it, Adam, I can jug it."

Adam is a master in the art of sloth and torpor but he surpassed everyone with his recent record-breaking speed ascents on El Capitan which prepared him well for this very situation. Now, on the sharp end, he slugged his way up corners and wide cracks with ease. When I arrived at the belay he would have tied-off the rope and be halfway up the next pitch. In this way we climbed hungry and reached a tormented summit which we could barely hang onto. It was 4.30 pm on August 13. A little later on the same day nine people, including friends, were blown off K2, just a few miles north, but we wouldn't know this for ten more days. What we endured for three days took three hours to descend by rappel. Sometimes the ropes would be stuck for just long enough to get us worried and then, with a tug, come falling down. Back at the shoulder the Americans met us with hot brews and food and I collapsed, more ill than elated, into the tent. I kept Adam awake all night with my bubbling lungs which he said sounded like I was smoking a bong.

13 ... on the collection of exotic ailments ...
I had never had pulmonary oedema before. It wasn't very pleasant at the time but it was definitely one for the collection. Now I have lots to talk about at dinner parties – of how, just before this trip, I had recovered from a very rare heart virus I'd picked up on Baffin Island, of how I'd got dysentery in Bolivia, cerebral oedema in Gangotri, hepatitis in Hampi and now a dreadful case of bubbles on Trango. The next day I just wanted to stay in my pit and deteriorate but, thankfully, Adam forced me to get on the ropes. That evening back at camp, safe and almost well, we could now afford the luxury of laughter as our anecdotes, that will last a lifetime, took shape.

14 ... on luck and fate ...
A few days later, as we sit in camp eating porridge full of weevils, a huge rockfall rakes our gully and a plume of dust rises a thousand feet. We could smell the cordite. Mohammed, a porter friend, has just come down half an hour earlier with my abandoned haulbag. He looks up at the dust and then down at me and says with a grin, "Acha. Good."

15 ... on getting banned from Pakistan ...
"A Pakistani expedition would never abandon a leader who was dying from oedema. Perhaps these people you call your friends are not really so."

The head of the mountaineering division seemed to be enjoying this debriefing. I'm sure he was relishing toying with us, that feeling of power he must have been getting.

"Why did you not stop them leaving? You are their leader."

"Things are different where we come from. I cannot order people around, I can't force them to do things against their will."

"But the rules clearly state that an expedition must stay together at all times."

I tried to reason by saying that lots of other trips split up in the same way without any problems at all.

"But you were in a war zone. How do we know that members of your team are not spies for the Indians? How do we know that they were not taking pictures of important military installations?"

I almost giggled as I tried to imagine how those ramshackled groups of army tents on the Baltoro or those falling down bridges, that hundreds of tourists see every day, could be classed as important military installations, but before I could compose myself and answer he jumped in with a self-satisfied request.

"Please can you give us $400 for your abandoned equipment."

"But isn't it bad enough that I've lost thousands of dollars of equipment in the avalanche without having to pay more?"

"The mountain is not interested in how much your equipment costs. Now please pay and sign here. And could you please give Captain Jamal $400 for food."

"But the captain ate with us for the whole expedition. We fed him well."

"That is irrelevant. You signed here your agreement. Look, please."

The head of the mountaineering division held up a scrap of paper with my signature on it and smirked. He'd got us again. I couldn't remember, but I had obviously signed our money away in the delirium of the 45-degree heat on the way in. I despondently handed over our last wad of notes and then this man, from whom I was now trying to hide my frustration, enthusiastically threw his final punch.

"I am sorry," he smiled, "but you have left me no choice but to ban you and your team from Pakistan mountain climbing for four years."

We arose, limply shook hands, and left the office feeling well and truly stitched up.

Deep Players

On the Shark's Fin
with Philip Lloyd

There are always a multitude of reasons on a big mountain for not going on but the most powerful, the one which decides above all others, is the lack off will.　　　　　Joe Tasker, *Savage Arena*

IN SEPTEMBER 1993 a small team of mates went to the Gangotri valley of the Garhwal Himalaya to attempt to climb to the untrodden summit of what we called the Meru Shark's Fin.

Few of you reading this will have heard the name Philip Lloyd. Why should you? He was a beginner in life, only just realising what his body and mind were capable of. Like the rest of us on that trip, he was only just shedding the confusion of youth but still held a willingness to experiment and learn. It was our first experience of high-altitude alpinism on a big wall. We'd climbed 6000-metre peaks before but not overhanging ones! Some of us were dealing with a new and radically different culture, reacting in

many ways – puzzlement, disbelief and outrage. New relationships were formed. We met characters unlike any we had met
before. We befriended Hindu ascetics, pestering them for
knowledge. We became especially close to Om Giri – Mountain of
Power – who lived in a cave and sat naked in deep snow. We had
the curiosity of children, living with open, seeing eyes, senses
linked to our minds, perhaps not understanding all, but willing to
absorb and ponder. Sponge and stone. And we had, it maybe, the
naivety of children; Dave decided that the slope was too prone to
avalanche and, very bravely, decided not to go. We saw the spire
in the clouds and the romance became entwined with the fear.
And it exhilarated us, this climbing on eggshells. Before, I had sat
with Philip in a forest in Patagonia and talked of dreams and
plans.

"Trango?"

"Later." We could go there anytime, But Meru Central! An
unclimbed peak by its hardest line. And we would try and free it.
Naive? Maybe. Then I hope we never 'grow up'.

We looked further into the future. Trips to all corners of the
world – Asgard, Dickey, Antarctica, the Trangos, Spitzbergen. The
plans spiralled and I reckon we shared the same broad vision of
what these trips meant. Not single accomplishments one after the
other, but an urge to explore deeper and deeper. Elemental forces
and toil. But the dreams of future adventures, which want to turn
into granite plans, can, it seems, become as ephemeral as a dream
in the dawn hours.

This is about Philip as a part of a team, on this climb and on
others, and he was like us. We came from Britain and he from
South Africa. He was a qualified lawyer but he soon found that
the mountains gave him the food for which he hungered.

On that trip all was shared – the *dahl*, the load-carrying, the
close calls and the exhilarating sights. How close we have all come
– the day on the glacier when the sun was so hot it made our
heads spin. I sat under an overhung boulder which gave shade
whilst Phil was on top of it stashing gear. When we came back six
hours later the huge rock had toppled. We joked of charmed lives
and good omens for the climb, but I chilled momentarily as I

looked in the direction of Bhagirathi 3 and recalled my other brush with granite when a rock dropped hundreds of metres landing on my arm and ending my climb.

While resting at camp, we received a letter from the parents of a Spanish girl who had been swept down in an avalanche on Meru North. They requested of us that we cement a plaque to an appropriate boulder. Philip was alarmed at the idea of a plaque on such beautiful rocks. What finer monument than the mountains themselves? But the plaque was fixed in place.

And the shared sensations. The jumps in the cardiograph pattern which make a life special, load-carrying in the gully at night on those eggshells, trying not to wake the sleeping snow, careful not to talk too loudly. The torchlight in our footsteps illuminating crystals of snow, white electricity flashing over Shivling, breathing in moments of adrenaline too numerous to recall.

At the top of the gully we hacked out an ice cave in a peculiar spherical sérac that we named the hanging globe of pleasure. Noel couldn't make it that far because of his 'bad altitude problem', so he started drawing up plans for the LAMC - the Low-Altitude Mountaineering Club.

One night we talked of the past. I first met Philip in Patagonia when Noel and I were attempting the Central Tower of Paine with Sean Smith and Simon Yates. He was working, like others all over the world, just to finance more climbs. A collector of experiences rather than of things. But I guess the experiences collect themselves.

A sponsor said to me recently, "Isn't it about time you lucked out and got up something." You try your hardest, but topping out matters even less than the amount of experiences you gain. Phil had already climbed twenty big Bolivian peaks and on his days off work he climbed the North Tower of Paine and La Aleta de Tiburon which, coincidentally, translates as the Shark's Fin. We teamed up for some intense free ascents. Intense for the speed with which we had to climb and walk to complete each route in a day. How easy it would be to miss the climbing partner who complements your mood and skill so well. With this man there was no argument, no indecision, only laughter and swift movement.

I was fit then but I found it hard and challenging to keep pace with Philip. He loved to read Tilman. He was his hero and, like Tilman, he was hard on himself, as his uncle said, "allowing no room for mediocrity". Later Philip made an outrageous climb, Una Fina Linea de Locura, to the right of the South African dièdre on the Central Tower of Paine and a new route on the Painetta. He then went on a very adventurous winter trip to the Cordillera Sarmiento where he made the first ascent of the Fickle Finger of Fate at the head of the Fjord of the Mountains. With such strength, five languages and a law degree he became affectionately known to the Meru team as the Robot and every time he went to his tent we pictured him recharging his nuclear battery pack.

On the morning of our eighth day of upward movement on the Meru Shark's Fin, Johnny accidentally dropped his plastic boot whilst trying to get it on his foot. With the sight of a falling boot fell the vision of a summit ridge. Phil gave Johnny a hug and rigged up the rappel anchors. There was no place for anger over a dream which was misplaced in the night. Destiny can't be side-stepped.

An image flits by of the big man carrying two enormous haul-bags full of kit back towards our advance camp, whilst Johnny and I struggled behind with one rucksack each.

Back at camp, knackered: "Hey, Phil, I think we need to get straight back on this next season."

"Count me in."

Then he went off and soloed Bhagirathi 2 in less than twenty-four hours, camp to camp. Camp was about seven miles from the start of the route.

Who knows what the future would have witnessed. With him other climbers' dreams are lost. Dreams of repeating more Lloyd routes. There have been others in climbing's short history; John Hoyland fell in the Alps in 1934 at the age of nineteen and he had made some of the most audacious leads of the time on Cloggy and Glyder Fach. His peers waited to see what he'd do next but, like Phil, he never had the opportunity to face his limitations.

The team, as others, will always carry his inspiration and I will hold on to some of the stoic and perhaps sometimes dangerous refusal to be budged into retreat which only developed, for me, in our partnership.

Philip lost his life in December 1993 when a rappel anchor pulled as he retreated from the Towers of Paine in a storm.

He knew Paine.

Accidental Hero – Silvo Karo

I'VE NEVER really had a climbing hero. There's people I've respected, people I've thought crazy. There are people who've fired me up with their actions and I've wanted to emulate them. And then there's the odd climber from deepest history who perhaps I've credited with being slightly more superhuman than they really were. But there's no one great name for whom I've actually felt a nervousness about meeting. No one whose image (the image I have created) has elevated them above the other great climbers so that they have become 'obviously' invincible and their feats, their legacies almost divine. Well perhaps there was just one ...

In September '96 Johnny Dawes and I waded around below a huge Himalayan wall, well out of our depth. Rocks whirred and whistled through the air like helicopters and bombs. Neither of us had been mountaineering before but we had come to try the unclimbed West Face – *thud* – of Bhagirathi 3. A rock impacted the slope nearby and vanished into the soft snow. The rubble was falling from the shale cap of the mountain a thousand metres above and the barrage increased as the sun swung around the sky to edge onto the wall. Pathetic little mites with a gigantic monster looming over them. Just as we had decided that our objective was incon-ceivable the whirr of one spinning lump of shale grew much louder than the others and I was smashed down the slope. Johnny helped me get back down to camp with a knackered arm and we both agreed a wall like that would be sheer suicide.

When we returned to Delhi we found the report of a Slovene pair who had just climbed the wall seven days before we had arrived. Straight up the centre, no fixed ropes – straight up the shale for God's sake. These people weren't like us. They must live at a different level of commitment, their skill must be complete mastery and, God, they must be single-minded. Silvo Karo. Janez Jeglic. Who were they? Since then the names have always jumped out at me from the pages of journals and magazines. Hazy black and whites of Cerro Torre in old copies of *Mountain*, dark figures grimacing out from the walls. That was them. As I researched my own Patagonian trips, I discovered that their names were synony-mous with that wild place. Jim Bridwell wrote that the South Face of the Torre was the hardest ascent ever made in Patagonia, a place where I soon learned you can just about substitute the word epic for the word ascent. As you wander around the Fitz Roy massif, Karo's routes stand out. The biggest lines on the biggest peaks. If, like me, you had read up on the place those routes dominate your view. The local experts, the annual big wall pilgrims from around the world, talk of his routes with a hint of humour, they are so audacious. Two of the routes, Devil's Dièdre on Fitz and Directis-sime de l'Enfer on Cerro Torre, are typified by great objective danger and are sometimes independently known as "that flushing Slovene death couloir".

In '93, whilst I was attempting a new route on the East Face of the Torre, we watched the avalanches and rocks roar down the corner line of his route every day. This just served to reinforce my image of this man's invincibility even more. I mean was he con-stantly dodging the rocks for weeks on end or were they bouncing off him? His name became a kind of joke to me and my friends. If it was too scary we'd "leave this one for Silvo Karo". Or if we saw a huge tottering pile of shale we'd say, "Look, there's a Silvo Karo route." His Eastern European origin added somewhat to the mystique, as here in Britain we have all too often lumped the Poles, Czechs, Russians, Hungarians and Yugoslavs together as another world of crazy climbers with no sense of self-preservation. I have even heard climbers bemoan the Eastern European bravery and try to demean their achievements: "How can we compete with psychos?" or "They only go for it so much because of the rewards they can reap off the state if they are successful." This attitude stems from deep-seated ignorance and is why even now many Eastern Europeans, even if they are doing the most important ascents in the world, receive hardly any financial help from the big companies. But somewhere out there was a man who beyond the mystique was only human, someone who took his craft very seriously. I wondered would I ever meet him.

❄

The phone rang. He was here in Scotland and apparently interested in climbing with me. I began to feel nervous. Me and my friends laughed uneasily. What would he be like? Would his shoulders fit through the door? His hands must be like shovels. Imagine getting into a fight with him! I drove at night through the snow to where he was staying. On my way over a deserted moor I came upon an upturned car with its lamps on. This was turning into a surreal evening. Bricking it, I shone my torch through the window expecting to see a blood-spattered corpse. There was nothing. Phew! Then I began to have the ridiculous idea that perhaps these kind of events surround this man's life. Like climbing those couloirs, perhaps he saunters through his life while chaos reigns around him.

I pulled up at a remote house and knocked. I wiped my palm and prepared to meet a legend. I was led through to a room where a short well built man was sitting on the sofa. He rose and we shook hands. Just as I expected this hurt. "Hello. I am Silvo." He spoke like Dracula and seemed quite edgy. Without any further pleasantries we got down to talking of the big walls we had climbed in far off places. I felt like I had nothing to offer and everything to learn but due to his modest disposition I became less starstruck as the night ran late. I asked him how he had first come to go to Patagonia. He spoke slowly and with difficulty.

"We always went to Italy to buy shoes. Under Tito we could not get these things in our country. There I saw a poster of Fitz Roy and I thought this was a most beautiful mountain. In November of '96 I went with my friends, Francek Knez and Janez Jeglic, and we make a very hard new route, mixed. It was from the summit that we saw Cerro Torre."

I had seen the Devil's Dièdre, the flushing couloir. It still hasn't had a repeat.

"We climbed in poor equipment and very bad clothes," he continued. Up until recently Silvo had made do with fur hats, stripy Eastern block tracksuits and 'Russian Gore-tex' (nylon).

That night we debated long over the Maestri affair. Silvo knew every shred of evidence for and against Maestri's claim to the first ascent of Cerro Torre. The debate was obviously one of his favourite cerebral pastimes, yet he wouldn't commit his opinion. I detected a dubious smirk though.

We arose at dawn to a puncture on my old motor. Silvo quickly replaced it with the bald spare and for the rest of my Scottish winter I never found a garage who could take it off to put a new one back on, so tightly did he screw the nuts up. After that his finger-strength became instantly legendary within the team. And so it was off to the Cairngorms, passing the wrecked car en route.

Below the Shelterstone we roped up and set off. Though feeling under pressure to perform, my pitch went OK, dot to dotting up clumps of turf on a protectionless slab. Silvo lead through, moving fast and determinedly. I watched closely to see what I could learn from his movements. At first I was almost disappointed to see him thrashing and using his tools so heavily but then it made me glad. Yes, he was 'only' human after all. Perhaps we could all aspire to these things ... A hundred feet above me, with no gear in, he's out of sight. A barrage of junk snow falls on me and I hear a muffled cry. I brace myself on the belay and one of the two pieces I am on pops. I scramble back onto the stance. No falling body appears above me, so I frantically begin rebuilding the belay whilst those preconceptions begin to creep back into my mind. Maybe he is an Eastern European psycho after all ... But the rope continues to run out steadily and I follow him up a pitch of hideously rotten snow. "Good lead, Silvo. Bad conditions, very Scottish." We moved together up the last hundred metres of our climb and clambered onto the flat summit. It was a rare, perfect day and there where people, scurrying dots, all around below us in the fresh snow, making the most of the sunshine. We smiled and shook hands.

"Our first climb. But perhaps not our last."

No way. Did I hear right? Does that mean that the great man might want to do a proper route with me one day? I could hardly contain myself as we sat and admired the view. I pestered him with questions about his life and his culture. I began to piece together a life story from his stilted English learned from base camps around the world.

Silvo was born in 1960 on a little farm near the town of Domzale, the second of four children. He grew up happily, working hard, caring for the animals and getting the crops in. "A hard worker will always make a good climber," he had said. His family lived in the mountains, so it was only natural for him to walk and scramble amongst them. He then went on to join the climbing club and begin the courses. I learned that the main work of the clubs under the communists was to take novice youths and train them to become mountaineers. In turn, they would train other novices. He progressed rapidly until, at nineteen, national service stole one and a half years from him. He hated the army and longed to be free to get back to the Julian Alps which he loved. Silvo then talked of his friends, his companions on some of the most treacherous walls in the world ... Whilst in hospital recovering from a broken leg received during a military exercise, he looked out of the window and saw a man climbing on the stone wall of the building. Back and forth he went repeating the same moves over and again. Silvo befriended him and credits the slightly older Francek Knez with being the first Slovene to train and climb really hard moves. A little later a young Janez Jeglic joined the club and the trio made a tight group, climbing the hardest routes of the day in the Julian Alps. All their climbs were made with the pitons and wooden wedges all other Slovene climbers were using in the early eighties.

In 1981 the team visited America on an exchange. It was an exhilarating time. They used nuts and Friends for the first time. They saw just what was possible and had a chance to compare their ability, which was considerable. They were soon racing up the hardest routes on Devil's Tower, Eldorado Canyon and the Needles of South Dakota, making new climbs and first free ascents. On return to their home Silvo, Francek and Janez turned their attention to Triglav, the highest point in their country. On consecutive weekends they made three new winter ascents on the 800-metre North Face, Silvo returning to his mechanics job in the factory mid-week.

"And then it was to Fitz Roy, our first expedition."

We waded over the Cairngorm plateau and out of the mist appeared Sneachda. It was quite late in the day but I thought we could squeeze another route in.

"What are all these people doing?" Silvo chuckled and began snapping photos. "They will laugh in Slovenia when they see this."

"But this is the most popular crag in Scotland," I replied feeling protective.

"Why do they not wait for the snow to go from the rock before climbing?"

"It's the Scottish speciality. Mixed climbing. Don't you have cliffs like this in your home country?"

"Yes we have ... But we do not climb on them. Let us go and drink coffee."

Fair enough, I thought. Must seem pretty tame after the East Face of Torre Egger.

These climbers were bringing new levels of difficulty to Slovenia now, making routes that were unimaginable with only pitons or without the new found strength reaped from dedicated training, but Silvo was taking more and more time off from his factory job. This was frowned upon but, unlike other communist regimes, Tito's government wasn't nearly so oppressive. In 1985, after an attempt on Kangchenchunga with a giant Yugoslavian expedition, on which Tomo Cesen topped out and Borut Bergant disappeared, Silvo decided he needed to take a year off to fulfil his climbing goals. He found his small-scale trip to Patagonia had suited him much more than the enormous machine of the Kangchenchunga expedition.

Not surprisingly, he was informed that if he took a whole year off work he would have no job to come back to. So he made his bed, and it was a good year. In November '85, after two months of fixing ropes and risking avalanches the three friends, along with an upcoming Slavco Svetetcic, Peter Podgornik and Pavle Kozjek made the first ascent of the East Face of Cerro Torre. It is an evil-looking route, Directissime de l'Enfer. I timed avalanches down it at one every twelve minutes! Silvo and Janez didn't know then that this was only the beginning of a long affair with Cerro Torre. July saw Silvo experimenting with high altitude again when he reached the summit of Broad Peak via the Austrian route. But that wasn't where his heart lay. Later that year and back on the small scale with his two old friends, he made what he describes as his finest route. Psycho Vertical, despite starting in the routine 'couloir of death' follows a dark thread line of thin cracks all the way to the top of Torre Egger, that slender hourglass of granite and snow that Don Whillans said looked like a newly opened champagne bottle.

During our talks Silvo never spoke of close shaves or epic retreats. It was like all his ascents had been executed first time, with skill and thought. Or perhaps the hard times were just part of the game – I was kept guessing. He seemed to prefer talking of his friends. They were close to him and he was as proud of their achievements as he was of others from his country. He liked to talk of Svetetcic with whom he made the second ascent of Rolling Stones (named for obvious reasons) on the North Face of the Grandes Jorasses in the fast time of one and a half days.

"Slavco could not free climb, 5+ at the most, and yet he soloed the Eiger Harlin route in a day and he went back to solo Rolling Stones. If he had succeeded on Gasherbrum 4 it would have been the greatest climb in the world." (Svetetcic disappeared whilst attempting to solo a new route on the West Face of Gasherbrum 4 whilst we were on the South Face of Trango Tower).

That evening Silvo gave a slide show in a local hotel. Despite the publicity, it was a small turn out. Not many people have heard the name Silvo Karo in Britain. Pictures of a beautiful land dissolved into one another upon the screen, unspoiled alpine meadows draped below the hulks of Triglav, Travnik and Sité. The film of Cerro Torre's South Face brought nervous laughter from the audience. Is this for real? But that snow is chest deep! They're actually climbing through waterfalls! The film made up for all the impressions that could not be put across with our lack of a solid common language. It said it all. And then a story Steve Gerberding told me flashed through my mind; Gerberding, a veteran of seventy El Capitan ascents and many Patagonian routes, was shopping in a crowded Yosemite deli when he saw Karo queueing up with a bag of bagels. Gerberding couldn't believe his eyes. He fell to his knees, prostrating himself at the visitor's feet and began shouting, "We are not worthy, we are not worthy", much to the embarrassment of Karo.

Sat on a pool table after the show, with glasses of dark beer, Silvo talked of his wife Alma and his son Jan. He had a sparkle in his eye when he spoke of them and recently he has given up big trips to spend more time with his family. He met Alma after his Bhagirathi 3 trip or, I should say, after his Everest trip because he and Janez went straight from their success in the Gangotri to attempt a traverse of the highest mountain. Not surprisingly Silvo was run down and developed health problems but he displayed remarkable will power. Since his marriage he has still found the will to climb hard sport climbs on the fine Slovene limestone and the hardest aid climbs on a family holiday to Yosemite. He also has made two disastrous trips to Bhagirathi 4, both times being thwarted by the Indian government's lack of organisation.

"Two times I pay for a permit and arrive in India to be told I cannot climb."

He was dismayed by the Kafkaesque bureaucracy which has to be surmounted to climb in India now and looks forward to trips to

Chile or other easy countries. His last trip to India, with big wall ace John Middendorf, resulted in Silvo being banned from the country because, in frustration, he went to attempt the wall anyway. Liaison officers with other expeditions made sure he didn't get to climb, though.

I mentioned that we might get an early start tomorrow for a big day out in the Cairngorms and said my goodnight. It was a slightly later start than I had anticipated. After a leisurely breakfast and shopping for whisky, I eagerly pulled my equipment out of the back of the car. The car park was heaving with skiers in fluorescent clothes shielding their faces from the wind-blown fog. As I laced my boots up the great man, the man that never backs down, sat still in the front seat.

"What's wrong, Silvo? Do you feel OK? Would you like to go somewhere else?"

"I have seen enough bad weather in my life. I think we should go and drink coffee."

A Lesson in Healing from Andy Parkin

CREAG MEAGHAIDH, March 1996.

"OK, so this is called a brake plate. You put the rope in like this and clip it through there. If I fall, which is highly unlikely, you pull this hand back and the friction will stop the rope running through. Just give me loads of slack, so as you don't accidentally pull me off."

Without another word I traversed off rightwards around a sharp arête and back into the gully. A full pitch of dripping ice lay above me. Grade V said the guidebook – no problem, I can climb fives in any condition. I was feeling particularly confident today, nothing could stop me. The first seventy feet was off vertical, pretty easy. It had a few patches of cruddy, slushy ice but I could soon scrape past them to the other patches of chewy thawing ice. I tunnelled behind a gigantic icicle for a rest and screwed a screw in. I couldn't see my partners. They where out of sight and I, as I later realised, was out of my mind.

I swung out onto the front face of the icicle and into the vertical. Ten feet of bomber Scottish ice and I got another screw which went in a little too easily and wobbled when I tugged on it. Oh well, I was feeling good. Great, in fact. I'd just carry on and see what came. I moved up into eggshell ice. My boots kicked straight through into the soft wet snow behind and my axes pulled out the odd time. I was used to dealing with this patchy sort of stuff and I could see a better looking area higher up. Limb by limb I crawled up the thin shell, keeping my chest right against the surface so as not to put too much weight on my arms. I was a long way out now ... *Whoosh.* My body shudders and my heart starts to pound. The vibration makes my footholds collapse a tiny bit and I realise that it would be possible to come unstuck on this stuff. *"I hate jet planes"* I shout into the ice and briefly consider what I will write in my letter of complaint to the RAF. Dear Whoever: One of your pilots almost killed me on Creag Meaghaidh yesterday blah blah.

Come on, get on with the climb. Each move now seems more insecure than the last. The eggshell is getting thinner and at one point I smash through and dig as far back as I can but find no purchase. The gaping hole I've made in front of me now makes it extra difficult to get higher but I manage, using a mixture of fear and bad style. Now I'm committed – I can't climb back down that slop. With my ice screw seventy feet below, it would be way too risky a manoeuvre. I stop being scared and start to feel a bit like a cardboard cut-out. There's a bulge above me with a reasonable looking patch of ice above it. I'll aim for that. I edge left with my tools right in front of my face, standing on the tip of a thin crust. I go up into the bulge. At a reach, I slam my left axe into the good looking ice and to my detached disappointment it shatters like a breaking mirror. I sigh and can already feel the bad luck descending upon me. I stay motionless, calmly having a schizophrenic debate in my head. One of me wants just to go for it, just start fighting. It's worked before, it could work now.

"No, stay still and wait for Nick to get around the top and drop a rope."

"That would take ages. Longer than this brittle shell will last."

"Reverse?"

"Is that possible?"

"Well, each move down is a move nearer to the screw and it looks even worse above."

"OK, down it is."

"This is a mistake," I say out loud.

I take out my right boot and go to kick it in lower down. As I swing my foot back my left foothole breaks and my body slumps down. I brace myself on my axes ... But they start to rip. They slow down for less than a moment and I kick in my foot ... Then they go. The ice falls away from my face and I throw my axes at it in one last attempt to retain contact. I knew it was futile. I remember beginning to scream, very loudly. Deeply at first, then getting higher in pitch. A mass of white flashes past my eyes, no slow motion here. I don't touch anything as I rocket past my companions on the belay. I hit the end of my fall fully conscious and spring back up the gully on the stretchy 8.5. The wobbly ice screw has held.

"Are you all right?" Nick shouts from above.

After some time wheezing in a winded state, I look up and see a blurred Nick. I clutch at my, judging by the symptoms, broken body. "Why do I never learn?" was all I could say.

❄

Moving through your small house I have to mind not to knock your belongings over. But you don't really care if they break. You didn't pay for them – you made nearly all of these things. You haven't said it to me but I think you have a clear idea of just how ephemeral all of this is. Like your stained glass mountains or the leaping salmon or, above the sink, Cerro Torre painted with a wall roller, the wire sculptures and the photo of the Peigne and Pelerins to help you recall your most frightened moments. Walking through into the front room my way is barred by haunted faces, crushed together, staring out at me from a large blue canvas. Kenya? India? Nepal? Where isn't so important. I can feel the heat and the clamour. It has similar aspects to the canvas you made in Hampi:

We dragged ourselves out of our mosquito nets extra early this morning in a futile attempt to beat the trickling humidity to the boulders. The rocks sat like giant potatoes on a broad smooth dome. They were already shimmering. We began to move excitedly, stiff from the long train journey which had brought us here from the cold granite of the Gangotri. There Andy had climbed Shivling with Sean Smith, while I had sat in camp with a knackered arm. In contrast, this rock felt to the fingers like the crust of a hot loaf fresh from the oven. We suffocated and traversed as local men made their morning ablutions nearby.

Andy set off to climb to the top of the first Hampi boulder. He had a different climbing style to the rest of us. His right arm and leg would always move first and then pull his thin ripped torso up a stop to allow his left limbs to locate the nearest edge or pocket. It seemed to me the movement of a very graceful crab. At the last move of the problem, as he hauled on a jug with his right arm, the rock broke and Andy fell to the ground. He was only a few feet up and for most of us a short ground fall would be no big deal, but for Andy with his fused hip the feline landings of a carefree youth are a hazy memory. He hit the bare rock with pencil straight legs and cracked his heels.

He didn't try to hide the agony as we carried him to a nearby café (many hardy mountain types would be ashamed to show such a weakness to pain). He began to retch as we fed him sweet tea and in the heat we all felt some of his delirium. A pair of white eyes moved in the darkness at the back of the room and, as they neared, a bald Tamil materialised. His skin was incredibly black. The man squatted at Andy's feet and, after much gesticulating, took the left foot in his hand and began his examination. We made room and watched. He squeezed and explored the heel and, feeling the pieces of loose bone floating, looked up at Andy, whose knuckles were now turning white in acknowledgement. Our man then moved over Andy's body, squeezing and manipulating every joint. Occasionally he would gasp in surprise and then assume a worried look when he fingered a bolt or plate under the skin. Slowly he broke into a proud smile. He had found an excellent subject with which to work. Then he tried to force the frozen elbow to straighten out and met with fierce opposition from a squirming Parkin. There, dazed and naive in all the heat and excitement, it is so easy to be sucked in by the many experienced con merchants but in the Swiss hospital Andy had felt the hands of the world's finest physiotherapists and quickly recognised that our friend, the temple masseur, had a gift.

Over the coming weeks our Tamil friend was to be Andy's constant companion, packing his feet in mud and administering herbal relaxants. During one particularly heavy bout of massage he pulled and twisted Andy's foot to extreme angles; "Stop, please, *stop!*" No effect. In a reflex response to the torment he kicked the man around the head and he fell backwards across the room. But he wasn't too put out – it was just the effect he was looking for. Andy was philosophical. He had spent so much of his life injured that he had a well rehearsed mental system for coping with such mishaps. He threw himself into his painting, as he had done before. The result, amongst lots of studies and portraits, was a huge bazaar scene on canvas. The many faces, like the faces in all Andy's crowds, look as if they know something. Something that not all are aware of – of course this is to my untrained and romantic eye.

Early in his career and on the Sheffield scene Andy had been a superb free climber. In '82 he went on a road trip to the States with Thierry Renault and made first on-sight ascents of many of the hardest routes of the day, including Leavitt's Hot Flyer in Boulder Canyon.

"All these blokes were saying 'Why don't we try this?' but that wasn't the way I thought. I said 'Why don't we do this?'."

In '83, after Lobsang and Broad Peak, he almost succeeded on a new route on K2 with Doug Scott. Then, in Cham, he made the first true winter solo of the Walker Spur on the North Face of the Grandes Jorasses. The Japanese alpinist Hasagowa had soloed the route in the late '70s but had resorted to siege tactics and fixed rope. Andy's one and a half day solo was made in a purist style.

"I wanted to honour Cassin and invoke some of the sense of discovery that he might have felt, walking over from Italy to make the first ascent. I climbed mostly free solo and without a route description. It was using this style that got me lost whilst soloing the Shroud."

The following season, whilst guiding on the Riffelhorn in Zermat, a belay failed when the rock gave way and Andy fell ninety feet onto a flat slab. The list of injuries was terrific, the most serious being a ruptured pericardium. I do not, and neither would Andy, wish to dwell on these injuries. It is better to dwell on the future than the past. This also goes for each and every route. Once a route is behind you (and especially with a poor memory) the experience may never have existed. The joy of climbing comes from the participation. Andy knows this and I reckon he won't be hanging up his boots, sitting by the fire and getting lost in reminiscence too early.

After the best part of a year in a Swiss hospital he was utterly broken. He assumed he would never climb again, and climbing was his life. He had hardly thought about anything else for years. This is the part of the story I needed to listen to. Then he began to paint. Mountains and people. The years passed and his body recovered. His choice of sites from which to paint became more adventurous as he moved further away from home and memory to find a suitable view. And, after time amongst the mountains, a desire to climb was instilled once again.

"A few years later I woke up and knew I was better. First I was a climber, then I was a painter and now I need both."

Now his painting and his climbing evolve side by side. Sculptures made from rubbish found on the glaciers form a significant part of his recent work.

"We found this airplane wreck on the Boissons and turned it into a huge elephant. An endangered species from human detritus."

In Patagonia Andy would spend days building cairns in the mountains or mobiles in the forest. He wouldn't take any photos and after a while the wind would take them back into the earth. Again the joy coming from the participation, and the mind looking to the next creation. That is not to say that Andy finds recounting past experiences disagreeable. It is the sheer size of these experiences, rather than his yarn-spinning abilities, that leaves me riveted. I was aghast when in his Chamonix house, he matter of factly told me of his three days alone, bivouacked at 8300 metres on Everest without oxygen or, more recently, when he modestly described his climb of Pelerinage on the Peigne with Christof Beaudoin:

On the tenth pitch after lots of difficult mixed climbing Christof took a belay and Andy led through on one-centimetre water ice.

"I was balancing on little ledges I was manufacturing with my ice pick to balance my front points on."

The angle was 80 degrees, unprotected and very delicate.

"At thirty metres I found a Friend on two cams and the climbing continued to be the hardest ice I've ever done. At sixty metres I still hadn't got another piece in and I was tip-toeing on verglas. There was no belay in sight, so I just kept going."

Out of rope, Christof began climbing also. After a further fifteen metres Andy was on or off and Christof was fighting desperately to stay on the face, now with even less ice after Andy had scratched up it.

"There was a spike above me which I couldn't quite reach, so I lunged for it. If I'd missed, the two of us would have gone. I just caught it. I couldn't believe the release of stress. I've never done anything like that – well perhaps on the Mermoz."

Patagonia has become a strong source of inspiration for him. For his painting and for his climbing. The depth and space of the sky and landscape are a challenge to paint and the frontierland atmosphere, the stories of Saint-Exupéry and the early explorers, have captured his imagination.

Andy's first ascent solo of Vol de Nuit on the East Face of the Mermoz caused quite a stir amongst the teams of international climbers camped at Rio Blanco. The weather had been dreadful and everyone was waiting for Fitz Roy. Then one day, one of those kind of OK days that everyone knew would bag out before tomorrow, a lone climber was spotted through the binoculars picking his way up near vertical-looking mixed ground. Thin 90-degree ice and irreversible moves were again the hallmark of the climb and also a difficult aid section. As the young Argentinian hot-shots looked on, they commented with obvious respect, *"Andy es locisimo."*

"That climb was near the limit for me. One of those rare times when you experience that inner flight."

These recent climbs herald the beginning of a new era in Andy's life.

"I don't like to talk about that accident but these modern hard things I have done feel like part of a healing process to me."

These routes convey a level of self-trust and coolness of head that can only be achieved by someone utterly in touch with their body. And after being forced to listen to his body for so long this could definitely be said to be the case for Andy.

He settled his tumbler of wine on the table top.

"You'll get better, kiddo. That time I lost everything. I lost my girlfriend, she looked after me for ages but I got so down, so distant, that she finally gave up. I lost my mind, for a while."

I nodded, trying to relate all this to my own sorrowful state. "But if I can't climb what can I do?" I had a lump in my throat. I needed his help.

"As you get older you'll realise that climbing isn't everything. Other opportunities will present themselves to you and to grow you have to explore them.

"The next season I was in the Bridwell camp waiting for Cerro Torre."

When the weather window came he and his mate François began a new route on the South Face of "the hardest mountain in the world". The line they had chosen was a steep and technical ice gully and much of the climbing was on rotten crud. They moved swiftly to lessen the risk of being taken out by the band of séracs above. After a thousand metres they at last arrived at the Col of Hope, in plummeting air pressure. They made it to the Helmet ice formation when the storm hit. After bivouacking, they began their descent and decided, upon reaching the Col of Hope, that it would be asking too much of fate to chance rappeling down the séracs. There was no choice. They rappeled the Ferrari route onto the Hielo Continental, the Patagonian icecap. They had no food left and no map of the icecap. After jettisoning most of their hardware, days of walking ensued. They stumbled off the snout of the Tunnel Glacier and onto the Pampa in a hallucinatory state and kept going by eating dandelions.

I know it was all a mistake, but that's the kind of experience I have always looked for. Andy remembers seeing horses prancing around him, mocking him, and this experience provided the mental material for his recent horse sculptures made from wire or cut from sheet metal with a blow torch. After another day on the featureless expanse of the Pampa they met gauchos who gave them cooked beef.

"That made me sick. After nine days out I think I had done my internal organs some damage."

Andy showed me his paintings of the Torre. Before his climb the mountain had rounded edges and a classic mountain look with light coloured, almost warm, granite. And after, it looks brooding and Gothic. Higher, darker and sharper. That exercise showed him that the act of climbing a mountain can change one's perception of that mountain for ever.

The French chose to give Andy and François the Golden Piolet award for the 'adventurous spirit' of their climb, A La Recherche du Temps Perdu. He had hidden the tacky trophy out of sight, but he did admit that the prize money would be useful for the forthcoming Alaska trip. Don't ask me how old he is. Really he is ageless. For him there is no time to lose but that is not to say that he rushes and loses sight of the reasons for doing what he does. Amidst the exhibitions and commissions, the sculpting of human waste, the climbing and skiing and the planning of imminent trips to K2 and Patagonia, and what inspires me most, this man still finds time to revel into the night.

❄

Summer '96

I've just finished my morning stretches, they take about an hour, and I move on to my mail. It's a little package from – Andy! A book on homeopathy. And a card:

Hey Paul

I found this in a book shop while I was visiting my mother. I know people who've had wonderous effects with it. Look into it, maybe it can help with the broken back and sternum. I'm getting slowly ready for the other hemisphere. Loads to do and life is buzzing. Cham is buried deep in snow and I've just started X-country skiing to get fit for sitting around in Patagonia. Leave around 8th Jan. Look after yourself, Kiddo.

Hasta la vista *Andy*

Author's Glossary
of less common climbing terms

Climbing terms needing a precise definition and modern climbing terms or slang. Plus a chapter-by-chapter table of British colloquialisms needing definition for American readers.

abseil, rappel To descend a rope using a friction device.

aid climbing The opposite of free climbing. Using your equipment to assist upward progress and not just for protection.

alpine-style A pure style. To ascend as a contained unit with no fixed rope or camps.

ascender A clamp for ascending a rope.

barring Using your knee or elbow in opposition with your foot or hand to ascend wide fissures.

bashie, copperhead, circlehead Soft metal swages for moulding into incipient cracks to provide support for subtle aid climbing, though rarely strong enough to hold a long fall.

Bird Beak Oddly shaped piton for tapping into the thinnest of rock seams.

capsule ascent A compromise between alpine-style and seiging for big climbs that are too technical and prolonged to be done in one continuous alpine-style push. The party is self-contained using a camp or camps on the wall or face, pushing the route forward without returning to the valley.

crimp A small finger edge on a rock climb.

diedre, dihedral A corner feature in a rock wall.

drive in A type of ice piton.

dyno A dynamic move where the whole body parts from the rock to catch a hold.

EBs, PAs The most popular rock-shoe (French) until the early eighties when they were rendered obsolete when stickier rubber was introduced by Spanish manufacturers.

egyptian Turning side on to the rock to get more weight onto your feet.

Friend Camming device. Trade name of the first device of this type which is sometimes used generically for all similar devices.

Gri-Gri Trade name for a belaying device.

ground up, on-sight The finest style of climbing. Ascending a climb with no pre-inspection and therefore no knowledge of what horrors await you.

hand drilling Placing bolts or rivets by manual means. Ethically more respectable than power-drilling, particularly on Big Wall routes.

hook, bat hook Device for hanging on tiny edges on the rock's surface.

Jumar See *ascender*. In common with the "Friend" a generic term taken from the first device of this type.

jumaring, jugging A bout of climbing a fixed rope using an ascending device such as a Jumar.

nut A general term for any metal wedge (fitted with a wire or rope sling) that is hand-placed into a crack or slot to provide protection or aid. Types include: Hexes, wedges, stoppers, curvers, spuds, Moacs, sliders, RPs.

piton, peg, pin Metal spikes of many sizes which are hammered into fissures in the rock. Types include: angles, Lost Arrows, blades, bongs, rurps, knife blades etc.

portaledge Hanging tent which climbers sleep in on a vertical wall.

power-drilling Placing bolts or rivets using a power drill (either by rap-bolting or during an on-sight climb or by retro-bolting after an aided lead). This is increasingly done by some European and American big wall climbers to leave solid protection to allow pitches (that would otherwise need to be aided or semi-aided) on a big-wall climb to be freed by an athletic follow-up team and thus leave a climb more likely to attract sport climbers. Often controversial, particularly during on-sight big-wall climbs.

rap-bolting Placing bolts in the rock using a rope from above.

redpointing Making a climb after rehearsing all the moves on a top rope and pre-placing all the quickdraws.

retro-bolting The adding of bolts to a climb after the first ascent. Considered ethically unacceptable by most climbers.

rivet Small metal pin driven into a shallow drilled hole for artificially climbing blank rock. Quicker and more lightweight than fixing a bolt on an aid climb and, providing it is done sparingly, it is presently thought to be visually and ethically preferable than equipping blank passages with bolt ladders.

seiging Climbing a route from a secure base camp, with repeated ascents and descents (sometimes with intermediate camps) to and from the high point to push the climb forward. Less committing than an alpine-style or even a capsule-style ascent.

skyhook Steel hook for hanging on a rock edge. Usually for aid climbing but also used on Wales's most dangerous free climbs.

slap Dynamic lunge for a hold.

sport climbing Convenient, safe climbing with drilled bolts for protection. A derivation from proper climbing – initially an attempt by normal climbers to push standards but soon evolved into a broader movement to process rock-climbing into a more athletically orientated, sanitised and measurable procedure by removing its main dangers and logistical complexities. Controversial, except on some (not all) extremely overhanging and crackless cliffs that are difficult or impossible to free-climb by other means. In other circumstances it is thought by many to represent a threat to the uncertainty and adventure of the cliffs that lies at the centre of making climbing a uniquely rewarding pastime. Dates from the easy availability of cordless drills which made such climbs feasible to establish. Supported by a growth in guiding, hut wardens, manufacturers, media and educational interest in the commercial exploitation of rock activity. Environmentally destructive.

CHAPTER 1
"bricking it" – scared stiff
"paggered" – beaten up or punched or feeling that way
"spends" – money available for spending
Youth Training Scheme – Government scheme to gainfully occupy the young unemployed

CHAPTER 2
"fifties for the leccy meter" – 50 pence pieces required for a pay-as-you-use electricity meter
"lashed up" – drunk, intoxicated
tannoy – loudspeaker in a factory or other crowded location
Giros – Government cheques issued (on the Giro Bank) to registered unemployed
"skint" – out of money, stony broke

CHAPTER 3
"Gobsmacked" – stunned, surprised or amazed (usually about something nice)

CHAPTER 4
"hacked" – getting there fast
"knackered" (as in a car being knackered, or even a person) – totally used up, tired, utterly spent (derived from Knacker – one who buys and slaughters spent horses)
"get a ton out" – squeezing 100mph out of a car

"celidh" – a Scottish dance and drinks party usually with accordion music

CHAPTER 6
"Wendy house" – a play house big enough for children to enter
MEF – Mount Everest Foundation based at the:
RGS – the Royal Geographical Society in London
"barny" – an argument or private row

CHAPTER 8
"gurning" – pulling a face sometimes through a horse bridle (an old Devonian custom)

CHAPTER 9
Wackford Squeers – a route named after the headmaster in Dickens's "Nicholas Nickleby"
Moac – an early and classic British nut design, a slender four-faceted wedge

CHAPTER 12
"bottling" (abbr. from "bottling-out") – running out of courage, "bottle" being a cockney term for courage

CHAPTER 13
"hoolie" – a strong wind

CHAPTER 14
Gemini – a make of bivouac tent

Notes about the Essays

FIRE STARTER. The gritstone quarries of Bolton are dismal places but to me they were everything. Since my childhood, I have always felt summoned to such places of industrial dereliction to practise my art or simply to explore the past. Previously unpublished.

RUBBLE MERCHANTS, SLATE HEADS AND OTHERS. I moved to that capital of British climbing, Llanberis in 1986 to follow the path of full time climber. It is both fortunate and unfortunate that things can't always stay the same. *On the Edge* 69 (1997).

LOST IN THE BROCCOLI GARDEN. Gogarth epitomises British sea cliff climbing. When you make contact with the rock you can feel the history seeping into your fingers. I have loved Gogarth and I have hated the place. I feel I grew up a little on the Red Walls. *High* 1987.

A PIECE OF DRIFTWOOD. Ed Stone was part of a close-knit team of friends in Llanberis who shared many good times. He died solo climbing on the Trinity face of Y Wyddfa in 1994. Previously unpublished.

ON THE BIG STONE. The first of many trips to Sron Ulladale. I later climbed Knuckle Sandwich (E7) with Johnny and Moskill Grooves (E6) with Johnny and Ben Moon. Ten years later the Scoop has been climbed in a day, but with pitons in-situ and a description of where the climb goes, it is a much more feasible proposition. *On the Edge* 49 (1995).

BHAGIRATHI DIARY. In 1990 I went on my first mountain climbing 'expedition' with Johnny Dawes, Joe Simpson and Bob Drury. We travelled in tandem with another British team who were attempting Shivling and made a feeble attempt on Bhagirathi 3. It was all so new to me, Bob and Johnny and we set about the task of organising a big expedition with enthusiasm. Now, a few years later, it's difficult to recapture that magic. Expeditions are now called holidays and though I need them I have a more relaxed approach. Previously unpublished.

EL REGALO DE MWONO. My first big wall climbing experience and the beginning of a nine-month road trip. I forsake the Yosemite training and jumped in at the deep end. The route is 1200m long and the grade is 6, 5.11, A4 and Scottish ice V. Team members were Noel Craine, Sean Smith, Simon Yates, Hanneke Steenmetz and myself. *American Alpine Journal* (1993).

EL CABALLO DE DIABLO. The best free climb I ever made was marred by feelings of guilt. This climb means more to me, perhaps, than any other. The day, the company, the style of ascent, everything gelled to make the perfect climb. The descent was another story, a story from which I learnt a few lessons. To me it is sadly ironic that Philip should have later died on this mountain. We graded the climb ED+, E5, French 7A, 550m. *On the Edge* 59 (1996).

JUST PASSING THROUGH. Another stop on a long journey through South America. *On the Edge* 61 (1996).

THE DOCTOR AND THE WITCH. In 1992, whilst feeling homesick in Bolivia, I went down with amoebic dysentery. I had just arrived from Brazil where my Basque, Catalonian and Argentinian friends and I had made a fabulous wall climb. In my fever the present and the near past became intertwined. *On the Edge* 65 (1997).

A GAME ONE CLIMBER PLAYED. In 1993 I came unstuck at Gogarth whilst trying to make the second ascent of Pat Littlejohn's direct start to Games Climbers Play. My Australian friend, and partner for the day, Glenn Robbins, pulled me out of the water, resuscitated me and sat with me for three hours until Oliver Saunders, who was out walking, happened to pass by. Glenn shouted to him and he ran to call a rescue. *Mountain Yodel* 6 (1997).

ADRIFT. In May 1994, with Steve Quinlan, I climbed a new line on the East face of El Capitan, Yosemite. The essence of the climb for me was here, on the UK Cowboy pitch. We got down off the climb and headed straight to Baffin Island. Grade 6, A4, 5.9, 1000m. *On the Edge* 60 (1996).

HYPERBOREA. Asgard West Face, 1994. Simon Yates, Sean Smith, Keith Jones, Steve Quinlan, Noel Craine, Jordi Tosas, Paul Pritchard. Grade 6, A4, E4. 1000m. *On the Edge* 45 (1994).

A SURVIVOR'S AFFAIR. Teo Plaza died in an avalanche on El Tronador with other friends whilst training to become an Argentinian guide. He was the most talented of the young Bariloche set. *On the Edge* 50 (1995).

MAKING CASTLES IN THE SAND. Trango Tower mixed men and women's expedition 1995. Donna Claridge, Celia Bull, Geraldine Westrupp, Kate Phillips, Noel Craine, Adam Wainwright, Andy Cave, Paul Pritchard, Ali Hussain Abadi, Ismael Bondo, Captain Jamal Mohammed. The Slovene route is 1000m long and has been free climbed in fine style by Wolfgang Güllich and Kurt Albert and later, for a film, by Catherine Destivelle and Jeff Lowe. The grade was 5.12b. With ice in the cracks we were forced to use some aid and for us the grade stood at 6, 5.10, A2. The first ascent was made in 1984 by Francek Knez, S. Canker and B. Srot. *On the Edge* 53 (1995).

ON THE SHARK'S FIN WITH PHILIP LLOYD. In 1993 Philip Lloyd, Johnny Dawes and I tried to climb the Meru Shark's Fin in Gangotri. We were repulsed after Johnny accidentally dropped his boot whilst trying to get it on after a bivouac one morning. A reminiscence of my last time with Philip. *Mountain Review* 7 (1994).

ACCIDENTAL HERO – SILVO KARO. A tough man from a tough world. An inspiration. *On the Edge* 58 (1996).

A LESSON IN HEALING FROM ANDY PARKIN. On Centre Post Direct Finish I came unstuck and fell 50 metres sustaining four crushed vertebrae, a broken sternum and a fractured skull. Nick Kekus lowered me and four clients down a thousand feet of gully and stayed with me while the others went to call for a helicopter. From Andy I learnt how to re-build life (and maintain sanity) when all seemed devastated by injury and illness. A combination of articles in *On the Edge* 48 and 57.

Note: Most of the articles have been substantially edited and developed since their first publication.

The Fables of
KALILAH AND DIMNAH

*Adapted and translated from the Sanskrit through the
Pahlavi into Arabic
by
'Abdullah ibn al-Muqaffa'
AD 750*

Translated from the Arabic by
Saleh Sa'adeh Jallad

MELISENDE
LONDON

First published 2002
by Melisende
39 Chelmsford Road
London E18 2PW
Tel: 020 8498 9768
Fax: 020 8504 2558
www.melisende.com
Second Printing 2004

ISBN 1 901764 14 1

Drawings and cover design by Myriam Misk Saikaly

Edited by Leonard Harrow

Printed in Cyprus by Lithostar Ltd.

Table of Contents

3

To the memory of Saadeh and Sarah Jallad,
my father and mother, from whom I learnt
how to teach our children Sa'ad and Tala
the value of the Mythos and the vitality of the Logos,
and how to differentiate between them.

Acknowledgements

Many good friends have helped over the course of translating and preparing this work. To them I express my deepest gratitude.

However, I must express my heartfelt thanks firstly to my wife, Leila, for her patience and tolerance encouragement and constructive criticism during the development of this project.

I must also convey my profound gratitude to Fr James T Burtchaell, C.S.C. Our friendship has grown stronger since we first met in Jerusalem in 1963. Though I am grateful for his being *inter-alia* the efficient copy editor of the book, it is his devoted friendship that my wife and I cherish most.

I would also like to mention Professor Issa J Boullata not only for his moral support, but also for being my outstanding teacher of Arabic Literature at St George's School in Jerusalem long before he became the distinguished professor he now is at McGill University in Montreal.

I also wish to extend my thanks to Professor John Esposito of Georgetown University in Washington DC and Director of the Center for Christian-Muslim Understanding for his invaluable advice and continuous encouragement.

I am also indebted to Nora A Shawwa whose continuous advice played an important role in the final production of this book.

I would like to note my appreciation for Myriam Misk who managed to prepare the illustrations and the cover design with profound sensitivity that depicts the real subtle meanings of the Fables.

I am particularly grateful to Kaity Papadakis and also for Eliana Saba for their tireless assistance in the preparation of the material and suffering the heavy burden I too often placed upon them.

Saleh Sa'adeh Jallad
Athens, October 2001

7

Note on spelling

The spelling of proper names and other terms from Arabic always poses problems for English readers. Indeed, many of the names in *Kalilah and Dimnah* are not Arabic in origin. Nevertheless, in this work the spelling of proper names aims to reflect the pronounciation most familiar to generations of Arabic speakers.

No attempt has been made to use a transliteration system which indicates vowel lengths or shows those Arabic consonants which do not form part of English phonology. However, *ʿayn* is indicated by ʿ, and the Arabic 'feminine' ending by *-ah*.

Translator's Foreword

Background

Among all the European and Levantine peoples of the early Middle Ages, the Arabians and the Arabic-speaking peoples were the most significant contributors to human civilization, notwithstanding the reduced role assigned to them in the historical record and in recent geopolitics. Were it not for the endowment of tremendous energy resources, they might still be relatively obscure.

Arabia is the origin and the nursery of the Semitic family. The peoples of Arabia migrated at different times and in different waves to the Fertile Crescent including Mesopotamia and became the Canaanites, the Phoenicians, the Akkadians, the Babylonians, the Assyrians, the Arameans and the Hebrews of antiquity. Within Arabia the fundamental elements of Judaism and Christianity are founded later. Early in the 7th century AD, Arabia again produced a people who swiftly conquered the majority of the then known civilized world within a period rarely paralleled in history. It also gave birth to a unitarian religion, Islam, which is based on similar principles to Judaism and Christianity. Like them, peace is one of the cornerstones of its objectives and success. Even its name is rooted in the Arabic word that means 'peace'. It claims today the adherence of almost one sixth of the world's population and was the fastest growing religion in the 20th century. At any hour worshippers somewhere in the world heed the call to prayer facing Mecca in Arabia.

Within a century of the death of the Messenger of Islam Prophet Muhammad in AD 632, the Arabs became the masters of a vast empire that extended from the Atlantic Ocean in the West, including Spain and in due course Sicily, to the boundaries of China. It was larger than the Roman empire at its zenith. It assimilated into its Islamic faith and Arabic idiom perhaps the greatest amalgam of peoples ever gathered, before or since.

They left the desert of Arabia with only four basic elements, which together contributed to their amazing success. The first was an

9

immense aptitude for conquest, the second was an all-embracing Islamic faith, the third was a flexible and useful language and the fourth was an unlimited, inquisitive mind with a strong will of assimilation and implementation.

The Arab nature of the empire soon subsided, but more importantly a world culture slowly developed within its boundaries. Both conquest and culture influenced to a considerable extent the shape of the world then and extended even into modern times. The Arabs are heirs of the great ancient civilizations that developed and flourished to an amazing level in Mesopotamia, around the River Nile and on the eastern shores of the Mediterranean. Likewise, they absorbed the fundamentals of the Greco-Roman culture prevailing in the areas they conquered. They developed it, applied it, improved on it and acted as an honest medium for transferring that legacy to medieval Europe. The Renaissance process that underlies the awakening of Europe had its foundations entrenched in the Greco-Roman heritage that was assimilated and transmitted by the Arab civilization particularly through Spain and Sicily (AD 750-1492).

Conquest created the need for the framework and for the mechanism of a new social order that was enveloped by Islam. It allowed the peoples in its empire who enjoyed diverse histories, variegated social mores and traditions, different races and creeds to interact positively among themselves and with the new conquerors as well. Thus it nursed the variables that together contributed to the creation of the new social order. Philip Hitti in his *The Arabs in History* states, "the invaders from the desert brought with them no tradition of learning, no heritage of culture to the lands they conquered. In Syria, in Egypt, in al-Iraq, in Persia, they sat as pupils at the feet of the people they subdued, and what acquisitive pupils they proved to be."

The Arabs brought with them Islam—a fundamentally Arab achievement, which acted as a necessary condition for the creation of the new social order and culture. Muhammad the Prophet of Islam managed within the last twenty years of his life to destroy tribal kinship as the fundamental bond of Arab relationship and replace it with the new faith which proved to be solidifying at a higher level of sophistication and a more far-reaching paradigm that was conducive to the building of a more universal nationhood, the *Ummah*. For the first time the Arab tribes were united and a kind of *Pax Islamica* was inaugurated for Arabia. Islam simply annulled the past. It declared among many other things that all Muslims regardless of their ethnic and racial affiliations are brothers. Under the new order all shared the expected responsibility and benefits equitably. Slaves and masters are equal under the new regime, but of equal importance it laid down the principle of the universal family of the human race.

"O mankind! We created you from a single (pair) of a male and a female, and made you into nations and tribes, that you may know each other (not that you may despise each other). Verily the most honoured of you in the sight of God is he who is the most righteous of you" (*Surat al-Hujurat* 49, 13).

"People of the Book", i.e. Christians and Jews, however, were not encouraged to convert, but if they chose to maintain their faith, they were rendered unprecedented tolerance, respect and protection. Perhaps Islam considered itself the legitimate inheritor of the older Semitic faiths of Judaism and Christianity, and that its teachings embodied a genuine synthesis of their major postulates, particularly the principles of the Oneness of God, the Resurrection and the inevitable Day of Judgement. Like them it is also the spiritual outcome of the Semitic life and experience in Arabia. With few differences a devout Muslim could agree with most elements of the Christian faith, particularly with the teachings of certain Christian sects that flourished in Arabia at that time. It is not therefore surprising that the Qur'an, the Holy Book of Islam, contains many parallels in both the Old and New Testaments, such as Abraham, Moses, Isaac and Jacob, Jesus Christ and his message and miracles, and his Mother, the Virgin Mary. It is also interesting to note that the Qur'an addresses largely the adherents of both faiths. Moreover at that time the Arabian Peninsula included a considerable percentage of tribes that followed Christianity and Judaism and who had extensive tribal kinships in the Fertile Crescent as far as Mesopotamia. Later these tribes played a significant role, if not decisive in the military, political, social, economic and cultural success of the Arab and Islamic civilization.

Islam envisaged itself as the framework within which the totality of the human life, behaviour and dynamics were manifested in this new social order. The relationship between God, the community and the individual was typical of the Bedouin and desert culture, clear, simple and direct. God alone was the central element that can know and judge all what people might do. People were expected to *live* practically in the Muslim world that was based on a pluralistic society that was functional and useful. It was not enough to profess a creed only or merely perform motions of piety. Consequently, the Canon Law of Islam *(Shari'ah)*, which upheld the fabric of the new society and culture was staunchly protected and persistently confirmed more than theology.

When the Arabians settled in the conquered areas outside Arabia, they faced problems and conditions that were alien to them, far beyond their capabilities, and foreign to their tribal traditions and primitive way of life. But one thing they always emphasized during their ascent, regardless of whatever they acquired from the subdued cultures and societies: namely Islam and its purposes. It must be stressed that the process of creating a new culture also influenced Islam itself, as it freely incorporated in its thought and practice a considerable amount of the thought and practices of the various peoples it controlled, particularly those of the Hellenistic intellectual culture. The pursuit of knowledge and learning is not only an individualistic and social attitude in Islam, it is also religious. It is revealing that the first words of *Surah* 96, *Al-ʿAlaq*, of the Qurʾan, which is the first *Surah* that declared the inauguration of Islam as the all-embracing faith in the new social order, called exclusively for reading, writing and the accumulation of knowledge, without limitations, as a fundamental prerequisite for faith. This is an unusual and probably unparalleled way of starting a revolutionary paradigm. The first words in Islam were:

> "Read in the name of thy Lord and Cherisher, the Creator
> Who created man out of a leech-like clot
> Read and thy Lord is most bountiful—
> He who taught (the use of) the Pen
> —Taught man that which he knew not."
> (*Surat al-ʿAlaq* 96, 3-5)

The Arabs had a long relationship with Rome and the influences ran in both directions. From the 3rd century AD onward the Arabs interaction with the Roman world intensified. Emessa (Homs) in Syria was the nursery for the empresses of the imperial dynasty established by Septemius Severus, the Phoenician from Leptis Magna (Libya). His wife, the famous Julia Domna, was of Arab origin from Syria and the mother of the emperor Caracalla. The mothers of emperors Elagabalus and Severus Alexander were also Arab and relatives of Julia Domna. More strikingly, Philip "the Arab" (244-249), who was of full Arab stock from Syria, became emperor and was most probably the first Christian emperor. In the latter half of the 3rd century, the ascent of the Arab factor in the relationship with the Roman world, is clearly reflected in the role of Odenathus and Zenobia of Palmyra (Tadmor) in Syria. Moreover, in the centuries that followed, as Christianity became the official and dominant religion in the Roman empire in the West as well as in the East (Byzantium), the 'Arab' influence reached its climax within the Holy See. During the 7th and 8th centuries, five Syrians became popes of Rome. They were John V (685-686), Sergius (687-701), Sisinnius (708), Constantine (708-715), and Gregory III (731-741). Sergius and Gregory are acknowledged as saints.

Whatever the early appearance of significant 'Arabs' in Rome, the later Muslim polity's substance, its character and its origin were Arab. This was never lost nor could it be. Its prophet is Arab, its basic emphasis of community lies deep in the ancient Arab tribal life; its language and its expression is Arab. However, it must be emphasized that Arab here has no relation whatsoever to a political or national entity but merely to a set of common characteristics. Even though Arab rule receded over a short period of time, and Arab prominence as an ethnic group in the culture they created reached its nadir, yet the Arab impact on Islam could never be eliminated. As long as the Muslims' leadership as well as the community held to the principles of a working pluralistic society, its ascent was almost guaranteed. As soon as deviation from the spirit and these guidelines occurred, its ability to accommodate further inevitable changes and progress faltered. The Muslim polity and society simply disintegrated but the wide-raging principles of the Islamic paradigm survive and attract new adherents.

Thanks to the distinctive qualities of the Arabic language that the civilization and thought produced in the Muslim world, it is still referred to as Arab, long after the Arab polity faded and despite the prominence of its non-Arab contributors. The gradual ascendancy of the Arabic language as the medium of communication in philosophy, science, technology, commerce and all other facets of civilization required more than the mere strength of conquest or the sheer benevolence of religion. Had it been proven that Arabic was not conducive to the challenge of change and progress; it would have been naturally obliterated shortly after the capitulation of the Arab polity. Instead, its wealth of vocabulary, its ability to produce many new words from the existing basic tri-consonant verbal roots (analogical derivation), its flexibility in condensing conceptual meanings into clear and eloquent expression, its intense disposition to metre and rhythm with rhetorical effects and its beautiful calligraphy among many other attributes, have contributed to and influenced the distinguished character of Muslim culture. It smoothly harnessed the knowledge, efforts and genius of philosophers, scholars, scientists, inventers, artisans, theologian and jurists, statesmen, musicians, mathematicians, physicians and any type of craft or profession that a fully developed civilization requires and manifests. The majority of such contributors were of non-Arab origins, and many were Christians who lived in the Fertile Crescent. Whether they were Persian, Indian, Buddhist, Zoroastrian, Hurrian, Jewish, Christian, or of any other affiliation or colour, they all had the freedom and opportunity to excel. In their quest to manifest their contribution to the Arab civilization, the Arabic language acted as a beneficial medium of communication, but more importantly it gave them the opportunity to share in and influence the dynamics of a common

13

intellectual, productive and operational social order. The non-Arab share in influencing the Arabic language as well as the intellectual and religious Islam is a dominant factor in Arab civilization.

The life of ibn al-Muqaffaᶜ

ᶜAbdullah ibn al-Muqaffaᶜ is singled out as one of the earliest representatives of the Arabic culture as described above. His ethnic, religious, professional and social background and achievement satisfies almost all the factors that contributed to and are reflected in the dynamics of the new Muslim paradigm.

ᶜAbdullah ibn al-Muqaffaᶜ was one of the most prominent exponents of the intellectual awakening and literary development enjoyed by Arabic prose in the period between the 8th and 11th centuries. The naturalization of the culture from the older Greek/Hellenistic, Persian and Indian civilizations, after they had been incorporated through translation into Arabic, and adaptation and refinement into Islamic civilization, had a pervasive and irreversible influence on almost every facet of economic, social, political and religious life, cresting during the first half of 'Abbasid rule, around AD 850. Islamic culture thus served as a carrier of considerable philosophical and scientific knowledge from antiquity, which, with innovations and developments, was later handed onto Christian Europe and contributed to the flowering of the Renaissance. The translation and adaptation of the 'Book of Fables', *Kalilah wa Dimnah* (i.e., 'Kalilah and Dimnah'), from the Sanskrit (Indian) through the Pahlavi (Middle Persian) into Arabic is an example of that legacy.

Our author was born as Ruzbih, at Jur, modern Gur in Iran, near Firuzabad in the province of Fars in the year AD 720 to a family of the Persian gentry. His father had been a tax collector in Fars under the Umayyad administration of al-Hajjaj and later Khalid al-Kasri of Iraq, *circa* AD 725-30. He was accused of misappropriating funds, then tortured and maimed, which gained him the new surname: al-Muqaffaᶜ, 'the Cripple'.

Ruzbih became a convert to Islam as a young man, and changed his name to ᶜAbdullah. He had been brought up in Basrah not far from the mouths of the Tigris and Euphrates, which was then the reigning capital of literary Arabic, and the centre of intellectual ferment until Baghdad was founded in AD 762 and developed to become the seat and symbol of Islamic civilization. In Basrah, he spent his formative years learning the foundations of the Arabic language, while refining a prodigious knowledge of his own Persian language and civilization, and benefiting from a significant exposure to Greek philosophy most probably through his contemporary Christian theologians.

Ibn al-Muqaffa' began his adult career at about 20 years of age as the scribe of the Umayyad governor of Kirman in southeast Iran, Dawud ibn Hubairah, during the reign of the last Umayyad caliph, Marwan ibn Muhammad. This position provided him with considerable wealth, and a privileged familiarity with the social and political forces during the unsettled years when the heavily Arab Umayyad regime came to a violent end.

It has been stressed by many historians that of all the Islamic issues, none has brought more bloodshed than succession and the struggle for the caliphate, a dictum that is largely true until recent times. True to such an axiom, the 'Abbasids under the leadership of al-Saffah ('the Blood-Shedder') brutally toppled and massacred in AD 750 their Umayyad cousins who had ruled the empire since AD 661.

Ibn al-Muqaffa' managed to communicate with the 'Abbasids. His fame gained him the position of the scribe for the three uncles of al-Saffah: 'Isa when he became the governor of Kirman, then as the educator of the sons of Isma'il, when he was the governor of Khuzistan (Ahwaz in Iran) north of Basrah, and finally as the secretary of Sulaiman when he was the governor of Basrah. His presence close to 'Abbasid decision-makers intensified his political knowledge, insight and instincts. However, his problems surfaced when al-Saffah suddenly died of smallpox in AD 754. A bloody family feud promptly erupted over the succession. The reason was that al-Mansur ('the Victorious') proclaimed the caliphate for himself after his brother's death. But his fourth uncle 'Abdullah, one of the two heroes of the 'Abbasid cause and now the governor of Syria, rebelled against his nephew, the new caliph. Al-Mansur defeated his uncle who escaped and hid under the protection of his brother, Sulaiman, the governor of Basrah. Al-Mansur removed Sulaiman from his position in AD 756, and demanded the immediate surrender of his rebel uncle.

Al-Mansur's personality and governing style neatly fit the profile of the benevolent despot. To him is the credit for the founding of Baghdad as the capital of Islamic civilization and he probably became the *doyen* of the neighbouring cultures at that time. He built libraries, schools, hospitals and other innovative social institutions, and initiated the fervour for translation and importation of new ideas that swept the empire.

However, his cruelty was as pronounced as his cultivated intellect. He brutally destroyed anything and anyone he perceived as an obstacle to his absolute authority, including his uncles. He cunningly eliminated his rebel uncle 'Abdullah, and anyone else he thought might usurp his throne. Just like the earlier Umayyad caliphs, his rule was based on that right to absolute rule by virtue of his position as caliph, the successor to the mantle of the Prophet in all features of government, including finance. He believed—along with his antecedents and descendents—that as the successor of the Prophet only God can displace him. To the dismay of a considerable number of his subjects he continued the hereditary caliphate introduced earlier by Mu'awiyah, the first caliph and founder of the Umayyad dynasty in AD 661-680. This compromised the Islamic tradition of *Shurah* and election by the consensus of the elders, established in the earlier time of the four orthodox caliphs, the so-called *Rashidun*, i.e. the Rightly Guided who had led Islam after the death of Muhammad and before the Umayyads seized power. The change which adopted dynastic monarchical model of the conquered Persian and Byzantine empires, had a profound impact on the various schools of thought that promptly sprang up within the empire. Under 'Abbasid rule, Arab leadership was reduced to an insignificant titular and ceremonial position. The prominence of non-Arabs became obvious, and the irreconcilable schisms in Islam, *vide* the entrenchment of the Shi'ah sect (which claimed the succession should lie in the family of the Prophet through his cousin and son-in-law 'Ali), were deeply established, particularly in Iran and Iraq, the seat of the ancient Sasanid Persian empire.

The accession of the 'Abbasid dynasty to the caliphate, and transferring the seat of power to Baghdad had another profound impact on the Islamic civilization. While under the Umayyads in Damascus, the Arabians looked for the Hellenistic Western civilization as an inspiration and a model, the Islamic civilization under the 'Abbasid in Baghdad became less and less Arab and looked more to the East, i.e. Persia, as their new model.

Ibn al-Muqaffa' spent most of his life between Basrah and Kufah, the two prominent cities of that time and region, and enjoyed the companionship of men of letters and wit, such as the famous poet Bashar ibn Burd, the master of letters 'Abd al-Hamid al-Katib, and others of lesser, or even shady reputation. This may have led some ill-disposed people to accuse him unjustly of *zandaqah*, religious heresy, and to raise the suspicion that his conversion to Islam had been a sham. All his writing, however, shouts down such claims.

His early tragic death in approximately AD 756, however, was probably provoked more by political and personal motives rather than by any religious uncertainties. The story of his murder is well known in Arabic literature. After an intense period of negotiations with the caliph, his masters, Sulaiman and 'Isa, the caliph's uncles, had ordered Ibn al-Muqaffa' to draft the text of an *aman*, or pardon, for al-Mansur's signature, in favour of their rebellious brother 'Abdullah, before he would surrender. Ibn al-Muqaffa' obliged them, and composed the text with tragic zeal. It daringly obligated the caliph to abide by the letter and the spirit of the cleverly drawn commitments, oaths and special promises in the pardon of the rebel. The distrustful caliph shrewdly discovered what was afoot, and determined to eliminate his uncle later, but signed the document. First, however, he had Ibn al-Muqaffa^c dismissed from service. Then, at his prompting, the new governor of Basra, Sufyan ibn Mu^cawiyah al-Muhallabi, who had a long-standing personal grudge against Ibn al-Muqaffa^c, lured him to his palace, where he tortured and murdered him at the age of 36. Ibn al-Muqaffa^c was survived by a son, Muhammad, who himself would one day become one of the secretaries of al-Mansur and a translator into Arabic of some major works by Greek philosophers such as Aristotle.

The intellectual legacy

During his short life, Ibn al-Muqaffa^c had produced a considerable corpus of original works and translations: books, discourses and treatises. Though his most famous and widely known work was the 'Book of Fables', *Kalilah wa Dimnah* (our *Kalilah and Dimnah*), other works of his were also influential. They included the *Khudaynama*, or history, chronicles and traditions of pre-Muslim Persia under the Sasanid dynasty, and the *A'innama,* which describes the customs, institutions and hierarchy of the court during the same period. The *Tajnama* describes the life of Khusru Anushirwan (Chosroes I), king of Persia. These would become later the standard sources and models of style as well as a source of information. Other works (which he is said to have written) included the *Book of Mazdak*, letters describing the Persian traditional religion of pre-Islamic Iran and a Manichean *apologia*, which describes some of the spiritual reflections of Ibn al-Muqaffa^c and many of his associates. Unfortunately, the majority of his works did not survive except in the references and refutations of others.

His surviving work includes three authentic treatises, which represent Ibn al-Muqaffa^c the political thinker as a match for Nicola Machiavelli, the later Florentine. The first is *Adab al-Saghir,* usually rendered "The Education of the Gentry", a book of wise advice for the growing class of gentry. The second is *Adab al-Kabir*, "The Education of the Courtiers", which offers practical guidelines and advice for the prince, his courtiers, and men who aspire to a career in government. The third is "Treaties on Public Administration", *Risalat al-Sahaba'*, thought to have been addressed to the Caliph al-Mansur himself, though without mentioning his name. It is a brilliant treatise on the political, social issues of the time, analysed with remarkable clarity and originality of thought. It includes proposals that could never have eluded or survived the attention of the ruthless and vengeful caliph. This treatise in particular, and his other works in general, including *Kalilah wa Dimnah,* may very well have contributed to Ibn-al Muqaffaᶜ's premature and terrible death.

It is worth noting that the controversial and persuasive doctrine for the time of Ibn al-Muqaffaᶜ of the superiority of reason and mind over faith emphasized throughout his works including *Kalilah wa Dimnah,* reflects the dominant thesis of the Muᶜtazilah school of thought that provoked the exasperation and vengeance of many caliphs, including al-Mansur. This doctrine held that faith and reason are always reconciled. If there were any conflict between the evidence of faith and reason as regards the existence and knowledge of God, then faith must be disallowed. It is reason and logical deduction which trump faith and its derivative norms and laws, and reason and logical deduction that is the dominant mode through which God is verified and is known. Through reason one can and must prove the unquestionable existence of God, not merely by faith. Thus man is already possessed of all the faculties he requires to discriminate between good and evil and has the power and will to act accordingly. He alone will face the responsibility of his actions. Some of these ideas developed slowly into critical thought and into the government theory of the Muslim world, which posed a direct threat to the core of the ruling dynasty's region over a long period of time.

These ideas have their roots in the classic Greek philosophers, and bear resemblance to some of the Christian thinkers of the time. The most prominent of these thinkers was St John of Damascus. A Syrian who spoke and wrote fluent Greek and Arabic. He came from a professional family that flourished during Byzantine rule over Syria. His grandfather maintained his position as the treasurer for Muᶜawiyah, the founder of the Umayyad dynasty, which was for a Christian an extraordinary achievement on its own. St John's father also occupied the same most important position in the Islamic empire. St John himself may have also inherited that post, but definitely was the companion of Yazid, the second Umayyad caliph after Muᶜawiyah. He spent a lot of time in the companionship of Yazid and his group of Christian friends, such as the celebrated Umayyad poet al-Akhtal. Yazid's mother was an Arab Christian, the famous Maisun the Kalbite. He relied heavily on the Christian military support of his mother's tribe and their kinsmen in his bloody feuds with the contenders to the throne, including the ᶜAlids (the followers of ᶜAli, the fourth caliph in Islam and the cousin of the Prophet), particularly his celebrated son, al-Husain, who after his death in battle became the battle-cry of the Shiᶜa sect of Islam. In his early thirties St John decided to give up all worldly life and its symbols, and retire around the year AD 730 to the monastery of St Saba on the outskirts of Jerusalem until he died in AD 748. He lived there as an ascetic and devoted his life to writing on Christian Orthodox theology. His influence on the Qadarite school of thought, which asserts the free will of the individual and his control of his actions, which was later incorporated in the doctrine of al-Muʿtazilah school of thought, can be easily traced. A comparison of the basic teachings of al-Muʿtazilah and the writings of St John leaves little doubt regarding his profound influence of this major and progressive school.

The lives of St John and Ibn al-Muqqaffaʿ (as well as that of Wasil ibn ʿAta', the founder of the Muʿtazilah) overlapped. It is therefore most unlikely that our author did not read St John's work. He must have been influenced by his famous arguments on free will and must have understood the Hellenic methodology of deduction used by St John. The prominence of the human faculties above all God's other creatures, and the responsibility they carry for their actions in this world and in the hereafter as well, spreads in many ways into the book of *Kalilah wa Dimnah*. Even one of the introductions attributed to Buzurjmihr the vizier of Anushirwan, in which the physician Burzawaih, who managed to copy *Kalilah wa Dimnah* from the Sanskrit in India, discussed the paradox of life, must have been written by Ibn al-Muqaffaʿ and may very well have been inspired partially by the life of St John of Damascus.

Adherents to the Muʿtazilah doctrine drew the wrath and vengeance of many caliphs besides al-Mansur during many decades of persecution. They presented a formidable challenge to the caliphs' governance and control over his subjects' and the wealth of the empire. On the other hand, when they were in the ascendant they were as vicious and brutal as their influence allowed. Their progressive doctrines, however, eventually fell victim to the power of the caliphs who were absolute rulers, and also to their own internal disputes and disintegration.

Kalilah wa Dimnah

Very few books succeeded in attracting as many people over the centuries, despite the geographic, social, racial, religious, economic and political barriers, as did Ibn al-Muqaffaʿ's *Kalilah wa Dimnah*. After the Qur'an, it was for some centuries the most popular book in the world of Islam. About three centuries later, it prompted a certain scholar named al-Yamani, to write a book comparing the proverbs and wisdom found in *Kalilah wa Dimnah* with Arab verse found in the poetry of the pre-Ibn al-Muqaffaʿ era, which was intended to discredit the originality of *Kalilah wa Dimnah* and abate its intense popularity.

Some two centuries later, it still maintained a significant influence that prompted one of the most prominent intellectual groups in the world of Islam to take its title from *Kalilah wa Dimnah*, namely "The Society of Pure Brotherhood and Friendship", *Ikhwan al-Safa'*. This comes from the fable of "The Ring-Dove".

ʿAbdullah ibn al-Muqaffaʿ translated the work from the original Sanskrit (Indian) through the Pahlavi (Middle Persian) *circa* AD 750, and this Arabic document is the oldest complete text of these tales now extant, since neither the original Sanskrit nor the earlier Pahlavi version has survived. A Syrian cleric named Periodeut Bud had previously translated it into old Syriac, *circa* AD 570. That translation, formerly found in the monastery at Mardin, is preserved in one incomplete manuscript in Paris. Its title in Syriac is *Kalilaj wa Dimnaj*, which came across in the Arabic translation two hundred years later as *Kalilah and Dimnah*. Both titles are a variant form of the old Sanskrit names of the two main jackals (who are the principal protagonists of the tales), Karataka and Dimnaka. But Ibn al-Muqaffaʿ managed to give them an Arabic originality. *Kalilah* corresponds to the Arabic word *Iklil* or *crown*, *Dimnah* to the Arabic word of the same spelling which means ruins. It could have been a spark of genius of Ibn al-Muqaffaʿ or merely a welcomed coincidence that both *arabized* words also depict in a subtle way the deep character of both jackals. *Kalilah*, has a sincere and good character that shines like a crown on the head. *Dimnah*—jealous ambitious and evil—reduces trust and friendship to ruins.

Largely through Ibn al-Muqaffaʿ s adaptation the work spread with amazing rapidity and breadth to other cultures. It has been further translated over the centuries, not only into the languages of the various peoples within the Islamic world, but also into the Romance group of languages including Hebrew, Syriac, Latin, Greek, Spanish, French, German, Italian, Slavic, Russian and English. With the exception of the Old Spanish, all other European translations were based on an early 13th-century Hebrew translation from Arabic. The Hebrew from Arabic was a free translation. By 1278, John of Capua, who converted from Judaism, had made a Latin translation of *Kalilah and Dimnah* based on the early Hebrew version, and gave it the title *Directorium Vitae Humane*. This translation received wide popularity and became the basis of most European translations. Most of the old translations were invested with the ethical values of the various translators. In any case, *Kalilah and Dimnah* had a significant effect on the literature of Christian Europe and largely influenced La Fontaine's *Fables*, through the French translation from the Persian version of *Kalilah and Dimnah* called *Anvar-i-Suhayli*, the "Lights of Canopus". The enrichment of the Indian fables by the Persian and the Arabic, seeped through European literature as independent fables like "The Dog and his Shadow", "The Talkative Tortoise", or within a collection like La Fontaine's or Giovanni Francesco Straparola's *Fairy Tales*. It is highly probable that the Arab traders carried with them portions of the fables of *Kalilah wa Dimnah* to Africa, whence the early African Americans introduced them to the New World where they matured into the *Br'er Rabbit* fables and *Reynard* the Fox.

The reason for the importance of *Kalilah wa Dimnah* and its international appeal lies in the powerful and universal subjects it addresses, and in the fascinating medium through which it manifests them. To a considerable extent, its persistent success tends to demonstrate the dynamic unity of human civilization regardless of time or space. The fables go back more than 2,000 years and are paralleled by the Greek fables attributed to the shadowy figure of Aesop. They are rooted in the books of wisdom intended as moral mirrors for princes of India. It has been suggested by some scholars, though not conclusively, that these fables were first collected and written around AD 300 in Kashmir. Similar themes are found today in the *Panchatantra* (the 'five books of wisdom') and the *Mahabharata*, and a few others scattered among other books. They treat natural human trials, traits and troubles, the constraints of environment and custom, the dark influence of evil and mischief, the haphazard presence of chance, and the powerful presence of human virtue, reason, passion, choices, rewards, and outcomes, both unpredictable and fair. There is an understanding of the learning experience that underlies human decisions, with both just rewards and haphazard outcomes. The old themes are all here: righteousness and evil, friendship and animosity, jealousy and devotion, honesty and deceit, forbearance and haste, wisdom and whim, lust and power, crime and punishment, decision-making and government, princes and subjects. However, the positive role of the scholar in government and in society is clearly highlighted throughout. The ritual dialogues in each fable between Baydaba the Philosopher and Dabshalim the King signal this.

The Indian original and the subsequent Middle Persian translations were lost a long time ago. The Arabic version of *Kalilah wa Dimnah*, therefore, represents the only surviving manuscript bridging past and present. Even the modern editing of the Indian work, the *Panchatantra* is believed to have relied on the Arabic version. Experts on this work believe that Ibn al-Muqaffaᶜ was a translator who freely adapted his material to suit his own objectives—in a word, he was more than a translator. He intelligently wove into the major story, and some of the shorter fables, his perspective on controversial issues such as the delicate and unsafe subject of governance. Some of the fables are most probably his own creation. When this book of fables is read in conjunction with his surviving works, one can easily see the relationship between the dialogue in the fables and the message in his treatises, for instance the two main issues of superiority of reason in decision-making, and the characteristics of benevolent governance.

The mere fact that the various issues of wisdom were conveyed in a para-human genre of socialized beasts has probably added tremendously to *Kalilah wa Dimnah's* spread and fame. To the reader, these animals almost instantly became masked humans. People tended to relate to such a medium in an undefended way, with no prejudice to any person or society. This was helped by the careful choice of animals that corresponded largely to the universal human perceptions or imputations of their personalities. The proud but limited Lion King, the honest but dumb-witted Bull, the crafty Jackal, are well-depicted examples. People can easily project their feelings on the animal characters without self-defence or injury. They can also let their imagination roam intrepidly in social and political venues without risking social or political misadventure, as Ibn al-Muqaffaᶜ himself foretold at the end of his Introduction:

> There are fables where dialogue among animals is used. The reason is to entice young people to read them in a light-hearted way as animal roguery in an attractive and entertaining genre. There are colourful fantasies involving animals that even kings find amusing. Kings also ought to take care to keep this book alive and famous, as it may allow them to relax and freely deploy their imaginations. There are insights intended for royalty, the gentry, and common folk as well. It is intended for wide circulation, and will bring employment to the copyists and illustrators involved in its production. And there is a wisdom here ultimately and exclusively meant only for philosophers.

Kalilah wa Dimnah was imitated in Arabic by other men of letters more than once, and was probably translated from Pahlavi into Arabic by other hands and probably under other titles at different periods. This is suggested by the various available Arabic manuscripts, which differ from each other. But the literary style of Ibn al-Muqaffaᶜ is recognizable, and scholars have identified and asserted, up to a comfortable level, the authenticity of the available manuscripts. The oldest is one in Aghia Sophia in Istanbul, discovered by A Azzam in 1941 and dated AD 1221. The second oldest Arabic manuscript is dated AD 1339, found by the Jesuit scholar Fr Louis Cheikho in Dair al-Shir in Lebanon. Though all of the existing manuscripts include certain additions or alterations, the style and the core of the fables still maintain their discernible superiority. It is evident also that it contained artistic illustrations. Later, from the 12th century onward, this book inspired many artists in Syria, Iraq, Persia and India, as well as in the Mamluk and the Mongolian courts, and produced beautiful illustrations reflecting their various levels and schools of art.

Kalilah wa Dimnah was also composed in Arabic verse more than once, and a later Persian translation in verse followed suit. Today there is a surviving manuscript written in Arabic verse by Ibn al-Habbariyyah composed about AD 1100, and another by al-Saghani in AD 1242 whose manuscript is located in Vienna.

The book was first printed in modern times in Arabic by the orientalist Sylvestre de Sacy, in Paris in AD 1816. This became the basis of the Bulaq imprint (Egypt) of 1817; the Cairo (Egypt) imprint of 1835; the Beit al-Din (Lebanon) imprint of 1869; the Mosul (Iraq) imprints of 1874 and 1876, and the Beirut (Lebanon) printings of 1880-84. Today *Kalilah wa Dimnah* is published, with some editing, by almost all the major publishing houses in the Arabic-speaking world.

It has been translated four times into English. The first was from the Italian by Sir Thomas North–the translator of *Plutarch's Lives*–in AD 1570 under the title *Morall Philosophie of Doni* (Doni being the Italian translator of *Kalilah wa Dimnah*). It was based on the Hebrew version that was translated 'freely' by John of Capua from the Latin between AD 1263 and 1278. It is worth noting that this version, which was translated for Cardinal Ursinus, became the basis of all modern European translations. In 1819 the Revd Wyndham Knatchbull made another translation from the Arabic based on Sylvestre de Sacy's manuscript. In 1885, I G N Keith-Falconer published an English version based on the Syriac translation of a 10th- or 11th-century copy of Ibn al-Muqaffaᶜ's work. However, the Syrian cleric responsible for the translation had exercised considerable freedom and managed to give his work a Christian flavour. In 1980, Thomas Irving published an English translation based on the 1251 Spanish version of Kalilah and Dimnah. At that time Alphonso X 'the Scholar' was still heir to the Spanish throne and had established his school of translation in Toledo. The Spanish version is considered the first significant work of prose literature in that language. Irving's translation was collated mainly from the Arabic manuscripts discovered by Cheicho and from the less authentic work of al-Yaziji. However, his valuable work excluded the four different introductions, which are intrinsically important parts of the fables of *Kalilah wa Dimnah* in terms of literary, educational, ethical and entertainment values, and constitute about one quarter of the entire legacy.

This translation of *Kalilah wa Dimnah* from Arabic into English is based primarily on the popular Bulaq version as edited by various scholars. It is comprised of four introductions including that of Ibn al-Muqaffaᶜ, fifteen chapters, and the chapter on 'Mehrize, King of the Rats' taken from the old manuscript of A Azzam. The first two chapters, 'The Lion and The Bull' and 'The Investigation of Dimnah', are the only two inter-related stories. The names of the jackals in those fables give the entire book its title, according to the contemporary custom of naming the whole by a part. Each of the other chapters constitutes an independent fable with a different theme or lesson. Major fables include minor fables, analogies and proverbs to explain or emphasize a certain point in the dialogue.

It is worth noting that this translation does not include six minor fables which were most probably deliberately omitted from the original Bulaq print. It seems that those fables were somehow indecent analogies. Most probably they were not even in the original work of Ibn al-Muqaffaᶜ, as they fit neither his style nor his way of life. However, their omission does not affect in any way the context, the lessons or the literary style of the rest of the fables.

The first two chapters that follow the set of four introductions deal with friendship, a valuable trait among people, and how deceitful, crafty and jealous contenders destroy it. Greed and blind ambition can drive people to undermine everything in order they may achieve their objective of status and wealth. The jackal Dimnah represents this type. Kalilah is the opposite in every respect. However, those who pursue destructive ambitions will ultimately receive their punishment. Other than the first two chapters each stands on its own. Though independent, all of them together embody themes of human morality, and promote a high level of ethical guidelines for good management of human issues. All are based on efficient planning and persistent use of the mind, which is the highest attribute of creation. Ibn al-Muqaffaᶜ blends his tales and the fascinating dialogues among the animals with piercing Hellenic logical deduction and analogies, which echo the numerical influence of Pythagoras. In addition Ibn al-Muqaffaᶜ uses from time to time some strong statements even when they seem not to be called for. Sudden bursts of sharp criticism of rulers and the abuse of power are spread all over the fables. Tyrannical rule is abhorred and it could be the source not only of the misery of subjects but should contribute to the inevitable downfall of the ruler and the destruction of his domain. It is through compassion, benevolence and forbearance that a good ruler can prolong his rule and the welfare of his subjects. Furthermore, elements of tactics in dealing with acquaintances, friends, courtiers and princes, and the dynamics of individuals well as collective relationships are deeply discussed in the various chapters in a most interesting, logical and entertaining manner.

The four introductions that precede Chapter One, 'The Lion and The Bull', have their roots in the Indian, Persian and Arab traditions.

However, it is not surprising that Ibn al-Muqaffaᶜ may have written or freely adapted important parts of these introductions as well as the fables. Though there are certain controversies as to the main contributions of Ibn al-Muqaffaᶜ to Islamic civilization and literature, he still enjoys a most prestigious status among scholars at the end of the early Islamic period of Arabic literature. Prominent men of letters described him in that period as one of the ten most intelligent people in Islam and the most intelligent and learned man among the non-Arabs in the empire.

Poetry was and has remained the primary Arabic literary genre since the pre-Islamic era, as is familiar in many verbal and non-literate societies in human civilization. Arabic prose, however, found a classic expression in the work of *Kalilah wa Dimnah* by Ibn al-Muqaffaᶜ that has been blessed with variation and development ever since. Up to the present day, the impression of the style of Ibn al-Muqaffaᶜ, his vivid figurative language, extravagant elegance, and colourful expression are still eloquently manifested in Arabic literature. With this innovative and remarkable style he was able to make the Arabic-speaking world, which conquered his native land and consigned his forefathers' religion to oblivion, know and appreciate the cultural values of his own high civilization and that of other nations such as that of India. In addition to revealing the superiority of Persian civilization in an elegant style that he created with the language of his country's conquerors, he also led a decent, polished and cultured way of life. His moral life and devotion to his friends, even to the extent of sacrificing his own life for them, is well documented in the Arabic annals. On the other hand, by emphasizing his ethnic cultural traits, he set a model—perhaps unintentionally—for future scholars and literary figures who shared his blood and culture. They flourished during the ᶜAbbasid period as staunch proponents of the ethnic movement of *Shucubiyyah*, (which might be translated as chauvinism, fanatical ethnicity).

When all is said, ᶜAbdullah ibn al-Muqaffaᶜ stands out both as an outstanding author and an original thinker. Without any doubt, he is one of the most eminent literary scholars in the history of Arabic language and literature.

Kalilah and Dimnah

This work I have read many times at different stages in my life. Our parents used to tell us the fables in Arabic when we were youngsters. We acted them out in plays at school. We were drawn to them at any age because they continued to be entertaining and amusing as we grew. I found myself telling the same stories to our son Saᶜad and our daughter Tala in English, since our children are more fluent in that language. This is probably what impelled me to translate them and share our beautiful experience with as many English-speaking people as possible. I had come to realize that the amusement opened us to a wisdom that grew more perceptive as we grew able to perceive it. I found myself calling on the fables to provide insight in our business, social, political, and family lives. Even now, when our children come home from their universities, they remind *us* of the pleasure the stories gave them. I am counting on their abiding affection for *Kalilah wa Dimnah* as they grow more maturely capable of taking them in.

SELECTED BIBLIOGRAPHY

Armstrong, Karen, *A History of God*, Phoenix Press, London 2001

Armstrong, Karen, *Islam: A Short History*, Weidenfeld and Nicolson, Orion Publishing Group, London 2000

Armstrong, Karen, *Mohammad: A Biography of the Prophet*, Harper, San Francisco 1993

Azzam, Abdulwahhab, *Kalilah wa Dimnah*, Almaᶜaref Publishing House, Cairo, Egypt, 1941

Ball, Warwick, *Syria: A Historical and Architectural Guide,* Melisende, London, 1997

Badeau, John S *et al*, *The Genius of Arab Civilization: Source of Renaissance*, MIT Press, Cambridge, Massachusetts, 1983

Bottingheimer, Ruth B, *Fairy Godfather: Straparola, Venice and the Fairy Tale Traditions,* University of Pennsylvania Press, Pennsylvania, 2002

Bustani, Butros, *Arabic Literature during the Abbasid Period*, Maroon Abboud Publishing House, Beirut, Lebanon, 1979

Chiekho, Fr Louis, *Kalilah wa Dimnah*, Almashreq Publishing House, Lebanon, 1994

Cowen, Sancia Jill, *Kalila wa Dimna, An animal allegory of the Mongol Court: The Istanbul University Album*, Oxford University Press, 1989

Encyclopedia of Islam, 2nd edition, E J Brill, 1978

Gregg, Kenneth, *The Arab Christians. A History in the Middle East*, Westminster/ John Knox Press, Louisville, Kentucky, 1991, USA

Glubb, Sir John, *The Life and Times of Muhammad*, Scarborough House, Chelsea, Michigan, USA, 1970

Hitti, Philip, *History of the Arabs*, Macmillan, London, 1970

Hourani, Albert, *A History of the Arab Peoples*, Faber and Faber Limited, London, 1991

Ibn Khaldoun, A, *Al-Muqaddemah, Prolegomena*

Ibn Khillikan, Ahmad, *Wafayat al A'yan, and the News of the Peoples of the Past*, Dar Al Sayyad, Beirut, Lebanon, 1969

Irving, Thomas Ballantine, *Kalila and Dimna*, Juan de la Cuesta, Newark, Delaware, USA, 1980

L Keith-Falconer (trans.), *Kalila and Dimna or The Fables of Bidpai*, London, 1885

Knatchbull, W (trans.), *Kalila and Dimna: or The Fables of Bidpai*, J Parker, Longman, Hurst, Reese, Orme & Brown, London, 1819

Najm, Muhammad Yusuf, *Analogy between Kalilah wa Dimna and the proverbs used in the old Arab Poetry: A study on the work of Al-thayerfah Publishing House*, Al Yamani, Muhammad Ibn Husain Ibn Omar, Beirut, Lebanon, 1961

Salibi, Kamal, *A History of Arabia*, Caravan Books, New York, 1980

Sa'ad, Farouk, *Kalilah wa Dimnah*, Dar Al Afaq Al Jadidah, Beirut, Lebanon, 5th edition, 1992

Shahid, Irfan, "A prolegomenon to the Study Byzantine and the Arabs", *Rome and the Arabs*, Dumbarton Oaks, Washington DC, 1984

Shadid, Irfan, *Byzantium and the Arabs in the Fifth Century*, Dumbarton Oaks, Washington DC, 1989

Shadid, Irfan, *Byzantium and the Arabs in the Sixth Century*, Dumbarton Oaks, Washington DC, 1996

St John Damascene, The Greek Orthodox Archdiocese of Australia, www.cygnus.uwa.ed.au

The Fisherman and the glittering shell

The Introduction to the Book
'Abdullah ibn al-Muqaffa'

The scholars of India compiled the book of fables, *Kalilah and Dimnah*. It contains the most elegant proverbs, parables and analogies. Scholars from various schools, after long toil, brought out the best of their thoughts and embodied them in a most creative manner. This culmination of their deep reflection expressed their wisdom in fables using animals as their main characters. They managed to express the full range of their wisdom in ways that allowed any theme to be highlighted for special attention. The book thus infuses wisdom with amusement. Wise men chose to read it for its wisdom, while the common folk read it for entertainment. Whoever has learned from his own experience and that of others, and remembers and appreciates what he has learned, may appreciate these fables and take them to heart without knowing in advance how and when he will draw upon them. He knows only that he has gained a variety of insights that could be useful at any opportune time. He is like a youth reaching mature manhood, who suddenly finds that his parents had left him vast wealth, and sources of further income that would spare him the hard work of earning his livelihood. This is the case with persons of deep insight. The wisdom gained from this book should supply both present and future needs for further knowledge in other types of the sciences, arts and letters.

It is imperative that the reader of *Kalilah and Dimnah* should grasp the meaning beyond the text, and understand the reasons for having animals as the main characters. The insights are embodied in proverbs, anecdotes, parables and analogies. If the reader does not comprehend that, then there is no benefit gained, and no intelligent inference can be made from the valuable wisdom offered in this book. Reading *Kalilah and Dimnah* without insight will thus be time lost.

Any person who accumulates knowledge of the arts and sciences and spends his time reading books without patience and insight, exhausts himself in vain. His reward will be similar to the man who found a treasure as conveyed in the following anecdote cited by the scholars of times past.

A man was crossing the wilderness, and spotted a place where he thought he might find a treasure. After digging for some time he found a treasure of wealth hidden in the ground. He figured that if he were to move the treasure by himself, it would be cumbersome, require more time, and entail more risk of discovery. It would be more efficient to hire workers to do it for him. Naturally he planned to supervise them and make sure that nothing would be left unguarded, and everything transported to his house. This would save him both the work and the risk. So he hired some porters to do the job. They came, and each one carried his maximum load. However, since no one supervised them once they set out, each went to his home instead of unloading the treasure at the owner's house as agreed. Once the treasure had all been carried off the man who had found it went home, but to his dismay he found nothing there. The porters had exploited his short-sightedness and stolen the entire treasure because he failed to think his own plan through to the end. His only reward was frustration and fatigue.

A like frustration awaits anyone who reads this book of fables without comprehending both the apparent and the implicit ideas within. Such a reader will not benefit from the text on these pages, which offer no real value on their own except through the meaning they embody. He would be like a person who is given a walnut, but is unable to enjoy it without first cracking the shell.

He might also resemble the man who approached an expert in the art of rhetoric and asked for instruction. The expert wrote all what he knew of this art on a yellow scroll. This student would read it thoroughly and regularly, but without grasping the real meaning of what he read. One day he conferred with a few scholars and experts in the arts and sciences, and they discussed various subjects. At one point he made a grammatical error, and an expert among those present pointed out his mistake. But the student rejected the opinion of the expert: "How can I be mistaken, since I have diligently and thoroughly read the yellow manuscript which is in my house at this moment?" His defence was worse than his mistake, and made manifest how these fascinating arts were closed to him by his vain ignorance.

When a sensible human being comprehends this book and digests it well, it is only prudent that he should act morally according to what he has learned from it, and consider it as an ideal on which to model his behaviour. If he fails to do so, the results will be painful.

This is like the learned man who awakened from his sleep when he sensed a burglar was breaking into his house. He decided to stay put, pretend to be sleeping and wait to see what the burglar would do. At just the right moment he would leap up, seize him and foil his scheme. The thief began collecting various valuable things while the owner waited. But after a while the drowsy owner went back to sleep. The thief took all he wanted and left the house safely. In the morning, the man realized his folly: knowledge alone was no help, and he had only himself to blame. This man's knowledge was useless when used ineffectively.

Knowledge is not complete without practical application. It is like a tree, and performance is its fruit. A person cannot be described as wise unless he utilizes his knowledge to some benefit. If a human being knowingly walks down a dangerous street, he is simply called ignorant. If he should ever reflect on it, he might admit that his choice was grounded on a capricious whim, since he had known the risk involved. But if another person walked down the same street unaware of the danger, we would consider him less stupid than the first.

Any person who directs his actions by whim, instead of by what he has learned from experience or from others, is very similar to a sick person. Though he can differentiate between foul and pure food and water, and heavy food versus light, he consumes the unhealthy and leaves the wholesome, due to his craving and gluttony.

Among the people who avoid worthy actions and do the opposite, the knowledgeable ones are less excusable. They are expected to have insight and discretion, and to act accordingly. It is like two persons who have fallen into a pit. One is blind; the other, not. Down in the pit they share the same predicament, but the blind man has more justification since he cannot see, while the other can. One therefore may justify the follies of the unaware, but not the foolish failures of the well-informed.

A scholar must therefore begin with his inner self, and cultivating it and refining it with the arts and sciences at his disposal. He should not accumulate such things for their own sake only. He should be like the spring from which people drink, expecting no rewards. Or like the silk worm which produces fine silks but does not benefit from them. Hence those who strive to accumulate knowledge must first educate themselves, and then teach others. Knowledge and wealth are two goods that should be first amassed and then distributed. They are both sources of kind generosity. Hence it is not appropriate for a scholar to rebuke anyone for a deficiency with which he himself is afflicted. Otherwise he will be like a blind man who scoffs at the blindness of another.

In addition, whoever seeks something should have rational limits, and refrain from seeking to excess. It is said that whoever races his mount without any set course will always be a loser. No one should exhaust himself by pursuing the unattainable. Likewise one should not regret the frustration of unattainable desires, since they have no meaning in this life or beyond. A person who does not burden himself with extravagant hopes will experience less pain when they are not attained.

There are two functions that are appropriately related: namely, worship of the divine and the accumulation of legitimate wealth. It does not befit a rational person to feel remorse over failing to achieve what was never attainable anyway. Perhaps God has planned better opportunities that this person is unable to recognize. A fable for this situation is the following:

Once there was a Pauper who was hungry and destitute. No one of his family or friends assisted him. One night, he was pondering about his life. Suddenly a Thief broke into his cabin. The Pauper murmured to himself, "Let the Thief do whatever he wants. I have nothing in here of any value. He will only be frustrated." While searching in the dark, the Thief stumbled on a bag of wheat in a jar. He said to himself, "I don't like to go home empty-handed from my night's work. Since I may not find anything better, I might as well take this bag." He proceeded to make an apron of his cloak to put the wheat in. Seeing this, the Pauper became more alert and thought, "If this Thief gets away with the wheat, which is all I have, I will be left destitute: already unclothed, and now hungry as well! No one lives long who lacks both food and clothing." So he laid into the Thief with a stout stick. For fear of injury the Thief bolted, leaving the wheat and his cloak as well. To his surprise, the Pauper ended up both clothed and fed.

However, people should not rely on Destiny alone to achieve their aims, nor should they fail to exert themselves to earn their daily livelihood, and leave the matter to chance. I am sure a few people will do so, but the majority will toil, and attempt to gain their livelihood by hard work. A person should both care and work in order to reap the benefit of his industrious efforts. On the other hand, he should not expose himself to needless pain and trouble. Otherwise, he may become like the pigeon that lays its eggs, but after they hatch, sees her youngsters taken and eaten. She nevertheless comes back again to lay her eggs in the same place, and the cycle is repeated until she too is eaten.

It might be said that God, the Almighty, has set a limit for everything in this world. Anyone who attempts to go beyond those limits will never succeed. It is also said that whoever strives for both this life and the eternal home, should know that good deeds performed in this life are counted in his favour, while the evil ones are counted against him.

People speak of three important things a person should carefully consider in this life: his daily livelihood, his relationships with others, and a good legacy by which people can remember him with kindness. There are three other characteristics that will handicap one's employment in any vocation. The first is negligence; the second is the squandering of opportunities; and the third is trusting people without ensuring their dependability, for many people are not honest.

A rational person should suspect his own passions and not follow them blindly, but act only when the right alternative has been confirmed. He should not act like a traveller who wanders off the planned route and simply carries on without correcting his mistake, thus making it worse. Such a person will only add to his exhaustion, and go further astray with every step. He may also be like a person who has a foreign body in his eye and does not stop rubbing it, thus risking the loss of eye and eyesight together.

It is imperative that a rational being believe in Destiny, and be firm about it. He should do to others what he wishes others to do to himself, and should not take gain from other people's losses. Otherwise he endures what befell a certain merchant at the hands of his deceitful partner. The story is told as follows:

Two Merchants stored their goods in a shared warehouse. One decided to steal a sack full of merchandise that belonged to the other. He was afraid that if he came at night, he might confuse the sacks and carry off one of his own. So one day the Merchant laid his cloak on one of his colleague's sacks as a mark for him to pick it up later at night, and off he went. Just as he left, the second Merchant came in to arrange his goods and found the cloak of his partner thrown on his sacks. He thought: "This is my friend's cloak, and I am sure he forgot it here. I should do him a favour and put it on his own goods, so if he comes to the store ahead of me tomorrow, he will find it immediately." He did so, locked up and went home.

That night the Deceitful Merchant came with an accomplice to help him, in return for part of the loot. When in the dark of the night they dimly saw the cloak on one of the sacks, they quickly hoisted it on their backs and rushed towards his home. Exhausted, he threw himself on his bed and rested without inspecting the sack.

In the morning, he saw the sack, was dismayed to discover it was one of his own, and deeply regretted what he had done. He dashed to the store, but found his colleague was already there, and much distressed. The Honest Merchant had arrived earlier, and found that the Deceitful Merchant's sack was missing. He was lamenting and saying to himself:

"Alas, I am disgraced. My good colleague has entrusted me with his wealth, and now some of it is gone. How will he react? I am sure he is going to accuse me of stealing! But since the safety of his merchandise is my responsibility too, I must pay whatever amount he may demand for the lost goods."

When the Deceitful Merchant entered the store and saw his colleague in distress, he sheepishly asked: "What is the matter?" The Honest Merchant told him about his missing sack of merchandise, and offered to pay for it since it had also been entrusted to him. But the Dishonest Merchant addressed him in a regretful manner and said:

"Don't be sad, my brother. Betrayal is the worst thing any human being can do to his colleagues. Cheating and deceit can never lead to any good end. Anyone who thinks otherwise lives in an illusion. The evil consequences of such actions will always end up with those who initiate them, and I for one have cheated, deceived and tricked you and many others too."

When the Honest Merchant sought an explanation, his dishonest colleague told him the whole truth. When he finished, the Honest Merchant said, "Your case reminds me of the story of the Thief and the Merchant."

"How does the story go?" asked his dishonest colleague. The Merchant recounted it to him:

"Once upon a time a Merchant kept two huge jars for storage in his house. One jar contained wheat; the other, gold. A Thief spent some time watching him and studying his movements. One day the Merchant had some other business that delayed his return home. The Thief broke in, but instead of stealing the jar that contained the gold, he stole the less valuable one that contained the wheat. When he discovered what he had done, he ended up frustrated."

The Deceitful Merchant said, "That story is not far from what I have done, and the fable is correct. I confess to my fault and my vile actions towards you. It disturbs me that things went this way, but many times the evil in oneself prompts a person to act shamefully.

The Honest Merchant finally accepted his apology, and forbore to scold him, but ceased trusting him as well. The Deceitful Merchant regretted his lowly actions and extreme ignorance of the lessons in life.

The book of fables, *Kalilah and Dimnah*, is not written for entertainment only. If one scrutinizes it thoroughly and meditates on the meanings embodied in the fables and analogies, he will surely become of the same mind. The reader should therefore spend time on understanding every fable and every word in the book.

He should act like the Youngest Son of the man who left considerable wealth to his three sons. He divided it equally among them. The first two squandered their shares. The Youngest Son observed the futility of his brothers' attitude towards wealth. He reflected, and said to himself: "A person accumulates wealth from any available source in order to sustain his livelihood, improve his welfare in this world, augment his prestige in society, and manage his life without having to rely on others. He should therefore spend it wisely: particularly on needy relatives, on his children, and generously on his friends. Whoever spends his money wrongly should be considered a pauper, even if he remains wealthy. If he saves and invests it well, he will enjoy his life and also the gratitude of those who are around him. But if he squanders it, his wealth will quickly dwindle, causing him deep regret and profound sorrow. Therefore I had better save my wealth, that I may with God's help use it wisely. I will also take care of my brothers: after all, we share the same father. And if it is true that we should assist poor relatives before assisting others, then since my brothers are my closest relatives I should begin with them."

So he summoned his brothers, and shared his wealth with them.

The reader of *Kalilah and Dimnah* with all its fables should therefore spend careful and tireless time on understanding it. One ought not conclude that it is merely an assemblage of anecdotes about two animals, or a dialogue between a lion and a bull or the like, lest one read the book entirely out of focus. Then he would be just like the Fisherman and the Glittering Shell.

One day a Fisherman threw his net in the water and caught a fish large enough to feed him for that day. But suddenly he spied a Glittering Shell in the water. Mistaking it for a valuable jewel, he let the fish go free and lunged to catch the shell. When he caught it and opened it, he found it empty. He regretted his greed and grieved at losing his daily food.

The next day the Fisherman went to another area in the bay, and cast his net there. He caught a fish even greater than that of the previous day. But he also saw another Glittering Shell beside it. Thinking that it also would be empty, he paid it no heed and returned home. Meanwhile another fisherman passed by, retrieved the Shell, and to his joy he discovered in it an extremely rare and precious pearl.

Similarly, people who miss the point of this book and do not comprehend its deeper meanings, but are satisfied by the superficial, are like the ignorant fisherman.

Moreover, those who concentrate only on the amusing aspects of this book of fables would be like the Farmer who had healthy seeds and good productive land. He promptly planted the seeds and painstakingly watered the land as well, until the plants flourished and grew. However, at the same time he also began devoting his efforts to rooting out the thorns in the field, and picking the wild flowers that usually grow around them, and thus neglected tending his plants. The result of his negligence was the destruction of the plants and the loss of his produce. It would have been far better and productive for him to spend more time on the plants than on the thorns or the flowers.

As for its structure, *Kalilah and Dimnah* has four elements. There are fables where dialogue among animals is used. The reason is to entice young people to read them in a light–hearted way as animal roguery in an attractive and entertaining genre. There are colourful fantasies involving animals that even kings find amusing. Kings ought also care to keep this book alive and famous, as it may allow them to relax and freely deploy their imaginations. There are insights intended for the royalty, the gentry, and common folk as well. It is intended for wide circulation, and will bring employment to the copyists and illustrators involved in its production. And there is a wisdom here ultimately and exclusively meant only for philosophers.

Dabshalim the King and Baydaba the Philosopher

Dabshalim the King
and Baydaba the Philosopher
'Ali ibn al-Shah al-Farisi
(Scholars are fundamental to society)

Bahnud ibn Sahwan, known as 'Ali ibn al-Shah al-Farisi, wrote the Introduction to this great book. There he states the reason why Baydaba, the Philosopher of India and Chief Brahmin in the reign of Dabshalim the King of India, wrote the book called Kalilah and Dimnah, *narrated as animal stories. His purpose in writing this book of fables was to shield his ideas from the vulgar, and mask their meaning from the rabble.*

The book embodies wisdom and her arts, her beauty, and her sources. To the philosopher, it is like a spring from which he may satisfy his inquisitive thirst, and an open field where his thoughts may roam. It instructs those who love it, and ennobles those who seek it.

In his Introduction, Bahnud mentions the reasons why Khusraw Anushirvan ibn Qubadh ibn Firuz (or Chosroes I), King of Persia, sent his Chief Physician, Barzawayh, to India to obtain the book of fables, Kalilah and Dimnah. *He also describes the patience of Barzawayh. Once in India, he waited until he found a man who would withdraw the manuscript of this book and others from the King's treasury, so that Barzawayh could copy them in the still of the night. Bahnud mentions the members of Barzawayh's delegation, and what was required to perfect their understanding of the text. For if readers do not study it well and scrutinize its hidden meanings, they will not benefit at all from this book. He also reports the presence of Barzawayh when the book was publicly read, and the reason why Buzurjmihr ibn al-Bakhtikan, the King's Vizier, was commissioned to write an independent Preface entitled "Barzawayh the Physician". In it his birth, life, education, and his love and pursuit of wisdom were described, and inserted just before the chapter of the "Lion and the Bull", which originally began the book.*

'Ali ibn al-Shah al-Farisi tells the following story in his Introduction.

To understand the reason why Baydaba the Philosopher wrote the book of fables, *Kalilah and Dimnah,* and presented it to Dabshalim the King of India, one must go back to the Eastern Campaign of Alexander of Macedon, the "Greek King with the Two Horns". After Alexander conquered the kings and countries in the Western world, he proceeded eastward to master the monarchies in Persia and beyond. He fought and conquered them one by one, defeating them in combat or bringing them to terms. His challengers were routed and scattered to remote areas. He then proceeded towards China, but this required him first to subdue India, which lay in his path.

The monarch of India at that time was King Fur. He enjoyed great authority, resolve, strength and experience. Upon hearing of Alexander's advancing forces, Fur began to mobilize huge armies in preparation for a decisive war. He consolidated his power over all of India, and energetically united all the kings and princes of the country. He swiftly equipped himself with military resources, including specially trained elephants and lions, finely apparelled horses, and horsemen fully armed with sharp swords and bright lances. The Macedonian was aware of these preparations, and realized they exceeded those of any of the monarchs he had vanquished. He thought it wise not to rush into a conflict he might lose.

Alexander was a leader of sharp cunning, with a brilliant tactical mind, a sound gift for command, and much practical experience. He decided to spend more time on planning. His first act was to dig a trench around his perimeter as a barrier against attack. He then devoted most of his time to preparing plans and perfecting his strategies. Alexander also solicited the advice of his astrologers regarding the timing of his battle against the King of India.

He came up with an ingenious plan. He ordered his artisans and engineers, whom he had selected from defeated nations and incorporated into his army, swiftly to cast a considerable number of life-sized bronze horses, fully equipped, with figures of mounted horsemen on them. He then instructed his artisans to fill their bellies with naphtha and sulphur, and position them at the forefront of his striking force. The horses were mounted on small wheels that allowed them to be moved forward at a good pace. Once battle was joined, and the Indian army attacked Alexander's, the petroleum and sulphur in the bellies of the horses would be ignited, making the bronze ferociously hot. As the attack elephants attempted to wrap their trunks around the molten horses, mistaking them for real ones, they would be abruptly and painfully burned, and stampeded in all directions.

On the eve of the day set by set by Alexander's astrologers for the battle, he sent envoys to King Fur, asking him to yield and submit. King Fur refused, and determined to fight. Alexander, "the Two-Horned King", made up his mind forthwith and gave the word for battle. As expected, King Fur placed his elephants at the forefront of his army. Alexander's soldiers pushed the bronze horses and horsemen towards the attacking Indian forces. The elephants wrapped their trunks around them.

Alexander conquers India

When they felt the excruciating heat radiating from the bronze horses, they shook the howdahs off their backs, stomped them with their gigantic feet, and stampeded through the ranks of King Fur's advancing army, sparing nothing and no one from the wrath of their agonized fury. Confused by this, Fur and his army dispersed in panic, unaware of what had befallen them. Alexander's soldiers vigorously pursued them and mercilessly killed and maimed them.

Then suddenly, in a thundering voice, Alexander bellowed: "King of India! Come out and face me alone! Keep your family and children alive, and do not provoke their needless death and extinction. It is not an act of chivalry for a king to send his family willingly into risk and hazard. On the contrary, he should protect them with all his wealth, and even with his own life. So come out and face me alone, apart from our armies. We two will fight, and winner take all."

When Fur heard what the "Two-Horned" Alexander said, he was lured to accept the challenge, in the hope of prevailing. He simple-mindedly thought that this was a great opportunity to emerge victorious. Both men mounted their magnificent horses, and fought with their swords furiously through most of the hours of that day. At the end Alexander, seeing no end to this fight since King Fur was a brave and skilful warrior, resorted to another of his tricks. Suddenly he let out a terrifying scream that shook the very earth and the armies standing to. Fur fell for the trick and fatally turned round in his saddle, fearing that Alexander's troops had surrounded him and his soldiers from behind. In an instant, Alexander swiftly lunged and struck Fur a ferocious blow that made his body arch from the top of his horse. He followed it with another that flung Fur from his horse onto the ground.

When the Indian soldiers saw what had befallen their king, they resolutely charged Alexander and his army, afraid of nothing, least of all death. But Alexander finally prevailed, and went on to conquer all of India. He spent some time there to unite the country under his rule, and ensured that order and stability prevailed. He then appointed one of his trusted leaders as vicegerent, and marched out of India in search of more worlds to conquer.

After Alexander and his army were far away, busy with further pursuits, the Indian people had a change of heart towards Alexander's appointee. They were determined that no foreigner would rule India. Neither the nobility nor the common people could accept such a situation. They therefore agreed among themselves to select one of their own as king. They finally chose a King named Dabshalim, and deposed Alexander's appointee.

No sooner had Dabshalim the King taken the reins of power

than he became a tyrant: oppressive, arrogant, and brutal towards his subjects. He successfully raided all the kings and rulers around him and destroyed them. The people of India submitted to his rule, but with fear and resentment. When Dabshalim saw that, he became even more abusive and authoritarian. He played havoc with his subjects and treated them with contempt. The more he oppressed them, the happier he became. Such was the situation under his rule, for quite some time.

It happened that a Brahmin philosopher, who was righteous and wise, lived in India during Dabshalim's reign. He was well known in the kingdom, and his wise decisions on many issues were widely accepted among the people. His name was Baydaba. When he witnessed the King's behaviour and his oppression of the people, he started to consider how to reform the King and return him to the path of justice. After deep and serious thought, Baydaba gathered his pupils around him and said to them: "I asked you here to consult about a grave problem. You must be aware by now that I have thought deeply of Dabshalim's actions: his unjust and evil acts, his misconduct, and his oppressive rule. All of us here train ourselves to take courageous decisions whenever kings conduct the business of government in such abusive ways. We all submit to strenuous training in wisdom and learning, to find ways and means of reversing such a situation, and making kings return to righteousness and justice.

"If we refuse to act, and neglect our duty to reform the kings, misfortune will afflict our society and danger will stalk us. The ignorant will conclude that we scholars are more ignorant than they are, and they will look on us with contempt. I must admit that the thought of emigrating to other countries crossed my mind, but I categorically decided against it, as an ineffective gesture. But it is intolerable to watch the King continue in his deplorable conduct and despicable government. On the other hand, we have nothing but words as weapons. Even if we wished to seek the assistance of others, we are neither ready nor able to withstand his violence. And if the King ever suspected that we oppose him and his regime, he would surely eliminate us.

"You may agree with me that even if this land is bountiful and life here is generally good, it is unwise and self-deceiving to live at close quarters with the lion, the dog, the serpent or the bull. Even a philosopher's wits should be trained to protect him from possible harm and dangerous risks, to avoid unnecessary fears, and to pursue the main chance. I heard about a philosopher who once wrote to his pupil:

"To befriend evil people and dwell within their society is like travelling by sea: whether or not one drowns, he must endure the uncertainty that he might.

"So anyone who willingly sojourns in dangerous places and

exposes himself to fearful risks can be likened to a jackass, which has no soul at all. We know that animals instinctively understand what is good for them, and shy away from what is harmful. We never see them rushing willingly into dangerous areas where they might perish. When they sense danger nearby they instinctively draw back from it in order to survive.

"I have gathered you here, my dear pupils, to discuss this very matter. You are my family, my trustworthy friends, the heirs of my learning. You are my support, the staff I lean upon. Whoever acts alone, upon opinions unshared, and convictions he dare not speak of and about which he seeks no opinion from his colleagues, forfeits all support. But anyone who takes early counsel and uses his wits to plan with forethought may accomplish what armies of soldiers and waves of cavalry could not achieve. In this matter the fable of the Lark and the Elephant may be revealing:

Once upon a time a Lark laid her eggs in a nest that happened to be in the path of an Elephant. The Elephant was in the habit of walking along that path towards his favourite drinking place. One day, while walking along, he accidentally stepped on the Lark's nest. The eggs were crushed and her young were instantly killed. When the Lark saw what happened, and realized that the Elephant alone was responsible for this catastrophe, she flew up and landed on the Elephant's head crying: "What have you done, my King! Why did you crush my eggs and kill my chicks while I was under your protection? Was it because I am too small, and so you despise me?" The Elephant answered arrogantly: "Yes, that is why I did it."

The Lark left him forthwith, rallied a group of other birds, and angrily protested the Elephant's actions to them. Their first reply was that there was little they could do to the Elephant since, after all, they were only tiny birds. So the Lark asked the magpies and the ravens to join her in gouging out the eyes of the Elephant and blinding him. She admitted to them that this would be her first venture in retaliation. They agreed, and together they descended on the Elephant and pecked at his eyes until he was blinded. Now he could no longer find his way to the drinking place, or forage for food beyond the reach of his trunk.

When the Lark saw what they had done, she went to a pond full of friendly Frogs and complained to them too of what the Elephant had done. The Frogs also replied: "What can we do against the might of the Elephant? We would never be able to hurt him."

The Lark responded: "Come with me to a nearby pit. There you can croak and make a lot of commotion. When he hears you he will be convinced there is water there, and will surely stumble into the pit.

The Frogs agreed. They all gathered at the bottom of the pit. The Elephant heard their croaking, and being very thirsty he hurriedly

قنـبرة

فيل

ضفدع

The Lark, the Frogs and the Elephant

walked towards the pit, toppled in, and could not climb out.

The Lark circled over his head and cried: "You arrogant and powerful tyrant! You despised me because I was puny and you were huge. Your arrogant bullying was as monstrous as your huge body, but despite my tiny size, my clever plan was more than your match."

"Now, in light of that fable, I ask each one of you to offer me your reflections and advice."

The pupils addressed Baydaba in unison: "Our righteous, wise and just philosopher, you are our leader—more capable than any of us. Our opinions are inferior to yours, and so is our knowledge compared to yours. But we do know that swimming with the crocodile is fatal, and the blame lies not with the crocodile but with those who put themselves at such risk. Likewise, whoever extracts the poison from the fangs of the snake and tastes it to test it, has himself to blame and not the snake. Furthermore, anyone who enters the lion's den ought not imagine he will be safe from his attack."

The case is the same with Dabshalim the King, who failed to foresee the disaster you described, and has hitherto learned little from his experience or that of others. Neither you nor we are safe from his brutal tyranny. But we are afraid that he will react violently if you confront him with what he may dislike.

Baydaba answered: "You have spoken truthfully, and for that I commend you. But anyone who has a firm and wise decision should not consult further with anyone else, whether above or beneath him. Every private opinion will risk either the hostility of the gentry or opposition by the common people. Despite what I have heard from you, and the advice you have offered with concern for my welfare as well as your own, I must now tell you that I have made up my mind to meet with Dabshalim. I have a settled judgment with which I must confront him. You will know soon enough of my discussions with the King and my answers to him. The moment you hear of my return from the King, let us confer again together here."

Baydaba dismissed his pupils. They left, bidding him farewell and praying for safety in his endeavour.

On the day Baydaba resolved to meet Dabshalim the King, he garbed himself in the distinctive Brahmin habit and went to the King's palace. There he spoke with the chamberlain and requested audience with the King. "I am a person who has valuable advice for the King," he explained.

The chamberlain approached the King and asked for permission for him to enter: "There is a Brahmin called Baydaba waiting outside, who claims to have some valuable advice for the King, and wishes to deliver it in person." The King agreed.

Baydaba entered, covered his head, prayed, and prostrated himself. He then stood erect, but remained utterly silent. Dabshalim pondered this strange silence, and said to himself: "This man is approaching me for one of two things: either to ask for some material wealth, or to request my protection from some harm."

He then addressed Baydaba and the Court: "In my opinion, scholars have greater credit in the kingdom for their wisdom than monarchs have for their governance. Wise men are richer than rulers by virtue of their wealth of knowledge alone, while rulers are not richer than wise men by virtue of their material wealth alone.

"I have come to the conclusion that wisdom and modesty are inseparable. When one is lost, the other follows. They are just like best friends: when one departs, the other prefers not to remain and endure the pain of separation.

"He who does not respect scholars, show them the utmost generosity and reverence, recognize their superior importance, protect them in weakness and shield them from disgrace, must have lost his mind and forgotten the purpose of his life. He has slighted the dignity of such wise men, and belongs back among the ignorant multitude."

Then the King looked up and queried Baydaba: "I have watched you standing here in silence; you have neither submitted a petition nor stated your purpose. Since you have been standing so long in silence, I thought you might be intimidated, or somehow fearful. I have been trying to read your mind, but since I know you, Baydaba, I knew you would not have approached me this abruptly without good cause, for you are the wisest person we have in the Kingdom. I ask you, then, to please explain to us the reasons for which you have come before us. If it is some injustice that has befallen you, I will be the first to give you immediate relief, and any assistance that will reaffirm your honourable status and accomplish your respected hopes.

"If your concern is temporal, I will award you immediate satisfaction. If, on the other hand, you are here to raise a challenge to my governance, to challenge the goodwill of the King, I will deal with your challenge thoughtfully, evaluate the situation, and impose any punishment you may deserve.

"I know, however, that people of your station will not claim the right to question how kings should rule. If your reasons are related to the people and how to manage them, or how I should care for them, then I am ready to listen. For I know that scholars always offer their counsel and advice for good purposes, while the ignorant usually do the opposite.

"I now welcome you, Baydaba, to speak freely."

When Baydaba heard the words of the King his fear vanished and his spirit was put at ease. He prayed again and prostrated once more before his King. He then stood and addressed the Court: "I beseech God, the Almighty, to give our King long life and an everlasting and mighty monarchy. The King has bestowed upon me an honourable status that favours me over all the scholars who will succeed me, and a remembrance within the circles of wise scholars until the end of time."

He then turned to the King, and faced him. He was full of peace, tranquillity and happiness, and spoke directly to him: "The kindness of the King, and his gracious generosity, overwhelm me. My presence here, which also carries the grave risk of addressing the King, was for the purpose of delivering my advice to him, advice I would give to no one else. All those who are close to the King will know that I have never been timid in voicing my opinion regarding the responsibilities of the scholars towards their master. Should the King scrutinize my words and comprehend them, he has the authority to react however he sees fit. Even should he reject my advice, I shall have fulfilled my obligation honestly, and can declare myself absolved from any future blame."

The King responded: "Baydaba, say whatever you wish. I will hear you out and be forthcoming; I will listen well until the end, and respond as you deserve."

Baydaba replied: "May it please the King: I have observed that, of all the creatures from the animal kingdom, the human being was singularly endowed with four distinctive traits. They are Wisdom, Reason, Virtue, and Justice. These are all the traits required in this world. Wisdom includes knowledge in the sciences, arts and letters, honesty and conscience. Reason includes tolerance, patience and gravity. As for Virtue, it includes generosity, modesty and humility, consistency and dignity. Justice includes honesty, benevolence, self-control, dependability and good temperament. All of these are advantages to a human being, while their opposites are clear disadvantages. When these traits are found in a person he is assured that his good fortune will continue to increase, and will not be compromised by the follies of his offspring. He will not brood over those who perish before him, nor will Destiny's adverse effects on his wealth sadden him. He will not be undone even should harm befall him. Wisdom is a treasure that will never give out, however much one draws upon it. It acts as a reserve which will ensure whoever possesses it that he will never find himself a pauper. It is like a beautiful gown that can never wear out. It is an endless source of elation and bliss.

"When I first came here to present myself, my silence expressed my profound reverence for the King, whose status and honour have surpassed that of all who preceded him.

"Ancient Wisdom emphasized that there is safety in silence, and taught that those who babble will stumble into confusion. The old story about the King who asked four of his scholars to offer him, in few words, the fundamentals of the moral life, is still very popular and relevant:

"The first said: 'The most beneficial medium of knowledge is silence.'

"The second added: 'One of the most beneficial things for a human being to know is the limit of his reason and intellect.'

"The third asserted: 'The most beneficial thing for a human being is to refrain from talking about issues that do not concern him.'

"The fourth responded: 'The most reassuring thing for a human being is to yield to Destiny.'

"It was also reported that sometime in the past the Kings of China, India, Persia, and Byzantium met and conferred. They agreed that each should give a statement whereby he might be remembered till the end of time.

"The King of China stated: 'I am more in control of the words that I do not utter, than of those I have already spoken.'

"The statement of the King of India was: 'I wonder why people talk about things which risk loss but offer no gain.'

"The statement of the King of Persia was: 'When I utter a word it owns me; but if do not, then I own it.'

"The King of Byzantium's statement was: 'I have never regretted words that I never uttered, but greatly regretted many that I did.'"

Baydaba continued: "To monarchs, silence is preferable to babbling, and more rational and more dependable than what the tongue may often disclose unwittingly. But since Dabshalim our King—May God prolong his life—graciously has allowed me to speak to him in Court, it prompts me to offer him the fruit of my advice, and to let him reap its benefits even before myself. The value of my words lies in the their effect upon the King. While the benefits and the morality inherent in my words will redound to him, my only reward is the simple satisfaction that I have done my duty."

Baydaba paused, and then went on: "Consequently I have this to tell you, O King. You now rule this Kingdom, which was founded by your fathers and great-grandfathers. They built strong forts and fortified castles to protect the kingdom. They established law and order in the country, led the armies, accumulated arms and cavalry, and lived with their people in harmony. All that did not stop them from leaving a happy legacy among the people, nor did it hinder the public from offering them profound gratitude on all occasions until this very day. They were kind to their subjects and gracious with their vassals. They acted benevolently and respectfully to all, while promptly executing their responsibilities.

"As for you, O King, whose forefathers are exalted and whose future is bright, you have inherited their lands and their cities, their wealth and their palaces. You have settled in this kingdom with legions of soldiers and great wealth that were provided to you as a legacy. But you have not executed your duties truthfully and efficiently. Instead, injustice has been the norm. You have acted unfairly, arrogantly tyrannized your subjects throughout the kingdom, and thereby damaged your legacy among your people and made them live in unbearable fear. It would have been more becoming of you to emulate your ancestors, and follow their path in governing this kingdom. It would have been more appropriate had you emulated their good deeds and refrained from embracing shameful and dishonourable actions. It is with kindness and care, not oppression, that you might have captured the respect of your people.

"It would have been better for you to legislate and enforce just laws and regulations, which would result in prolonging peace and stability in the kingdom and leave a praiseworthy legacy for yourself. The arrogant and ignorant person is the one who takes reckless decisions that could lead to bloodshed, but the firm and shrewd ruler is the one who reigns over his kingdom prudently, with the utmost care and kindness.

"I ask you, O King, to consider deeply what I have laid before you. I must repeat that my intention was not to provoke you, nor to ask for relief from any private affliction. I did not come before you to claim rewards for any good deeds that I have done. I came to provide you with considerate advice that might be of great benefit to you."

By the time Baydaba had delivered his advice and finished his discourse, the King was aflame with rage. He gave him harsh answer, scorned him, and belittled his purpose. In his wrath he said: "You know that you have spoken to me with an insolence no one in my kingdom has ever dared use, and confronted me with a disrespectful audacity as no other has ever dared or done. Who do you think you are, Baydaba? You are but a commoner who has managed to insult the dignity of the King, and gone far beyond your rights with your abusive words. I reckon that the best way to forestall others like you is by punishing and torturing you severely. That should make an example of you for any who may be tempted to emulate you, and reproach their King thus when the Kings graciously allow them in their courts."

Dabshalim immediately ordered the death of Baydaba by crucifixion. But when his soldiers had seized Baydaba and led him off, the King realized he had made his decision in anger, and changed his mind. He ordered that Baydaba be shackled and imprisoned instead. Dabshalim the King determined to punish Baydaba's pupils as well, but on hearing the news of Baydaba's Destiny they promptly fled the Kingdom to remote islands and countries.

Baydaba remained in prison for some time. No one ever dared to utter his name in the presence of the King. But one night Dabshalim could not sleep, and lay for a long time staring at the stars. He pondered their movements, their orbits, their shapes and patterns. He meditated on some of the principles of astronomy. Then, suddenly, he remembered Baydaba and his speech, and realized that he might have made a mistake in punishing this wise man. He thought: perhaps I have wronged the Philosopher, and in my anger hastily treated him unfairly. Scholars once said that there are four properties that should never be found in the character of a King. The first is anger, as it is the most repulsive trait. The second is stinginess, since his extreme wealth does not justify it. Thirdly, dishonesty, for all people despise liars. The fourth is fury in debate, since abuse and insolence do not belong in peaceable dialogues.

Baydaba came to me to offer advice, not to press a request. It appears now that I treated him contrarily to what he deserves, and rewarded him with a punishment rather than with the honour that is his honest due. It was wrong of me to do so. It should have been my duty to listen to him and be guided by his counsel.

The King immediately sent his servants to bring Baydaba back to the Court. When the Philosopher arrived the King addressed him: "Baydaba, are you not the man who attempted to show me how incompetent I was in ruling the Kingdom, and demonstrated to me how ineffective my record was?"

Baydaba answered: "What I have set before you, O King—the truthful and merciful, the honest and the kind—was for your own good and the good of your subjects, and intended to prolong your reign."

The King then told him: "Baydaba, I want you to repeat all that you uttered then, word for word, without omitting a single word or syllable."

Baydaba then repeated his discourse while Dabshalim listened carefully, thoughtfully tapping the floor with the staff in his hand. Then he lifted his head, bade Baydaba be seated, and said to him: "I am pleased by what you have said, and my heart is at ease now. I will study what you have advised, and will follow your guidance."

The King ordered his soldiers to unbind the Philosopher, and he was given back his freedom and his Brahmin habit. Baydaba replied, "You, O King, should realize that concealed in my advice are principles that challenge your reason and understanding."

"You are quite correct, Baydaba, and a most praiseworthy wise man. I have decided that you will become my Vizier and ruler over all of my Kingdom," Dabshalim declared.

"I am grateful, but I beg you, O King, to relieve me of such a grave responsibility, for no reform in this kingdom can succeed unless conducted by you," Baydaba answered.

The King granted him his wish. But after Baydaba had departed from the Court the King changed his mind, summoned him once more, and told him: "I have given enough thought to my offer to have you rule the Kingdom on my behalf. My anticipated reform cannot succeed unless conducted by you. I can find no one better than yourself to carry this responsibility. So I ask you not to disagree with me in this great matter."

Baydaba then willingly accepted the King's offer and commenced his duties as the King instructed.

It was customary at that time that when the King appointed a Vicegerent, or Vizier, he would be crowned and make an official progress throughout the kingdom. Accordingly, the day Baydaba was confirmed as Vizier was declared as a national holiday in India, that is observed to the present day. He ruled with justice and fairness. In his court the rights of the commoners were secured from the aggression of the nobles. Weak and strong were equal before the law. He was always ready to discuss petitions and grievances with the people, and decreed equitable and just laws and regulations. He was kind and generous to a fault.

When his pupils heard the good news about their Philosopher, they came back from exile, delighted that God had renewed the King's faith and trust in Baydaba. They thanked God for Baydaba's success in reforming the misconduct and mismanagement of Dabshalim the King.

When Baydaba found leisure and time from his service under of Dabshalim, he devoted himself to writing books on politics. He wrote many books with detailed suggestions and political finesse. The King followed Baydaba's guidance diligently, first of all in administering justice and kindness towards his people. This won for him the support of other neighbouring kings. Order, stability and happiness prevailed in the Kingdom.

Baydaba did not forget his pupils. He called them together and rewarded them generously. He also made them commitments regarding their future. He spoke as follows: "I am sure that when I first decided to meet with the King, you thought that Baydaba had lost his wisdom and his thoughts had come to nothing, since he had decided to challenge the brutal tyrant. Now you have seen the soundness of my opinion and the strength of my intellect. I did not go to him in ignorance, for I had learned from scholars before me that kings could have a level of uncontrolled violence similar to that of intoxication. Kings cannot be revived except through the guidance and preaching of scholars, and through the cultivation of knowledge and civility by wise men. As it is the duty of the kings to be guided by knowledgeable scholars, so it is the responsibility of the scholars to reform the kings with their speeches and lectures, and to guide them with their wisdom. They should show the kings the clear evidence for their ideas to deter them from any deviation from righteous conduct, and dissuade them from enacting unjust laws.

"My interpretation of what the scholars said is straightforward. Wise men have an absolute duty towards their kings. They must attempt to wake them up from their deep slumber. Their responsibility is just like that of the physicians who are experts in maintaining health: namely, prescribing the right medicine to cure the sick.

"I was hoping that neither the King nor I would die before I could face him and deliver my advice. Otherwise all the people in the world would say, "Baydaba the Philosopher lived in the reign of Dabshalim the tyrant and did not persuade him to reverse his evil actions and restore justice and equitable rule."

"They might also have said, 'He had no courage to speak because he feared for his life, and thought it better to escape to another country and endure the pain of longing for his homeland.' So I determined to offer my life for what I believe in, and the learned men who follow me will understand and appreciate what I have done. Consequently I exposed myself to death for the sake of duty and commitment, as you have witnessed.

"In the words of a proverb, it was understood in the past that one is driven to achievement by three motives. The first is a reaction to hardship. Another is a loss of wealth. The third is a strong set of beliefs one sustains even in the teeth of harm, so that people will ultimately realize his character. He who does not venture to overcome challenges may never be able to achieve his aspired objectives.

"I must tell you that Dabshalim the King has given me leave to write a book that contains all types of wisdom. So let each one of you write on whatever subject you choose, and present it to me. I will evaluate the level of intelligence and wisdom and knowledge expressed, and will act accordingly."

The pupils replied: "Our virtuous, rational and intelligent Philosopher: we swear by Him who bestowed on you wisdom, reason, knowledge, and virtue, that we have never doubted your courage. You are our leader, and our most venerable ideal. We will diligently follow your guidance."

It fell out then that for many years Dabshalim the King conducted the affairs of his kingdom well with Baydaba as helmsman. Peace and stability prevailed in and around the kingdom, and Dabshalim had the time to concentrate on reading the books written by the previous philosophers of India, which they had prepared for his ancestors. He in turn wished to have a book written to immortalize himself, and to describe the history of his reign. He was sure that only Baydaba could write such a book. So he called him and said: "Baydaba, you are the Wise Man and the Philosopher of India. I have given deep thought to the books of wisdom that are found in the Treasury of my ancestors. Every king had a book describing the history of his reign and his knowledge in the arts and sciences, as well as that of his subjects. Some kings wrote their own accounts. Others were written by the knowledgeable scholars of that time. I am afraid to pass on without leaving such a book in my Treasury. I would leave nothing for future generations to remember me by, and by exception nothing would be attributed to me. Hence I wish you to write a book of great eloquence. On the surface it must show my policies on how to rule and how to discipline the people. Implicitly, however, it should prescribe the behaviour and morality of the kings, their methods of government, and their ability to beget loyalty among their subjects. It should manifest how both the rulers and the ruled were spared the rigors of governance. I want this book to be my legacy."

When Baydaba heard the King's request he immediately prostrated himself, then said: "The King's wise forefathers must be happy with him. May his auspicious stars shine bright in the sky; may potential misfortune be staved off; and may his good days be prolonged. He who has endowed you with sharp insight and profound reason has also motivated you towards sublime objectives, elevated you to the highest levels of honour, and stretched your thoughts to the furthest limits. May God keep you happy and assist you in keeping your promises and your strength, and help me in attaining what I intend to do. Command me, and I will comply."

Dabshalim the King replied, "Baydaba, you are still known to be of sound faculties and loyalty to your King. I for one have successfully tested you, and therefore I want you to write this book. Spend the best of your intellect on it and use any means to complete it. Let it contain gravity, comedy, amusement, wisdom and philosophy."

Baydaba prayed for the King, prostrated himself again, and said: "I will fulfil my task—may God prolong your days—but I shall need time to finish this book."

"How long?" the King asked.

"A year," Baydaba answered.

The King agreed, and ordered that a handsome stipend be given Baydaba to enable him to complete the book. Baydaba gave great thought to how best to begin, what style to use, and what the final product should be. So he gathered his pupils around him and said to them, "The King has chosen me to do something that I shall be proud of, and I am sure you and the whole country will share with me the resulting honours. That is why you are here with me."

He then described the King's request and the purposes of the book. But he recognized that his pupils did not in the least understand what he was about. He pondered some more, and was convinced that such a mission could not succeed without his own personal dedication to the task, and the utter concentration of his reason and insight. He thought to himself: "A ship cannot negotiate the high seas without a crew, for they are the ones who are able to manoeuvre it to safety. But it is the captain who has the knowledge and the experience for command. If the ship becomes over-crowded with passengers, or weighed down by surplus crew, the risk of sinking becomes greater."

So he finally decided to write the book alone, assisted by only one of his trustworthy pupils. The two of them sequestered themselves with enough food to eat and paper to write on for a whole year. They spent that time in a closed room, laying out and writing the book.

Baydaba dictated the text and the pupil served as his scribe. They continually reviewed it until the book was complete. It contained fourteen separate chapters. Each chapter dealt with one issue, and a story line to guide the readers in orderly fashion. Baydaba collected the fourteen chapters in one book and called it *Kalilah and Dimnah*. It was a book of fables. He also put dialogue into the mouths of animals such as beasts, predators, lions and birds, in order to amuse both the cultivated and the common people. But ultimately it was written to educate the intellectual elite. He also included various guidelines for the people to follow within their families, and other generalized rules required for their religious and worldly welfare. Issues such as loyalty to and intimacy with kings, and avoiding them when necessary, were discreetly dealt with. The book initially looked like other books of wisdom. Animal roles were an amusing novelty, however, and what they uttered was a wisdom appropriate to the highest level of the sciences, arts and letters.

Baydaba began the book with the issue of friends and friendship. Central to the first chapter were friendships between people, how they should treat each other, and how intimate friendship can be eroded by the trickery of jealous schemers. Baydaba instructed his pupil to write as if he were narrating it under instruction by the King, with an amusing style yet full of wisdom. Both teacher and pupil laboured hard and long, until they decided on two jackals as the lead characters. While the animal dialogue was amusing and comic, the theme was one of astute wisdom.

55

Thus scholars would focus on the wisdom in it and leave the amusement to others. Scholars would easily comprehend the strategy of the book. As for the laymen, they would enjoy the fables recounted by the animals, and enjoy its purposeful amusement. They would not be aware of the deep meaning it concealed, nor would they appreciate the objective of the book. The Philosopher intended to portray the strength of friendship, and how friends should avoid falling into the many traps their enemies may plan for them, and benefit from the experience and its implied lessons to keep their friendship strong and intact at any cost.

A whole year passed during which Baydaba and his pupil composed their book. At the set time the King summoned Baydaba, who requested that all the people should be gathered in order to hear him recite the book in public. The King had it announced throughout the Kingdom that his people must gather from all over India to listen. A throne similar to that of the King was prepared for Baydaba to sit on. Baydaba was dressed for the occasion. He wore his ceremonial black habit of the Brahmins. His pupil carried the book gracefully. The crowd and the King were standing in gratitude and respect for their Philosopher.

"Lift up your head, Baydaba. This is a day of tranquillity, happiness and pleasure," the King declared, and bade him be seated and begin reading. The King frequently interrupted Baydaba's recitation to question him about the apparent or subtler meanings of each chapter.

The more Baydaba read, the greater was the admiration and elation of the King. When all was finished, the King addressed him: "Baydaba, for this magnificent task I will reward you generously. You have satisfied my request beyond my wildest dreams. Ask whatever you wish and it shall be granted!"

Baydaba prayed for the King, wished him happiness and long life, and said: "May it please the King: As for wealth I have no need for it. As for clothing, I will choose nothing over my convenient attire which I wear now, and I do not need anything from the King ... except one boon."

The King said, "Tell me, Baydaba, and I will provide it to you."

Baydaba said, "I ask the King to order that this book be copied just like the others which were written for his predecessors. Let him instruct his servants to use special care to safeguard this precious book. I am concerned that it could be smuggled out of India and end up in the Persian treasury. This book should never leave the House of Wisdom located in the King's Treasury."

Baydaba also called in his pupils and provided them with generous gifts.

It came to pass that when Khusraw Anushirwan ruled Persia, he was deeply involved in the arts and sciences, and history. He also happened to know about the book of fables *Kalilah and Dimnah*, and determined to have it at any cost. He could not be at peace until he sent his physician, Barzawayh, who patiently and skilfully spirited his translation out of India and finally deposited it in the Treasury of Persia.

The Mission of Barzawayh the Physician to India

The Mission of
Barzawayh the Physician to India

The most fundamental and abiding truth is that God the Almighty created this world with His mercy. He has endowed its creatures with bountiful nourishment, and provided its peoples with adequate sustenance. He has also given them ample guidance for their spiritual salvation, to prepare for the eternal home. But His highest endowment for human beings was reason. It is the foundation of everything in this world. Without it no one is ever able to earn a living, obtain any benefit, or protect himself against any evil. Through reason people are able to know right from wrong, and pursue their spiritual salvation and happiness. However, experience and knowledge of the arts and sciences are required for the mind to advance in insight and achievement.

Inherent within reason is an instinct for excellence that resembles the fire concealed in the flintstone. A spark of fire will not leap forth until someone strikes the flint. Only then can the nature of fire be manifest. In the same way, new knowledge is brought forth from reason only when it is struck by learning. The further knowledge and experience progress, the more vigorously they must be struck forth. Whoever is gifted with a sound mind, and perfects his reason through continuous learning in the arts and sciences, will ultimately achieve happiness in this world and beyond.

God had endowed King Khusraw Anushirwan with the best of minds, abundant knowledge, sound comprehension of complex issues, honourable comportment, and the most advanced methods of scientific research and investigation. He surpassed all other kings in the attainment of advanced knowledge in the arts, sciences and philosophy. While searching for further knowledge he heard about the book of fables, *Kalilah and Dimnah*, located in India. He was convinced that it was an authority for all the arts and sciences, a guide for prudent judgment in this life, a key to the eternal home and the revelation of its dread recompense. King Anushirwan immediately instructed his Vizier, Buzurjmihr, to find a shrewd and scholarly person fluent in both the Persian and Indian languages, and devoted to the pursuit of knowledge and wisdom. The Vizier found such a man: Barzawayh, the royal physician. Barzawayh was immediately summoned to the Court.

When Barzawayh was in the King's presence, he first prayed and prostrated himself. The King then addressed him: "Barzawayh, due to your qualifications and accomplishments I have chosen you for a most challenging mission. My advisors tell me you are a man of virtue, knowledge, and reason, and that you pursue learning diligently wherever it is found. It has come to my attention that there is a magnificent book in the Treasury of India which is of great interest to us."

The King then briefed him on all that he had discovered. He then said: "Prepare to leave for India. Use your own judgment and devise a plan to obtain the book. Thus both you and we shall benefit from it. In addition, bring back with you whatever other books you can carry. Take all the money you need, and do not hesitate to spend whatever may be required to acquire such precious resources. My treasury is at your disposal for any venture that may assist us in acquiring further knowledge. Go as soon as possible, and return safely and quickly."

Barzawayh took with him twenty bags of money, each containing ten thousand dinars, and embarked on his mission, blessed and guided by the Court astrologers.

Upon his arrival in India, Barzawayh set out to make the acquaintance of as many people as possible at the Indian Court, and among the public as well. He befriended the courtiers around the King: the nobility, scholars, scientists and philosophers. He visited them in their homes and received them in return with graciousness and civility. He introduced himself as a stranger in pursuit of further learning in the arts and the sciences of India, and asked for their guidance and advice. He persevered for quite a long while, accumulating knowledge as if he had known nothing before. He made many new friends from all sectors of the society such as the nobility, the philosophers, the scientists, the merchants, and the common folk.

One man, who happened to be the Treasurer of the King, became his trustworthy friend. After quite some time, during which Barzawayh appraised the honesty and loyalty of his friendship, his knowledge, his character, and his kindness, he resolved to reveal to this man the purpose of his mission. He faced him and said: "My brother and friend, I do not wish to conceal my secret any longer. I should like to tell you that I came to India for a purpose I have kept private. A shrewd man can learn the secrets of others by watching their eyes carefully. The eyes can exhibit insight, and I see you have such insight within."

The Indian Treasurer replied solemnly: "Despite the fact that I never talked to you about your secret objective, and your careful avoidance of disclosing who you really are, I knew the truth about you. But because I wished to be your trusted friend, I was reluctant to disclose what I had learned. Now that you have taken the initiative and revealed your mission to me, let me tell you what I have already discovered, which may be a good deal more than what you might think.

"You came to India on orders from your King to steal our intellectual treasures and take them back to your country. You arrived here with dishonest objectives and furtive plans. I have been observing your patience and persistence, and have been impressed by how meticulously you have avoided all risk of discovery until now. These qualities, however, were what attracted me to you as a friend, confirmed my trust in your competence, and prompted me to treat you as my brother. I have yet to find a man who is more purposeful or more knowledgeable than you, more diligent in pursuing the arts and sciences, or more discreet about his secrets. There is great strength in your character, especially as a stranger in a foreign land, and a newcomer to the morals and manners and of its people.

"My friend, I believe that the soundness and genius of the mind is manifest in eight properties:

"The first is kindness.

"The second is to know and respect oneself.

"The third is loyalty to the King, and readiness to investigate what things may satisfy him.

"The fourth is to know who is worthy of your trust, and how to share secrets safely.

"The fifth is to behave correctly in the royal court and earn entrée to higher levels.

"The sixth is to safeguard one's secrets and those of one's confidants.

"The seventh is to discipline one's conversation, and discuss confidential matters with only a trustworthy few.

"The eighth is to offer no more information than is asked.

"These personal traits are essential to both success and good fortune. And in my observation you have been endowed with them all. May God protect you and give you all the assistance you need to succeed in your mission.

"My friend, even though your endeavour will rob us of our intellectual treasures, and cost me my honour and my learning resources, I will gladly help you to obtain what you came here for, and to accomplish your mission."

Barzawayh listened attentively, and then replied: "I had prepared myself to disclose to you the full tale of my life and responsibilities, and to offer arguments and justifications for my mission and my tactics. But you have insightfully discovered all of this, and I have little left to explain. So I shall be brief. I am thankful for your assistance: so generous and loyal to your new friend.

"As you know, if ideas are laid before a philosopher, or secrets are confided to an intelligent and respectful person, they are closely held, as priceless treasures are safeguarded in strongly built vaults."

The Indian Treasurer replied: "Nothing supersedes intimate friendship. Pure friendship generates a sense of unity with one's counterpart. Friends will never hide anything from each other, or keep any secrets to themselves alone. Secrets are the exchange of civility and refinement. No secret shared by two can be secured. For if two people discuss a secret, then there is no guarantee that a third person from either side might not hear of it. And whenever three persons know about anything, it is bound to be known by the multitude, and the original trustee may not be able to defend or deny it.

"There is an analogy to this in the clouds. Once even a single person points out that they have broken open, the sky is there for all to see. I feel a profound and unmatched happiness when we are together. I also realize that by entrusting your secret to me you have exposed us both to the danger of death. I expect that our secret will inevitably become public knowledge someday. When it does, all my wealth will not suffice to shield me from the wrath of our King. Our King is harsh, rude, and brutal, and he normally punishes us for the smallest mistake. I cannot imagine the severity of his punishment for such a great crime as this! Our intimate friendship prompts me to provide you with the assistance you require to succeed in your mission, even though I know that nothing in this world will save me from the brutal punishment of the King."

Barzawayh then said: "Scholars and learned men have praised and commended the man who helps his friend by protecting his secrets. The success of my mission is now in your hands, and I hope I shall enjoy your confidential support for my mission. I now trust your generous nature and your estimable intellect. We are not wary of each other, but share a single wariness of the people around us. They could discover our venture, and then hand you over to the King. Yours is the life at risk, since I shall depart while you remain here. So let both of us stand by our promise not to reveal our shared secret to any other person."

Both agreed to be loyal to each other and maintain an inseparably intimate friendship.

The Indian Treasurer provided the book of fables *Kalilah and Dimnah* to his friend Barzawayh, along with many others. In light of the risk that the King of India might send for the books while they were in

Barzawayh's keeping, he concentrated day and night on translating them industriously from the Indian into the Persian language. He spent all his mental and physical energies towards this purpose.

When Barzawayh had completed translating *Kalilah and Dimnah*, and some other selected books, he wrote to Anushirwan the King of Persia, informing him of his accomplishment. The King was carried away with joy, but feared for his retainer's life, so he ordered him to leave India immediately. Barzawayh promptly complied. When he arrived back in Persia Barzawayh was weary and pale from the severe strain and fatigue, so the King bade him rest for seven days: "You are our loyal servant and will definitely reap what you have sown. Rejoice and be happy, for I am going to award you my highest honours."

On the eighth day, the King of Persia ordered all the princes and all the scholars to assemble before Barzawayh. The physician then read the book to the assembly, who had come from all corners of Persia. They were elated by the wisdom they heard, thanked God for such a gift, complimented Barzawayh and praised him. The King ordered that the coffers full of pearls, rubies, aquamarines, gold and silver be put at the disposal of Barzawayh, and said to him, "I now decree that you shall sit on a throne like mine, wear a crown, and rank ahead of all the nobility."

Barzawayh prostrated before the King, then said: "May God honour the King in this life and in the eternal home, provide him with recompense, and reward him with kindness. By God's help, I have no need to accumulate wealth. But since it was your wish to do so, I shall take a few things in deference to your command."

He went through the treasury of robes, picked several of the royal gowns made in famous Khurasan, and addressed the King: "May God prolong the King's life, and bestow on him His gracious generosity. It is imperative for any human being to offer his gratitude to those who treat him with grace and kindness! After the exhaustion and hardship I have undergone, I am satisfied that the King is well pleased with the outcome of my mission. I assure him that I will perform all tasks and duties entrusted to me, regardless of hardship or difficulty. This I do with the utmost pleasure and eagerness, since I know they will augment the King's honour and recognition, and that of his royal house as well. I pride myself on my absolute loyalty to the King. Tasks that seem otherwise hazardous become easy for me, and what may be hardship for others gives me profound satisfaction when done at his command. Exhaustion and pain turn into tranquillity and pleasure every time I feel he has been satisfied by my fulfilment of duty. But I have a request to place before the King, which I pray he will grant. It is a small thing in itself, yet there is a great benefit in granting it."

King Anushirwan responded: "Ask, and I will fulfil any of your wishes, the least of which is sharing with us in the rule of our Kingdom. Do not be shy; everything is granted to you."

Barzawayh replied: "The King should not be concerned about my attempts to satisfy him, nor question my single-minded loyalty. I am his faithful servant, and would give up my life for him with no prospect of reward.

"It is not his duty to reward me, nor was my task all that difficult. But it is due to his generosity and honourable nature that he rewarded me, and elevated me and my family to the highest honour in the Kingdom. I am sure that if the King had the power to bestow such honours on me in the eternal home he would have done that too. May God provide him with the best reward He might choose.

Anushirwan then asked him to state his wish, and Barzawayh replied: "My request—may God elevate the King's renown still higher—is that he instruct his Vizier, Buzurjmihr ibn al-Bakhtikan, on oath to make it his first and most consuming concern to write a chapter describing my mission, with whatever grace he can. I ask the King to assure that, when finished, this chapter immediately will precede the chapter on 'The Lion and The Bull' in the book of fables, *Kalilah and Dimnah*. If the King grants this, I shall consider that he has accorded my family and me the highest honour and prestige, and assured our everlasting legacy as long as the book is read."

Khusraw Anushirwan and his nobility were gratified by this request, and approved, since it focused on the honour and memorable legacies that reward good people. Khusraw agreed and said, "It shall be done, with pleasure. I shall honour you by granting your request, Barzawayh, for you are a worthy person. Your wish is modest, your satisfaction is great, and my compliance is wholehearted."

Khusraw then turned to Buzurjmihr and instructed him as follows: "You have long known of the attentive advice rendered to me by Barzawayh for many years. You are also aware of the hardships and hazards he recently endured on my behalf, his single-minded determination to please me, the priceless benefit he has provided me, and the wisdom and arts and letters he has brought me from India, which will be our pride forever. You also saw that I opened our coffers for him to choose whatever he wished, and he declined. He solicited a single favour as his reward and tribute.

"I therefore command that you fulfil his wish and raise his name in honour before our entire people. In honouring him you will be pleasing me. Spare no effort, no extravagant expression, and compose a chapter fit to join the others in the book of fables, *Kalilah and Dimnah*. Give Barzawayh the credit, recount his accomplishments, and cover him with glory. You should describe his mission to India under our sponsorship, and how it has benefited our kingdom over others. Describe in detail the obstacles he encountered in Persia, commend him for his deeds, and enlarge upon it all as best you can, so that Barzawayh and my subjects will be pleased with my generosity. Barzawayh deserves this tribute from me, from you, and from all the people in our Kingdom. Ensure that the lustre of this chapter exalting Barzawayh exceeds that of anything known to either the common folk or the gentry, in any genre of scholarship. You will be the happiest of all the people when you comply with my request. Let me know, and I will convoke the people of the Kingdom and you shall read it to them. Thus they will appreciate your own merits, diligence, and loyalty to me. This chapter will become your boast."

When Buzurjmihr heard the King's injunction he prostrated himself and said, "May God prolong the King's life, and elevate Him to the status of the most righteous, now and in the eternal home. The King has bestowed on me an everlasting honour."

Buzurjmihr left the King forthwith and set himself to writing the chapter. He described the life of Barzawayh from the day his father first sent him to the tutor, through his first trip to India to study the preparation of medicine, and how he learned the Indian language. He also detailed the mission to India and his quest to obtain the book of fables, *Kalilah and Dimnah*, as requested by Khusraw Anushirwan. He did not recite any credit or merit attributed to Barzawayh without enlarging upon it with elegance.

When he had finished his assignment he informed the King. Khusraw Anushirwan declared that all the nobility and their families, along with the people of his Kingdom, be invited to hear Buzurjmihr read out the book, with Barzawayh sitting at his side. They all attended the occasion. When the recitation ended, Buzurjmihr's wisdom and knowledge had pleased the King. All, from the King to the lowest, paid tribute to the Vizier and thanked him for the excellent tribute. The King rewarded him with abundant gifts and wealth, but Buzurjmihr accepted only one beautiful royal gown.

Barzawayh thanked him heartily, kissed Buzurjmihr's head, hands and face, and said to the King in gratitude:

"May God bestow on the King the utmost happiness and long life, for he has lifted me and my family to the highest levels of honour anyone might hope for, by commissioning Buzurjmihr to write my biography as my everlasting legacy to posterity."

The Paradox of Life

Barzawayh
according to Buzurjmihr ibn al-Bakhtikan

Barzawayh, the Chief Physician of Persia, who copied the book of fables, *Kalilah and Dimnah* and translated it into the Persian language from the Indian books as mentioned before, dictated all that follows here ...

My father was in the army and my mother belonged to a noble family from the Persian clan called the Al Zamazimah. I grew up in a comfortable environment. My father took extra care in my upbringing and education, and I thought I was his favourite among all my brothers. He entrusted me at the age of seven to a good tutor who taught me the art of writing, and for that I thank my parents deeply.

Then I focused on the sciences. I studied medicine, as it was my first choice. The more I learned, the more I craved to perfect my skills, and the greater effort I exerted to learn as much as there was in this fascinating field. When I first began my practice, I argued with myself which of the four objectives sought by the majority of the people I should strive to attain through my career: wealth, fame, pleasure, or peace in the eternal home? I learned from the medical books that the best physician is the one who focuses on his medicine, and pursues good deeds now to attain happiness in the life after death. I decided to become a physician so I would not be like the merchant who bartered a priceless ruby for a cheap bead. I also found out in the old medical books that a physician who follows a path that will make him happy in the eternal home, does not in any way forgo the enjoyment of this life. His state is comparable to that of the farmer who tills and prepares his land for the fruit and other useful produce and not for the grass, since a variety of wild grass will naturally grow around healthy plants in the field.

So I began my practice with the hope of attaining happiness in the next life. I treated all my patients equally, with bias towards none. My hope was always to ensure that all of them got the maximum benefit from the medication, and an even share of my time dedicated to their exclusive welfare. I harboured no ulterior motive, nor did I look for a wage or a reward for my work. I never envied any of my colleagues in the profession who were inferior to me in knowledge, but superior in prestige and wealth, or in other ways which had no bearing on anybody's health, or on my good conduct and reputation in word or in deed. I must confess that a few times, deep down in my soul, I did have a great desire to join their ranks and emulate them, but I fought these temptations fiercely, and many times scolded myself for my inward envy.

I would chide myself, saying, "Since when have you lost the ability to differentiate between what is beneficial and what is detrimental? When will you quit longing for worldly pleasures? Despite the painful labour one exerts in their pursuit, and the misery that follows their loss, the moment they are achieved they lose their satisfaction.

"O, my poor soul, don't you know yet what will follow this life after we depart? If you do, isn't that knowledge good enough to restrain you from the greedy and gluttonous attitudes you incubate? Aren't you ashamed to share such thoughts with the immoral and the ignorant, and indulge in the pleasures of this perishable world?

"Ownership of any material wealth is only an illusion. Even if it appears to be true, it will not be so for long, for death will ultimately put an end to all that we cherish. Only the misled could imagine that what they now seem to own is theirs forever. Take heed, my wretched soul, and look to your own best interests. Abandon all foolishness. Consolidate your strength and energies and follow virtue and avoid evil. Remember that by nature our body is plagued with various diseases and is full of corrupt fluids, products of life, which itself is only perishable and terminal.

"It is like a statue whose limbs are held together by one single nail. When the nail is removed everything falls apart."

I always tell my poor soul to be more sophisticated, and not to be conceited with the many friends it has, and the acquaintances that it wants to covet. Despite the pleasure and happiness it may obtain from such friendships, the painful consequences of separation will ultimately prevail. Life is like a wooden ladle; when it is new it is used to serve the soup, but when it is broken it becomes good only for firewood.

"My dear soul, do not let your family and relatives impose on you strenuous demands that you cannot easily satisfy. Otherwise, you will be like frankincense: it burns itself to extinction while producing an exquisite aroma that is enjoyed only by others. You should always think of the future life beyond this short one. Beware of the attractions of immediate pleasures lest you end up selling yourself cheap. If you do, you will be just like the foolish merchant who had a great amount of sandalwood for sale. Unwittingly he thought that if he sold the whole lot by weight, as was customary, it might take a long time to sell the batch. He stupidly decided to sell the wood in individual lots, and

based each unit's price on his haphazard estimates. He inevitably ended up selling the sandalwood at a loss."

I have seen many people—each with different opinions and quirks, each against all, surrounded by many enemies and acquaintances— whose occupation was to stab each other in the back. Each opposed the other just for the sake of being different. When I saw all this, I was sure I would not wish to seek anyone's acquaintance. For I was sure that if I believed any of them, I would surely be like the Hoodwinked Thief who believed in the unbelievable.

They tell of a Thief and his gang who decided to rob the house of a Wealthy Man. When they climbed onto the roof of the Wealthy Man's house, he woke up at the sound of their footfalls and alerted his wife. He told her to pretend she had just awakened, and ask him in a loud voice how he had accumulated his vast wealth, and to persist even if he tried to hush her.

The wife complied and demanded in a loud voice to know the story of his wealth, so that the thieves could clearly hear their dialogue.

He told her: "You know, dear wife, Destiny has brought you enormous wealth through me. So put aside anxiety, eat, drink and be merry but do not inquire about secrets which I do not want any one to know."

But she persisted, and said loudly, "You can tell me. No one is here listening to us." The thieves were listening quietly.

The Wealthy Man continued: "I will tell you. I have accumulated this great wealth through stealing. "And how did you do that?" she inquired.

He continued:

"I became very skilled in robbing others. It was so easy, and no one ever suspected me. I used to take my gang and climb onto the roofs of wealthy people. Normally I did that on nights with a full moon. We used to wait until the rays of the moonlight passed through the skylight of the house. At that moment, I would climb the moon's rays and repeat seven times a spell that I learnt: 'Sholom, Sholom.' Stealthily I would slip down the rays and into the house. No one even noticed me. I took all I could carry and returned quickly to the moon's rays, embraced them again and repeated once more, 'Sholom, Sholom,' seven times. They usually carried my gang and me back to the roof. We would all then return safely to our homes."

The thieves thought this might prove to be a very successful night, and expected to collect a lot of loot using this spell. After a decent wait, the Thief who led them embraced the moonlight passing through the skylight and recited, "Sholom, Sholom," seven times. He then let himself glide down the rays, expecting them to carry him to a smooth landing

inside the house. Instead, he found himself fallen on his head and the householder beating him with his thick club.

"Who are you?' the Wealthy Man demanded angrily.

The Hoodwinked Thief replied: "I am simply someone who was deceived by believing the unbelievable. This is the result of following an illusion."

I, too, stopped believing in the impossible, and was afraid to believe in people lest they destroy my soul. This prompted me to turn to the study of religions, and to look for justice in them. But it was all in vain. I never did find anyone who could provide me with the right answers, nor were any of the religions satisfactory to my quest. They did not attract me, or make any sense to me.

Thus, as no religion provided me with the trustworthy knowledge and satisfaction I sought, I turned again to the religion of my ancestors hoping to arrive at the right answers. But, alas, after thorough investigations I concluded that even my ancestors' religion did not satisfy my inquisitive reasoning and rational thinking. I found myself focusing merely on the investigations of religions, and arguing and scrutinizing them in vain and going nowhere.

Then suddenly I began wondering about the closeness of the end, and the immensity of death as a definite eventuality with or without the presence of any medical disorders. The thought of extinction was a frightening finality.

Fearing that I might spend my time going in many confusing vicious circles, lurching from one thought to another, I decided to avoid anything or any idea that could harm me. Killing, fighting, harming others, anger, stealing, betraying, lying, duplicity, and defaming others are abhorrent actions that must be stopped immediately. So I promised myself never to hurt anyone, and not to reject the doctrines of the awakening and resurrection after death, and the punishment and reward expected in the eternal home. I avoided evil people and attempted to mingle only with the selected and the righteous.

I found that righteousness is not equalled by any other trait, and with God's help the return on this investment should be considerable. Righteousness always points us to do well and directs us to correct decisions just as one offers good advice to a friend.

It was established long ago that righteousness is not a perishable commodity. On the contrary, it is constantly replenished. Righteousness has amazing qualities. Neither the powerful, nor even the ruler, can seize it from anyone. Water and oceans cannot drown it. Fire cannot burn it. Thieves cannot steal it. Predators among all the animals and vultures cannot ravage it.

It was also observed that a negligent and heedless person prefers a few immediate but terminal pleasures to the attainment of future but everlasting happiness. Such a person will incur an agony, similar to that which afflicted the merchant who had to pay the wage of the master craftsman for a task he never undertook.

Once upon a time a Merchant owned a unique jewel. He hired an expert Jeweller to drill a hole in it and fashion it into a valuable pendant. Both agreed on a wage of one hundred dinars. The Jeweller went to the Merchant's house to do the work. In one of the corners of the house he saw a stringed instrument called the *sunj*. The Merchant invited him to play it if he could. The Jeweller was delighted, for he was gifted in that art as well. So he played the *sunj* so beautifully that both were carried away, right up to the end of the day. As the Jeweller took his leave, he demanded his wage of a hundred dinars. The Merchant objected, "What have you done to earn your wage? You have not worked on my jewel at all.

The Jeweller replied: "I have done exactly what you ordered. I was employed by you, and whatever you requested, I obliged." He persisted in his argument until the Merchant gave in and paid him his wage. But, alas, his jewel remained intact, and not drilled or mounted as planned.

The more I reflected on the pleasures of this world, the more I restrained myself and abstained from any indulgence in them. The path of austere asceticism seemed to me the best way to prepare myself for my final end. It felt like a father carefully nourishing and developing his children to maturity. It resembled an open gate to everlasting tranquillity. An ascetic manages his affairs through abstinence and solitude, and succeeds in seasoning them with gratitude and humility. With his deep humility and profound contentment, he has no need for any extras. He is satisfied with his life; hence he worries about nothing. When he rejects worldly pleasures, he escapes from so many hazards, and purifies himself from unwarranted lust. When he abandons jealousy, love comes instantly to replace it and transforms him into an all-giving person.

By using his reason and intellect, the ascetic develops sharp insight in his actions, and frees himself from any feeling of guilt or self-reproach. He fears no one, and needs no one. Hence he secures himself safely against the harmful actions of others.

The more I became involved in asceticism the more strongly I was attracted to it. It became almost my way of life. At that point, however, I was terrified that if I decided to make it my whole life, there was no guarantee I might not weaken at some future moment. If in the meantime I refused to perform tasks that normally generate good returns to me, and are vital to my welfare in this world, I would end up with a miserable life.

Such a situation reminded me of the dog who had a bone in his mouth. One day while he was passing beside a river, he saw his reflection in the water. He plunged into the river to seize the bone that he thought he saw there. The result was that he lost the real thing he already had and found nothing in the river, as it was only an illusion. Hence, I became wary of asceticism, and fearful of the potential boredom that it would impose on me. So I decided to continue with my own life, and to live in the manner to which I was accustomed.

However, in order to satisfy my reason, it was prudent to review my situation, and to anticipate carefully the potential harm that might befall me in the future. If I have to choose any course of life, I need to compare the distress and harshness of the ascetic life with the calamities I am bound to encounter if I choose the material and worldly style of living.

My mind at that time was overwhelmed with the thought that all the pleasures of this world inevitably degrade into harm and suffering. Life in such a case resembles salt water: the more one drinks it, the thirstier he becomes. Perhaps it is also like a bare bone that retains the scent of meat. When a dog catches the bone he persistently chews it in an attempt to get the full satisfaction of finding and eating the meat in the bone, which is all gone. The dog is left with only the scent. He may gnaw until his mouth bleeds, but still find nothing to eat.

Life also reminds me of the bird called the kite, which caught a piece of meat and held it tightly in its beak. Many other birds were attracted to it and all whirled around it in an attempt to steal the morsel. The kite diligently tried to avoid them, veering in all directions until it was exhausted. Finally it gave up, and lost the piece of meat to the other birds after toiling so hard to find and catch and keep it for itself. It ended up with nothing to eat.

Life may also resemble a jug full of honey, which contains at the bottom some fatal poison. One may enjoy the sweet honey while tasting it, and may even ask for more. But, alas, one will quickly die of the poison mixed with that honey.

Life is a sweet dream, the joy of which will cease upon awakening.

As those thoughts came back to me, I chided myself again for my recklessness in wishing to attain the seductive attractions of this world. So I returned again, in my thoughts, to the prospect of attaining peace in the eternal home through abstinence and asceticism in the here-and-now. I was very disturbed by my inability to accept once and for all a path to follow. My situation looked like that of a judge who first heard the case for the plaintiff alone and judged in his favour. However, later on when he heard only the case for the defendant, also alone, he rendered judgment against the plaintiff and for the defendant.

The Dog with a bone and his reflection

But my anxiety did not stop there. Again I scrutinized the burden of asceticism and its harshness. I reflected long upon the relatively small amount of suffering required by asceticism compared to the comfort of my soul in the eternal home.

Initially I had a feeling of peace. But when I looked at the gluttonous pleasures of this life I was daunted by how much pain I must endure by forgoing them in this life. Even though it may lead to everlasting suffering and punishing sorrows, I still had an innate appetite for such pleasures.

Yet, how could a man not be attracted to the idea of bartering a few bitter moments experienced now, in order to enjoy the sweetness of a happy eternal home? How could he willingly exercise, instead, the option of enjoying a few immediate pleasures as a price for immortal suffering and perpetual pain?

I asked myself: What if a man were given a choice to live for one hundred years, provided his worldly pleasures were proportionately withdrawn, day by day. Then at the end of the hundred years, he would be cleared from all pains and face no harm forever, and would live in everlasting peace and tranquillity.

I believe that any person should truly accept such a proposal, and not even consider these years as part of his life, but as a small sacrifice relative to his total happiness in the eternal home. For how can a person be impatient with respect to a few days of austere asceticism and painful abstinence, if it will result in his everlasting peace and happiness?

It has been acknowledged everywhere that the world is made up of pain and suffering. Isn't it a fact that man starts a painful journey from the moment he is conceived to the last day of his life on this earth? Look at the facts carefully. As a baby he is afflicted with all kinds of sufferings: left unfed when hungry, unsuckled when thirsty, and not rescued when in pain. In addition, imagine the child's hardship during pregnancy, delivery, cleansing and anointing and wrapping. When laid on his back he is not at liberty to move into any direction, and sometimes suffers agony during breast-feeding. Over the following years, as he grows up, he tastes the torment of education, including the severity of teachers, the restlessness of studying, and the boredom of writing. Simultaneously, one should not forget the pain caused by fever, irritation and the pain of the various medications, and other unforeseen incidents and afflictions that he will experience while growing.

Later, upon reaching manhood, he labours to obtain and accumulate wealth. He also strives to educate his children regardless of the risks involved, while pursuing all kinds of work and exerting all types of efforts to achieve his objectives. Over the passage of time, man will

always be subjected to further physical problems and diseases related to the yellow and black bile, gases, mucous, blood, etc. He is exposed to deadly poisons and troubled with the fear of snakebites or attacks by lions and other predators, or being destroyed by other natural factors such as extreme heat and cold, torrential rain, tornadoes, and so forth. Furthermore, he will inevitably experience the different sufferings and pains of old age, if he survives that long.

Even if a person is not frightened or worried by such issues, and has no anxieties about his dismal situation, he will still worry about the hour of his death. At the time of his departure from this life he will without any doubt imagine the catastrophe that will ultimately fall upon him. Such thoughts may include the sorrow of separation from his family, his loved ones, all that was dear to him, and the thoughts of the imminent horror of death itself and beyond.

He who fails to reflect deeply upon these issues is rightly considered frivolous, and excessive in his lust for vice, and he will surely have no one else to blame but himself.

Who in his right mind, knowing the realistic facts about life, would not resort to every possible ploy that helps him prepare himself for the eternal home! Who cannot but reject whatever factors or reasons drive him to indulgence in the immediate pleasures of this world and its vanity! The case becomes more serious particularly at this age and time, when life appears to be tranquil while in reality it is troubled.

It may happen that we find a king who is firm and prudent and enjoys great capabilities, such as superior judgment and far-reaching insight. He may also be just, honest, grateful, and a keeper of promises. He may be generous and caring towards his people, and persistent in providing them with an adequate level of welfare. In addition, he may know his subjects well and understand the issues that are close to their hearts. He may encourage them to pursue more knowledge, condone good actions, and praise the generous and reward the scrupulous. Perhaps the King himself is also firm in punishing the oppressors, courageous in his decisions, and is a strong leader who grants his subjects with generosity, and defends them against all harm.

However, we might just as reasonably see our world through other eyes that see all honest actions and sound doctrines eradicated from among the people. Life then is lopsided. What was ample in the past has become scant. The few defects that were harmful to society, then, have festered and flourished and become rampant today.

Goodness is dwindling and evil thrives. Perception and comprehension would seem to have lost their bearings. Right disintegrates and disappears and is invariably replaced by destructive falsehood.

Rulers of today are occupied by lust and gluttony, and are adept at losing their authority over their dominions. The oppressed today accept and submit to injustice, while the unjust enjoy the long reach of their oppression and wrongful acts. Greed and avarice prevail and are like an insatiable predator whose jaws are agape and ready to swallow whatever moves past.

Contentment is a stranger in this land and an unknown quality among the people of today. Evil people and wrongdoers seem bound for heaven, while the good and the just appear to be heading towards hell.

The qualities of chivalry and magnanimity are rejected and the lofty and lowly together slander those who begot and cherish them. Instead, baseness and contemptible deeds are more honoured and are successful in attaining a better life nowadays. Authority and power are transferred from the shoulders of the respectable and prestigious to those of the ignoble and inferior.

The world seems to react with pleasure and happiness, rejoicing at this lopsided state of affairs, as if approvingly crying with ecstasy that "The good is vanquished and evil now reigns."

Consequently, I delved further in my thoughts and pondered more deeply about this world and in the various troubles that arise. I recognized that the human being is the noblest of its creatures and the most efficient. However, he seems to be always in harm's way and is overwhelmed by incessant anxieties. Hence I wondered with awe why rational people who know about their worries still refrain from employing their faculties in finding rational solutions, which could assist them in attaining their salvation.

Then suddenly I discovered that the reason for such a failure lies in a relatively few and base set of pleasures originating in and transmitted by the senses of smell, taste, sight, hearing, and touch. Hoping that he may attain even the minutest portion of such pleasures, man carelessly indulges himself to the fullest in their attainment, neglecting and paying no attention to any plan that could save him and his soul in the future.

I found the perfect fable that could describe man's predicament in this life.

A Man was fleeing from an enraged and violent Elephant, found a Well, and decided to hide in it. He dangled from two branches growing out of the shaft. Suddenly his feet felt a strange body clinging to the sides of the well. He looked down cautiously, and to his horror he saw four Snakes poking their fearsome heads out of their nests in the walls. Peering deeper into the darkness, he saw at the bottom a terrifying Dragon with its mouth agape, ready to ravage its prey. When he turned his eyes upward he saw, to his further dismay, two Rats, one black and the other white, determinedly gnawing on the two branches that kept him from falling. Amid all these dangers, a nearby beehive containing natural Honey suddenly caught his attention. He tasted it and found it quite delicious. He continued tasting the sweet Honey and wanting more of it. But while enjoying it, his attention was naturally distracted from the real and imminent dangers awaiting him, and how he might escape.

His attention was diverted from the four Snakes who might fatally bite him, and the two Rats, Black and White, gnawing on the roots that alone held him from falling into the mouth of the Dragon.

The seductive taste of the Honey thus prolonged his distraction from these mortal hazards long enough for him to fall to his ghastly death in the Dragon's mouth.

The fable is clear. The Well is a figure of this world, which is full of hazards and dangers, anxieties, handicaps and obstacles. The four Snakes are analogous to the four natural elements that are mixed in a fine balance in the human body. If any one is distempered, it will destabilize the human body with deadly results, just like the deadly poison concealed in a snakebite. The two Branches evoke the limited term of one's life on this earth, which is a sure eventuality. As for the Black and White Rats, they reflect the night and day which will incessantly and regularly alternate, and thus will slowly but surely consume man's term on this earth. The Dragon is the final destination of man. No one can ever escape from his final moment of death. The Honey however, resembles the minute pleasures of this life. Through his senses he may eat, hear, smell and touch and be absorbed by temporary joys. But he may also forget himself, and his more lofty objectives, thus creating unwarranted obstacles that will hinder him from achieving his real purpose in life. The results could be most serious, with profoundly detrimental consequences.

All of these different thoughts were agonizingly and confusingly mixed in my mind.

Consequently I decided to be safely content with myself and my normal behaviour. My intention then was set on doing my best to reform and perform my earthly responsibilities efficiently. Furthermore, I hoped that I might be guided to do the right things, control my will, respect myself, and develop and acquire the ways and means which will render myself adequate support, to strengthen my situation now, as well as in the eternal home.

So I stayed in India for a while and successfully copied many books full of wisdom. Then, as soon as I finished copying the book of fables *Kalilah and Dimnah*, my mission was successfully accomplished, and I left India for Persia.

The Lion and the Bull

Chapter One

The Fable of
the Lion and the Bull

(Jealousy turns friendship to animosity)

Dabshalim the King addressed Baydaba the Philosopher: "Provide me with a fable that describes how intimate friendship is turned into animosity and hatred through interference by the crafty and the untruthful."

Baydaba replied, "If two dear friends are subverted by the crafty and the untruthful, their bond will ultimately be severed and destroyed. The following is a clear example ...

Once upon a time there was a sage living in Dastawand, in Persia. He had three sons who lacked the skills to earn their own living, and were consuming their father's wealth instead. One day the sage summoned his sons and admonished them for their shiftlessness. This is what he told them:

"My sons, earthly goals are of three kinds, and can be achieved by only four means. The three goals are to accumulate wealth, to raise one's status, and to prepare for the eternal home.

"The first of the four means is to earn income through honest work. The second is sound economic management of income. The third is its effective investment. The fourth is to spend one's wealth on wholesome, comfortable living, and on family and friends, in a way that would contribute positively to one's eternal home.

"Whoever fails to utilize these means will not reach his goals. For if a person does not work, he will have no wealth to sustain his life. If a person works and earns a handsome living, but does not manage his wealth well, it will dwindle and leave him a pauper. If he keeps his wealth dormant and fails to invest it properly, it offers false security because it will lose its value. It will be like kohl: only a tiny amount of powdery eyeshadow clings to the stick, and the rest is wasted. If he spends his wealth in the wrong cause, or unreasonably squanders it, a similar poverty awaits him. Furthermore, unforeseen disasters and diseases that come his way will inevitably deplete his wealth. It is just like a water tank. If water continues to pour into the tank without an outlet, pressure will gradually increase and burst the tank, and all will be lost."

Hearing what their father said, the three sons took his message to heart, and appreciated the benefit of his advice. They deeply regretted their previous indolence and decided to change their lives accordingly.

The eldest son, who was a merchant, migrated with some of his companions to a region called Mayun. He travelled in a cart drawn by two bulls; one was called Shatrabah; the other, Bandabah.

After they had gone a considerable distance, the cart became mired in a muddy ditch. He and his companions tried to extricate the cart and the bulls from the mud, and managed to free everything but Shatrabah the Bull, who was hopelessly mired. When it seemed impossible to free the Bull, the eldest son decided to go on. He left one of his companions there to guard it in hopes that when the mud dried, Shatrabah could climb out. However, the man guarding the Bull grew weary. Fearful of being alone in the strange place, he left Shatrabah the Bull and rejoined his companions.

He told them the Bull had died, and said: "If one's days on this earth reach their end, and one's hour of death has arrived, there is no way one can escape that Destiny. On the contrary, one should accept his Destiny and not to try to avoid it, for his struggles may confound him all the more. He might end up like the Man who was wandering in a dangerous wilderness, aware that it contained various wild and hungry predators."

Suddenly a ferocious Wolf attacked him. He looked left and right, and spied a village ahead of him, just across a valley. He ran towards it as fast as he could. Since there was no bridge over the river he dived in and tried to make his way across to the village, but unfortunately he could not swim. Had it not been for one of the villagers who rescued him, he surely would have drowned.

By the time the Man regained his breath and his wits, the Wolf had evidently given up. Setting off again down the valley the Man saw a lonely house where he thought he might rest awhile. But when he entered the house he was surprised to find a gang of robbers who had just seized a merchant and were about to kill him and divide his money. Fearing for his own life, the Man dashed out and fled towards the village.

By the time he arrived there, he was exhausted. He sat down by a wall, hoping to have a few minutes to recover from exhaustion and fright. Unfortunately, an old fissure in the wall gave way at just that moment, collapsed, and killed him on the spot.

The merchant's son replied, "I believe you, for I have heard the story before!"

As for Shatrabah the Bull, he eventually managed to clamber out of the dangerous ditch, and settled down beside a fertile field provided with grass and water. Shortly after the companion guarding him departed, his strength and energy returned, and he began bellowing loudly and happily.

It happened that the field was on the outskirts of a forest full of predators, including wolves, jackals, foxes, leopards and tigers. Their unchallenged leader was a large Lion, the King of that part of the forest. He was an absolute monarch, highly opinionated and not inclined to solicit anyone else's views. The Lion heard the strange bellow of the Bull, and could not identify it or imagine what it could be. He had never heard the bellow of a bull, nor seen one before. He had never ventured beyond his domain, nor did he even hunt or labour for his daily bread. His food and prey was always fetched and served to him by his soldiers, the other predators.

Among the beasts in the domain of this Lion King were two Jackals. They were very knowledgeable in the arts and sciences, and quite shrewd and crafty as well. One of the two brothers was called Kalilah, and the other Dimnah.

The Jackal Dimnah asked his brother Kalilah, "My brother, why is it that our King the Lion does not roam beyond his immediate domain, and is never active?"

Kalilah answered in a warning tone: "What is it to you, Dimnah? This is none of your concern. We are in the Court of a King. We will defer to his whims, doing what he likes and avoiding what he dislikes. We are not of the same level as the gentry who belong to the social class of the kings, and can freely fraternize with them. So please refrain from such discussions and take note that those who comment on or meddle with matters that do not concern them may not emerge unscathed. If you take to heart the Fable of the Monkey who was beaten by the Carpenter, you may understand my point."

Dimnah inquired, "How does the story go?"

Kalilah began as follows: "Once upon a time a Monkey observed how a Carpenter was sawing a log of wood and forcing two wedges into the cleft as he sawed. Meanwhile he was standing on the very log he was splitting. The Monkey liked what he saw and waited for an opportunity to join in. One day the Carpenter left his workshop to take care of some errands. The Monkey, who had no business being in the Carpenter's shop, mounted the log as the Carpenter had. But he mistakenly let his tail flop into the split of the log. The Monkey then pulled out the wedges, and the two halves snapped together on his tail, causing the most excruciating pain. When the Carpenter returned and saw what had happened he became enraged. He began to beat the Monkey fiercely with his stout staff, and the pain from the staff was even worse than the pain from the log."

نجار

قرد

The Monkey and the Carpenter

Dimnah replied: "I listened to your story and I understand it. But you should know that not all who approach kings do so for selfish motives. Some approach them to obtain favours that help their friends or restrain their enemies. Those who lack high station in this world may be content with whatever they may have, and modest additional boons: like a dog that is pleased with a dry bone. But the noble-hearted and chivalrous will not be so easily satisfied, for they have high aspirations. They are like the lion that has just caught a hare but will toss it aside to chase a camel, not like a dog who wags his tail continuously ... for a scrap of bread. Notice the eating habits of the mighty elephant: he will consume his fodder only after he receives a large helping of attention and flattery.

"Whoever has wealth and is generous to himself, his family, and his friends will be remembered for a longer time after his death. But one who lives in hardship and misery, and is unable to spend adequately on himself or his relatives, is better dead than alive. However, someone who works selfishly only to satisfy his basic desires and needs, is not very different from a mere beast."

Kalilah then said: "I grasp your point. But think further. Everyone has a certain status and dignity. If a person is settled in his position and status, he should be content with it. That will not compromise the prestige and dignity that he enjoys."

Dimnah answered: "Every person does indeed enjoy a certain level of status and prestige, and might as well be content with it. We have no reason to believe that our social position will bring us disgrace."

Dimnah replied: "Positions and status are the focus of strong competition that is very much related to magnanimity of character. A person's magnanimity may elevate him from a lowly position, but the reverse is also true: those who are not magnanimous may fall from exalted heights to the pit of ignominy. One rises to a high and honorable status with great effort; falling is so much easier. A person may find it difficult to heft a heavy stone onto his shoulder, but letting it fall to the ground is no strain at all. For us, the ambition to excel is highly appreciated. Why should anyone be content with the level where he finds himself, if the opportunity to pursue higher ambitions is wide open?"

Kalilah replied, "I understand. So now, tell me what your plans are."

Dimnah said, "I will find a way to meet the Lion at an opportune time and befriend him. The Lion, you know, has his weaknesses. If I approach him he might grant me a lucrative position. Then I will enjoy the status and influence I crave."

Kalilah asked, "Why do you assume that the Lion is as pliable as you claim?"

Dimnah replied, "Through my senses and my insight. I just know it. A person with sharp insight can understand the condition of a friend or an acquaintance, and sense deeper traits that do not show on the surface."

Kalilah rejoined, "And how do you plan to have access to the Lion when he is not even your friend yet? You don't have any experience or knowledge of how to behave in the presence of a king."

Dimnah stressed the point: "A strong and durable man will not be deterred from carrying heavy loads even if he is not accustomed to do so. But a weak person will not even try to shoulder such loads, even when it is his duty to do so."

Kalilah then said to Dimnah: "The King's dignity may not permit him to fraternize beyond his social circle. He will naturally befriend those who are familiar. It is said that a King is like the vine that clasps and climbs the nearest tree. So, how would you plan to find favour with the Lion, who has never even heard of you?"

Dimnah replied, "I take your point; you are correct. However, you should also realize that one who is close to the King but lacks the qualities appropriate to that position or status, is at a greater disadvantage than someone determined to gain access to the Court who lacks only experience at that level. Through persistence, such a person can manage to win the King's respect. In any case, I promise you that I will succeed. I will attain the status and position of the nobility through my own efforts. For it was also said, 'Only those who forego their pride, endure harm and injury, and restrain their anger, are kind to others, respect their confidence, consort with kings, and fulfill their ambitions.'"

Kalilah said, "Suppose you succeed and gain a hearing from the King. What chance do you have of gaining his favour and obtaining the position you hope for?"

Dimnah replied: "If I study him and take enough time to understand his behaviour, then I assure you I will manage well, and he shall like me. I will appease, rather than oppose him. Whatever he thinks is right, I will make it look even better, and appreciate the results, and cheer him on. I will make sure that he is pleased with whatever he chooses to do.

"On the other hand, if he makes a poor decision I will identify his mistake and its consequences, and point out why it should be reversed, as best I can. The more effective I become, the more my credit with the Lion will rise. He will see in me what others lack. A refined and knowledgeable man can easily justify an illicit act and discredit a rightful one. A skilful artist can paint a scene on the wall that appears in high relief, then paint the same scene to appear engraved. The methods are contrary; but the artistry and appeal are the same."

Kalilah was disturbed: "Nevertheless I am worried about you, and afraid for your safety. The company of kings is risky. Scholars warn us of the three things that only imprudent people risk, and rarely with impunity. One is the friendship of kings. Another is entrusting women with secrets. The third is drinking poison to test its strength. Scholars also compare kings to a mountain too difficult to climb. It may offer delicious fruit, precious stones, and plants with useful medicinal powers. Yet it is also a place full of lions, tigers, wolves and many harmful predators. It is too difficult to climb, and even more difficult to inhabit."

Dimnah answered: "I grant you that. But it is known that whoever refuses great challenges will never claim valuable rewards. Whoever backs away from satisfying his ambition for fear of risk will not go far in this life. It was also said in the past that three matters cannot be achieved except through persistence, strength, and daunting challenges: first, the duties and responsibilities of a king; second, the art of sea-faring; third, combating an enemy. Scholars also taught that the most challenging human endeavours are to enjoy the grace and company of kings, and to worship with monks. This reminds me of the elephant, whose beauty and splendour are manifested in either of two places: in the wild, or as a mount for kings."

Acquiescing to Dimnah, Kalilah said, "May God provide you with all the assistance you may require to pursue your quest."

Dimnah then watched for his opportunity, and approached the Lion while he was sitting amid his Companions. He saluted him. The Lion asked one of his acquaintances, sitting beside him:

"Who is this?"

"He is Dimnah, the son of someone we know."

The Lion then said, "Yes, I used to know his father."

Looking at Dimnah, he asked him, "And what of you?"

Dimnah answered: "I have been waiting outside the King's gate for a long time, watching and hoping that one day he might notice me, and assign me a task whereby I can earn my way. I know there are many responsibilities in the King's Court that require an unimportant person to perform them. Thus even the most unimportant person may be of some use. Even an uninteresting stick that is thrown on the ground and left to rot may one day prove useful, and be picked up by a passer-by to save for a future need."

The Lion listened to Dimnah's reply, and liked it. He thought that Dimnah might have opinions or advice that could be of some use to him.

The Lion turned to his guests and said: "A magnanimous and knowledgeable man may have a humble status and thus be unknown. His real status, however, may be quite honourable, and his potential might claim respect. Thus he could enhance his rank by his performance and raise his prestige to the level he deserves. He could be like fire, which reaches upward to the sky despite attempts to beat it down."

When Dimnah realized the Lion was pleased, he said, "The King summons his Companions to Court in order to draw on their considerable knowledge. It may be said, however, that excellence is manifest in two ways. The first is the excellence of a fighter facing an opponent. The second is the excellence of a single scholar surrounded by others.

"Too many inexperienced aides could prove counterproductive. Success at work may depend, not on the number of administrators and assistants, but on their quality. One thinks of a man who exhausts himself unearthing a terribly heavy rock, only to find it has no value at the market. A person interested in studying the trunk of a tree finds all the branches around it a bother. Therefore the King is right not to despise the gracious qualities found in a man who may be of lowly status. Such a commoner, once given the opportunity, might come up with great achievements. He may be very much like the nerve that is plucked out of a dead body and strung into a bow, thus becoming valuable. The bow is vital to the King for sport, and in the battlefield as well."

Dimnah wanted the group to know that the Lion King had honoured him for his gallantry, knowledge and judgment, and not simply because he had known Dimnah's father, as he said. So he went on: "A king does not recruit persons for his court just because he previously knew their fathers, nor does he exclude them because he did not. He scrutinizes everyone.

"The closest thing to a man is his body. Yet the body is often infected with harmful illnesses that can be cured only by a medicine brought from afar.".

The Lion King was much taken by what he heard from Dimnah, and presented him with many gifts. The King then addressed his Court and said: "A king should not persist in trampling the rights of his people, for they may be divided into two types. The first type is belligerent, like a poisonous snake: it may not strike the first time it is stepped on, but the deadly bite will surely come if he is stepped on again. The second type of person is simple, and resembles sandalwood. If it is subjected to prolonged friction it will become hot enough to burn anyone who touches it."

Over time, Dimnah became a trusted friend of the Lion. One day when they were alone, Dimnah asked him: "I have observed that the King remains at home and shows no interest in going out. Is there some reason for this?"

While he waited for an answer, the loud cry of a bellowing Bull suddenly rang through the forest. The Lion was uneasy but would not

طبل

ثعلب

The Fox and the Drum

admit it to Dimnah. Dimnah, however, understood that the bellowing of the Bull had made the Lion fearful and tense.

Dimnah asked the Lion: "Is the King fearful of the sound he heard?"

The Lion replied: "I have never been more afraid."

Dimnah said: "A king should never give ground merely because of a sound like that! Scholars in the past confirmed that not all sounds should cause real fright."

The Lion asked for a fable to illustrate such a statement. Dimnah obliged:

Once upon a time a Fox was wandering through the thick forest. It happened that someone had left a huge Drum hanging on a tree. Every time the wind blew, the branches of the tree swung and beat the Drum, which produced a great throb, heard throughout the forest. The throb of the drum attracted the Fox, who approached it inquisitively. When the Fox saw the enormous size of the Drum, he was sure that it contained a lot of meat and fat for him to feast on. So he set upon it energetically and tore it open. To his surprise he found it empty. So he said to himself: "Perhaps the bigger the body, and the louder the sound, the more empty it is."

"I offered the King this example that he might know that this seemingly frightening sound could prove less significant than supposed, once we get closer and understand it. Therefore, if it please the King, I will go and investigate the sound and its source, and will report back. There will be no need for the King to leave his home."

The Lion agreed and permitted Dimnah the Jackal to go and investigate the strange sound. But after Dimnah had left, the Lion regretted his decision. He thought: "I may have made a mistake in sending Dimnah away to investigate. He first appeared loitering outside my Court, ambitious for an opportunity. One must be cautious of anyone who waits so long outside the Court of the King, without a summons or a complaint in his hand. He might simply be an opportunist looking for help. Or a criminal facing punishment and trying to obtain my mercy. He might be a plotter trying to turn the King's harm to his advantage. He could be a friend of the King's enemies, and therefore an enemy to the King's friends. Such people are always suspect, and I should have been more wary. I engaged Dimnah without testing his reliability. After all that waiting at our gate, he might have become resentful enough to deceive me and help my enemies. He may well find that whoever is out there bellowing with the strange voice is stronger then I, and be lured into joining forces against me."

The Lion anxiously left his palace and paced back and forth. He relaxed, however, when he saw Dimnah approaching, and asked nervously: "What have you seen, and what have you done?"

Dimnah calmly said, "I found the Bull who was bellowing so loudly in that strange voice."

The Lion then wanted to know, "How strong is he?"

Dimnah answered, "The King should not worry. The Bull has no might at all. I tested him in many ways, and wrangled with him, but he was no match for me!"

The Lion said, "Do not be fooled by what you see, and underestimate no one. For the mighty wind normally passes over the weak weeds, and then destroys the huge palms and other large trees."

Dimnah countered: "The King should not be afraid of him, nor exaggerate. I shall bring him to Court and he shall be the King's loyal servant."

The Lion King said, "Go ahead, then."

Dimnah rushed back to Shatrabah the Bull and addressed him fearlessly, "The Lion has sent me to bring you to him, and ordered me to tell you that if you submit and come to pay allegiance to the Lion willingly, he will guarantee your safety in his presence, and forgive you for failing to visit him until now. But if you refuse, then I shall have to leave you here and inform him of your decision."

Shatrabah asked Dimnah, "Who is this Lion who sent you to me with this message? Where is he, and how would you describe him?"

Dimnah replied, "He is the King of the Beasts, and he lives close by. He has a huge army of his own kinfolk."

Shatrabah was terrified at the mention of lions and predators. He told Dimnah, "If you swear to ensure my safety, I shall come with you."

Dimnah promised, and asked the Bull to trust in him. So they left together for the Lion's Court.

It happened that the Lion took an instant liking to Shatrabah the Bull and received him graciously and respectfully. He asked him, "When did you arrive in this country? And what brought you here?"

Shatrabah told the Lion his story. The Lion then requested Shatrabah in a very amiable way: "Stay with me and do not leave me. I will always honour and respect you." The Bull thanked and complimented him.

As time passed, the Bull's prestige and standing with the Lion increased to the highest levels. He quickly became the confidential friend of the Lion, his bearer of secrets, and his trustworthy advisor. Each day, the Lion's admiration of his friend the Bull deepened, until he became truly his closest Companion.

Envy then began to gnaw at Dimnah. He saw how quickly the Bull had attained the highest status, though so recently an unknown stranger. Dimnah fell victim to acute resentment and pain. One day he poured out all his frustrations to his brother Kalilah: "Don't you ever wonder, my brother, about how I have changed lately? How misguided I was to devote all my care and concern to Lion, while I neglected myself! I have allowed the Bull to befriend the Lion, and now he has become more prestigious and closer to him than I.

Kalilah asked, "What do you plan to do?"

Dimnah said, "I am not so much concerned about rising higher in the Lion's confidence, but I would like to reclaim the position I already enjoyed. A rational person should look into three matters, and attempt diligently to learn from them. First, he should review past events and distinguish the useful from the harmful. He should learn from the harmful so that he will not repeat it, and accept the useful as a good example for the future. Second, he should preserve the useful lessons of the present and evade the harmful ones. Third, he should construct a plan how to achieve the useful and avoid the harmful.

"When I considered what might help restore me to my previous status, and pondered the reasons for my failure, I resolved to have this grass-chewer, the Bull, eliminated. That is the only way to regain my position with the Lion. It may also serve the Lion well, since his excessive friendship with the Bull is odd and possibly compromising."

Kalilah tried to reason with Dimnah: "I do not see any harm coming to the Lion from his friendship with the Bull, nor is the prestige and status that the Bull enjoys creating any risk."

Dimnah grudgingly replied: "There are six things that might weaken a ruler and make him dangerously vulnerable. These are isolation, temptation, dissipation, brutality, time, and stupidity.

"Isolation leads one to ignore wise aides, advisors and politicians, and to keep others who enjoy insight, courage and honesty from participating in the decision-making process, thus barring them from providing the ruler with their sincere and experienced insight. Unworthy opportunists will take their place, and weaker policy will result.

"Temptation is the source of feuds that end up turning allies into enemies.

"Dissipation is a weakness for carousing, gossip, entertainment, drinking, hunting, and the like.

"Brutality is the unrestrained use of excessive force, which tempts one to forego the patience and self-control needed to avoid conflict.

"As a ruler ages and draws near death, he is inclined to be improvident about resources, or to rely on raids to compensate for them.

"Stupidity inclines a ruler to resort to leniency when force is required, and vice versa.

"The Lion is definitely infatuated with the Bull and that will expose him to shame and harm."

Kalilah replied, "How can you now rival the Bull when he is stronger than you, more honoured by the Lion, and has more supporters in the Court?"

Dimnah answered: "Do not let my size or my seeming disadvantage deceive you. Success has little to do with weakness or strength, or the relative size of one's body. Through careful planning and cunning many small and weak creatures have achieved more than the stronger ones. Haven't you heard of the weak Crow who craftily tricked and killed the poisonous Black Viper?"

"How does the story go?" Kalilah inquired.

Dimnah obliged:

Once upon a time a Crow lived in an eyrie on a tree atop a mountain. Nearby lived a Black Viper. Every time the Crow's eggs hatched, the Black Viper ate them. This greatly distressed the Crow, who complained to her friend the Jackal.

"I need your advice," she told him.

"About what?" the Jackal asked.

"I intend to sneak up on the Black Viper while he is asleep, and peck his eyes out. Perhaps then I can live in peace," the Crow said firmly.

The Jackal responded in a concerned voice: "Your strategy is all wrong. You should indeed have your way with the Black Viper, but without any risk to yourself. Never emulate the Drake who attempted to kill a Crab and ended up killing himself instead."

"How does the story go?" asked the Crow.

The Jackal proceeded to tell the story:

Once upon a time a Drake lived happily in the jungle next to a creek rich in fish. As time passed and he aged, the Drake became feebler, until he could no longer catch his daily ration of fish. Starving and weary, he sat pondering one day how he might ease his situation. A Crab happened to pass by, and saw him depressed and frustrated. "Why are you so depressed and sad?" he asked the Drake, who gave this response:

How can I not be depressed after what happened today? I overheard some fishermen talking to each other. One of them said he had seen many more fish in another creek at the far side of the jungle than in this one. His fellow fishermen replied that they ought to fish there first, and come back here only after they have a full catch from the

The Drake and the Crab

other creek. If that happens, you can appreciate that I will definitely die of starvation.

The Crab scurried over to the other creek and warned the schools of Fish there what to expect. A group of Fish decided to meet with the Drake and discuss the matter with him. At that meeting, they said, "We come to you for advice, for we believe that in situations like this, it is reasonable to take counsel even with the enemy."

The Drake said, "If I were you, I could not tolerate the threat of the fishermen, nor could I overcome them. I see no alternative for you but to move to some other creek nearby, one where the water runs high and is bordered by thick reeds. If you agree, I will ferry you there to safety. You will thereby do yourselves a favour, for you can multiply light-heartedly and swiftly in the new environment."

The entire fish population agreed to the Drake's proposal. The scheme worked very well for him. Every day he collected two Fish, but instead of placing them in the creek as agreed, he flew into the nearby hills and ate them. This went on for some time.

One day, while the Drake was on the way to get his two Fish, the Crab stopped him and said: "I too am bored and lonely in this place. Why don't you take me to the new creek?"

The Drake obliged. He picked him up him and flew over to the hill where he had eaten all the fish. The Crab looked around and saw a heap of fish bones. He immediately recognized the trick, and understood what the Drake had been doing all along. But he also realized his own danger: the Drake intended to eat him as well. So he thought: "If one finds himself facing death, he has nothing to lose by resisting, if only to satisfy his pride and honour."

So the Crab suddenly clamped his strong, biceps-like arms on the neck of the Drake, and squeezed hard and long until the Drake fell dead. The Crab then scurried back to the remaining Fish in the creek and told them all that had happened.

The Jackal then continued his explanation to the Crow: "I told you this fable simply to make you aware that sometimes a scheme can be self-defeating. Now, then, I will show you a way in which, if carefully followed, you can kill the Black Viper without risk, and ensure your own safety."

"How do I go about it?" the Crow queried.

The Jackal then explained: "Scan the countryside carefully until you are lucky enough to find some piece of lady's jewellery. Snatch it up and continue flying in a very conspicuous way, so that all the people notice you. Carry on until you find the viper's hole, and then drop the piece of jewellery into it. When the people see the jewellery fall to the ground they will all rush to retrieve it. I can assure you that in the process, and without any prompting, they will get rid of the Viper once and for all."

The Crow followed the Jackal's instruction. He flew at low range in circles, searching for the right target. Suddenly he saw a rich woman bathing on a rooftop with her necklace and clothing laid aside. The Crow dived down, snatched the necklace, and flew back into the sky at a height where all the people down below could see him. The people who had seen the incident ran after the Crow until he dropped the necklace into the Black Viper's hole. They rushed over to retrieve it, and in doing so they had to kill the Black Viper as well.

Dimnah the Jackal continued his justifications to Kalilah: "I have recounted these fables to let you know that when strength fails, one can still reach his goals by shrewd planning."

Kalilah then said: "Yes, but the Bull is not simply strong. He is also determined, and he has a good brain. So how can you manage to overcome him?"

Dimnah answered: "True, the Bull has those other qualities, but he rightly owes me respect, gratitude and trust. Believe me, I will have his life, just like the Hare who managed to kill the Lion."

"How does the story go?" Kalilah inquired."

Dimnah explained:

Once upon a time there was a very fertile land, rich enough in streams and pastureland for all the beasts and animals living there to enjoy an adequate life. But they had no peace, for they lived in unsettling fear of a right fierce Lion in the neighbourhood. One day, all the beasts met together with the Lion to discuss the situation. This was their proposal: "We realize that you spend your time hunting, and appreciate how much labour and exhaustion it must cost you. We want to put forth a suggestion that may benefit us all. If you offer us your solemn oath that you will not attack us, but let us live in peace, we promise to deliver to your den, every day, an animal for you to feed on to your satisfaction."

The Lion agreed with the beasts, and all parties honoured their undertakings. It happened, however, that one day a Hare drew the crucial lot and realized it was his turn to be served to the Lion. The Hare then appealed to the rest of the beasts: "If you could have the kindness to be patient with me, I will rid you of the Lion for good."

The beasts asked, "What would you like us to do?"

The Hare replied, "Please order the beast responsible for my delivery to the Lion's den to take his time, so that we arrive late."

They agreed to that. The Hare then began walking towards the

The Lion, the Beasts and the Hare

Lion's den, but daringly and deliberately he slowed his pace. As planned, he arrived late for the Lion's normal lunchtime. While the Hare proceeded, slowly and alone, the Lion had become desperately hungry and burning with rage. When he did see the Hare, the Lion charged him and shouted angrily, "Where did you come from?"

The Hare replied: "I am the beasts' messenger. They sent me with another rabbit for your lunch as agreed. Alas, another lion stalked us and seized the rabbit, and then arrogantly said to me, 'In this land, I alone have the priority over all beasts.' I explained, 'Please, this is the King's lunch, which the beasts entrusted to me for delivery. I beg you not to annoy him.' When the lion heard that, he cursed you and your ancestors. I hastened here to give you the bad news."

The Lion angrily ordered the Hare: "Come with me and show me this insolent lion."

The Hare took the Lion to a deep cistern, full of clear water, and told him his adversary lived there, and that he need only peer into the cistern to see him. The Lion saw both his own reflection and that of the rabbit, and believed the story. He plunged into the cistern to attack and kill the new competitor, but drowned instead. The Hare lost no time running back to the beasts to recount what had happened, which meant they were now free to live without fear.

Kalilah then replied, "If you could kill the Bull without hurting the Lion, then that would be your business, since I too believe that the Bull has harmed me, and you, and the Lion as well, and many others of the King's soldiers. But if you cannot kill the Bull without harming the Lion, you should refrain from it since this would amount to a betrayal by both of us."

Dimnah agreed, made his decision, and began to implement his scheme. For several days he abstained from visiting the Lion in his Court. Then, while the Lion was sitting by himself, Dimnah sheepishly approached him. The Lion asked: "What kept you away so long? I hope it was something profitable."

Dimnah replied, "I suppose so. At least I hope it was good, though one can never tell."

The Lion suspected something and inquired, "What happened?"

Dimnah replied, "What happened is something that I do not believe the King or any of his Companions and soldiers expects to occur!"

The Lion insisted, "What was it?"

Dimnah said, "Atrocious talk, O King."

"Tell me!" the Lion demanded.

Dimnah then told him: Here, then, are words that are abhorrent to whoever hears them, and do not bear repeating. The King is a gracious King. I am sure the King realizes how painful it is for me to repeat what he may hate to hear. But I also trust his sound judgment and confidence in my advice. I assure the King that his safety and welfare, as far as I am concerned, comes well before mine. It has occurred to me, however, that he may not believe what I am about to tell him. Yet when I reflect how dependent our lives as beasts are upon the King, I have no other alternative but honestly and truly to serve him. Whether or not he asks my advice, or I fear he will reject it, let me remind the King of what our elders confirmed in the past, namely, that 'Whoever withholds his advice from the King and his opinion from his Companions, will definitely betray himself.'"

The Lion asked: "Tell me immediately what it is you have learned."

Dimnah continued in his sly manner: "The King should know that a very trustworthy friend informed me that Shatrabah the Bull met with some of his military officers and spoke as follows: 'I have observed the Lion carefully, and now I understand very well his policies, capabilities, and strength. It is clear to me now that they are based on real weakness and frailty. Soon he and I will have to confront each other and I will show you his real mediocrity.'

"When I heard this, I was convinced that Shatrabah was a deceitful traitor. Despite the King's generosity and respect towards him, and his special treatment of him as a royal peer, he has started to believe that he actually is the King's equal and that if the King is deposed he will succeed to the throne. It is through the King that he would achieve his ambition.

"But our elders in the past believed that if someone else becomes as strong or as prestigious as oneself, particularly the King, then one should promptly kill him; otherwise he himself will be slain. Shatrabah has become widely knowledgeable, very eloquent, and skilful in all of our public affairs. A sensible person will forestall trouble before it arrives. It is true that one can never be sure when troubles will come, but equally true that one is never sure of overcoming them when they do.

"It was said in the past that there are three types of men: the decisive, the more decisive, and the indecisive. The decisive man is not surprised when trouble comes, and will not lose heart or be overwhelmed by fear. He will always have alternate plans and methods to cope with his troubles. The more decisive man has the insight to foresee the timing and the gravity of troubles in advance. He will then focus on them, and devise ways to cope when the trouble occurs. In fact, he will keep the medicine at hand before the onset of the disease, and so eliminate it before an outbreak. As for the indecisive person, he is the one who cannot act in crisis. He wastes his time on whimsical hopes that things might not happen, but when they do, whatever solutions he may think of will be too late to implement. This resembles the fable of 'The Three Fish'."

The Lion asked, "In what way?"

Dimnah continued:

Once upon a time a school of three Fish lived in a creek. They were called the Canny, the Cannier, and the Uncanny Fish [?? 'Wise', etc, – a lot of fish end up in cans!]. The creek was located on high ground and very few knew of its existence. It emptied nearby into a small river.

It happened one day that two fishermen were passing by, saw the creek, and agreed that they would return soon with their nets to fish extensively there. The fish overheard their conversation.

The Cannier Fish feared that the danger was imminent and that she would be caught, so she left the creek immediately and swam through its mouth into the nearby river.

The Canny Fish waited until the fishermen came. Seeing what they were about to do, she attempted to escape through the mouth of the creek into the river just like her friend, but she was too late. The fishermen had already closed that exit. She then thought, "I was negligent, and here I am now in this awkward situation. How shall I escape, knowing as I do that hasty moves in emergencies rarely succeed? Still, someone with good sense and a good mind should be optimistic, and always think positively and logically." She then pretended she was dead, and floated to the surface. The fishermen took her out and placed her in their creel where the creek opened into the river. At just the right moment, when she was quite close to the water, she surprised the fishermen, jumped into the river, and also escaped.

As for the Uncanny Fish, she swam frantically back and forth in the creek without direction or plan, and was finally caught due to her inability to foresee danger and failure to act promptly and prudently.

The Lion said, "I understand what you mean, but I do not think that the Bull will betray me and plot my death. Why should he do that when I have done him nothing but good? He never had a wish that I did not transform into reality."

Dimnah persevered: "Wicked people are known to maintain good manners and amiable behaviour until they are elevated to the position they crave but do not deserve. No sooner do they attain such a position than they are striving for further promotion. Most worrisome are those who harbour the base traits of lechery and betrayal. The sordid and treacherous man will serve and advise a ruler only out of fear. Experience shows, though, that whenever he loses that fear he will revert to his real self, like the dog's tail which, no matter how long it is bound, will always return to its natural crooked state when unbound."

The King must realize that if people reject the advice of their friends when it is difficult, their judgments and decisions will always be unreliable. It is like the sick person who rejects the medicine prescribed for him by his doctor because it may be painful or disagreeable, and foolishly takes what he likes instead. It is the duty of the Companions of rulers to proffer advice that will make the rulers shrewder, and to frame the advice as agreeably as possible. They should prevent the rulers from taking decisions that could harm or humiliate them.

The most dutiful Companion is the one least willing to sweet-talk and flatter the ruler.

Actions are as worthwhile as their results.

The most desirable women are those who defer to their husbands.

The more exalted the source, the sweeter the praise.

The noblest kings are those unspoiled by arrogance.

The highest code of ethics motivates people to be more devoted and loyal.

It was also said that a person who has fire in his pillow or snakes in his bed will never be able to sleep.

When one man feels another's animosity, they cannot be at their ease together.

The most indecisive kings are those who deal with daily matters carelessly, with no thought for their outcome. Such a king resembles a stampeding elephant that will do no one's bidding while enraged. When something becomes troublesome, he ignores it; then, when his neglect begins to cause damage, he blames his Companions.

The Lion replied: "You have been very harsh in your assertions. I shall simply take them as advice. If Shatrabah has become my enemy I shall regret it, but I don't think he can ever harm me. How could he? I am a carnivore: it is my nature to kill beasts and eat their flesh. He is a herbivore who eats only grass. He is my food, and I shall never be his. Furthermore, I cannot imagine him betraying me after I guaranteed his safety. I outdid myself in generosity and public praise. If I change my attitude now, without any grounds, I shall lose face in front of everyone. I would be blamed for naïveté, and would have a bad conscience besides."

Dimnah rejoined: "The King must not be misled by his own statement, 'He is my food, and I shall never be his.' If Shatrabah does not kill the King himself, he will surely get the support of others. Remember, it has also been said: "Never not trust a guest whose morals you do not know. You never know what he could do to you. You may end up being harmed as the Louse was harmed by the Flea."

The Lion asked, "How does the story go?"
Dimnah recounted:

Once upon a time a Louse lived for a long while in the bed of a wealthy man. She would suck the man's blood while he was asleep and unaware, so she crawled about at her ease. But things changed when a Flea decided to visit her. She invited the Flea: "Do stay with me and enjoy the delicious blood and comfortable bed." He agreed and took up residence. But when the man went to bed the Flea attacked and bit him so sharply that the pain awakened him. Unable to sleep, he got out of bed and ordered that it be inspected. The Flea leapt out and escaped unharmed, but the servants discovered the slower Louse and crushed it to death.

Dimnah continued, "I told the King this fable to show him that no one is safe from destruction by evil people, even if they are weak. So if the King does not fear Shatrabah, then he will have to be wary of his own soldiers, for Shatrabah has lured them into treason."

This time the Lion was ready to listen, and asked with dismay: "What do you think we should do? What do you suggest?"

Dimnah said, "If it please the King: the decayed tooth will continue to hurt until it is plucked out. Only vomiting will comfort a person with foul food in his stomach. And the only remedy for a fearsome enemy is to kill him."

The Lion replied, "You know, you have undermined my trust in Shatrabah as my friend. I shall send him a message telling him what you have explained, and instructing him to meet me later."

Dimnah did not like what he heard. He feared that when the Lion discussed the matter with Shatrabah and heard his account of things, Dimnah's plot would be exposed. Worse still, the Lion would be convinced of Shatrabah's innocence, and Dimnah's envious betrayal. So he said to the Lion: "Sending a message to Shatrabah may not be the best tactic, or the most decisive. Let the King consider what is likely to happen. When Shatrabah realizes the King intends to kill him he will naturally take the initiative and strike first, with all his might. He will be well prepared, too. If he flees and the King lets him escape without a battle, the King will be ridiculed and belittled by his peers. Canny kings do not usually pass formal judgment on anyone until he has been accused and convicted. Different crimes, however, have different remedies. Kings impose overt punishment for overt crimes, but covert punishment for covert ones."

The Lion replied, "But if a ruler punishes anyone for a crime without thorough inquiry, then both the guilt and the punishment are on his head, and deservedly."

Dimnah replied, "If that is the wish of the King, then I advise him not to allow Shatrabah to enter the Court unless the King is prepared. I warn the King never to let him out of his sight or allow Shatrabah to deceive him. I am sure the King will understand his sinister purposes when he sees him. The King will observe some changes in Shatrabah's appearance: his complexion has changed, and his limbs have become fidgety; he glances shiftily this way and that, and wags his horns as if preparing to gore and fight to the death."

The Lion answered, "I will be ready for him and take precautions, and if I observe any of the signs you mentioned, then I will be sure of his futile intentions."

Dimnah realized that he had managed to arouse the Lion against Shatrabah the Bull. He was confident of success, and expected the Lion to call in the Bull and slay him. He had planned to approach the Bull as well, in order to turn him against the Lion. But he decided to have the Lion send him straightaway as his spokesman to the Bull, lest anyone else leak the news, which could jeopardize his plan, and he, then, would end up as the one at risk. So he suggested to the Lion, "Let the King allow me to visit Shatrabah, scout out the situation, and listen to whatever he might say. If I can discover his secret plan I shall then tell the King whatever I manage to get out of him."

The King consented. Dimnah left straightaway for Shatrabah's place. He pretended to be sad and depressed. When the Bull saw him, he greeted him graciously and asked Dimnah, "What took you so long to visit me? I have not seen you for days, and I trust you were well."

Dimnah replied, "Those who do not control their own lives are never well. Anyone who is in the hands of the untrustworthy will always live in danger and in fear. Not an hour will pass without a feeling of an overwhelming insecurity."

Shatrabah asked, "What has happened?"

Dimnah replied in a morose voice:

The inevitable has finally come to pass. Who can challenge Destiny? Have you heard of anyone who attained great things and was still satisfied? Have you met anyone who achieved his goals and was content? Who has ever followed his whims and come to a happy end? How many have sought favours from contemptible people and been shown the door? How many people do you know who made common cause with evildoers and ended up safely? Haven't you also heard that all those who befriend rulers will never be sure of their security or their favour?

Shatrabah said with concern, "I gather you are suspicious of the Lion, and that great trouble is brewing."

Dimnah replied, "I fear so, though I am not the one at risk."

Shatrabah asked, "Who is in trouble, then?"

Dimnah answered: "You know the strength of our friendship and the trust we have in one another. You also know that it was I who persuaded the Lion to guarantee your safety, and received his pledge after I first met you. I think it is my duty as a friend to share with you what I have heard."

Shatrabah asked, "What do you know?"

Dimnah replied: "A trustworthy inside source has assured me that the Lion told his Companions: 'I like the Bull more than ever, now that he has been so deliciously fattened. Since I have no more use for him, it is time for us to feast on him.' When my source came to tell me what he had heard, it was clear that the Lion had renounced his oath of protection and betrayed you. So I rushed to warn you, to allow you to consider what to do."

When Shatrabah heard this, he was reminded of the part Dimnah had played in obtaining from the Lion the guarantee of his safety. It now seemed to him that Dimnah had been sincere and honest in his dealings with him, but that the Lion's fiercely brutal nature could never change. His distress was profound, and he said to Dimnah: "Since I have never been untrue to him, I never thought that the Lion would turn on me. I have never hurt any of his soldiers since we struck up our friendship. He must have been misled and turned against me by someone with ulterior motives. I know that the Lion has some evil Companions who lie to him frequently. He has believed their lies many times before. It is true that those who mix with evil people can project their own mistrust on certain good and honest friends.

"The Lion's weakness in being drawn in by a dishonest Companion resembles that of the Duck who once saw the light of a star reflected in a pond and mistook it for a fish. When the Duck tried to catch it, she realized that it was only an illusion and gave up. The next night, however, she saw a real Fish in the pond. But then she made the opposite mistake and mistook it for the illusion she had seen before. She made no attempt to catch it, and lost her meal.

"If the Lion has heard a lie about me and believed it, he might have believed similar lies about others as well. But if he heard no lies about me, yet decided to molest me, it would be strange since he has never behaved this way before. It was said in olden times that one might suspect something is amiss when a person counts on comradeship from his intimate friend but meets with aggressive rejection instead. Their friendship must somehow have disintegrated. Even if there were some cause for anger, the disconcerted would expect some appeal to their friendship, and some hope for forgiveness. But when anger erupts without apparent cause, there is no ground for expecting reconciliation. Only if the cause is known can there be a likely hope for reconciliation and peace.

"I have given deep thought to my situation. I have done the Lion no wrong, slight or grave. It is true that in friendships misunderstandings do occur: one can never be too careful. But a rational person will always review a conflict to determine whether it was unintentional or deliberate. He will incline to forgive his friend, unless it would be harmful or degrading. A true friend will resist blaming or reproaching someone for unpleasant incidents between them, and forgiveness is usually safest for both.

"If the Lion thinks I have done him harm, I am honestly unaware of it. I may have disagreed with some of his opinions; possibly he thought I was too blunt. Even so, that is surely no crime. Actually, I have rarely disagreed with him, and only on behalf of just decisions in court cases. I never shared my disagreements with his Companions or staff. I purposely waited until we were alone, and discussed them with him soberly, respectfully, and in private. It is my experience that rulers who seek only agreeable advice from their counsellors, or agreeable medicines from their physicians, or accolades from scholars, are unlikely in times of difficulty and uncertainty to welcome or even appreciate the profound benefits and value of knowledge. They will definitely aggravate their problems and place their Companions in an impossible situation.

"If the Lion is angry towards me without just cause, then perhaps he suffers from the addiction to power that often afflicts rulers. Despite their security, trust and patronage, rulers can be dangerous friends. If that is what lies behind my difficulty, then my greatest risk is the high status and prestige I have enjoyed in the Lion's Court. And if the cause of the Lion's change of heart towards me was not in fact caused in any of the ways I have mentioned, then the death I face must be related to my Destiny, which no one can avoid or challenge.

"That Destiny, however, rules the Lion's power as well, and one day it will take both his power and his life: something we must all expect. Destiny is so powerful that it can easily enable a weakling to be carried comfortably on the back of an enraged elephant. Similarly, it is Destiny that allows an ordinary man to de-fang a poisonous snake and spend a playful time with it.

"Destiny can transform an indecisive person into a decisive one. It weakens the strong and enriches the poor. It can provide courage to the coward and terror to the brave. Destiny embodies and embraces all challenges in this world.

Dimnah then stated: "The Lion's plan to slay you is due neither to the lies of evil Companions, nor to an addiction to power. It is due simply to the Lion's innate inclination to betrayal and lecherous behaviour. He is immoral, deceitful and treacherous, and an accomplished betrayer. His methods are calculated. He entices you with his delicious food, but you are unaware of the poison it contains, that will kill you afterwards."

Shatrabah replied with sadness: "It seems I have enjoyed the lovely but lethal hospitality of the Lion. And now I drift closer to that final, deadly end. Had it not been for dire need, as a herbivore I would never have kept company with the carnivorous Lion. My ordeal is just like that of the Bee that enjoys the sweetness and scent of the water lily and forgets itself. The night falls, the blossom closes, and crushes it to death. It seems that whoever is malcontent with his lot in this world, and so overwhelmed with ambition that he forgets or fails to provide for the uncertainties and chances of the future, will surely meet a futile end. He will be like the Fly, which is not content with life among the trees and roses. Instead it insists on lapping the water that trickles out of the elephant's ear, and so will surely be killed one day when the elephant smacks it with his huge ear. So is the case with whoever extends his love and advice to the ingrate. He is just like a Farmer who vainly sows his seeds in the swamps, where he will never reap a harvest. Anyone who advises the conceited might as well counsel the dead, or pour out his secrets to a deaf person."

Dimnah interrupted Shatrabah, "All this talking is a waste of time. You must find some way to save yourself."

But Shatrabah's concern was elsewhere: "All is lost now. How can I plan for my safety now that you have disclosed the Lion's thoughts and intentions for me? If he wants to devour me, he will do it. As you well know, even if he thinks well of me, his cunning and immoral Companions who wish me dead will have their way. If malicious plotters connive against an innocent person, they will succeed in killing him even if they are weak and their victim is strong. They will kill him in the same way the Wolf, the Raven, and the Jackal managed to kill their friend the Camel."

"How does the story go?" Dimnah asked.

Shatrabah replied:

Once upon a time a Lion lived in a jungle close to the main road. He had three friends: a Wolf, a Raven, and a Jackal. It happened that some herdsmen who owned a few camels passed by. One of the camels escaped from their caravan and wandered around lost. Soon he entered the jungle, and roamed about there until he reached the Lion's den. The Lion asked him where he came from.

The Camel said, "From a place nearby."

The Lion, the Wolf, the Jackal and rhe Raven

"And what do you want?" the Lion inquired.

"Whatever the King may order me to do," the Camel replied politely.

"Then you shall stay with us in this land of security, fertility and plenty," the Lion said.

Life was good to them for a long while. Then one day the Lion went out hunting but was attacked by a huge Elephant. They fought fiercely, and though the Lion finally escaped, he had been wounded by the Elephant's sharp tusks, and was bleeding from wounds all over his body. When he arrived in his den he collapsed and was unable to move. His hunting days were over. Because his friends, the Wolf, the Raven and the Jackal, were accustomed to eating the leftovers of the Lion's prey, they now went hungry, for they were too lazy to hunt their own prey. So they began to starve and became extremely weak.

The Lion understood, and said: "You must be exhausted and discouraged; you need to eat."

They answered: "We care more about our King than about ourselves. It hurts us to see what happened to him. If only we could find something for the King to eat so he could regain his health."

The Lion answered: "You are most kind. But it might be good for us all if you could forage for food that could nourish both you and me."

The Wolf, the Raven, and the Jackal left the Lion and reconvened in a secluded place to discuss the matter further.

They said: "What do we care about this Camel, a herbivore? We have nothing in common. He does not think the way we think, or belong to us. Perhaps we should talk to the Lion and show him the benefits of eating the Camel's flesh."

The Jackal objected: "No, we cannot mention this to the Lion since he gave him his word and guaranteed his safety."

The Raven interjected: "Leave this to me. I shall speak with the Lion."

He went immediately to the Lion's den, and the Lion asked him, "Did you succeed in hunting any prey today?"

The Raven replied bluntly: "If it please the King: only those who share in the effort and pursue their prey will succeed. As for us, we cannot exert any effort or concentrate any attention to the task, so intense is our hunger. Nevertheless, we have agreed upon an effective way to avoid starvation, if the King agrees."

The Lion asked: "And what is that?"

The Raven explained: "That herbivore, the Camel, has dwelt with us for a long time without being of use to anyone. He cannot defend us, or perform any useful service. He is thus the perfect candidate to be our food."

The Lion answered with anger: "Your solution is senseless, depraved, treacherous and ruthless. How dare you come to me with such a suggestion, knowing perfectly well that I have guaranteed the safety of the Camel, and taken him under my protection? Have you never heard that no charity is nobler than to protect a terrified person and spare his life? I have given him my solemn oath, and I do not intend to betray him."

The Raven took a firm stand: "I know exactly what the King means. But there are emergencies so dire that one person may rightly be sacrificed to preserve a household. And some emergencies may be so severe that a household must be sacrificed for the entire tribe. Indeed, an entire tribe might need to be sacrificed for the security of the nation. And ultimately the whole nation may be offered to save the King. In this case, it is the King who is now at risk and in need of this sacrifice. I will assure the King that I shall find a way to relieve him of his oath, so that he will incur neither guilt nor dishonour. We will achieve our objective without anyone taking the responsibility of giving the order to slaughter the Camel. We will develop a plan that will be ultimately useful and completely successful."

The Lion said not a word.

The shrewd Raven understood that his silence implied consent. He immediately rushed out to caucus with his friends: "I discussed the matter of killing and eating the Camel, on condition that all of us, including the Camel, meet together in the Lion's den. We shall recall what happened to the Lion and express our condolences. As a token of our friendship, each of us will offer himself to the Lion and flatter him. Then the other two will ridicule the offer by showing the harm in eating that particular kind of flesh. If we all collaborate, we shall all be safe and the Lion will be grateful."

And that is exactly what they did. They all came before the Lion. The Raven was the first to speak: "The King desperately needs food so that he can regain his strength. We sincerely offer ourselves for him, for we cannot live without him. If he should die, life would lose meaning for us. Therefore I give myself willingly to the King. Let him feast on me."

The Wolf and the Jackal immediately intervened. They asked the Raven to forego his offer, since his flesh could do the King no good, and could not satisfy his hunger.

The Jackal, however, went on to say, "But I can satisfy the King's hunger. I happily give myself to him."

The Wolf and the Raven shouted in unison: "You are filthy and you stink."

But the Wolf continued: "I am not like that. Let the King eat me: I offer myself."

The Jackal and the Raven rejected in their turn and said: "All physicians have confirmed that eating wolf's flesh is the surest method for suicide."

The poor Camel expected the others to find an excuse for him as they had for themselves. Therefore, in order to appease the Lion and save himself from future harm he made the same offer: "But I can satisfy the King's hunger. My flesh is delicious and my stomach is clean. Let the King eat me and feed his friends and servants as well. I willingly accept and I am happy to offer myself."

The Wolf, the Raven and the Jackal immediately approved: "The Camel has spoken the truth. He is very generous, and has put into words what is already known perfectly well to us all."

So they leapt upon him and tore him to pieces.

Shatrabah continued: "I have recounted this fable to show that if the Lion's Companions have already decided on my death, there is no way I can avoid it or protect myself. Even if the Lion disagrees with his Companions about me, it will do me no good. It may be said that the most gracious ruler is the one who rules with justice. But even if the Lion did regard me with mercy and benevolence, he will give way under the pressure of his Companion's lies and backstabbing tactics. The more hateful they become, the weaker his kindness and mercy will be. Does the King not observe that water is unlike words, and a stone is much harder than a human being? If water drips onto the stone long enough it will eventually wear a hole in it. And with enough time and persistence, words can do the same to humans."

Dimnah replied: "What are you planning to do now"?

Shatrabah explained, "I have no alternative but to persevere and fight. To someone whose cause is just, defending oneself is better than prayer to a praying person, alms to the alms-giver, or piety to the pious."

Dimnah told him: "No one should ever risk being killed if he can avoid it. A rational person will keep fighting as the last resort, but begin with craftiness and cunning. It was said in the past: "Never underestimate the weak and contemptible enemy, particularly if he has his wits about him, and adequate support." Of course you still may not prevail over the Lion, who in this case is courageous and strong. But anyone who underestimates a weak enemy could suffer the same Destiny that befell the Sea-Tide at the hands of the Sandpiper.

"How does the story go?" Shatrabah asked.

Dimnah told him the tale:

Once upon a time a Sandpiper and his Wife lived on the seacoast. When she was due to lay her eggs his Wife told him: "It would probably be better to hatch our eggs in a secure place. I am afraid that the Tide of the sea will take away our small fry with the tide."

The Husband replied: "Hatch them right here. The place is ideal for us, and we have fresh water and flowering bushes all around us."

She answered: "You are very careless. I am still afraid that the Tide will take our chicks. I am sure of it."

But he insisted, and ordered her: "Just hatch your eggs here. We are not going to move."

She replied angrily: "You are so obstinate and always look for the easy way out. Don't you remember how he intimidated and threatened you? Don't you realize how great your disadvantage is?"

The Sandpiper refused to listen further, but she persisted: "Listen: whoever ignores good advice will be like the Turtle who did not listen to the two Ducks who tried to help her."

The husband inquired: "How does the story go?"

She recounted:

Once upon a time two Ducks lived close to a creek lined by thick stands of grass. There they befriended a Turtle who lived in the creek. It happened one day that the creek began to dry up, and the two Ducks decided to leave and look for another place. So they went to bid the Turtle farewell. "Peace be with you," they greeted her. "With the creek drying up we have decided to move."

The Turtle replied, "But the drought affects my welfare more than yours. I am like a ship: I cannot survive except in water, and you can live wherever you want. Please take me with you."

They were willing, but the Turtle questioned how it might be done. "How are you going to carry me?"

They explained: "We will hold both ends of a reed in our beaks, and you will grasp the middle of the reed with your mouth, and thus we shall fly together. But you must not utter a word if people see you and start mocking you."

So the three set off as described. The people down below wondered at what they were seeing, and said: "What a weird sight! A Turtle is flying between two Ducks."

But the Turtle could not keep her mouth shut, and started to say: "May God gouge out your eyes, you silly people."

But, alas: the moment she opened her mouth she fell to her death.

The Turtle and the Ducks

The Sandpiper Husband replied: "I heard your story. Nevertheless, do not be afraid of the Tide. He will not harm us."

The Tide, however, rose and carried away their young as she expected. The Mother wailed: "I knew this would happen."

Her Husband replied: "Don't worry, I will take revenge on the Tide."

He went grieving to a flock of birds and appealed to them: "You are trustworthy friends to me and my brother. You must help me."

"But how"? they asked.

He suggested: "We shall go together to the rest of the birds, and complain to them of what the Tide has done. We will tell them that they are our kin, and owe us help."

So they went to the birds and received this reply: "Our Lady and Queen is the Phoenix. Let's all go and call her. When she appears, we will explain to her what the Tide has done, and ask her to avenge you with all her awesome powers."

They all went with the Sandpiper and summoned the Phoenix until she appeared. They told her the story and demanded her assistance, and she agreed.

When the Tide heard of the birds' firm intention to fight him under the command of the fearsome Phoenix, he was afraid to go into battle against such an overwhelming adversary. So he agreed to return the Sandpiper's young, and made peace with him. The Phoenix left him unharmed and returned home.

Dimnah continued his argument with the Bull and said: "I told you this fable only to show you that fighting the Lion is not a wise alternative."

Shatrabah replied: "Until I can be sure of the Lion's real intentions, I will not attack him, or scheme against him, or harbour any animosity against him. In the meantime, I shall maintain my friendship with him."

Dimnah did not like what he heard from Shatrabah. He was afraid that the Lion might not see the changed attitude of the Bull that he had previously reported. The Lion would then accuse Dimnah of high crimes, and cast him into agonizing disgrace. So Dimnah quickly advised: "You must go to the Lion and discern his intentions the moment he looks at you."

"How could I tell?" Shatrabah inquired.

Dimnah replied: "When you first enter the Lion's Court, you will see him sitting poised on his tail, throwing out his chest, and gazing sharply at you. His ears will be erect and his mouth wide open, all ready to attack."

Shatrabah finally agreed: "If I see those telltale signs, then I will believe you about the Lion."

After Dimnah had thus schemed to make the Lion and the Bull hostile towards one another, he went straight to his brother Kalilah who asked, "How far has your plot gone?"

Dimnah answered: "I am on the point of achieving what we both wished. Come along and watch it all happen."

Kalilah and Dimnah rushed together to witness the expected battle between the Lion and the Bull, observe the outcome, and react accordingly.

Shatrabah arrived in the King's Court. He saw the Lion poised on his tail just as Dimnah had described. He murmured to himself with awe: "How true it is that the friend of the ruler is very much like a person who keeps a snake as a house pet; he will never know when it will attack and bite him."

Meanwhile the Lion was looking at Shatrabah, and saw the signs Dimnah had described. He had no doubt then that Shatrabah had come to attack and kill him. So he forthwith attacked the Bull. They fought a ferocious and bloody battle. Both were severely wounded, but the Lion finally vanquished the Bull fiercely slaying him.

When Kalilah saw the Lion exhausted and bleeding, he angrily scolded Dimnah and said: "You are a mean, immoral and loutish creature. You have proven yourself ignorant of life's true lessons, and you will reap the baneful results of your vicious scheme."

Dimnah asked, "Why do you say that?"

Kalilah explained gravely: "The Lion is wounded and the Bull is dead. The most fateful deed is when a person with an ulterior motive arouses a friend to misbehave, by fighting with another friend and killing him. A rational person plans and evaluates all alternatives before executing them. Alternatives that may be securely accomplished are to be pursued, while others that are uncertain will be avoided. I am really afraid that the payback for your barbarity will be grave. You have spoken smoothly but acted savagely. You have reneged on your commitment to me, and caused harm to the Lion.

"It was said in the past that:

"Spoken words are void without matching actions.

"Justice is barren without loyalty.

"Almsgiving is meaningless without gracious intentions.

"Wealth is counterfeit without generosity.

"Honesty and loyalty are twins.

"A good life requires sound health.

"Nothing is secure without happiness.

"Knowledge replaces recklessness in a thoughtful person.

"It also augments rashness in the behaviour of fools.

"Do you not observe that the same daylight that increases the vision of those who can see, can blind the weak sight of other creatures like bats?

"What you have done puts me in mind of past wisdom. It was said if the ruler was righteous, but his viziers and aides were abusive, they would deny the people his generosity, and prevent him from getting closer to them. This resembles a pond full of fresh water and vicious crocodiles. No one could draw any water from that pond even when thirsty, for fear of the harmful crocodiles.

"Dimnah, you wanted the Lion exclusively for yourself, something that is neither proper nor possible. You know of the analogies given to elaborate on what I mean,

"The sea has its waves; the ruler has his Companions. Friendship is not durable without loyalty; The Eternal home cannot be attained through hypocrisy.

"Gaining by the loss of others is futile.

"My warning to you is found in the story in which the Man said to the Bird: 'Never attempt to rectify what cannot be set right, and never try to educate and refine those who are inherently and irreversibly dissolute.'"

Dimnah inquired: "How does the story go?"

Kalilah recounted:

Once upon a time a clan of Monkeys lived on one of the mountains. On a very cold, rainy and windy night they wanted to light a fire to warm themselves. They looked around and suddenly saw a Firefly flashing in the darkness. They mistook it for a spark of fire, however, so they hastily gathered a load of wood and piled it atop the Firefly. Then they began to blow on the wood in the hope that the imagined spark would set light to the pile.

A Bird perched on a nearby branch observed what they were doing. He cautiously hailed the Monkeys to alert them to their mistake. After they had ignored him awhile he decided to draw closer and explain to them what was wrong. At that very moment a Man was passing by and saw what the Bird intended to do. He advised him: "Do not waste your help on the stubborn. Don't you know that sabres are never tested on rock, and a bow can never be made of inflexible wood? So do not exhaust yourself teaching anyone as incapable of learning as those fellows."

The Bird refused to listen, and landed in the midst of the Monkeys to tell them face-to-face that a firefly is not a spark of fire. To his misfortune, the nearest Monkey grabbed him, flung him to the ground, and killed him.

"This is just like you, Dimnah. You are possessed by deceit and immorality, two evil traits, and deceit is the worse of the two. What you have done, Dimnah, could also be illuminated by the following fable, which you must hear.

Once upon a time a Swindler and a Simpleton became partners in trade. One day while they were travelling together the Simpleton strayed off the road and had the incredible luck to find a bag containing a thousand dinars. His partner, the Swindler, found out what had happened. After some discussion they decided to return home. When they arrived at the outskirts of the city they rested and discussed how to divide the money. The Simpleton suggested equal shares for each.

The Swindler, whose real aim was to take all the money, said: "Let us not divide it now. Sincerity and companionship are better served by sharing and discussion. Let each of us take some of the money for his immediate expenses, and then we will bury the rest at the base of this tree. It is safe here, and we can always come back and get more whenever we need it. No one knows of this place except the two of us."

The Simpleton agreed, and they each took some money, then together buried the rest at the base of the huge tree and returned to the city. Sometime later the Swindler went back alone, dug up the money and took it all for himself. He smoothed over the soil at the base of the tree as if nothing had happened, and went home.

After a few months the Simpleton came and asked his partner to accompany him to retrieve some more money. Both went to the tree and dug in the place where they had buried the bag. When they found nothing, the Swindler slapped the Simpleton in the face and shouted at him, "Sad to say, no one can trust a friend these days. You must have returned behind my back and stolen the money."

The more the Simpleton swore that he had never taken the money, and the more he cursed the unknown thief, the more the Swindler struck him in the face, saying loudly "You are the only person who knew the secret place, and no one took the money but you."

This went on for a long time, and finally they both complained to the Judge. The Swindler accused his partner, who rejected the accusation.

"Do you have any evidence of your accusation?" the Judge asked the Swindler.

"Yes," he replied, "Your Honour knows the tree, and it can vouch for the truth of what I say."

The Judge could not decide between the conflicting stories, so he insisted on hearing the alleged evidence from the tree itself. The Swindler had already planned a trick. He had his Father hide in the trunk of the huge tree beforehand. So they all went out to the tree, and the Judge asked it what had happened. The Father of the Swindler then said from inside the tree, "Yes, it was the Simpleton who stole the money."

The Judge's suspicion intensified, however. So he ordered his staff to fetch some wood and set the tree on fire. Once the fire was lit the Father began to shout for help from inside the trunk, and was finally extricated. The Judge had him explain what had happened and the Father told him the true story. The Judge dealt the Swindler a fierce blow, and slapped his Father's face many times. He ordered him to be paraded in disgrace before the people, fined him a large sum of money, and gave it all to the Simpleton.

Kalilah explained himself to Dimnah: "I have recounted this fable to show you that immorality and deception will often make a plotter into his own victim. And you, Dimnah, represent immorality, deception, and treachery, and I fear you will get exactly what you really deserve. You will never get away with it, for you are a deceiver and a chameleon. The fresh water of the river disappears when it pours into the sea; and the welfare of any home vanishes when a corrupter moves in. You are like a fork-tongued poisonous serpent, for your deceit is like poison running through your tongue. I fear for the poison you conceal, and for the disaster that is bound to befall you. It is only a matter of time.

"The corrupt man who pits friends against each other is like a person who has a serpent for a pet. He grooms it and handles it fondly, yet it will eventually strike him. There is truth in the saying, "Keep company with the rational and generous, but if you must choose, choose the rational."

"The perfect friend, of course, is both rational and generous. One who is rational but not generous may still be helpful, if you avoid his misbehaviour but learn from his good sense. One who is generous but not rational may be helpful as long as her resources last, provided that you do not follow her advice. But flee those who are both selfish and unwise, for they will both corrupt and destroy you. As for me, I am getting as far away from you as I can. How can your brothers and friends expect any generosity and love from you after what you have done to your King who trusted, honoured and respected you so generously?"

Kalilah went on: "You know, you are like the Merchant who claimed that falcons could carry off elephants if one believes that rodents could digest two hundred pounds of iron."

Dimnah asked, "How does the story go?"

Kalilah said:

Once upon a time a Merchant decided to leave town in search of business. He happened to have two hundred pounds of iron in his shop, and stored it with a Colleague. Eventually he returned and asked for his iron.

The Colleague said, "I am sorry to tell you that the rodents ate it all."

The Merchant replied, "Yes, I have heard that rodents can eat iron, because their teeth are extremely sharp."

The Colleague was relieved that the Merchant had believed him. On his way home the Merchant found one of the Colleague's younger sons playing outside. He took him to his home and locked him up. The next day, when his son did not return, the Colleague went to the Merchant and inquired: "Would you possibly have any information about my son? He is missing."

The Merchant answered, "When I left you last evening, I saw a Falcon carrying a boy, and it was probably your son."

The Colleague let out a shriek, and began striking his head in pain and agony and shouting in disbelief: "Listen to this, my friends! Have you ever seen or heard of a Falcon kidnapping boys?"

The Merchant immediately replied in a loud voice: "Yes, of course. In a place where rodents can eat two hundred pounds of iron, why should it be impossible for falcons to kidnap and carry away even elephants?"

The Colleague then pleaded and said, "Please return my son to me. I have cheated you and I will pay you for your iron, which I sold."

"This example, Dimnah, is for you: to appreciate that if you betray your friend, then you will be even more treacherous with others. And if one knows that his friend has betrayed others, he will know better than to trust him with his friendship.

"Nothing is worse than when affection is entrusted to the deceitful.

"Whoever betrays a friend will be more treacherous to others.

"If one knows his friend has betrayed others, he cannot trust him with his friendship.

"Nothing is more wasteful or more harmful than:

"Entrusting one's heart to the unfaithful

"Devoting oneself to an ingrate

"Teaching those who refuse to cultivate themselves

"Sharing secrets with those unable to keep them.

"Take note that friendship with chosen good people will bring out goodness in human beings, but friendship with chosen evil people will breed only evil.

"But friendship is just like the wind: when it flows over a perfumed garden it will spread the sweet and fascinating aroma. And after it passes over a garbage dump it carries only putrid smells."

Kalilah was weary by now, and he finally told Dimnah with deep sorrow: "I have talked at length with you, and probably disturbed and burdened you with my frankness."

Meanwhile, after the Lion had destroyed the Bull and had time to calm down, he began to reminisce about his old, dear and best friend, and how it was that he had slain him. "I am deeply distressed and in great pain for the death of Shatrabah," he reflected. "He had a good mind and sound judgment, and was a unique moral counsellor. Now I am not certain whether he was innocent and slandered, or really guilty of what he was accused of.

The Lion was depressed, and began to feel shame for what he had done.

Dimnah noticed the Lion's mood as it clearly showed on his face. He left Kalilah, approached the Lion, and craftily exclaimed, "Congratulations on the King's victory over his enemies, which he has attained through the grace of God. But why is the King sad?

The Lion answered, "I miss the companionship of Shatrabah. I really miss his sound opinion, amiable civility, and great knowledge."

Dimnah firmly replied, "Let the King waste no sympathy on the Bull. A rational person will not forgive anyone he suspects. A prudent person may sometimes detest someone, yet take him as a close companion for his great competence and shrewd judgment. It is just like the painful medicine that one must swallow to be cured. Similarly, one may love a person very dearly, yet shun him or even kill him if he suspects possible harm from him. It is just like a person who cuts off the finger that was bitten by a snake, to save himself from the deadly venom."

The Lion was put at ease by what Dimnah told him. As time passed, however, he came to know the whole story of how Dimnah had treacherously betrayed his friend Shatrabah the Bull. And when he did, the Lion punished him with a most painful and savage death.

(The end of the Fable of the Lion and the Bull)

Dimnah in Court

Chapter Two

The Fable of
the Investigation of Dimnah

(Evil will be justly punished)

Dabshalim the King addressed Baydaba the Philosopher: "You have explained how a person can destroy an otherwise intimate and long-lasting friendship through cunning manipulation, lies and deception. You have also recounted to me what happened to Dimnah after Shatrabah's death. But what were the Lion's justifications when he reviewed his thoughts and judgments of the Bull, especially after he found out the truth about Dimnah's deception? And what had Dimnah to say in his own defence?

This was what the Philosopher had to say in reply.

After the Lion killed Shatrabah, he felt quite guilty and reproached himself deeply. He recalled how the Bull had been his bosom friend, and that they had enjoyed a very special relationship. Shatrabah had been his closest friend, and unlike his other Companions he always gave him the best advice.

It happened one night that the Tiger, who was the next best friend of the Lion, was passing by the house of Kalilah and his brother Dimnah. As he drew close to the doorway he overheard Kalilah reproaching Dimnah for what he had done, blaming him for his crafty and fatal slander, and accusing him of fabricating lies regarding the nobility. The Tiger also learned of Dimnah's treasonous actions. In fact, he managed to listen to the entire discussion between the brothers.

Kalilah had addressed Dimnah: "You have committed a very treacherous act, and put yourself in a very compromised situation. You have committed a dangerous offence that could bring on your own destruction. You will face execution if the Lion finds out your secret, especially your deadly perjury and betrayal. You will have no ally, and your life will surely come to a disgraceful end. Everyone will join forces against you, because they will all fear your wicked scheming. All will coalesce, with you as their common enemy.

"As for me, from this day forward you are no more my friend, nor my confidential Companion, nor my sharer of secrets. Scholars in the past warned us when they said, 'Avoid those you do not like.'

119

"It is more proper and safe for me not to have anything more to do with you, and to make my own peace with the Lion after the agony you have caused him."

When the Tiger heard all this he quickly went to see the Lion's Mother. He made her promise on oath not to divulge to a living soul what he was about to tell her. Then he told her all he had heard between Kalilah and Dimnah.

The next morning, while the Lion was sitting alone, depressed and morose about Shatrabah's Destiny, his Mother entered his chamber and said, "What is distressing you so?"

He answered, "I am desolate because I killed Shatrabah. His intimate friendship and devoted service to me are a powerful memory. He consistently gave me honest advice, and I felt at ease with his counsel, which was always loyal."

His Mother responded: "The most devastating accusation a person can face is his own confession of crime. What you have done is a grave mistake. How could you kill the Bull without any knowledge of the facts or any evidence of crime? I would have a great deal to tell you about it, if scholars did not insist that divulging secrets is criminal and dishonourable!"

The Lion said, "The teachings of scholars have many meanings and many interpretations. I know what you say is right, but I need to know whatever you may have learned. If anyone has shared a secret with you, then share it all with me."

His Mother told him everything except that the Tiger had been her source. She said, "I am aware of the severity of punishment scholars assign to the violation of secrecy, and the disgrace it entails. But I wanted to tell you what I know for your own good. If the fatal mistakes of the wicked and their malicious results were to become public knowledge, their habitual betrayal of the King and avoidance of punishment will encourage the common people to justify their own shameless actions and take foul play in high places as a sanction for their own worst mischief. Thus they hold up the guilt and treachery of the ruling authorities as an excuse for their own foul play."

After his Mother had her say, the Lion called his Companions and soldiers to court. He then sent for Dimnah. When he was brought in and saw the desolate state of the Lion, he began to speak: "What is wrong? What has distressed the King?"

The Lion's Mother turned on him and replied with contempt, "It is your presence—even for the space of a wink—that upsets the King. I promise you that you will never see another sunrise."

Dimnah replied: "Evidently the winner does take all. The first will seize all and leave nothing to the last. They used to say that people who take the most pains to ward off evil always seem to be the first struck by it. Therefore I implore my King and his soldiers not to set an evil example for future generations.

"They also used to say that whoever knowingly consorts with the wicked consorts with disaster. That is probably why ascetics secluded themselves from all God's creatures, and preferred isolation to society. Their motive for pious deeds has actually replaced their love of earthly pleasures. Only God can reward good deeds with further benevolence, and charity with greater benefaction! Whoever exacts rewards from people for his good deeds to them truly earns their rejection instead. For it is evil to perform good deeds other than for love of God, and for His sake only. And if that is one's motive, it is wrong to expect rewards from any human being. The most any of our King's subjects can hope for is a virtuous character, an honest reputation, and a gracious way of life.

"Scholars have also stated: 'Whoever prefers lies to truth is mad, mindless, pitiable and contemptible.' That is why the King must not rashly accuse me of any suspicious act. I do not say this for fear of death, since that is a calamity no one can escape. Every living soul will one day face the end. I can assure the King that if I had a hundred souls, and he wanted them all exterminated, I would gladly yield to his wish."

At that point one of the King's soldiers spoke out: "He is saying all this to save himself, not out of any real love for the King."

Dimnah retorted: "What a fool you are! Is it wrong to attempt to save myself and offer every possible defence? What is more urgent than trying to save my life? You betray your obvious jealousy and hatred. All who heard you now know that you wish well to no one. You are truly your own enemy. Is there anything in the world more precious than oneself? You belong in the King's stables instead of the King's court."

As soon as Dimnah flung this rebuke at him, the soldier left in disgrace and frustration at his inability to reply.

The Lion's Mother then spoke: "I am amazed at your overwhelming guile, your impudence and insolence, and your shameless answers to anyone who confronts you."

Dimnah replied, "That is because you always see me with one eye only, and hear me with only one ear. Though the devious reputation of my grandfather cast a shadow over me from the start, many have spread lies and rumours about me, and misuse the King's trust and generosity. They underestimate the patron of their wealth and good life. They do not know their place, or when to speak and when to remain silent.

The Lion's Mother appealed to the court, "Do you not see how this fool feigns innocence while his guilt is so grave?"

Dimnah quickly replied, "Those who perform the duties of others will never succeed—like a farmer who uses ashes in place of soil and manure; or a man who wears women's clothes or *vice versa*; or a guest who claims he is the master of the house; or the uninvited person who harangues a meeting on irrelevant matters. The fool is one who does not comprehend people's real issues, and thus he cannot ward off any real danger."

The Lion's Mother broke in: "You are truly a crafty traitor. Do you think that by speaking thus, you will deceive the King and escape imprisonment?"

But Dimnah replied, "The traitor naturally resorts to deception when desperate, and will not hesitate to eliminate his accuser at the first opportunity."

The Lion's Mother angrily replied: "You are a traitor, and a liar as well. Do you really believe that you will be saved from punishment, and that your craftiness will help you, despite the seriousness of your crime?"

Dimnah lashed out at her, "A liar is one who reports what never occurred, and quotes what was never said, and claims accomplishments that never happened. But my words are clear and true."

The Lion's Mother addressed the court, "The scholars among you will get to the bottom of this matter, and have the last word."

With this she angrily left the court. The Lion delivered Dimnah to the Judge and instructed to lock him up. The Judge put a rope around his neck and threw him in prison.

Kalilah knew by midnight that Dimnah was in custody. He visited him in disguise. When he saw Dimnah shackled and confined, he wept and said: "Deceit and trickery are what landed you in this misery. I tried sincerely to dissuade you from executing your wicked scheme. Warning and advice were all I could offer you. How I wished you had become an honest man! But each occasion has its message, and each event its proper setting. Had I failed to advise you when you were in your normal health and strength, I would have considered myself your accomplice in your crime. But ambition overcame your mind and disabled your judgment. I have offered you many examples, and reminded you of the teaching of our scholars. But the scholars also said, 'Crafty traitors usually die before their time.'"

Dimnah replied to Kalilah: "What you say now is quite true. The scholars also said: 'Do not complain of the punishment for a crime you planned and executed. It is far easier for a person to suffer the consequences of his crime in this world, than to endure the punishment and guilt hereafter in Hell.'"

Kalilah then said, "Yes, but your crime is so grave, and the Lion's punishment is so harsh."

Kalilah visits Dimnah in prison

It happened that a Leopard was imprisoned nearby and overheard the conversation between Kalilah and Dimnah. They were not at all aware of his presence. He realized very well why Kalilah was reproaching Dimnah, and heard the details of the whole story as repeated by Dimnah, confessing to his crime and to the enormity of his action. He carefully remembered what was said in order to testify if called before the court as a witness.

Kalilah was exhausted at that point, so he bade his brother Dimnah farewell, and sadly returned home.

Early the next morning, the Lion's Mother entered her son's quarters and addressed him, "O King, and Lord of the Beasts, it is your high duty not to forget what was said and done yesterday. You promptly resolved to imprison the jackal Dimnah, and thus you have satisfied God, the Lord of all Creatures. Our scholars correctly said in the past, 'One must never slacken in the pursuit of piety, and never defend the guilt of a scheming criminal.'"

When the Lion heard his Mother's words, he summoned the Tiger, who was also the Supreme Judge, and asked him together with his uncle, called the Just Lion, to look into Dimnah's case and investigate the matter thoroughly. Their assignment was to produce the evidence of his guilt, but only after meticulous, accurate and close examination and challenge according to legal custom and precedent. All ranks of the Army would be present in the court and listen to the deliberations. They were also to report to him all their findings on daily basis. Both the Tiger and the Just Lion complied with the King's orders.

Three hours later the Judge brought in Dimnah for questioning in the presence of the entire assembly. When everyone was ready, the court officer announced: "You all know that since he killed Shatrabah, the Lord of the Beasts has suffered from severe depression and apathy. He believes that he killed Shatrabah without any just cause, but was provoked to it by the lies and backstabbing deceit of Dimnah. The Judge has therefore been ordered to convene the court and investigate Dimnah's case. Whoever knows anything of Dimnah's actions, whether good or evil, let him say so now in front of the assembly and other witnesses, that his testimony may be assessed. Should Dimnah be condemned to death, there must be enough evidence to sustain it. We believe that haste is an unsuitable emotion in such proceedings, and favouritism is absolutely inappropriate."

At that point the Judge said, "You are all to abide by the instructions of the Lord of the Beasts that no one withhold anything you may know about Dimnah's case. He has strictly warned everyone not to perjure himself on Dimnah's behalf. There are three instructions you should bear in mind:

"First and most important: You must not underrate this hideous crime and treat it as a misdemeanour. The greatest sin is to execute an innocent person on evidence that is perjury and fabrication. Whoever knows the truth about any liar who has accused an innocent person, and schemed and fabricated lies that led to his death, and covered up afterwards, is considered an accomplice to that perjury and will share the same punishment.

"Second: If a defendant confesses to his guilt, it is better for him. The King and his officers may forgive him, or even set him free.

"Third: Never appease those who defame and slander others but live immorally themselves. Both the authorities and the common public must disavow such people. Whoever knows anything about such a crafty schemer must give evidence before the assembly and the witnesses. They will be treated as witnesses for the prosecution. I must remind you all of what was confirmed in the past: 'On the Day of Judgment a clot of fire will choke whoever conceals testimony in favour of a dead person.' Therefore each one must deliver his true testimony."

When the assembly heard the Judge's warning no one uttered a sound, until Dimnah addressed them and said: "Why are you so silent? Say whatever you know. But remember that I will have the right to challenge every statement made. I would remind you of what our scholars stated: 'Whoever testifies with respect to an act that he never saw, and says anything regarding issues of which he is ignorant, will face the same Destiny as the Physician who claimed competence in matters of which he was ignorant.'"

The assembly asked, "How does the story go?"

So Dimnah told them the story:

Once upon a time a knowledgeable and kind Physician lived in a city. He was very skilful in preparing fine medications. But this Physician became very old, and lost almost all his eyesight. A King ruled the city where he lived. The King had a daughter who was married to his nephew. One day she felt some of the pains typical of pregnancy. The Physician was called to examine the woman. He diagnosed her disorder and said, "If I had better vision I could mix her the correct medicine since I know all of the ingredients, but I don't trust anyone else to do it."

It also happened that a man known for his bravado lived in the same town. He had heard about the pregnant daughter of the King and her need for the medicine. He pretended to have full knowledge of medicine and to be expert in mixing pharmaceutical compounds. The King summoned him and sent him to the royal pharmacy to prepare the right prescription. Of course he knew nothing about any of the chemical or medical ingredients. Nevertheless, the Impostor haphazardly chose a few he found on the shelf, including one dose of poison. Ignorant of what he was doing, he mixed the chemicals with the lethal poison and gave the concoction to the pregnant woman, who died forthwith.

When the King heard of his daughter's death, he summoned the impudent Impostor and forced him to drink his own potion, which promptly killed him too.

"I have given you this example to show what happens when an informer alleges that someone has committed a wrong act, basing his information on mere suspicion, and thus becomes an offender by his accusation. Any one of you, therefore, who goes beyond the limits of his knowledge of the facts will face the same Destiny as the Ignorant Impostor, and has only himself to blame. Remember, the scholars have said in the past that 'Many a time the words people utter are visited upon them as evidence, either for or against them.' Now it is your turn to speak."

The Lord of the Pigs was present in the assembly. He enjoyed a special position and status before the Lion's court, which he now addressed: "Honourable scholars, listen to what I shall say and understand me well. When scholars in the past discussed matters relating to honest and righteous people, they believed that they could be identified by their pleasant countenance. I am sure that you, by virtue of your keen judgment that was God's gift and blessing to you, are able to judge righteous people simply by their looks. You can infer the larger picture from the small details. If you focus on this wretched creature, Dimnah, who stands before us accused of hideous crimes, you can easily observe the clues in his overall appearance that give evidence of his guilt."

The Judge interjected, "You have made it clear to me and to all the audience here that you know the signs that confirm the guilt of a person from his own appearance. Please elaborate, and verify your theory in the case of this villain."

The Lord of the Pigs proceeded to vilify and assail Dimnah and said, "A long time ago, scholars asserted that if one has a left eye smaller than the right, and twitches continuously, and if he also has a nose tilted slightly to the right, that creature is definitely a crafty scoundrel."

Dimnah replied sharply, "You are indeed astonishing. As if it were not enough to be a filthy creature, with repulsive physical features that are so conspicuous! What is more amazing, you still have the audacity to dine with the King, and visit with him despite your filthy, ugly physique. We all know your defects, yet you dare to ridicule pure bodies that are free of such faults. I am not alone in seeing your defects; the entire assembly here can confirm the facts. Our friendship has hitherto kept me from pointing this out. But now you have perjured yourself to my face, disclosed your real animosity towards me, and hurled slander in the presence of the assembly. Thus you give me no choice but to expose your defects to this assembly here and now. I can truly and honestly insist that those who know you well should prevail on the King to disinvite you from his table and his company.

"If you were assigned any agricultural responsibility, you would be a complete failure. All the more reason you should not try any useful trade: you should be neither a tanner nor a cooper to either the common folk or the gentry."

The Lord of the Pigs replied angrily, "You dare to speak to me in this way and treat me in this manner?"

Dimnah cut him short and said, "Indeed I do, and what I tell is the truth about you. What is more: you limp so badly because you were born with a broken and crooked leg. Furthermore: your paunch is repulsively flatulent and your lips are everlastingly slit. All in all, your appearance is as disgusting as your character is malicious."

By this time the face of the Lord of the Pigs was contorted, and displayed his severe distress. He wept for shame, stammered, stuttered, and was contemptuously humiliated before the entire assembly.

Dimnah went after him all the more aggressively when he saw him mortified and weeping: "You will cry even longer when the King notices your filthy features, disinvites you from his table, dismisses you from his service, and banishes you from his court."

The Lion had a very trustworthy Jackal stationed there among the assembly, with instructions to memorize all the dialogue in the court and report back to him. The Jackal went immediately to the Lion and told him all that transpired. The Lion then ordered the Lord of the Pigs relieved of all of his responsibilities, and directed him never to visit him or show his face again in court.

The Lion also ordered Dimnah remanded to prison. By now most of the day had elapsed, while all these events occurred. All the court proceedings were recorded and sealed by the Tiger, and everyone went home for the night.

It also happened that another Jackal named Rawzaba was a bosom friend of Kalilah, the brother of Dimnah. Rawzaba also frequented the Lion's court and the Lion greatly respected him, and was very generous to him. It happened at that time that Kalilah was severely depressed by Dimnah's situation. He became seriously ill and finally died of distress over what had become of his brother Dimnah. So Rawzaba went straight to Dimnah and conveyed to him the sad news of his brother's death. Both were sad and wept. Then Dimnah said to Rawzaba: "What shall I do in this world now that now my pure brother has departed and left me alone? I thank the Most High God that Kalilah did not die without leaving me another kinsman, a friend who is like a brother to me. I put all my trust in you, and in God's grace and His benevolence towards me, for the care and attention you have given me. I know you are my hope and my support through all this torment. Please do not fail me and do not refuse my overture, as I want to reward you for such deeds. Kindly go to a certain place which I shall describe to you accurately, and fetch me the wealth that by God's will my brother and I accumulated over the years by our hard work."

Rawzaba the Jackal did what Dimnah requested. When he brought the money, Dimnah gave him a share of it and said, "You can approach the Lion easier than anyone else. So as a favour to me, please listen carefully to everything said about me in the Lion's presence, and of what happens between my adversaries and myself as reported to the Lion. Be attentive to the Lion's Mother and her attitude towards me, and the Lion's responses, and whether he opposes her on any point. Please consign all of this to memory and then report to me."

Rawzaba the Jackal took the money and agreed to do as Dimnah requested. But he went home first and hid the money.

The next morning the Lion was sitting in his chamber. Two hours later his Companions asked to visit with him and he agreed. They entered and placed the confidential transcript of the court proceedings in front of him. He read all that had transpired in the court, and by now he was apprised of their proceedings and of the interventions of Dimnah. After he finished, he called his Mother and read it all to her. When she heard it, she shrieked at him: "Do not blame me if I speak harshly, for you seem unable to distinguish between what is good for you and what is harmful. I have consistently asked you to refrain from listening to him. These are the words of the criminal who deceived us and betrayed our trust."

She left in anger. Rawzaba the Jackal saw and heard everything, and hurried to Dimnah to report it all. At that moment a messenger arrived and took Dimnah before the Judge in court. The Judge called the court to order and said: "Dimnah, an honest and truthful informer had told me the fact of your guilt in this case, and there is really no need for us to prolong our investigation.

The scholars confirmed that God the Almighty made this world a prelude to and a proof of the eternal home. It is the home of prophets and of God's messengers, who point us to goodness, guide us to Paradise, and preach to us the knowledge of God. Your indictment and guilt have been proven to us, and this trustworthy person has already told us the

truth. However, our Lord the King has instructed us to review your case, and re-investigate it even though the evidence of your guilt is established beyond any doubt.

Dimnah replied, "I see, O Judge, that you are not familiar with the jurisprudence of our courts. It is an injustice for the King to force the oppressed and innocent to be tried by a corrupt judge like you. On the contrary, the judge should protect and defend them. How could you decide that I should be executed, without a challenge or defence? Only three days have passed, and now you want my death merely to satisfy your whims and emotions. But what has been said in the past in such circumstances is still true: 'He who has habitually performed acts of charity and tolerance is inclined to continue, even if such acts prove harmful to him in the end.'"

The Judge replied, "It has been written in our ancient books that a Judge must recognize the acts of good people and those of the wicked. Each will be rewarded or punished according to his deeds. If the Judge upholds this axiom, then good people will want to increase their benevolent acts and the wicked will be discouraged from performing their evil acts. It is therefore up to you, Dimnah, to consider what you have brought upon yourself, confess your guilt, confirm it, and repent.

Dimnah said, "Righteous judges do not hand down judgments based only on suspicion, nor do they make decisions founded on assumptions alone, when either gentry or common folk stand accused. They know that mere suspicion is no replacement for the truth. If any of you thinks I am a criminal, then I will only say that I know myself better than anyone else. My knowledge of myself is doubtlessly the truth, and your knowledge of me is twisted with suspicion and doubt.

"The nub of your criminal indictment is that I betrayed another person. Can you imagine the shame I would endure if I perjured myself and lied, thus exposing myself to your sentence of death? I am innocent of the crime of which I stand accused. What you should be doing is commending me for my integrity and honour. My chivalry, magnanimity and faith would never allow me to entangle you in the sort of injustice you are trying to impose upon me, by confessing to a crime I never committed. I have no right to ask you to inflict injustice, so how could I conspire in it myself?

"Please, Your Honour, refrain from such requests. Even if it were merely advice from you, it would be wrong of you to offer it to me. On the other hand, if it is a trick, then let all take note that the most grievous tricks are attempted by those who are assumed to be above such methods.

"But I know, Your Honour, that neither righteous judges nor pious rulers indulge in crafty schemes and deceit. You must know, Your

Honour, that whatever you decide will be taken as a precedent by the ignorant and the wicked. Honest people will cite honest precedents in the courts, while wrongdoers, the reckless, and the wicked will cite wrongful precedents. I fear, Your Honour, for your own sake, that your unsustained accusation of guilt will have a catastrophic impact. The catastrophe is that you still enjoy the same prestige, respect and status with the King, his army, the gentry and the common folk. You are esteemed for your opinions, convincing in your justice, satisfying in your decisions, your virtue, and your benevolence. How then could you forgo all these qualities when it comes to my case?"

At this point the Judge recessed the court and reported to the Lion what had happened. He then called in his Mother, who said to her son the Lion: "Now I am even more concerned, for Dimnah may succeed by using his great cunning and end up killing you, or manage somehow to destroy you. I worry that he may end up doing more mischief than what he already did through the deceit and slander that drove you to kill your friend without any cause."

The Lion listened intently and replied, "Then you must tell me who told you the truth about Dimnah's crime. That is the only way I can get the evidence to eliminate him."

She replied, "I hate to divulge a secret that has been entrusted to me. I shall never be at peace about Dimnah's death when I recall later how scholars have repeatedly prohibited us from revealing the secrets of others. But I will request the person who confided this secret to me to release me, and will ask that he himself reveal what he truly heard."

She left her son's court and immediately summoned the Tiger. She reminded him of his responsibility to assist the Lion in finding the truth, and that he should not refrain from being a witness, nor conceal his testimony, particularly since he enjoyed such high status. She also insisted he must uphold the rights of the oppressed and confirm the evidence of truth for both the living and the dead. For according to the statement of scholars, "Whoever conceals any evidence in favour of a dead person, will miss his own on judgment day."

She went on trying to convince him of his duties until he finally consented and went straight to the Lion. He reported everything he had heard of Dimnah's confession as he had memorized it. When it became known that the Tiger had testified against Dimnah, the Leopard, who was in jail and had overheard Dimnah's confession, sent a message to the Lion that he too wished to testify against Dimnah. When both the Tiger and the Leopard had testified, the Lion asked both of them, "What made you withhold your testimony, even though you knew our deep interest in the determining Dimnah's guilt?"

They both replied: "We were aware that according to the law, one witness is not enough for a judge to deliver a binding verdict. With this in mind, we were reluctant to come forward. But once the first came forward as a witness for the prosecution, the second was encouraged to complete the evidence as the Law requires."

The Lion accepted their explanations. He then ordered that Dimnah be executed in prison in the most ignominious manner.

Anyone who looks deeply enough into this case should know that whoever attempts to obtain personal gains with sweet talk and guile, and causes harm to others, will sooner or later be rewarded for his deceit, in the worst possible manner.

(The end of the Fable of the Investigation of Dimnah)

Friends are supporters and comforters

Chapter Three

The Fable of
the Ring-Dove

[The Ring-Dove, the Rat, the Deer and the Raven]

(Pure friends are supporters and comforters)

Dabshalim the King addressed Baydaba the Philosopher: "I have listened to the fable that describes how a dishonest person maliciously destroyed a sincere and intimate relationship between two friends by planting false reports. I appreciate the awful justice such a liar faces when his actions and intentions are ultimately discovered and promptly punished. Tell me now, if you please, about pure and honest friendship. How do people beget a close friendship, and come to enjoy each other's company?"

The Philosopher replied: "For rational beings no other relationship can be equated with true friendship. Close friends are the support for one another's good fortunes and welfare, and comforters when disaster strikes. This can be vividly appreciated in the fable of the Ring-Dove, the Rodent, the Deer and the Raven."

The King inquired, "How does the story go?"

Baydaba then began his tale.

Once upon a time in a land called Sakawandajeen, near a city called Dahar, there was an area ideal for all sorts of hunting, the favourite area for many hunters. A Raven lived there in a nest perched in one of the huge trees with many branches and thick foliage. One day while resting in his nest he noticed an ominous, skulking hunter, stout stick in his hand and hunting net on his shoulder, advancing towards the tree. The Raven was terrified and thought: "This bird-catcher is here for only one reason: my death or another's. I shall stay put and watch carefully what he is up to."

The Bird-Catcher spread his fine net and scattered some seeds on top of it. Once his trap was laid he hid himself in the undergrowth. After a little while a Ring-Dove, who was mistress of all pigeons in the neighbourhood, passed by with a flock of her friends. They failed to notice the trap, and began to feed on the seeds. Inevitably, the net caught them all. The Bird-Catcher was very pleased and began to advance towards them. Each of the pigeons tried on its own to break free from the strands of the net, but to no avail. Then the Ring-Dove rallied them: "In your anxiety to escape, do not forget to help one another. None of you in this situation should react selfishly and concentrate only on your individual safety. Instead, we should act as a team together. That way we might release the net, and all be saved."

The pigeons heeded the Ring-Dove's counsel, and with their combined strength they pulled the net free of its tether and soared into the sky, net and all. The Bird-Catcher was still hopeful, thinking they would not be able to fly far, and would eventually land and make it possible for him to net them once more. So he patiently pursued them.

The Raven had been watching, and decided to follow along and see what happened. He saw the Ring-Dove shrewdly observing the Bird-Catcher's persistent pursuit. After flying some distance, she told her companions: "The Bird-Catcher is persistent, and determined to catch us. If we continue flying in the open sky, he will keep us in sight and easily track us. But if we fly towards a town we shall probably lose him, and eventually he will leave us alone. I know a Rodent who is like a brother to me, and lives in a town not far from here. If we can get there, he will be able to cut the net and set us all free."

The pigeons agreed and directed their flight to the residential area. When the Bird-Catcher could no longer follow them he returned home discouraged, as they had hoped.

When the pigeons, led by the Ring-Dove, drew near her friend the Rodent, she ordered them to land. The Rodent had over a hundred holes in the area that allowed him to hide and escape when in danger. The Ring-Dove started to call out his name, which was Zirak. The Rodent heard his name and answered, "Who is calling?"

The Ring-Dove replied, "I am your dear friend, the Ring-Dove."

When he heard her voice he promptly emerged from his hideaway. He saw her situation, and immediately asked, "How did you fall into this awkward trap?"

She replied: "Don't you know that no good or evil befalls anyone without Destiny playing a decisive role? It is Destiny that put me in this awkward situation, as it has done many a time for others stronger and greater than myself. Even the sun and the moon can be eclipsed on orders from Destiny."

The Rodent, while listening to his friend's philosophizing, began to gnaw at the knots around the Ring-Dove with his sharp teeth. But she stopped him and said, "Please: first gnaw through the knots around the rest of the pigeons. Then when you finish, gnaw through mine."

She repeated her plea many times, but he paid no heed. Finally he gave voice to his curiosity: "You have persistently asked me to start freeing your friends. You seem not to be anxious about your own freedom, as if you had no care or concern for yourself."

She replied: "No, my friend. I am afraid that if you gnaw through the knots around me and set me free first, you may become bored or lazy and stop gnawing through the knots around the rest of our companions. But I know that if you start with them first, leaving me till the end, you will never abandon me no matter how exhausted you become."

The Rodent blurted out: "Your selflessness make me admire and love you all the more."

As the Ring-Dove requested, the Rodent then continued to gnaw through the knots in the net which entrapped each pigeon, until they were all free.

When the Raven observed what the Rodent had done, he was impressed and wished to befriend him. He flew over and loudly hailed him. The Rodent poked his head out of his hole and replied, "What is it you want?"

The Raven answered, "I would like us to become good friends."

But the Rodent replied, "You and I can never have a relationship. Rational beings must aim at what is possible and forego what is impossible. In our case, you are the predator, and I am merely your prey."

But the Raven pleaded with him: "It is true that you are my prey, but eating you will not make me significantly better off. Believe me, your friendship is far more important to me than having you as a meal. It is not fair for you to reject me. What made me seek your friendship were the genuinely ethical attitude and good manners I have observed in you. You were not trying to impress us or show off. A rational person will always disclose his superiority even when he tries to hide it. It may be concealed, yet nothing can stop the spread of its sweet fragrance, and compelling aroma."

The Rodent replied, "You must be aware that natural animosity between creatures is our most persistent and irrepressible instinct. One finds it in matched and mismatched forms. An example of a matched animosity is the natural, deep hostility between the Lion and the Elephant. When they fight, their strengths are matched. The Lion may end up killing the Elephant or *vice versa*. On the other hand, animosity is mismatched when their relative strengths are as different, say, as those of the Cat and myself ... or, for that matter, between you and me. Our animosity could never bring you to harm, but it would surely be the end of me. It is like water: even when heated to its boiling point, water will still quench fire. Any person who befriends such an adversary and makes peace with him, resembles someone who keeps a viper up his sleeve. My conclusion is that a rational person will never befriend a crafty enemy."

The Raven persisted: "I understand what you say. But I am

appealing to your native goodness to believe the truth of what I tell you. Do not make it so difficult for me and tell me there is no way we could ever become good friends. Rational and generous persons normally do not look for any reward from the good deeds they perform. Friendship between good people can be renewed easily and quickly even after long separations. It is just like a jug made of gold. Though hard to break, it is easy to repair. On the other hand, friendship between wicked people resembles a jug made of pottery. It is easily broken and impossible to repair. An amiable and generous person can befriend his own kind, but the mischievous and evil person harbours no love or friendship for anyone except out of fear or need. The reason why I am in need of your friendship and your favour is that you are good-hearted and magnanimous. I am going to stay right here by your door, and will eat nothing until you and I become bosom friends, as close as brothers."

The Rodent replied: "All right! I accept your friendship and we shall be as close as brothers. I have never turned away anyone in need. Please understand that I had to say what you heard, to test you and assure myself that you are trustworthy. I hate to think that if you ever deceive me, you might say that the Rodent was too easy a prey."

The Rodent then came out of his hole but remained just beside his door. The Raven asked, "What keeps you from coming over to enjoy my company? Do you still doubt my intentions"?

The Rodent replied: "People in this world interact in two different ways which both foster friendship. One is the interchange between their souls, and the other is the exchange of their physical needs. Those who give and take soul-to-soul are the pure people. But those who negotiate to supply their needs entangle their friendships with considerations of cost and benefit. Their acts of giving and their efforts to satisfy others are just like the Bird-Catcher who scatters seed to the birds. He is really interested in his own welfare, not that of the birds. Hence friendship based on the benevolence of the soul is far better than that based on worldly motives. I trust your intentions and the goodness of your inner soul, and share with you the goodness of mine. But it is your friends and acquaintances that bother me. Their inner nature is as bad as yours, and they do not share your high opinion of me."

The Raven rejoined, "One mark of close friendship is that one's friend is also a friend to one's friends, and an enemy to one's enemies. I guarantee that I have no companion or friend who would not like you, and I assure you that I can easily turn my back on all those whose nature I share."

After the Rodent heard this, he approached the Raven and shook hands with him, and they felt at ease with one another. They lived amicably for a few days. Then one day the Raven addressed his new friend, the Rodent: "You know, your burrow is very close to paths that are frequented by humans. I am afraid that one day some boy may throw a stone at you and hurt you. Now I know a secluded spring near here, where a Turtle friend of mine lives. There is an ample supply of fish that could feed us both, and we could live happily there. Let me take you with me there and we can live in peace."

The Rodent agreed and said, "I have so many stories to share with you when we reach our destination. So make whatever arrangements seem best."

The Raven took the Rodent by the tail, flew off with him, and landed at the designated place. As they were approaching the spring, the Turtle was at first alarmed to look up and see a Raven arrive carrying a Rodent. She was put at her ease when the Raven called her by name. She then realized he was her friend, and emerged from her home to greet him.

"Where did you come from?" she inquired.

The Raven recounted the story of the pigeons who had been trapped, how he had followed them, how they had been saved by the Rodent, and all that had led to their arrival.

When the Turtle heard the story of the Rodent, she admired his wisdom and his loyalty to his friends. She then asked him, "What brought you to our neighbourhood?"

But the Raven broke in and urged the Rodent: "Tell us the stories and the news you promised before we arrived in this neighbourhood. That will be the perfect prelude to the answer to my friend the Turtle. Please treat her as you do me."

So the Rodent began to tell his story.

My first home was in the house of an Ascetic in the city of Maroot. He had no family or children. Every day a basket full of food was brought to him. I used to observe his behaviour very carefully. He was in the habit of eating from the basket what he needed, and then hanging it up, with whatever food remained. After he left I would hop into the basket and eat my fill from it, then feed my fellow rodents as well. The Ascetic tried his best to hang the basket somewhere to protect his food, but to no avail. This went on until one night a friend of his came to visit. They supped together and began to converse. The Ascetic asked his Guest, "Where did you come from and where are you heading?"

The Guest, who seemed to have travelled across the world and seen its wonders, described the many countries he had visited, and the wonders that each offered. But the Guest eventually became annoyed by the Ascetic who would periodically clap his hands for no apparent reason, and interrupt him. Of course he was clapping to drive me away from the basket of food every time I got near it. Finally the Guest grew cross and said to the Ascetic: "I am talking to you in a civil way, yet you make sport of me. Why did you ask me to share with you what I have seen in this world?"

The Ascetic answered apologetically: "I was clapping to drive away a Rodent who has been a nuisance to me, but I don't seem able to get rid of him. He eats my food without leaving any for me."

The Guest said, "Is it just one Rodent, or more?"

The Ascetic replied, "There are many here in this house, but there is one Rodent in particular that I cannot outwit. I have run out of tricks to scare him off."

The Guest then said to the Ascetic, "You need to learn from the woman who agreed to barter shelled sesame for the cheaper unshelled."

The Ascetic inquired, "How does the story go?"

The Guest explained. "Once I stayed with a gentleman as his guest. After dinner he prepared my bed and went to sleep. But he was restless that night, and unable to sleep. Near morning I overheard him say to his wife, 'I have invited some people for lunch tomorrow. Please make them some food.'

"His wife told him angrily, 'How could you invite people to eat with us when we have nothing to feed our children? We spend all the income you make, and you never save.'"

"The man replied, 'Do not regret spending anything to feed us or others. Saving and hoarding may have terrible results, just like what once happened to the Wolf.'"

"His wife asked, "How does the story go?"

"The man said, 'Once upon a time a man went out hunting. A while later he saw a Deer. So he quickly readied his bow and arrow and neatly killed the Deer. He slung it over his shoulder and headed for home. Suddenly a wild and fearsome Boar blocked his way. He promptly shot it with his arrow. Unfortunately for the Hunter, the wounded Boar did not die instantly, but attacked and gored him so fiercely that the bow was knocked from his hands, and he finally died. Meanwhile the Boar too died of his wounds.

"Later still, a Wolf passed by and saw the three corpses lying on the ground. He thought happily, 'This Man, the Deer, and the Boar can feed me for a long period. But I shall start by eating the bowstring, and save the rest for later.' He gnawed on the bowstring for some time until it was severed. But unfortunately this released the tension on the bow so powerfully and abruptly that it struck the Wolf a fatal blow on the throat.

"The man paused for a while and went on speaking to his wife, 'I gave you this example to emphasize how the accumulation of wealth and savings may also have terrible results.'

"She replied to her husband, 'Well said. But we do have rice and sesame enough for six or seven people, so I shall start cooking while you invite whomever you wish.'

"The next morning the woman shelled a measure of sesame and spread it outside to dry in the sun. She instructed one of her young boys, 'Take care of the sesame, and do not let birds or dogs come near it.'"

"She went back to the kitchen to finish her cooking. It happened that the boy neglected her instructions and did not keep an eye on the sesame. Meanwhile a dog had passed by and fouled it. The woman, seeing that the sesame had become tainted, was loath to make any dish out of it. She took the peeled but tainted sesame to the market, and bartered it for an equal amount of the less expensive unshelled sesame. All this happened while I was standing in the market observing everything. Then I heard a man saying, 'There must be some reason why this woman bartered the more expensive shelled sesame for an equal amount of the less expensive unshelled sesame.'

"That is very similar to the story of your Rodent. You have told me that this apparently impoverished Rodent has been able to make a nuisance of himself. Well, let us see about that. Get me an axe and I will dig out his hole and discover some of his secrets."

The Ascetic complied with his guest's request and got him an axe, which he borrowed from his neighbours.

I was in my hole at the time, along with a bag of a hundred dinars, and had no idea who had hidden it there. When I overheard their conversation I became very concerned. Then suddenly the guest applied the axe to my burrow, and dug through until he reached the bag with the hundred dinars. He took it out and said to the Ascetic, "You know, this Rodent could have never succeeded in getting the jump on you and robbing you of your food without the resource of these dinars. Wealth has given him the extra support for physical strength, good thinking, and efficiency in planning."

The next morning all my friends the Rodents gathered and addressed me: "We are famished, and you are our only hope."

Hearing their pleas, I left with them and went to the perch from which I used to leap and get our food from the basket. I tried reaching it many times, but in vain. My weakness now was apparent to the rest of my associates. As they left me I heard them saying, "Leave him with whatever he has. He is so poor now that he needs someone else to support him." So they left me, shunned me, and even joined my enemies.

So I thought, "Only wealth can attract acquaintances, supporters and friends. I learned the hard way that a pauper is unable to achieve his objectives. His situation resembles rainwater that stagnates in the wadis and ditches, and cannot flow into a river, or anywhere. The result is that the earth will absorb it uselessly then and there."

I also discovered that without friends one is like a person without a family: a person without children has no posterity to honour his memory. What is more, a person without wealth also forfeits his intellect and his motivation, both here and in the eternal home. For when a person is reduced to poverty, his relatives and his friends will all abandon him. A pauper who is always is in need of others is like a tree in a swamp, consumed from every side.

Experience taught me that poverty is the prime cause of all calamities. It is the source of all immoral acts and the harbinger of disaster. I found out that when a person is reduced to poverty he becomes suspect to those who previously trusted him. Those who held him in high regard before he was poverty-stricken become distrustful. When anyone commits an evil deed, he is the first to be accused of the crime. All traits that are considered commendable in the wealthy become objectionable in the pauper. Bravery among the wealthy is recklessness among the poor. Generosity among the rich is considered squandering among the poor. If a poor person is patient, people see it as a weakness, and if he is really venerable, he will be thought of as senile. Death, therefore, is far preferable to asking for help from the unscrupulous and the stingy. It is easier for a conscientious person to seize the jaws of a serpent, milk its poison and drink it, than to request any assistance from a vile miser.

The Rodent paused, and then resumed the story he was recounting to the Turtle:

When the Guest found the bag of dinars he divided the money equally with the Ascetic, who wrapped his share in a piece of paper, and kept it beside his head when he went to sleep that night. I thought that I might still have a chance to get back part of that wealth, and store it in my hole in order to regain some of my lost strength. I could then attract back a few of my friends who had abandoned me when they learned my wealth was gone. I crept up to the Ascetic while he was sleeping, quite close to his head. Only then did I realize that his guest was still awake, and clasping a stout stick in his hand. He promptly struck me on my head. It was so painful that I rushed back to my hole. After a while when the pain subsided, greed and determination prompted me to have another try. This time the guest hit me so hard I was a bloodied mess. It left a memory so painful that it made me hate wealth; my body would shiver instinctively every time I remembered any wealth.

I realized then that problems in this world are caused by greed and unwarranted ambition. People who cherish this world will always be in a state of exhaustion and fatigue from incessantly attempting to achieve their material desires. I also came to the conclusion that emigrating to distant areas in order to obtain wealth is far better than begging, even from generous people. Moreover there is nothing equal to contentment in this life. This is how I convinced myself to be satisfied and gratified by my lot in this world, and why I decided to move out of the Ascetic's house into the wilderness.

There I happened to make friends with a Pigeon, and through him I befriended the Raven. The Raven recounted your friendship with him, and said he wished to visit you. I asked him to bring me along to meet you. Life without friends is synonymous with loneliness, and a desolate experience. I believe there is no joy in this world that equals friendship. Nothing is as dismal as its absence. I have tried so many things in this life, and now I know better. I know that a rational being should seek only the basic resources that defend him against all evil. That is to say: adequate food and drink to assist in maintaining good health of body and tranquillity of mind. If a person is offered the entire world with all it contains, he still requires only a minimal amount of basics to defend himself against need. That is why I accompanied the Raven, and I consider myself your brother and friend, and I wish and hope that you will also consider me as such.

When the Rodent finished his story, the Turtle replied with profound grace. "I listened to you and was elated by what you said. But I sense that you may still be somewhat inhibited. I must emphasize to you that rational words and talk mean very little if not ratified by successful actions. Imagine a patient who knows exactly which medicine can cure him but does not use it. In that case his knowledge is not worth anything, and his sickness will still prevail.

"Therefore use your faculties well and never worry about a want of wealth. You must know that a magnanimous person may be honoured even if he does not have any wealth, just as the lion is dreaded even when he is lying down at rest. The reverse may also be true. A wealthy person who lacks magnanimity may be despised, just like an outcast dog is shunned even if they adorn him with golden anklets. Do not let the distress of departure from your homeland overcome you. You must be like the lion who moves around with his innate strength intact whenever he settles. If you know yourself well, the natural slopes in life will allow exquisite rewards to flow towards you like the gathering of rainwater. You must understand that priorities in this world accrue to the more knowledgeable, the more reflective, and the more determined people. What is more, no goodwill ever rewards the idle and wavering person.

"It was said in the past that there is no longevity or constancy in the following:

"The shade of a summer cloud,

"The friendship of wicked people,

"The stability of buildings without foundation, and

"Abundant and extensive wealth.

"A rational person therefore should not grieve over his lack of wealth. The fortune of a rational being is his faculties, and his good performance in this life. He can be sure that no one will ever rob him of what he has already done, nor would anyone blame him for something he chose not to do. Such a person is not apt to be cheated of the final chapter of his life, for death comes only by surprise, and has no accurate or defined time.

"Permit me to say that though you may have a lot of experience and knowledge in life, which may render all I have told you less valuable, I considered it an obligation to explain to you our understanding of things.

"Since you are now our sincere brother and intimate friend, all our advice is humbly offered to you."

When the Raven heard what his friend, the Turtle, had shared with the Rodent, and heard the kindness she showed him throughout her discourse, he was elated. He told her: "Your attitude towards our friend has pleased me, and you have honoured me by your courtesy. I pray that you will be as happy as I am. The people in this world worthiest to achieve happiness are those whose home and circle of acquaintance are full of friends and honest confidants. There are always a few among them that will make each other's lives tranquil and happy, and can willingly assist each other in times of need. Only magnanimous and noble-minded individuals can lift up their noble-minded friends when disaster strikes their lives. Only other elephants can pull out an elephant trapped in a deadly muddy pit."

Just as the Raven was speaking, a Deer suddenly came rushing towards them. The Turtle plunged into the water, the Rodent scurried back into his hole, and the Raven flew off and perched on one of the trees close by. Then the Raven took a turn high overhead to see if anyone were pursuing the Deer. When he saw no one, he called the Rodent and the Turtle to come out, since all was safe. When the Turtle saw the Deer looking intensely into the water in the spring, she understood and addressed him kindly, "If you are thirsty, go ahead and drink without fear, for you are safe in this place."

The Deer drew near and drank. The Turtle cordially welcomed him and asked, "Where have you come from?"

The Deer replied, "I was roaming in the Sahara, but hunters with lethal arrows hunted me and I was chased from one place to another. Today I saw a figure far off, and feared he might be one of the hunters, so I ran towards this place as fast as I could."

The Turtle gently calmed him down: "Fear not: we have seen no hunter here. Please feel at home among us, and be good enough to accept our friendship. There is plenty of water here, and ample grazing fields. We wish you welcome."

The Deer accepted, and stayed with them. As time passed, it became customary for these friends to sit together each day in the shade in their favourite spot, chatting and discussing the events and news. One day the Raven, the Rodent and the Turtle were sitting and talking in the shade as they did every day. They began to worry when the Deer did not appear. They were worried that some harm might have befallen him. Both the Rodent and the Turtle asked the Raven, "Could you please go up and look for any sign of our friend? Please search in all directions."

The Raven promptly flew high up in the sky, and to his dismay he saw the Deer tied down by ropes. He quickly dived back to rejoin the Turtle and the Rodent and told them what he had seen. Then both the Raven and the Turtle turned to the Rodent: "This is a matter only you can handle. You must assist your friend and rescue him."

The Rodent accepted the mission and promptly rushed to the Deer. He asked, "How did you, with all your intelligence, fall into this muddle?"

The Deer sadly replied, "And since when can intelligence displace Destiny?"

At that point the Turtle arrived. The Deer told her with anxiety: "It was not wise of you to come here. The Rodent may free me from those ropes, and if the Hunter surprises us, I can outrun him, the Rodent can disappear quickly in one of the many holes, and the Raven will simply take to the air. But you are very heavy and slow, and I am afraid the Hunter will harm you."

The Turtle answered firmly, "Life is meaningless when sincere friends part. If dear and devoted friends leave each other, it is as though one's heart has been wrung, and one is denied any happiness, and is blinded as if a thin film has clouded his eyes."

The Turtle had just finished her statement when the Rodent

managed to cut the ropes and free the Deer. But then the Hunter suddenly appeared. The Deer ran away, the Raven flew off into the sky, and the Rodent dived into one of the nearby holes. Only the Turtle was left standing there. The Hunter approached the trap and saw that his ropes had been cut. He looked to left and right and saw only the Turtle slowly crawling off. He caught her and tied her up. It did not take long before the Raven, the Rodent and the Deer got together and observed the Hunter binding the Turtle, and they were greatly distressed.

The Rodent lamented: "What a life! The moment we overcome one calamity we suddenly find ourselves thrown in the midst of a worse one. It is truly said that 'a person will continue firmly and smoothly in this life until he stumbles and falls, for whatever reason.' From then on, it seems, he will succumb to further troubles and obstacles, and his road to success will be full of hurdles and impediments even when things otherwise seem to be clear.

"I care dearly for the Turtle, the best of friends, not for any expected reward or ulterior motive but because of our deeply honourable friendship: a friendship better than any between father and son, and so strong it ends only with death. Woe to this body, which is fatally threatened by disasters, subject to the damage of time, and without permanency. Matters are then taken out of our hands abruptly and quickly, for nothing lasts forever. The rising stars will not go on ascending, nor will the setting stars go on falling. Those that rise will one day fall, and those that fall will one day rise again.

"Separation from our intimate friends is so painful: sharp like severe cuts and deep slashes, as excruciating as serious wounds."

Then the Deer and the Raven addressed the Rodent: "Neither our care, nor yours, nor your eloquent words alone, will be of any help to the Turtle just now. People, it is said, are put to the test when they face real challenges. Honesty is confirmed only when real transactions occur. Love, and care for one's family and children, are promptly tested when need arises. Likewise sincere and devoted friends prove their loyal friendship uniquely when disasters strike."

The Rodent then replied: "I have a plan to get us out of this predicament. The Deer must stay in view of the Hunter, and pretend to be wounded and limping. The Raven should then fall upon him and act as if pecking at his wounds. As for me, I shall stay close to the Hunter and watch him closely. He may possibly leave his weapons and the Turtle and pursue you in hopes of catching you. As he comes closer, start limping slowly enough to make him hope to overtake you. He needs to believe he will eventually succeed. Draw him as far away as you possibly can. I hope that will give me enough time to gnaw through the ropes binding the Turtle, and save her."

Both the Raven and the Deer followed the instructions of the Rodent. The plan worked, and the Hunter followed the Deer and the Raven for a good distance. The Rodent finally succeeded in gnawing through the ropes and freed the Turtle.

Exhausted and weak from following the Deer and the Raven, the Hunter decided to quit his pursuit. He returned to where he had left the Turtle but was stunned to find only the severed ropes. Then all of a sudden he thought of the strange things that had happened, like the Deer who had walked with a limp all the time he followed him. He became confused and thought that he was losing his mind. He also recalled the Raven who was feeding on the Deer. He could not imagine how his strong ropes had been mysteriously severed. He was spooked by it all, and murmured, "This land is odd. It is an abode either for magicians or for the Jinn and demons."

Perplexed, he abandoned his gear and ran off, too frightened even to look back over his shoulder. Meanwhile the Raven, the Deer, the Rodent, and the Turtle went back to their newly secured and shady place. There they lived happily ever after in untroubled tranquillity ...

Baydaba the Philosopher paused briefly, and then reflected: "It is fascinating to observe that these small, weak creatures were repeatedly able to save themselves from harm and even death. What made that possible were their sincere and pure friendship, their courageous and wholehearted loyalty, and the profound gratification they experienced in the company of each other, without any ulterior motives.

"If these beasts could do it, it is worthier still for human beings to become dear and sincere friends, each providing the other with the necessary support and required strength. All the more so since they are provided with rational faculties and intelligence, and the ability to differentiate between good and evil, and are uniquely endowed with knowledge and judgment.

"What I have recounted to the King is an example of how people should perform in a pure, sincere and untainted environment of honest brotherhood and pure friendship.

(The end of the Fable of the Ring-Dove)

The Ravens and the Owls

Chapter Four

The Fable of
the Ravens and the Owls

(Beware of the deceptive deference of the enemy)

Dabshalim the King asked Baydaba the Philosopher, "Now that I have heard the fable of the sincere, loyal and intimate friends who became closer than brothers, I understand how they should co-operate with each other. Would you please tell me a fable about an enemy that should never be relied upon or trusted, even if he exhibits submissiveness, deference and flattery?"

The Philosopher answered, "Anyone who is deceived by an inveterate and aggressive enemy will surely end up in a calamity like that inflicted on the Owls by the Ravens."

"How does the story go?" the King asked Baydaba.

Baydaba then began his tale.

Once upon a time a thousand ravens nested in a huge tree, and had chosen a Raven as their King to rule them. Beside their abode was a cave that served as the habitat of a thousand owls, and they had chosen an Owl as their King to rule them. These two groups, and their respective rulers, sustained a deep and lasting animosity towards each other.

One night the King of the Owls and his army raided the nests of the ravens, and killed and captured a good number of them. In the morning, the surviving ravens assembled with their King and said, "The King is now aware of what the King of the Owls and his army have done to us. Some have been killed, and the majority of those remaining suffer wounds, broken wings, torn feathers, or severed tails. But the worst of it is their familiarity with our abode, and their bold and insolent attack on us. We are sure they will attack us again, and will continue to do so now that they know our habitat so well. We are loyal to the King, and will follow his guidance. May it please him to consider the situation, and then tell us what to do for his safety as well as our own."

At that time there happened to be Five Ravens known for their sound knowledge and judgment, who were especially reliable about critical decisions and serious policy matters. The King of the Ravens always solicited their advice when facing crises or disasters.

The King asked the First of his Five Advisors, "What do you think we should do?"

He replied, "My opinion is not new, but based on what our scholars advised in the past. They agreed that the only response to an angry enemy is to leave our land and flee in order to save ourselves."

The King then turned to the Second Advisor and asked, "What do you think of this matter?"

The Second replied, "My opinion is similar to that of my colleague. We should escape with our lives."

The King then stated: "I really cannot accept such a strategy. We should not succumb to our enemy and leave our land and home as soon as disaster strikes. On the contrary, we should unite and prepare ourselves to fight our enemy and intensify our resistance. We should be on the alert so as not to be taken by surprise, but to meet them fully prepared, and to fight them from strength so as not to lose the war and be forced to retreat. We should plan to fight with everything we have, and ensure that our wits match those of the enemy. We must defend ourselves in our stronghold and outmanoeuvre the enemy, sometimes with patience and delay, other times by engagement, until we find the opportune moment to win this war and defeat our enemy once and for all."

Then the King turned to the Third Advisor: "Now what is your opinion?"

He answered: "I do not agree with the opinions expressed by my two colleagues. I suggest instead that we send spies and informants to feed us the right information about the enemy. Simultaneously, we should dispatch a delegation to find out if the enemy wants peace, war, or ransom. If we find that the real motive of this raid was to obtain money, then we might conclude a peace treaty in which we commit to pay them a certain annual tax, and then be safe and secure in our own homeland. It was said in the past by many kings: 'If the enemy has achieved the upper hand in any war, and our kings fear for their lives and their lands, they should use their wealth to shield their country, themselves and their subjects from further harm.'"

Then the King asked the Fourth Advisor the same question. He replied, "I do not share that view. My advice is to leave our homeland. To tolerate the suffering of homelessness and to persevere under the resulting hardships of our daily life is far better than losing our dignity and self-esteem, and preferable to submission to an enemy that is beneath us in status and honour. I am sure that if we follow what my colleague has suggested, the King of the Owls will never accept less than exemplary punishment. It was said in the past: 'If you conciliate your enemy, offer no more than the minimum to obtain your objectives. You should refrain

The Advisors devise a plan

from full rapprochement with the enemy; otherwise he will abuse you, weaken your army, and humiliate you. The situation will then resemble a wooden pole erected under the sun. If you tilt it slightly its shadow will be lengthened. If you continue tilting it, however, beyond a certain angle the shadow will begin to be drastically reduced.'

"I say therefore that our enemy will always slight and humiliate us, even if we fully reconcile with him. It is our duty to express our opinion to you, but your exclusive responsibility is to defend the country, even by waging wars.

Then the King turned to his Fifth Advisor and asked, "What is your opinion and what do you choose? War, peace, or abandonment of our homeland?"

The Fifth Raven said, "One should not go to war against those who are superior in strength. It could be truly said, then, that a person who does not evaluate his own strength and that of his enemy, and fights those who are stronger than himself, will be fatally vanquished. A rational person never undermines or belittles the capabilities of his enemies; otherwise he would unwittingly deceive himself and invite a decisive defeat. Personally, I am afraid of the King of the Owls and his army, even if they do not take the offensive. My fear of them was already strong even before their most recent attack. A prudent person will never trust the enemy whatever the circumstances. If the enemy be far, one will always fear his reach. On the other hand, if he be close one can never be safe from his sudden, sneak attack. And if the enemy be alone, one should not underestimate his cunning and deceit.

"The most shrewd and efficient people are those who detest going to war simply to avoid tax and tribute. The cost of dealing with an enemy without waging wars will normally be measured by the expenditure of money, equipment and labour. However the cost of warfare includes the further cost of the souls and bodies of those involved.

"I therefore advise the King not to declare war on the owls. Whoever fights a stronger enemy courts his own destruction. If a king protects all his secrets, selects his viziers carefully, maintains deep respect among his people, and is personally above reproach, then he can never be deprived of the innate goodness and effectiveness he possesses. I believe that our King is the kind of person I have described.

"The King has consulted me and expects my answers. Some of what I have to say is for the public ear, but certain strategic matters must be treated confidentially. And even secrets and confidentiality are ranked. A few could be shared with close friends and associates; fewer still, with select confidants and aides. But there are certain issues that should be known by only two persons. My final proposals are that confidential and not to be shared by more than four ears and two tongues."

The King agreed. He rose immediately and met with his Fifth Advisor for some time behind closed doors.

The King asked first, "Do you know how the hostility first arose between the owls and us?"

The Advisor replied, "Yes. Some unwise and unwarranted words were spoken in the past by one of the ravens."

The King then inquired, "And how does the story go?"

The Fifth Advisor Raven then offered his account:

Once upon a time a group of cranes had no ruler, and for some reason they agreed to choose an owl as their new king. While they were still in discussion a Raven happened to land nearby, and they thought it might be a good idea to consult the Raven on the matter. When the Raven drew near they requested his advice. He said, "Even if all the birds begin to die out from region to region, and the peacocks, the ostriches, and the pigeons are vanishing from face of the earth—even then, you should never feel compelled to appoint an owl as your king. The owls are the ugliest of birds, and possess the worst behaviour, the least intellect, and the deepest hostility. They are the farthest from compassion. They harbour such traits in addition to their blindness and their inability to see during the daytime. But their worst and most repulsive traits are their insolent incompetence and antagonistic behaviour. I am sure it would be far better for you not to let owls rule you. You can rule yourselves well enough and use your own faculties and good judgment, just like the Hare who claimed that the Moon was her King, and acted accordingly."

The cranes asked, "And how does the story go?"

The Raven replied:

Once upon a time a land long inhabited by the elephants gradually became desolate as its water dwindled and its springs dried up, its plants withered and its trees dried out. As the elephants became unbearably thirsty, they went and complained to their King. He then sent his messengers and his experts in all directions scouting for water. One of them came back, reported that he found a spring, and described its exact location. Its name was the Moon Spring. The King and his subjects headed happily and swiftly towards the spring to quench their thirst.

It happened that this spring was in a land belonging to the Hares. In their stampede the elephants crushed many of them to death. The surviving Hares then assembled urgently with their King and demanded that something be done. They said, "The King is aware of the calamity inflicted on us by the elephants."

The Cranes seek a king

He answered, "Let each one present me with his opinion on this matter."

A Hare named Firuz, whom the King knew to be of sound thinking and judgment, came forward and said, "I ask the King to dispatch me to the King of the Elephants, along with one of his confidants, to report to him what he sees and what I tell him."

The King of the Hares replied, "You are very trustworthy and we shall accept what you advise. Go to the elephants in my name and deal with them as you see fit. But you must understand that the judgment, the reasoning, the intellect, the flexibility, and the grace of the messenger should reflect the strength and wits of the person who sent her. So you must treat the elephants with the utmost gentleness, kindness and patience. It is the deferential messenger who can relax the fury of the enemy, and the harsh messenger who will aggravate him."

When the full moon was at its brightest, Firuz the Hare set out to meet the King of the elephants. As she approached, she was afraid they might crush her tiny body with their gigantic feet, even if unintentionally. So she decided not to go very close. She climbed to the top of a mountain overlooking them, and from there she called down to the King of the Elephants: "The Moon has sent me to the King with a message. Please understand that a messenger should not be blamed if the message contains harsh words."

The King of the Elephants asked, "What is the message?"

She replied: "Thus says the Moon: "Whoever knows that he is stronger than the weak, but presumes he can bully and fight still stronger beings, will surely be swallowed by disaster. You know your strength with respect to the rest of the beasts. But you have been deluded into supposing you can do anything and harm anyone you choose. You have paraded down to the spring dedicated to me, and drunk from it, and defiled it."

The Moon has therefore sent me to warn you never to do that again. If you do, I will blight your eyesight and destroy you. If you doubt my message, come to the spring now and I will meet you there.

The King of the Elephants was nonplussed by the words of the Hare. So he agreed, and left with Firuz the messenger to go to the spring.

When he arrived and looked into the spring he saw the reflection of the Moon's rays in the water. Firuz told him, "Draw some water into your trunk, wash your face, and then kneel to the Moon."

The King of the Elephants plunged his trunk in the water, and as the water was stirred the reflection was jostled, and he imagined that the Moon had trembled. Puzzled, he asked, "Why did the Moon tremble? Is he angry because I put my trunk in the water?"

Firuz the Hare said firmly, "Yes."

الأرنب

الفيل

Firuz the Hare subdues the Elephant

So the King of the Elephants knelt once more to the Moon, apologized for what he had done, and vowed that neither he nor any of his subjects would ever repeat what they had done to the Hares.

The Raven continued addressing the cranes: "In addition to what I said about the owls: they specialize in slyness, cunning and deceit. Of all kings, the deceitful one is the worst. Whoever has the misfortune of serving such a king will face an end similar to that of the Hare and the Corncrake when they went to the Cat for arbitration."

The cranes asked, "And how did that come to pass?"

The Raven began:

Once I had a Corncrake as a neighbour, and he lived in a tree very close to my nest. We used to be very good friends. Then one day he disappeared. I did not know his whereabouts, and he stayed away for a very long time. Some while later a Hare came by and dwelt in the Corncrake's home. I did not wish to dispute with the Hare, so I said nothing. She stayed there for some time. Then one day the Corncrake returned to his house, only to find the Hare occupying it. So he told her, "This is my house, so be good enough to move out and find a place of your own."

The Hare replied, "No. This is my house and I already occupy it. You are an imposter. If this is really your house as you claim, then prove it."

The Corncrake responded, "The Judge lives nearby; let us go and see him."

The Hare said, "Who is he?"

The Corncrake replied, "On the coast near us there is a very devout Cat who prays a great deal. He fasts all day, and spends all night praying. He harms no beast and sheds no blood. He lives on the grass he eats and whatever is cast up by the sea. If you like, we can go to him and agree to his judgment."

The Hare answered, "If he is as you describe, I will gladly accept his judgment."

The Raven then said, "I followed the two of them to see how those known to fast and pray reach their judgments."

They all journeyed together to see the Cat. When he saw both the Hare and the Corncrake approaching, he promptly stood up and began praying. He appeared serene and displayed the utmost deference and humility. Both were impressed by what they saw, approached him respectfully, and saluted him. He ordered each to present his or her case. When they finished he said, "You must realize that I am growing old, and cannot hear so well. Please come closer so I can understand more clearly what you are saying."

The Hare, the Corncrake and the Cat

Both approached him further, repeated their pleas, and awaited his judgment. Then he spoke: "I understood what you said. But before giving my judgment let me give you a piece of advice.

"First, I must admonish you to fear God, and never ask for anything beyond your true rights. Those who seek the right thing will achieve it, even if they have to die for it. Anyone who wrongfully seeks what is not rightly his will ultimately lose, even if the judgment goes for him. A person who lusts for the goods of this world owns nothing in reality. Nothing is worth more than righteous deeds: neither wealth nor friends. A person of sound mind will seek the possessions that he can keep forever, whose benefits are enjoyed in the future. He should refrain therefore from craving worldly possessions.

"The value of wealth for a rational person is no more than pieces of clay or stone. But the value of people for him lies in the good he wishes for them, and the evil from which he protects them, as he would wish for himself."

The cat continued his smooth talk until both trusted him completely. They relaxed, and drew very close to him. At the opportune moment, he leapt on them both and killed them instantly.

The Raven then resumed his advice to the cranes: "The owls combine all the ugly omens and shameful traits. Hence never even think of having an owl as your king."

After the cranes heard the Raven's advice, they decided against the Owl.

The Owl himself was present at the meeting, and had heard everything. He approached the Raven and addressed him angrily, "You have done me irreparable harm; yet I cannot recall ever having harmed you. There was no cause for what you have said and done.

"You know that when an axe cuts a tree, the tree can still grow, and when a sword slashes the flesh, it will eventually heal. But the wounds made by the tongue, by the spoken word, never heal. The arrow that pierces the flesh may be plucked out, but the sharp darts of the tongue hold fast when they hit the heart. You may know that for every fire there is a quencher. Flame is extinguished by water, poison by medicine, and sadness by patience; but the fire of hatred can never be smothered. Therefore you and the race of ravens have planted between yourselves and us owls the tree of resentment, animosity and hatred."

At the end of his speech the Owl left in a rage. He conveyed what had happened to the King of the Owls, word for word.

Later on, the Raven regretted all he had said, and reproached himself: "I have surely committed a serious breach, and brought upon myself and my fellow ravens unwarranted animosity and hatred. I sincerely regret having given the cranes any advice, or told them anything hostile about the owls. Probably most birds have more experience than I in worldly matters, and have acquired more prudence in dealing with such issues. I am sure they would have refrained from using such words, in order to avoid what I failed to avoid. They must have more insight, and see more clearly where such follies would lead. Words can injure both speaker and audience, and plant hatred and rancour. Such harsh words are not mere words, but sharp arrows and pointed spears."

"A rational person who is confident of his strength and his superiority should never use them to provoke enmity. A person who has an antidote in his possession should not thereby feel free to swallow poison. On the other hand, an effective person who has misjudged an issue may later focus his judgement more keenly and perform more shrewdly in crisis. Others who sound impressive before a crisis may flounder when it arrives.

"I am an unfortunate whose words have driven him to disaster. My stupidity made me speak beyond my experience, because I was unwilling to listen to those who knew better. I am the sadder for being a speaker but not a listener.

"Whoever fails to obtain the advice of the more experienced, and hastily decides to act without patiently reviewing the situation, may face unpleasant results. I could have done far better than my performance today, and could easily have avoided falling into this unwarranted and awkward state of affairs.

The Raven continued blaming and reproaching himself and went off in a dejected state.

The Fifth Raven Advisor then said: "The King has asked me how the antagonism between us ravens and the owls began, and I have told him the story. I have also given my judgement and my reasons for it. But I have another scheme that may, God willing, relieve us. For many a people has planned and schemed in a discreet and clever manner, and ultimately achieved great goals. This is illustrated in the fable of the gang who robbed the Ascetic of his young goat."

The Raven King asked, "And how does the story go?"

The Raven Advisor began his tale:

Once upon a time an Ascetic bought a healthy kid in order to sacrifice it. He was leading it along the street when a scheming gang of thieves saw him and decided to take it from him. One of the gang approached him and said, "You, Ascetic, what kind of dog do you have?"

Another came by and commented, "This is not an ascetic, for

ascetics do not have dogs."

They continued harassing the Ascetic in this manner until he was persuaded that he was leading a dog and not a kid, and that the person who sold it to him had used a spell on him. So he turned the kid loose, and the gang carried it off.

"I cited this fable to illustrate that we may be able to achieve our purpose through patience and a well-considered plan. What I would request from the King is that he peck at me in front of a crowd, and pluck out all my body-feathers and my tail-feathers. Then he should dump me at the base of this great tree. He and all his army should then immediately go off to some secure place. I hope that I will then have the patience to find out the plans of the owls and study their defence systems. My hope is to deceive them. At the opportune time I shall find a way to come to you, and we shall execute our plan to attack and defeat them, by God's will."

The King asked the Raven seriously, "Do you really agree to what you have suggested?"

The Raven confirmed, "Of course, how could I not agree to whatever might relieve my King and his soldiers?"

The King then pecked the Raven all over his body and followed through with the plan, departing with his soldiers.

The Raven began to moan and groan until the owls heard and saw him, and informed their King. The King went to the Raven to enquire about his kinsmen, the ravens. When he reached the Raven he asked one of the owls to interrogate him. The owl asked, "Who are you, and where are the ravens?"

The Raven answered, "I am only an unimportant raven. As you can see, my condition reflects the fact that I am not one who is privy to confidential matters."

Some of the owls recognized him and said to the King, "He is the Vizier of the King of the Ravens, his chief counsellor. Let us find out from him what crime he had done to deserve such a severe punishment."

When asked, the Raven replied, "Our King solicited the advice of his counsellors on how to respond to your recent ultimatum. I was present when he requested our opinion and told him that, frankly, we are unable to fight the owls. They are stronger and more courageous than we are. I suggested seeking peace, and offering a reasonable ransom. If the owls agree, I said, that is fine, but if they do not then we will have to go into exile from our land. If war between the owls and us is good for them and destructive for us, then peace is the better alternative. I urged the ravens not to go to war with you, and gave them a number of examples. I assured them that our enemy is powerful and that nothing can contain his might better than capitulating to his will. I even told them, 'Don't you observe how the grass in the ground survives the forceful wind? Because it is slim, it leans with the wind.'

"Alas, they ignored me and claimed they preferred to fight. They even accused me of collaboration with the owls against them. They defied me and shouted down my advice. Then they tortured me, severely. The King and his soldiers left me in this awful condition, and I have no idea where they went afterward."

When the King of the Owls heard the Raven's explanations, he asked his viziers about their opinions and demanded what action should be taken in his regard.

The First Vizier said, "I believe we should kill him here and now. This is the best way to defend ourselves against the ravens. By killing him, we avoid his shrewd craftiness, and the rest of the ravens will be deprived of his advice. I remind you of what was said in the past: 'When all the factors of success suddenly become available, in perfect proportion, at one moment, it is not wise to let the opportunity pass. People who aspire to achieve great things, and labour and struggle towards their planned targets, but fail to seize the moment, will irretrievably waste an opportunity that may never be repeated. Similarly, if one finds his enemy in a weak situation and spares his life, he will regret it later when the enemy develops the necessary strength and wields more power.'"

The King then requested the opinion of the Second Vizier. "What should be done with this Raven?"

He answered, "I think the King should not kill him. A humiliated enemy without supporters is worthy of our mercy and forgiveness, and his life should be spared. The enemy who is fearful and asks for our protection should be worthy of our trust."

The King of the Owls then asked the Third Vizier, "What do you think should be done?"

The Third Vizier replied, "I think the King should keep him and treat him well. He could be a good advisor. One may reasonably consider that when our enemies are fighting each other it constitutes a victory for the King. When he finds that his enemies are divided among themselves it is a major relief for him. He could be saved, just like the Ascetic was saved from the Thief and Satan.

The King asked, "How does the story go?"

The Third Vizier of the Owls said, "Once upon a time an Ascetic was given a very productive cow. She could produce an abundance of milk for him to live on. He led her home, but a Thief saw him and decided to steal her. At the same time Satan stood by, and he planned to kidnap the Ascetic.

"Satan asked the Thief, 'Who are you?'

"The Thief replied, 'I am a Thief. I want to steal this cow from the Ascetic as soon as he goes to sleep. And who are you?'

"Satan answered, 'I am Satan. I intend to kidnap the Ascetic when he goes to sleep and take him with me.'

"So they both followed the Ascetic and entered his house after him. The Ascetic tethered the cow in the corner of his house, ate his supper, and went to sleep.

"The Thief and Satan discussed their plans, but disagreed as to who was to make the first move. Satan told the Thief, 'If you begin by stealing the cow, the Ascetic may wake up. He will yell and the neighbours will then wake up and come to his aid. If that happens, I shall be unable to kidnap him. Therefore wait until I finish with him and then you can do whatever you want.'

"The Thief was afraid that the Ascetic would wake up when Satan attempted to kidnap him, and spoil his plan to steal the cow, so he disagreed. He told Satan, "No, you wait until I take the cow and then he is all yours."

"Both continued arguing until the Thief became disappointed and frustrated and started shouting, 'Wake up and watch out, Ascetic! Satan wants to kidnap you!'

"Satan also shouted, 'Wake up and watch out, Ascetic! The Thief wants to steal your cow!'

"Both the Ascetic and his neighbours got up, and wicked Satan and the Thief ran away."

The First Vizier, who had advised the King of the Owls to kill the Raven, said, "I believe you and the other viziers have been deceived by the Raven and foolishly accepted what he said. You have not provided the King with sound opinions but focussed on the wrong issues. I entreat the King not to accept their advice."

But the King ignored his advice and ordered that the Raven be taken to the habitat of the owls and treated generously and graciously.

Some time later the Raven addressed the King of the Owls in the presence of the Vizier who had recommended his death: "The King has seen what my people, the ravens, have done to me. I shall never be at peace until I avenge myself. I have given the matter deep thought, and realize that I am unable to do it because I am a raven. I recall that scholars once said that if someone agrees willingly to immolate himself by fire, that is the greatest sacrifice one can offer God, and thus all his wishes will be answered. If the King orders me to burn myself, then I will pray to God to change me into an owl. Thus I will acquire more hatred, more courage, and more resolve to fight the ravens. That is how I can gain the

satisfaction of revenge."

The Vizier who had voted for the Raven's death spoke: "You have a way of concealing evil behind a pleasant mask that reminds me of good wine contaminated by poison: it may taste sweet and smell good, but it will prove to be deadly. Do you really expect us to believe that if you burn your body with fire, you can change your vulgar native identity and its repulsive characteristics? Isn't it true that your moral traits are inalienable? Isn't it true that you will always be a menacing raven regardless of any pretended change? You remind me of the Mouse who was given the choice of marrying the Sun, the Wind, the Clouds or the Mountain, but finally chose to marry the Rat."

The King asked, "How does the story go?"

He said:

Once upon a time an Ascetic known to be so good that God always answered his prayers was sitting by the seashore. Suddenly a Kite passed by with a Mouse in her claws, and dropped her in front of the Ascetic. He had pity on her, wrapped her in a piece of paper, and took her home with him. Worried that his household would not take care of her, he asked God to change her into a beautiful girl, and that was precisely what happened when God answered his prayer. Instantly, he went to his wife and told her, "This girl is like a daughter to me; please treat her in the same way that you treat your son."

When the girl grew up into a very beautiful woman, the Ascetic told her: "My dear daughter, please choose whomever you like as a husband, and I will agree to give you to him in marriage."

She answered, "Since you have given me the choice, I shall choose as my husband the strongest of all beings."

The Ascetic told her, "Perhaps you mean the Sun."

He rushed to the Sun and said, "I am speaking to the great creature, the Sun: I have a young girl who is seeking the strongest being in this world as her husband. Would you marry her?"

The Sun said, "I will direct you to someone who is stronger than I: the Cloud. He covers me, and protects others from my painful rays, and filters the brightness of my light."

The Ascetic went to the Cloud and made the same request he had made of the Sun. The Cloud replied, "I recommend that you go to someone who is stronger than I: the Wind. He is the one who drives me forward and backward, east or west as he chooses, without my consent."

The Ascetic went to the Wind and repeated his request. The Wind answered, "I will direct you to someone who is much stronger than I: the Mountain. I can never move it from its place."

The Ascetic went to the Mountain with the same request. The Mountain answered, "I will direct you to someone who is much stronger than I: the Rat. I have no power to stop the Rat from drilling holes in me and making his home in those holes."

The Ascetic rushed to the Rat and pleaded, "Would you marry this beautiful girl?"

The Rat replied, "I am afraid that is a difficult proposition. My burrow is too small. Furthermore, Rats marry mice."

The Ascetic first secured his daughter's agreement, and then he prayed to God and asked that the girl be converted back to a mouse. God obliged, and the girl was immediately transformed into a mouse, her original and natural state.

The first Vizier turned on the Raven once more, and said, "What I have described is exactly your case, you crafty and deceitful creature."

The King of the Owls ignored his Vizier's advice, and gave orders that the Raven should continue receiving the most kind and generous treatment. As time passed, and the Raven became well fed and nourished, he regained his plumage and his health improved. He also had enough time to observe and study everything required to execute his plan. One day he found the opportunity to fly off and meet with his own King at the agreed-upon hideaway. He explained all that had happened and what he had observed. Then he addressed the King and boldly said, "I have accomplished my mission; now the King must listen to my instructions and follow them carefully."

The King replied, "The soldiers and I are under your command, so give the orders you see fit to secure our victory."

The Raven explained his plan: "The owls are encamped now on the mountain, near a flock of sheep tended by a shepherd. We shall carefully prepare some fire and throw it on the habitat of the owls. We shall strew dry wood on the fire and fan it with our wings until it feeds on the dry wood. In this way, the owls that attempt to leave their houses will die by burning, and those who stay will be suffocated by the smoke."

The ravens followed the plan precisely, and managed to kill every owl in the land. Once the ravens achieved their victory, they returned safely to their homes.

Later on, the King of the Ravens asked his Vizier, the Raven responsible for their victory, "How could you endure the company and trust of the owls, when we all know that good and evil people cannot maintain a rational relationship?"

The Raven explained: "What the King has said is true. But a rational and shrewd being will not fret and lose his patience when

burdened with a most crucial responsibility that may have severe consequences for himself or his own King. This is all the more true when one knows that his endurance will surely be highly rewarded, and is worthy of the pain and suffering incurred. In such a case, one should disregard any feelings of humiliation or disgust arising from the deliberate submission to the odious enemy. One must maintain this patience until he attains the worthwhile objectives. Such justified ends based on anticipated endurance should produce sublime happiness."

The King then asked, "Tell us about the mind of the owls."

The Raven replied: "I met no rational owl except the one that persistently sought my death. Though he pleaded with them many a time, they never agreed with him. They did not even bother to investigate my background, and failed to remember the status I had enjoyed among the ravens, and that I was well known for my sound judgement. Furthermore, the owls were too complacent, and underestimated my deep scheming and sound planning. They rejected all kinds of rational advice from others, and made me privy to all their secrets. A king must always protect himself from deserters and double agents, and should conceal his secrets from them."

The King answered, "I think what really defeated the owls was their oppression, the lack of sound judgment in their King, and his compliance with the poor advice of his viziers."

The Raven replied: "What the King has said is correct. To begin with, we have observed in life certain facts which we must take into consideration: Only those who accumulate wealth will be obeyed; most gluttonous people will become sick; and kings who trust evil and illogical viziers will come to a disastrous end. It was also said in the past: 'Arrogant people should not expect long-term praise. Foolish persons should not expect to have many friends. Neither should the misbehaving and dishonourable, the unbenevolent and uncharitable, the sinful and the wrong-doers. Nor should the dishonest King who is deceitful and lax in serious matters, and listens to weak and unscrupulous viziers who do not care for the stability of the kingdom or the welfare of the King's subjects.'"

The King said, "You have carried a very heavy burden while subverting the owls and deluding them."

The Raven replied, "We are assured that any person who endures hardship that leads him at the end to some gain or benefit, will undoubtedly achieve his desired objectives. But first he must uproot any inflexible pride and passionate zeal within himself, and train himself to patience and perseverance. He will then be like the Viper who reconciled himself to the idea of carrying the aging King of the Frogs on his back, and thus lived without hunger for a very long time."

The King inquired, "How does the story go?"
The Raven replied,

Once upon a time old age came upon a Viper. He lost his sight and became quite feeble. He could no longer hunt and therefore hardly ate. He decided to creep about in the hope of finding something to nourish his weak body. He arrived at a spring with plenty of frogs, a spring he used to frequent when he was much younger and where he had easily caught a few frogs every day.

The Viper stationed himself nearby. He remained immobile, and seemed depressed and sad. One of the frogs asked, "Why are you, the mighty Viper, looking so sad?"

The Viper answered, "No one has more reason to be in distress than I! My diet in the past depended on the many frogs I used to catch in my heyday. But now that I have been afflicted by a certain calamity, I have been forbidden to catch and eat them. When I meet a frog nowadays I am unable even to make an attempt to catch it."

The frog hurried off to his King and gave him the good news. The King of the Frogs decided to visit the Viper, and he asked him, "What has happened to you?"

The Viper explained: "One evening recently I was preparing to catch a frog. He fled to the house of an Ascetic. It was dark. It happened that the son of the ascetic was also at home. I felt something and thought it was the frog. So I bit it, but unfortunately it was the finger of the boy, and he died instantly. I fled from the house but the Ascetic ran after me, cursed me, and said, 'Since you have killed my son, belligerently and without cause, I curse you and pray that you will live the rest of your life in utter degradation. May the King of the Frogs ride upon you, and may you never catch another frog to eat. You shall depend entirely on the charity of the King and on his dole.' That is why I have come to you so that you can ride me, and I will be ever so glad to be your mount.'

The King of the Frogs liked the idea of riding on the Viper. He thought of it as the utmost in honour, pride, and prestige. So he mounted the Viper, and did enjoy it. Then the Viper told him, "The King knows that I am now his personal mount; may it please him to allocate a stipend for me to live on."

The King of the Frogs replied, "With pleasure, for if you are my mount you must be compensated!"

The King ordered that the Viper be allocated two frogs every day. As it turned out, the submission of the Viper to his insolent enemy did not harm him at all. On the contrary, it benefited him and provided some useful sustenance.

"As for myself: I tolerated the humiliating yoke of the enemy only to achieve and gain the great rewards of victory and security, and his final destruction. I came to the conclusion that victory achieved through resilient patience, attentive scheming, and flattering manners is far more effective than when attained through direct confrontation and inflexible force. It is well known that despite its burning heat, fire consumes only the portion of trees above the ground. But water, with its harsh and lucid coolness, can effectively eradicate what is below the earth as well. I recall it was said in the past that there were four things which, even in small amounts, must not be underestimated and left unattended: namely, fire, disease, enemies, and religion."

The Raven continued, "All we accomplished was due to the prudent judgement of the King, and his education, knowledge, and nobility. For it was also said in the past that if two persons plan to seek the same objective, the more magnanimous of the two would succeed. If both are equal in this trait, then the one who is more decisive would be the most suitable. And if the two also share this factor equally, then the one who enjoys more status and prestige will attain the aspired target.

"Moreover, the following was also passed down to us: One should not contend with a shrewd, resourceful, skilful and persistent king who resists vanity during good times, and despair in calamity. It would be a self-defeating endeavour, particularly when such a king is like ours: fully knowledgeable of the duties and responsibilities required to accomplish any task, and meticulously careful in balancing might with leniency and anger with benevolence. Our King knows when to act, prudently awaiting the most effective moment. The King deals with the present, with one eye on the future."

The King then addressed the Raven, "I must commend you on your profound good sense by which, along with your educated counsel and some good fortune, I have been able to attain the chosen objectives. Many a time one person endowed with a shrewd mind can be more effective against the enemy than a powerful and well-equipped army. I was deeply impressed by your persistent mission there amidst the owls, and the long harsh treatment you endured, indefatigably calm and utterly deliberate."

The Raven answered, "I followed the King's ideals, and succeeded in befriending all who were useful to me, using rough confrontation or exaggerated flattery as was required to exploit every opportunity."

The King interrupted and said amiably: "You became an efficient man of action, while the rest of the viziers and advisors were merely men of words without any practical follow-through. I am pleased to say that you are God's great gift to us. Before this gift, we never experienced the full delight in our food, or drink, or sleep, for want of any safety and security.

"I recall that in the past a sick person would not have relish for food or sleep until he recovered. Likewise the greedy person who has been provided by his superior and king with wealth and a job to perform would have no pleasure until he executed it well. By the same token a person who is pursued by his enemy, fearful of his power day and night, could never rest until rid of him, so his heart could be at ease. Whoever throws off a heavy burden will find relief, and whoever drives away his enemy and ensures his future defence will live in sweet tranquillity."

The Raven responded, "I pray to God, who vanquished the King's enemies, to grant him much enjoyment throughout his reign, and to provide for the welfare of his subjects and permit them to share the happiness and delight of his mastery of his kingdom. For if the King's subjects do not share in that happiness, then it is no better than the goat's beard, which the kid keeps on sucking in vain, thinking it a teat."

Then the King asked his Vizier the Raven: "Can you describe the King of the Owls, and their military strategy?"

The Raven answered, "His life was based on wantonness, vanity, arrogance, recklessness, and inefficiency, and displayed the ugliest possible traits. His viziers, advisors and friends shared these traits with him, except for the Vizier that counselled him to kill me. That Vizier was wise and resourceful. He was a shrewd philosopher and a scholar. His like is rare. He was magnanimous and enjoyed a very sound mind, and prudent knowledge."

The King interjected, "And which of his traits reflected his intellect?"

The Raven responded: "Two traits, O King. The first was his advice to kill me. The second was that he never withheld from the King and his Companions any advice, no matter how minor. He never used harsh and strong language, but spoke in a gentle and respectful manner, and he even pointed out some of own mistakes. He would frame his advice directly and literally, but resorted to examples and fables to show its cogency. He would explain the misgivings of others so the King might be able to see his own. That way his King would not misdirect his anger and punish him. I heard him once saying to his King, 'A king must never neglect his duties and responsibilities, for it is too grave a matter to leave them unattended. Very few people are given this singular opportunity of kingship.

'Such responsibility can never be fulfilled except through shrewd, prudent and timely action. Kingship is a precious trust. Whoever attains it should care for it and fiercely defend it. Its duration was likened by past scholars to the short shade cast by the leaf of the water lily. Monarchy can swiftly vanish, and as quickly be restored, only to disappear again; it is like the wind, which comes in sudden gusts. Its capacity to survive challenges is as durable as that of a sensible and reflective person to survive wicked and evil people. Yet it is as fragile as a raindrop hitting the ground.' What I have told the King shows how one should not underestimate natural enemies who pretend to be friendly, nor be deceived by their apparent deference."

(The end of the Fable of the Ravens and the Owls)

The Ape and the Turtle

170

Chapter Five

The Fable of
the Ape and the Turtle

(Never squander what has been painstakingly gained)

Dabshalim the King addressed Baydaba the Philosopher, "Now that I have heard that fable, tell me one about a person who seeks an objective, and achieves it, but then loses it."

The Philosopher replied: "It is much easier to pursue an objective than to sustain it once achieved. Whoever attains his objective but fails to sustain it will lose it and will experience what happened to the Turtle."

The King asked, "How does the story go?"

Baydaba began ...

Once upon a time when the King of the Apes, named Maher, grew old, a younger, stronger member of his family deposed him. Maher escaped and ran away, wandering until he found himself somewhere on the coast. There he found a fig tree and made it his new home. One day while he was picking the fruit a fig accidentally fell into the water. As the fig touched the water, it produced a pleasant sound. He enjoyed it so much that he continued eating and throwing more figs in the water.

It also happened that a Turtle was in the water just below him. Every time a fig fell in the water he ate it. After a while, when the falling figs became quite plentiful, it occurred to him that the Ape must be dropping them for him to feed on. So the Turtle felt that he should befriend the Ape. He engaged him in conversation, and liked his company, and so they became fast friends.

The Turtle's wife, however, began to fret about her husband. She told one of her neighbours, "I am very concerned and anxious about my husband's prolonged absence. I am afraid he may have had a fatal accident."

Her neighbour replied, "Your husband is fine. He is down at the shore and has developed a very close friendship with an Ape. He eats and drinks with him and the two have become inseparable. That explains his absence. You should realize, however, that he will never live with you again unless you find some way to get rid of the Ape."

"What shall I do?" the wife asked.

The neighbour replied, "When your husband arrives, pretend

171

to be sick. When he asks about your health, tell him that all the physicians say your death is imminent, and the only effective medicine is the heart of an ape."

A few days later the Turtle returned home. He was quite concerned to find his wife in a feeble condition. He asked her, "What happened to you?"

The neighbour answered, "Your poor wife is very sick. All the physicians we consulted have prescribed the heart of an ape. There is no other treatment that can cure her."

The Turtle answered, "This is an impossible request. How can we obtain an ape's heart when we live in the water? But perhaps I might deceive my friend, the Ape."

He went back to the shore to visit with the Ape, who greeted him: "My friend and brother, what made you so late in visiting me?"

The Turtle answered timidly, "My extreme shyness. I am overwhelmed by the generous and kind way you have treated me, and I do not know how to reward your beneficence. But in order to reciprocate your kindness and generosity, it would please me if you would join me at my house. I live on a nearby island full of fruit. I would be glad to mount you on my back and swim over to that island."

The Ape liked the idea and mounted the back of the Turtle. But just as the Turtle set off across the water, the burden of betraying his friend pressed on his conscience. He bowed his head in distress, and the Ape asked, "My friend, why do you look so sad and so concerned?"

The Turtle replied, "It is because my wife is dangerously ill, and that will interfere with my ability to enjoy pleasant discussions with you, and offer you my best hospitality."

The Ape answered, "I know you well enough, and am quite sure of your care for me. There is no need for you treat me ostentatiously."

A short while later, the Turtle stopped swimming. The Ape became curious and thought:

There must be something seriously wrong for the Turtle to act in this erratic way. I suspect he may have had a change of heart towards me. Perhaps he does not welcome my friendship anymore. And so perhaps he plans to hurt me. For we know that nothing is more fleeting or capricious than the feelings of the heart.

A rational being should never refrain from scrutinizing the inner feelings of his kinfolk, sons and daughters, brothers and friends—in each challenge, each moment, and each word. This should be habitual, whether one is energetically pursuing an objective, or in a more relaxed and leisurely situation, whatever the circumstances. That is how one can discern what the heart conceals. Scholars confirmed that when suspicion unsettles the heart of a friend, he should be prompt and direct in taking all necessary precautions and investigating the matter carefully. Should his suspicion prove true, he will be protected. If it be disproved, then his prudent and shrewd inquiry has cost him nothing."

Then he asked the Turtle, "What is troubling you so? You are hesitant and distracted, and seem to be pondering something troublesome."

The Turtle answered, "What really bothers me is that I am afraid you may not like my hospitality when you come to my house, since my wife is very sick."

The Ape said, "Do not worry so much, for anxiety and worry solve no one's problems. Instead you should make every effort to obtain useful medicines and nourishing food for your wife. Experience confirms that wealth should be spent generously on four needs: almsgiving, times of need, one's sons and daughters, and one's spouse.

The Turtle answered, "What you have said is true. My wife's physicians say that the only medicine that can cure her is the heart of an ape."

The Ape trembled at what he heard. "Oh, what a pity! Comfort and diversion have beguiled me in my old age, and drawn me into this precarious plight. Someone has truly said that the contented person will live in security and ease, while the voracious person spends his life in exhaustion and weariness. I must use all my wits now to survive this predicament."

Then the Ape addressed the Turtle: "Why did you wait this long to tell me? I could have carried my heart with me, had I known! It is a tradition among us apes that if one goes to visit a friend, he leaves his heart at home with his wife and family, or wherever he lives. This allows us to see the wives of our hosts without risk to our weak hearts."

The Turtle replied, "And where is your heart now?"

The Ape said, "I left it back in the fig tree. But you can take me back to fetch it and bring it with me."

The Turtle was elated and thought, "My friend is willing, so there was no need to betray him."

When the Turtle approached the shore, the Ape jumped off his back and hurried up the fig tree. When the Turtle noticed that the Ape was slow to return he cried, "My friend, bring your heart and come along. You are making me wait too long."

The Ape replied, "Not at all! Do you think for one moment that I would be like the Donkey who, as the Jackal claimed, had no heart or ears?"

The Turtle inquired, "How does the story go?"

The Ape explained:

Once upon a time a Lion lived in a forest. It happened that a Jackal also lived close by and always foraged among the Lion's leftovers. One day the Lion caught the mange and became so weak and weary he could not hunt anymore.

So the Jackal asked the Lion, "Lord of the beasts, what has happened to you? You have changed so dismally."

The Lion said, "This itching disease has exhausted and weakened me. I was told that there is no medicine to cure it except the heart and the ears of a donkey."

The Jackal replied, "This is a very easy task. I know a tailor who owns a donkey and uses it to transport the clothes he works on. I will fetch you that donkey."

The Jackal, then, sought out the Donkey, greeted him kindly, and said, "Why do you look so frail?"

The Donkey answered, "Because my owner does not feed me properly!"

The Jackal insisted, "And why do you stay with him in such miserable working conditions?"

The Donkey replied, "I have no choice, for it seems impossible for me to escape. Anywhere I go, there is always someone who beats me, exhausts me, and keeps me painfully hungry."

The Jackal said, "Come with me, and I will show you a beautiful place, isolated from human beings, with green pastures full of grass to feed on. You will also find a flock of well-fed donkeys there, enjoying unmatched beauty and health."

The Donkey replied happily, "Let us go, then. Nothing should keep us from living there."

The Jackal sent him off to the Lion. But he went on ahead of the Donkey, and explained to the Lion the exact whereabouts of the Donkey. The Lion then set out to intercept the Donkey and kill him. But in his extreme weakness the attack was unsuccessful and the Donkey managed to escape. Terrified, he ran away as fast as he could ever remember.

The Jackal reproached the Lion: "Have you become such a weak failure that you cannot even take your prey?"

The Lion answered with shame, "If you bring him back to me, he will never escape again."

The Jackal agreed, and went back to try once more. When he met the Donkey, the Jackal said, "What happened to you? One of the donkeys I described to you saw you coming, and being so gracious to strangers he rushed to receive you with enthusiasm, to show you his hospitality."

The Donkey, who had never seen a lion before, believed him

and agreed to return with him. Once more, the Jackal ran ahead of the Donkey and explained to the Lion what he had done. He told him, "Get ready for the Donkey. I went to great lengths to deceive him. Do not be feeble this time, for if he escapes he will never come back with me again."

The Lion's soul and heart were agitated as the Jackal upbraided him. He hurried to the ambush point, and as soon as he saw the Donkey he sprang on him and slew him with one mighty blow. He then addressed the Jackal: "My physicians insist that I do not eat any Donkey before washing and cleansing myself. Take care of it until I return and then I will eat his heart and ears, and I will leave the rest for you to eat."

As soon as the Lion left, the Jackal ate the heart and the ears. He hoped this would be interpreted as a bad omen by the Lion, who would then leave the rest untouched for the Jackal to consume.

Upon his return, the Lion inquired, "Where are the heart and the ears of the Donkey?"

The Jackal answered bluntly, "Don't you realize that if the Donkey had had a heart to understand with, or ears to listen with, he would have never come back to you with me, especially after he escaped the first time from real and imminent death.

The Ape went on talking to the Turtle. "I have recounted this fable to show you that I am not like the Donkey who, as the Jackal claimed, was without a heart or ears. You tricked me first, and I have tricked you back, and corrected my nearly-fatal mistake. It was said in the past that matters spoiled by ignorance must be redeemed by knowledge."

The Turtle replied pleadingly, "You are right. But a good person will always confess his guilt. Moreover, if he commits a shameful act, he will not resent or shirk his punishment, for he is always as true to his words as to his deeds. If he ever falls into a predicament, he can always pull himself out of it through his clever and nimble mind. He resembles a person who has the strength and the support to lift himself up when he stumbles and falls on the ground." ...

That was the fable, which describes a person who pursues something and then loses as soon as he attains it.

(The end of the Fable of the Ape and the Turtle)

The Ascetic and the Weasel

Chapter Six

The Fable of
the Ascetic and the Weasel
(Haste is waste)

Dabshalim the King said to Baydaba the Philosopher, "Now that I have heard this fable, tell me another which describes a person who acts in haste and without discretion or foresight about the possible outcome."

The Philosopher replied, "If one is not sure of the evidence, yet acts hastily, he may regret his actions and could face the situation of the Ascetic who unjustly killed his loyal Weasel."

The King asked, "How does the story go?"

Dabshalim continued ...

Once upon a time an Ascetic lived in Jurjan in Persia. He was married to a beautiful woman, but she was barren for quite some time. Fortunately, just when they were about to lose hope, his wife was found with child. Both were elated. The Ascetic prayed and asked God to bless him with a son. Then he told his wife, "I have good news for you. I hope we shall have a son who will be useful to both of us and will be our joy and delight. I shall give him the finest of names, and look for the best scholars to educate him."

His wife replied, "What makes you talk about matters that may or may not occur? Whoever does that may fall into the same awkward situation of the Ascetic who poured the best honey and butter on his head in foolish waste."

Her husband asked, "Tell me what happened."

She went on: "Once upon a time a merchant used to provide an Ascetic with a daily ration of honey, which was his main source of nourishment. The Ascetic was in the habit of eating one portion and saving the rest in a jar that he hung on a peg over his bed. One day he lay down on his bed with a cane in his hand. The jar full of honey and butter was hanging directly over his head. He began to think of the prices of honey and butter that had recently increased. He murmured to himself,

"I shall sell this jar of honey and butter for a dinar and buy ten goats with it. The goats will produce kids every five months, and in no time I shall have a herd of goats. Within a couple of years, they will

177

produce further and I shall end up owning more than four hundred goats. I shall then sell them all and buy a cow or a bull for each four goats. I shall also have enough money to buy a piece of land and some seed, and hire some farmers who can help me plough the land with the bulls and plant the seed. I shall profit from the milk of the cows, and their offspring as well. I am sure that within five years I shall accumulate considerable wealth from my plantations. Then I shall build a magnificent mansion and purchase male and female slaves. I shall marry a beautiful woman who will bear me a lofty and intelligent son. I shall select the finest name for him. As he grows, I shall attempt to provide him with the best education, and raise him with a firm hand to bring out the best in him; and when that fails I shall whack him with this cane like this!

"Unconscious of what he was doing, he swung his cane forcefully, knocked down the jar, and smashed it. All the honey and butter poured onto his head in total waste.

I have told you this story so you will refrain from talking prematurely about things that should not be even mentioned, since you can never know whether they will ever materialize."

The Ascetic was chastened and agreed with his wife.

It happened that his wife did give birth to a beautiful boy, and the father was overjoyed. A few days later came the time for her to purify herself at the public bath. Just before she left for the bath, she told the Ascetic, "Watch your son until I come back from the bath."

A few moments later, a messenger from the King arrived and gave the Ascetic an immediate summons to appear at the royal court. Having no one at that time that was able and ready to take care of his son in his absence, he had to rely on his loyal Weasel. He had domesticated the Weasel from birth, and treated him kindly and lovingly as his own child. The Ascetic went to the King after he had left the Weasel and his son at home behind closed doors.

Suddenly, a Viper crawled stealthily out of her hole and approached the boy. The Weasel attacked her ferociously in defence of the boy and managed to kill the Viper. He then chewed the Viper into pieces, staining his mouth with her blood in the process.

The Ascetic returned from the King's court and opened the door. The Weasel, wishing to show the master his pleasure and accomplishment in loyally defending the boy, rushed happily to the door. When the Ascetic saw the Weasel's bloody mouth and body, he panicked at the thought that the Weasel must have suffocated and killed his son. In his rage he must have lost his mind and rationality. He could not calm down, investigate the matter, and discover the truth. Instead, he harshly and impulsively smashed the head of the Weasel with his cane and killed him instantly. The Ascetic rushed into the house, only to find his son alive and lying next to the remains of the Viper. When he realized what had happened and understood the wrong he had done in his violent haste, he howled and beat his head with both fists in despair and lamentation. "I wish I had never been given this boy, and never committed such a treacherous betrayal!"

At that moment his wife entered the house and saw him in such this state. She asked, "What happened?"

The Ascetic explained what he had done and how wrongly he had rewarded the Weasel's good deed.

She said, "You will always reap the fruits of haste …"

That was an example of a person who acts with haste instead of patiently investigating the facts first.

(The end of the Fable of the Ascetic and the Weasel)

The Rat and the Cat

Chapter Seven

The Fable of
the Rat and the Cat

(Neither friendship nor hostility is constant)

Dabshalim the King said, "I have listened to this fable. Tell me one now about a man surrounded by many enemies and almost overwhelmed by them, who to save himself managed to appease and pacify a few of his enemies, then maintained his loyalty to those who befriended him, thereby attaining safety and security."

The Philosopher replied, "Neither friendship nor hostility is constant. They always fluctuate. Sometimes friendship is transformed into antipathy, and at other times the latter may revert to honest and firm loyalty. This happens in so many different ways. Prudent people will manage to respond to every new situation shrewdly and find the right justification for each alternative. When dealing with an enemy, the use of strength and fortitude are major factors of success. But when dealing with friends, courtesy and insight play the major role.

"However, a shrewd and rational person will not refuse to mollify his enemy, making peace with him, even requesting his help, if that can ward off larger danger or achieve a desirable objective. Moreover, if one performs wisely in such situations, he will definitely attain his goals.

"The Rat and the Cat provided an example of this when they fell into a certain calamity. By agreeing to make peace with one another they escaped deprivation and disaster.

The King inquired, "How does the story go?"

Baydaba then began ...

Once upon a time a Cat called Rumi lived in a hole in the trunk of a huge tree. A Rat called Faridun lived close by. That area was familiar to quite a few hunters who came there in search of many beasts and birds to trap.

One day one of the hunters spread his nets and ropes in the vicinity of Rumi the Cat, who was promptly captured.

Meanwhile the Rat emerged from his hole looking for something to eat, but as always was on the lookout for his enemy, Rumi the Cat. He quickly noticed the trap with Rumi the Cat entangled in it. He was delighted until he looked over his shoulder and saw the Weasel just about to catch him, and an Owl in the tree ready to snatch him. He was at a loss: afraid to move backward lest the Weasel take him, and afraid to move to left or right lest the Owl snatch him. If he went forward, the Cat would devour him. He thought: "This could be a total disaster. It seems that bad luck is sitting on my shoulders and trouble waits on every side. However, I still have my wits about me, and am not about to panic. The risk is great, but a rational person will never lose his nerve if he has a prudent mind and an alert intellect, whatever the situation. The faculties of the mind are like a sea whose depth is impossible to plumb. During disasters and trials, one's faculties can go slack and draw a person down. But in the midst of chaos one must stand by his original purposes and not be distracted by crisis.

"I see no way out of this predicament except to make peace with my enemy, Rumi the Cat. It appears that he is equally desperate. Perhaps he will listen to me and understand my position. He may observe and appreciate my honest and sincere approach to him, and see that it does not conceal any double-talk or deceit. He may be desperate enough to work with me, so that we both survive."

So Faridoon the Rat approached Rumi the Cat in his trap and said, "How are you?"

The Cat replied, "Just as you always hoped: I am caught in a tight situation."

The Rat continued: "Today I am your partner in calamity. I pray and hope that I can escape from my dilemma, and I do hope the same for you. I am telling you the truth, and not deceiving you. Look: the Weasel is waiting in ambush and the Owl has me on his menu. Both are your enemies as well as mine. Therefore, if you sincerely pledge my safety and promise no harm, I will cut the ropes that are binding you and set you free.

"Then we will each be saved with each other's help. It is just like a ship and its crew, both of which need to survive. A seaworthy ship can sail to safety only with a skilful crew; and the skilful crew can never safely bring the ship to port unless it is seaworthy. Each plays a complementary role in attaining a shared objective."

When the Cat heard the Rat's speech and felt he was sincere, he replied, "What you say seems rather true, and I share your desire to escape. If you cut my ropes I will be thankful to you all my life."

The Rat replied, "I shall cut all the ropes except one, then wait until I can assure myself of your sincerity."

The Rat began to gnaw through the ropes, but when the Weasel and the Owl saw the Rat approaching the Cat, they were both thwarted and wandered off.

At that moment the Cat felt the Rat ease up in his efforts to cut the ropes, and asked, "Why the delay? You do not seem so determined to cut my ropes. Perhaps now that your safety is assured you have changed your mind, and plan to back out of your promise. That is not considered honourable by decent people. An upright person will never renege on promises to his friends. A moment ago you claimed my friendship. It behoves you to reciprocate and save me, and not to recall my previous hostility. You must appreciate that the peace between you and me was authentic enough to wipe out the memory of our old antagonism. Furthermore, you should remember that honouring one's promise and word is always well rewarded, while harm and evil are the prompt rewards of betrayal. A magnanimous and generous person is thankful and grateful, and does not harbour grudges or hatred. One act of goodness should erase the memories of all evil ones. It is also said that the punishment for betrayal is swift. If one is appealed to for mercy and forgiveness, but refuses, that is what we all call betrayal."

The Rat answered, "I believe there are two types of friendship. One is by choice; the other, by necessity. Both, however, are in the pursuit of personal interest. In the case of friendship by choice, a person can always be familiar with his friend and trust him in all circumstances. But in the case of a friendship of necessity, which is resorted to in urgent circumstances, friends may be trusted sometimes, but at other times they must be wary. A rational person may well negotiate some friendship to provide himself with protection from certain dangers. The purpose of such pragmatic friendship is to yield its benefits as quickly as possible.

"I will honour my promise to you, but with great caution. I do not wish to fall again into the kind of desperation that compelled us both to accept a mutual peace.

"You understand that situation is critical to successful actions, and each action has its own appropriate moment. Actions performed at the inappropriate time can carry unwarranted results.

"I shall cut all your ropes except for one knot, to keep you restrained. I shall cut it only after I am sure that you are otherwise occupied by the movements of the hunters."

The Rat continued gnawing the ropes around the Cat. Then suddenly the hunter approached. The Cat said anxiously, "This is the critical moment! Cut my ropes now!"

The Rat exerted all his efforts and finished the last knot. The Cat jumped up on the tree, and the Rat dived into one of the many holes around. The hunter was astonished by what he beheld, then collected his damaged ropes and left in frustration.

Later the Rat came out of his hole but was wary of being too near the Cat. The Cat then hailed him: "My wise and courageous friend, what makes you reluctant to come closer so I can reward you for the good you have done me? Please come close and do not abandon my friendship. Whoever takes a friend, then abandons him and discards his friendship will forfeit its benefits, and his usefulness to other friends will be affected. You have been very generous to me and I will never forget your good deeds. Truly you deserve the best reward from me, and all my friends as well. Do not be afraid of me, and please believe that I will give you all I have."

The Cat insisted on oath that what he said was the absolute truth.

The Rat replied: "I know that many apparent friendships conceal a deep and hidden hostility far more potent than open enmity. Whoever fails to take enough caution in such a relationship will be like a person who rides on the tusk of a ferocious elephant and falls asleep, only to wake up after he has fallen under the elephant's feet and is being crushed to death.

"A friend is called a friend in the certainty of benefits he is expected to provide. An enemy is called an enemy for fear of the harm he would inflict.

"A rational person may extend his friendship to any enemy in prospect of a proportionate benefit. But if he anticipates any harm from a friend, he will then treat him warily. Haven't you ever observed how newborn animals follow their mothers seeking their milk, but when they are weaned they no longer follow? Perhaps, if one friend abandons another, there may be no reason for him to anticipate harm if the roots of that relationship had not originally been hostile. But if they were, and later became friendly only because of an urgent common need, that type of friendship will vanish with the need, for it could easily revert to its native antipathy. It is no different from water, which will boil on the fire, but always cools once the fire is removed.

"As you very well know, you are my most fearsome and harmful enemy. It was only need and expediency that prompted both of us to make peace. Now that the reason which forced us into peace and friendship has been eliminated, I am afraid our antipathy will resume. No benefit awaits the weak who fraternize with their enemies, or the humble who befriend their mistreating overlords. I know I mean nothing to you except as prey and food. And I have neither need for, nor trust in you.

"The weak person who is always wary of his strong enemy has a better likelihood of survival than the strong one who underestimates the weak and alternates arrogance with appeasement. A rational person befriends and makes peace with his enemy if the situation compels him to do so. He will treat him pleasantly and show him all signs of friendship and pay him hypocritical homage if he has no choice. But as soon as he finds a way out, he should go his own way. You must understand that the mistake of a person who quickly befriends the enemy may never be revisited.

"It is confirmed that a rational person will honour his word and promises to those enemies with whom he made peace. But he will never trust that enemy fully, and will never be safe if he attempts to establish an intimate relationship with him. On the contrary, he should distance himself as far as possible.

"As for me, I like you best from afar. I wish you safety and longevity much more than before. I do not expect or wish from you any reward for the good I have done to you. But I do expect that you would reciprocate if I fell into a similar situation. Beyond that, it is a fact that we can never be trusting friends. So Farewell, and peace be with you.

(The end of the Fable of the Rat and the Cat)

The King's Son and Fanzah the Bird

Chapter Eight

The Fable of
the King's Son and Fanzah the Bird
(Beware of the powerful who seek revenge)

Dabshalim the King said, "Now that I have heard the last fable, tell me another which explains how people should act when there is a serious feud among them, and how they should protect themselves from each other."

Baydaba the Philosopher replied …

Once upon a time, one of the Kings of India whose name was Baridun had a beautiful bird named Fanzah. The Bird also had a handsome and comely baby. The King loved and admired both greatly. He gave orders that Fanzah and his chick should stay with the Queen, and asked her to take good care of them.

One day the Queen herself gave birth to a beautiful son. Both— the King's son and the young chick—became inseparable friends, and played happily together. Fanzah the Bird used to fly to the mountain every day and bring back an exotic and delicious fruit. He always gave one half to the King's son and fed his own other half. This helped both of them to grow up fit and healthy. The King appreciated that and loved Fanzah even more.

It happened that one day Fanzah the Bird was away in the mountain collecting the exotic fruit. His young baby was playing with the King's son while sitting in his lap. The young chick let fall some of its droppings on the boy. The boy became furious and with a burst of rage he seized the bird and smashed it to death on the floor.

When Fanzah the Bird returned he was stricken with grief and pain by the death of his son and lamented: "Shame on the kings who honour no promise and renege on their commitments. Woe to those afflicted by the friendship of kings who have no affection or respect for others. Those kings do not cherish anyone, and do not act generously except to those whose wealth they may temporarily need, or whose knowledge they may urgently require. They treat them kindly until they obtain what they want. As soon as they do, they show no affection, friendship, intimacy, or any sign of goodwill. They would exhibit neither mercy nor forgiveness, nor attempt even to exercise justice. Their lives are built fundamentally on hypocrisy and corruption. They belittle the grave crimes they themselves commit, and visit their wrath on misdemeanours that thwart their whims. Among those Kings is Baridun, the merciless and ungrateful, who acted treacherously towards his companion and intimate friend.

Then Fanzah the Bird angrily attacked the boy's face and plucked out his eyes, then escaped by flying to the highest balcony of the palace.

When the King heard the news he was devastated. But he thought it would be better if he could beguile Fanzah the Bird into coming back. He approached him at the balcony and addressed him, "You have my word, Fanzah, that you are forgiven, and exempt from any penalty. Come down to me."

Fanzah replied firmly, "The King must know that the treacherous person is always punished in the genre of his own treachery. If he is not punished immediately, he will surely incur it at the end. The punishment may even afflict his children and his children's children as well. But punishment will be inexorable. Your son betrayed mine, so I carried out his punishment immediately."

The King said, "I agree that we have betrayed your son, and therefore you are justified in executing your right of revenge. You are immune to any retaliation from us, and we are also quit of yours against us. So come back and we shall be at peace with one another."

Then Fanzah declared, emphatically: "I will never come back to you again. Experienced people confirmed that one should never reacquaint himself with an avenger. The kindness, the soft words, and the generous behaviour of the malevolent but unrequited person will only augment suspicion and fear. One can never be too cautious towards an unavenged person. The offender fears him and is never at his ease. Nothing is better than keeping enough distance from him, and maintaining a close watch.

"It was said in the past that a rational being considers his parents as his friends, his brothers as his companions, his spouse as his mate, his sons as his legacy, his daughters as an expense, and his relatives as adversaries. But he always considers himself unique.

"I am therefore only a unique, lonely and outcast stranger who has accumulated at your Court a heavy burden of grief that can never be shared with anyone. I am going my way, so Farewell, O King."

The King replied: "Had you failed to avenge yourself, or had you been the offender and betrayed our trust in you, then I would agree with what you have said. But the case is clear. The evidence shows that we inflicted an outrage upon you first, and therefore you are free from any guilt. Hence nothing should keep you from trusting us. Come back and

I give you my solemn word that no one will ever harm you."

Fanzah answered, "It has been confirmed that hatred and grudges are painfully fixed in people's hearts. Words usually conceal the real intentions of the heart, while the heart is ultimately more honest than the spoken word. I am sure that my heart does not trust your words, any more than yours trusts mine."

The King said, "Do you not know that hatred and grudges afflict people everywhere? But those with sound intellect will sincerely attempt to eradicate rather than instigate and foment them."

Fanzah answered: "I agree with you. However, a cautious and prudent person should never forget that the embittered avenger is never forgetful of his hurt, and does not throw the issue behind his back. A rational person therefore must be circumspect and alert himself to the traps, trickery and deceit that such a person might be planning against him. He should be aware that many an enemy is deceived by soft words and a lenient approach, in the place of hostility and force. Thus the wild elephant is caught by using a tame one as bait."

The King continued: "A rational and magnanimous person will never abandon his friend or sever his relationship with his close companion. He will always retain his trust in them, even when he feels threatened and may worry for his own safety. This is well observed even in the behaviour of the lowest of beasts. They exhibit such noble traits. I have seen how dog entertainers slaughter their dog for dinner after they finish their act. The dog knows its destiny, but still maintains its loyalty and friendship throughout, and never renounces them or runs off."

Fanzah replied: "Rancour, wherever it lies, is always feared. But there is no rancour like that in the hearts of kings. They are known to cultivate revenge as an obligation, and pursue it with valour and pride.

"A prudent person should never be blind to the intense and deep-seated rancour that dwells in the heart. For it is like a firebrand that conceals its intense heat as long as it is not stoked. But it will always hunger for more wood to kindle. Rancour and hatred will always search for pretexts to flare up like a firebrand when fed with kindling. Neither soft words nor a kind and tender approach will extinguish rancour. Nor would any supplication, submission or appeasement damp its rage. Nothing but death can quench the rancour of a feud. Many a person has wished and hoped to discuss the grievance with the avenger in the hope of negotiating an amicable peace that would satisfy the avenger and protect the offender. But I am too weak to quell the hatred you harbour in your heart. Nor am I so sure that you possess the goodwill you profess. You will never be at peace. Fear, anxiety and dread will always haunt me as long as we are together. Therefore the most prudent solution for both of us is our final separation. Hence I bid you Farewell."

The King went on: "I understand that no one can control what happens to him. Nothing small or great can befall anyone that was not absolutely predetermined. The creation of a creature on this earth, its birth, and its destined journey are not obedient to its will, and so is its death and ultimate extinction.

"What you have inflicted on my son and what my son has inflicted on yours had been predestined and so we are both absolved from our wrongdoing. You and I were afflicted by a calamity, yet we should not be overwhelmed and trapped by what our Destiny determined."

Fanzah then answered: "Yes, Destiny is as you describe it. But believing in Destiny should not prevent the prudent person from protecting himself against any real danger, nor should he fail to take all precautions. One should plan and act according to a balance between belief in predestination and the responsibility for prompt, firm and prudent initiatives.

"I know very well that you talk to me gently, while your inner feelings are of hatred and violence. The matter between us is grievous, not negligible. Your son killed mine, and I plucked out his eyes in revenge. Now you want to avenge and satisfy yourself by deceiving and killing me. You want to rob me of my life. But the soul of a living person always resists death. It was said in the past that poverty, suffering, animosity, separation, illness, and old age are calamities. But the ultimate calamity is death.

"No one can know the extent of pain and suffering more keenly than the one afflicted with a similar ordeal. So I know exactly what drives your thoughts and intentions, for I suffer in the same manner as you. Therefore there is no goodness in our friendship. Every time you or I recall what the other has done to our child, our heart and attitude towards each other will regress."

The King insisted, "A person unable to turn away from a concealed evil, ignore it, forget it, and eradicate it totally from himself, is considered useless and vain."

Fanzah answered: "A fellow with an abscess on his foot will always feel the pain no matter how gingerly he walks. By the same token, when a person whose eyes are sore does not shield them from the wind, the soreness will only be aggravated. So with the person who has inflicted a disastrous injury on another but maintains a close relationship with him—the issue of revenge is always open and unsettled. So he exposes himself to certain death.

"A prudent and pragmatic person, therefore, should attentively safeguard himself against all hazards and risks. He must evaluate all matters rationally, and reduce his reliance on routine. He dare not underestimate those he does not trust. If he relies on his own strength, he may easily be drawn into danger and death. A person incapable of controlling his diet can overburden his body with food or drink, and put himself on a deadly path. If one stuffs oversize morsels into his mouth he will choke to death when he tries to swallow. So it is with anyone who allows himself to slacken his prudence and be beguiled by the sweet promises and talk of his enemy. He then replaces him as his own worst enemy.

"It is true that no one can really have certain knowledge of his own Destiny, or of the uncertainties of the future. However it is still imperative for him to act with prudence and accountability and carry out his duties firmly. A rational person will not trust anyone absolutely, and would never expose his life to danger if there were a safer alternative. I am a person who has different alternatives and I will always endeavour to choose the one most advantageous to me.

"There are five traits that are always useful to whoever has them. They will satisfy him in every aspect of his life. They will console him while he is away in foreign lands. They will bring closer what appears far away, and will cause him to gain livelihood and friends.

"The first is to refrain from harming others. The second is to adopt the most noble attitude, conduct and knowledge. The third is to avoid doubtful and suspicious situations. The fourth is to exhibit the utmost generosity and noble-mindedness. The fifth trait is to perform one's assigned work with absolute honesty and dedication.

"If a human being fears death he will never enjoy wealth, family, children or country. They are all desirable; but his life is essential.

"The worst type of wealth is that badly spent.

"The worst wife is one who does not accommodate her husband.

"The worst son is one who resents and disobeys his parents.

"The worst king is one who instils fear in innocent people and fails to protect and defend his realm.

"The worst country is one that is barren, unfertile, and provides no security or safety to its inhabitants.

"I am neither safe nor secure with the King or in his kingdom, and thus I must bid him farewell."

With that, Fanzah flew away with no intention of returning ...

This was an example of how the parties to a serious vendetta should never trust each other.

(The end of the Fable of the King's Son and Fanzah the Bird)

The Lion and the Jackal

Chapter Nine

The Fable of
the Lion and the Ascetic Jackal

(A wrong decision may be retracted when the evidence is sure)

Dabshalim the King addressed Baydaba the Philosopher: "Now that I have heard the last fable, tell me another which describes how a king should react when he reviews a case and discovers that someone had been wrongfully punished for a crime he did not commit, or harshly rejected though innocent."

The Philosopher replied: "A king must review and reconsider all cases of those who have been condemned, guilty or innocent, rightfully or wrongfully; otherwise the process of government could become harmful and destructive. The king should look into the cases of those who were afflicted by such calamities, and find what benefits might come of them. If the person involved is trustworthy and loyal, the king is right to rehabilitate him. A king needs faithful ministers and aides to advise timely restraint, sympathetic amity, and prudent counsel. But these qualities emanate only from those who are wise in judgment and exceptionally virtuous.

"The ruler has many duties and responsibilities, and therefore he needs a staff and many aides to assist him in performing his duties efficiently. But the fact is that very few people combine such good traits. To describe what I have just said, I shall give you the example of the Lion and the Jackal.

The King asked, "How does the story go?"

The Philosopher began to recount it ...

Once upon a time an upright and pious Jackal lived in a clearing in the jungle, together with other jackals, wolves and foxes. But he did not act as they did. He neither raided others, nor shed blood, nor killed prey, nor ate any meat. Consequently he fell out of favour with his colleagues, the beasts. They reproached him and said, "We are not satisfied with your behaviour or your ascetic attitude, even though your piety does not affect us at all. You should not set yourself apart, but be one of us and act as we do. What ever made you abstain from killing, to pursue a vegetarian way of life?"

193

The Jackal answered: "My friendship with you will not make a sinner of me unless I commit an evil act. Sins, however, are not identified by the places where they are committed, nor by one's acquaintances. They occur within people's hearts and actions. It is not right to assume someone was righteous simply because he lived in a sacred city. Neither should one be considered wicked because he performed his tasks at an impure place. Otherwise a person who murdered an ascetic in his *mihrab*, or prayer niche, would be considered innocent, but sinful if he failed to slay him on the battlefield. My close fellowship with you did not make you responsible for my life: my heart and actions belong exclusively to me quite independently of our friendship. Since I know the value of my own deeds, I have kept to myself, and pursued that upright path in this life."

The Jackal maintained his devout attitude, and his fame as a mystic and ascetic spread far beyond his neighbourhood. Within a short while his fame caught the attention of a Lion that ruled a certain distant region. He wished to meet this pious, pure, honest and upright Jackal. The Lion sent a messenger and invited him to his Court.

When the Jackal arrived, they discussed many issues and the Lion liked what he heard. After a few days, the Lion invited him in and said, "You are aware that I have many responsibilities, and many aides who help me fulfil them. Yet I need still further assistance. I have heard of your amazing purity, good behaviour, strong faculties, and deep piety, which made me admire you even more. So I wish to assign to you an extensive part of my duties, and elevate you to the highest rank in the realm. You will be a respected member of my own circle of advisers and counsellors."

The Jackal answered, "Monarchs have the absolute right and obligation to select their aides and assign them various duties and responsibilities. But they are always advised not to oblige anyone to serve. A forcibly selected aide will never perform his job with the required zest. That would be my situation, for I am not inclined to work for any ruler. Furthermore, I lack the required experience, and was never a Companion to any ruler. Being the King of the Beasts, the King can surely select from amongst them able and strong aides eager to work diligently and serve their ruler. If the King appoints them, they will be of real benefit to him and relieve him of the many burdens he carries. In addition, they will be proud of their achievements and rewards."

The Lion answered firmly, "Forget all that. I am not changing my mind."

But the Jackal persisted: "There are only two kinds of person that can serve the ruler, and I assure the King I am neither. The first kind is impudent and hypocritical; they attain their objectives through boldness, and protect themselves through flattery and cajolery. The second kind is stupid and thoughtless; no one envies them.

"Whoever serves the ruler with honesty and purity, and does not compromise that with hypocrisy, may put himself in dangerous situations. The enemies and the friends of the ruler may band together against his faithful counsellor, motivated respectively by animosity and jealousy. His old friends and Companions may join his foes and attempt to harm him, as they become his arch-rivals for influence. On the other hand, the enemies of the ruler will harbour all kinds of ill feelings and harmful intentions against him since he provides counsel to the ruler that may not be in their favour. When these two kinds of people combine against the advisor and counsellor of the ruler, the results can be disastrous."

The Lion said, "I hope your fear that my Companions may harm you out of jealousy will not stop you from accepting my offer to enter my service. Do not be afraid. You are by my side, and I will take care of you. I will elevate you to the highest status and furnish you with all the honour and bounty that ambition and endeavour could require."

The Jackal answered: "If the King really wishes to be generous to me, I ask only that he allow me to live in this wilderness in safety and security. I shall have very few worries to preoccupy me. The water and vegetables I obtain from this land will be adequate and should enable me to lead a satisfying life. I have learned from past experience that a ruler may inflict more fear and harm in a single hour than others might in a lifetime. Hence, a way of life based on security, safety, and peace of mind, however meagre, is preferable to a more flamboyant way of life exposed to fear, tension, and spite."

The Lion replied, "I have listened to your convictions. You need not be afraid, for your fears will not materialize. I see no alternative but to appoint you as my advisor."

The Jackal answered: "If the King insists on my service, I will accept: but only after I receive his solemn pledge. Conflicts may arise with any of the King's Companions, who will rank above me and thus be jealous, or beneath me and thus envious. They may seek to harm me unjustly by telling untruthful tales, or passing on gossip, to rouse your rage against me. The King must pledge never to take prejudicial action against me in summary judgment. I would expect him to investigate thoroughly whatever I might be accused of, to find evidence that is reliable and clear, and only then to reach a judgment. If the King can offer me this pledge, then I will exert my full efforts to assist in whatever way he please. I will loyally offer my honest counsel, and I promise that he shall never have cause to worry about my service."

The Lion replied, "You have my pledge, and much more." He

then appointed him to manage his treasury, made him his sole advisor, and ennobled and enriched him as no one else.

When the King's Companions and friends realized what had happened, they became angry, jealous, envious, and very disgruntled. They discussed the matter among themselves and agreed upon a combined effort to disenchant the Lion about the Jackal.

It happened that one day the Lion brought home quarry from the hunt and loved the taste of its meat. He ate some and decided to save the rest till later, giving orders it should be kept in a very secure place. His Companions acknowledged his orders, but removed the meat instead and hid it in the Jackal's house without the latter's knowledge. They planned to compromise him, and testify against him if the opportunity arose. The next day at lunchtime when the Lion requested that the meat be brought to him, it could not be found.

Among all the King's Companions sitting in counsel at court, the Jackal was the only one who had no idea what was afoot. The Lion then demanded his meat and insisted on an explanation. His Companions looked around at one other in feigned awkwardness. Then one of them said in a confidential tone: "We have no choice but to convey to the King bad news as well as good, even if the results are sometimes painful. I understand that it was the Jackal who took the meat to his home."

Another Companion said, "No, I do not believe he would do such a thing. However, it is fair to conduct a search and resolve the issue. It is often difficult to understand what goes on in the minds of others."

Another added, "I agree that concealed intentions are not easy to uncover. I am sure if you search in the Jackal's house you will find the meat. That should verify all that was said about his disqualifications and treachery."

Another concluded, "If we find the meat in his house it argues for more than treachery. It shows blatant ingratitude and bold usurpation of the King's authority."

Another suggested, "If the King wishes to send a search team to the Jackal's house, it should be done swiftly, for he has informers everywhere."

They continued in this vein until the Lion was thoroughly taken in. He summoned the Jackal and asked, "Where is the meat I ordered you to keep for me?"

The Jackal answered, "I gave it to the Chief Cook to prepare it for the King whenever you called for it."

The Lion summoned the Chief Cook, who was party to the plot against the Jackal. He testified: "No, he entrusted me with nothing."

The Lion then sent a trusted person to the Jackal's house, where he found the meat and brought it to the Lion. At just that moment a Wolf who had hitherto been silent approached the Lion. He adopted his best courtroom manner, exuding gravity and due process, and urging no conclusions but what the evidence could sustain. He then said, "Since the King has enough evidence with respect to the Jackal's treason, he should not consider pardon. For if he does, then the King will never be able to investigate the treachery of others, nor the crimes of the guilty."

The Lion then dismissed the Jackal from court, and he was promptly seized and imprisoned.

One of the counsellors spoke: "I wonder how, despite all his prudence and deep knowledge in such matters, the King was unable to perceive the Jackal's craftiness and deceit. Even still more amazing was his readiness, in spite of all that transpired, even to consider a pardon."

Meanwhile, the Lion had sent a messenger to the Jackal seeking some excuse, and an apology for his crime. But the messenger returned with insolent lies that he had fabricated and ascribed to the Jackal. The Lion flew into a rage and forthwith ordered the execution of the Jackal.

. The Lion's Mother, however, realized that her son had acted impulsively. She sent him word to stay the execution pending further instructions. Then she entered her son's chamber and addressed him, "My Son, what did the Jackal do that made you condemn him to death so swiftly?"

The Lion explained to her what happened. She then told him: "My son, I believe you have acted hastily. A prudent person avoids possibly regrettable results by acting quite patiently, after thorough investigation, and evidence that is unambiguous. Haste begets regret and anguish because of the poor judgment that accompanies it. In such matters as this, kings have more need than anyone else of patient and persistent search for the truth based on evidence.

"It is understood that the worth and status of a woman derives from her husband; those of the son, from his parents; those of the erudite, from their teacher; those of soldiers, from their commander; those of an ascetic, from his religion; those of subjects, from their kings; and those of the kings are from their piety. The virtue of piety resides in the intellect; and the worth of the intellect derives from its patience and persistence in pursuing evidence to establish the certainty of issues. And most important of all is prudence in judicial decisions. For a king, the prime need for prudence is in evaluating his aides and Companions. You should be able to identify, appraise, and classify them, each according to his standing among the others. The king should always suspect their intentions when it comes to their relationships with each other. It is a fact that no one of them will regret the destruction of the others if and when the opportunity arises.

"The King has already tested the honesty, the magnanimity and the sound judgment of the Jackal, and was consistently satisfied with him and praised him on every occasion. You should not betray him after all he has managed to the King's great satisfaction. From the moment the Jackal arrived he has given us no reason whatsoever to suspect his honesty. On the contrary, he exhibited sound judgement and sturdy virtue.

"You should not have been so hasty in pronouncing such a condemnation for a meagre dish of meat! It is most appropriate that the King should look further into the case of the Jackal. You will then find that Jackal would have never have touched the meat entrusted to him.

"Perhaps, on further investigation, you may find that the Jackal has many enemies who could have plotted against him. Maybe you will find that they were the ones who hid the meat in his house without his knowledge. You know that when the kite snatches a piece of meat and clutches it in its talons, the rest of the birds will hover around it. Similarly, dogs will always crowd around the dog that has the bone.

"Until today, the Jackal has been serviceable to the King and endured all manner of harm just to attain his aspired objectives to his full satisfaction, without ever concealing anything."

At this moment, one of the Lion's honest aides entered and verified the innocence of the Jackal.

The Lion's Mother then added, "You must ensure the effective punishment of the plotters; otherwise they may attempt more serious crimes.

"You should punish them severely and make them an example of those who might try similar acts in the future. A prudent person should not forgive or stay the punishment of the ungrateful, bold traitors, the insolent, or those who do not believe in the Day of Judgement. They should be punished for the acts they have committed. You realize the futility of quick anger, and the grave consequences of misbegotten judgement.

"Those who are ungrateful for little things will never be satisfied with greater rewards. Therefore it behoves the King before all else to reinstate the Jackal and show him the utmost kindness, to assure him that you will always seek his advice and counsel despite the egregious harm you have inflicted upon him.

"There are some people who should never be forsaken under any circumstances, and the Jackal is one of them. He has been known for his righteousness, generosity, loyalty, gratitude, faithfulness, friendliness, freedom from jealousy, and refusal to harm others, despite the heavy burden of the many demands of his friends and Companions in dire situations. On the contrary, the ones to be discarded are those known for their brutal aggressiveness, promise-breakers, the ungrateful, and the unfaithful. They are far from practicing compassion and piety, and they implicitly disbelieve the rewards and punishments on the final Day of Judgement, and the eternal home.

"The King has known the Jackal perfectly well by now, and has tested him successfully all through his service. Hence you should keep him as your truly cherished Companion."

The Lion then summoned the Jackal, commended him warmly, and said, "I hereby apologize to you and will reinstate you in your position."

The Jackal replied: "It has been confirmed that the worst person is the one who harms his friend or companion for personal gain, and fails to treat him the way he himself would wish to be treated. Then when his friend is in the wrong, he turns a blind eye: for other ulterior motives. Such incidents often occur among friends.

"What happened between the King and me is very well known, and I beg the King not to be harsh if I tell him what I think. I do not trust him anymore, and therefore I must resign from his Court. A King should never keep in his circle of trusted Companions those upon whom he has inflicted severe punishments. He should never have rejected them in the first place, but if a person with authority has been deprived of his position, he should be treated with all due generosity."

The Lion simply ignored the Jackal's argument: "I have observed your behaviour and character with satisfaction, and tested your faithfulness, honesty, and loyalty. I discovered as well the lies of the scandalous calumniators who deceived me in order to harm you. Therefore I am willingly and sincerely reinstating you to the highest ranks of the senior nobility. A magnanimous person should forget the many harmful incidents that face him, and focus instead on the one good event that befalls him. I have resumed my complete trust in you, and expect that you reciprocate and trust in me once more. Both of us will then regain our pleasure and happiness."

The Jackal then returned to the service of the King and performed his previous duties well. The King fulfilled his promise and doubled his rewards to the Jackal, who grew ever closer to the King as the years passed by.

(The end of the Fable of The Lion and the Jackal)

Elath and Bilath and Erakht

Chapter Ten

The Fable of
Elath and Bilath and Erakht

(Forbearance is fundamental to governance)

Dabshalim the King addressed Baydaba the Philosopher: "Now that I have heard the last fable, give me another which describes the methods a king should employ to protect his kingdom and consolidate his rule. They should comprise an ideal policy. Should wise forbearance, or bold courage, or chivalrous magnanimity, or prodigal generosity be the fundamental characteristic of the monarch's governance?"

Baydaba replied, "The best method by which a king can protect his realm and ensure his power throughout his reign is a policy of wise forbearance. It is the best overall approach for a king who wishes to manage his kingdom and rule his subjects effectively: the most important trait of any successful monarch. I have the following example to evoke what I have proposed ...

Once upon a time a king named Bilath had a Vizier called Elath. This King was very devout and followed an ascetical life. One night while sleeping, he had eight different and frightening nightmares. He woke up trembling with fear, and immediately summoned the Brahmin ascetics to interpret the nightmares for him. When they had arrived and taken seats, he joined them and recounted his dream. They responded: "The King's dream may contain grave implications. If we are allowed seven days, we will surely be able to offer him the true interpretation."

The King agreed: "Very well. You have seven days as requested."

After they left the Court, they conferred in the house of one of their number and agreed as follows: "Our mastery of the highest level of scholarship provides us the means to avenge ourselves upon our enemy, the King. We remember well how this King has thus far slain twelve thousand of our brotherhood. Now that he has revealed his secret and asked us to interpret it for him, we have the perfect opportunity. Let us be baleful in our speech and terrify him into complying with all our demands. This should be our conclusion: we have conducted a very thorough study of our sacred books, and found that a terrifying evil is about to befall the King. It is an evil he can avoid, however, under certain set conditions. He must hand over to us all those whom he cherishes, and who enjoy a special place in his heart, for us to kill. Only by allowing us to slay all the people we identify can the King be saved.

"Should the King ask, 'Whom do you want to kill? Give me their names,' we shall reply: first: Queen Erakht, the most cherished of all your wives and the renowned mother of Juwair. Second: Juwair, the most beloved and honoured of your sons. Also we must have your honourable nephew, and Elath, your Companion and counsellor. In addition, we require Kala, your secretary and most trusted comrade. Also your unique sword, and the admirable white elephant who can outrun the best of horses. Then we want your war-horse and the two white elephants that are inseparable from the great male elephant, and your swift and sturdy horse from Bacht. Furthermore, we want Kabareon, the wise man and the scholar, whose knowledge of issues is vast and unparalleled. (We mean to avenge ourselves on Kabareon for what he has done to us.)

"Then we should press further, and tell the King: it is imperative that the King execute all those we identify, and collect their blood in a basin in which he should then bathe. As soon as he emerges from the basin, all of us Brahmins will gather from throughout of the world and whirl around him in circles, chanting various incantations to break the spell that haunts him. We shall spit on him, then cleanse him from the blood and anoint him with the sweetest perfume. He shall then go into his glorious palace. Thus God will exorcise the evil that he rightly dreads. Should the King survive this rite, and agree that his own safety enjoys a more urgent priority than that of those he has always cherished, whom we have identified and propose to sacrifice for his sake, then the disaster that threatens King and Kingdom will be averted. His power and authority will be maintained intact, and he will be able to name an heir of his choice. But should he fail to fulfil these demands, we fear that someone will usurp the monarchy, and he will most likely be killed shortly after.

"Then, after the King complies and executes our requests, we shall kill him in the most ghastly and fitting manner we can devise."

On the seventh day, when their conspiracy was complete, they returned to the King and announced, "We have searched our books to enable us interpret the King's dreams, and have discussed the matter among ourselves. May the most pious and righteous King's generosity be maintained forever! We come to lay before him our interpretation, but this requires that we meet with him alone, without either Companions or counsellors."

The King instructed the rest of the Court to leave, and when they were alone the Brahmin Ascetics gave him the reply they had agreed upon. The King, in frantic distress, replied: "Death is far better to me than life if I must order the death of those I love as my own self. I am going to die in any case, and life is too short to carry such a burden. I shall not be King forever. Death, and separation from the ones I most love, amount to the same thing."

The Brahmins replied: "You are mistaken, O King, if you imagine that others' lives are more precious than your own. Your priority must be to preserve yourself together with the realm, and to pursue your great hopes and expectations with confidence and conviction. You should rejoice in your Kingdom and in the subjects who have honoured and admired you. You must not be overcome by the lesser issues and leave the graver ones unattended, lest you abandon those for whom you have manifested deep love and affection. You must understand, O King, that people love life only because they love themselves. No one loves another for any other reason than to enjoy his or her company while alive. Second to God only, your own person must come first before anyone else in this life. Your next priority must be the safety of our Kingdom, which you have blessed with your diligent and persistent efforts all through the years and months of your reign. You should not underestimate the value of your own person, nor sacrifice it for others. You should listen to us, follow your own hopes and ambitions, and ignore everything else. The King has nothing to fear."

Upon hearing the harsh and arrogant words of the Brahmins, the King's distress and suffering overcame him. He left them, fled to his chamber, and fell on his face weeping and squirming like a fish out of the water.

He murmured: "I do not know which would be more devastating: losing my Kingdom, or killing those I love most? In either case, I would never be happy as long as I lived. I know I shall not reign forever, and I am not obsessed with being a monarch. But I will forego all the pleasures of life if I lose Erakht. How can I administer my realm without my minister Elath? How could I bear losing both my white elephants and my great horse? More importantly, how can I be called King again if I kill those identified by the Brahmins? And what kind of life is left to me in this world if my loved ones are all gone?"

The news of the great ordeal and suffering of the King spread through the Kingdom. When Elath realized the deep suffering and pain the King was going through, he gave it deep thought. He brought to bear all the wisdom and perspective he had accumulated, in order to save the King from this predicament. This was his conclusion: "It would not be appropriate for me to visit the King and inquire about this matter without his invitation and permission."

So he decided to go to Erakht and speak with her. When he met her he said, "Since the day I joined the service of our King, he has never acted on anything before asking my counsel and opinion. Now I feel he is concealing something unknown to me, but I have no clue what it might be. I recall, however, that several nights ago he spent quite a long time behind closed doors with a delegation of Brahmins. I am worried that he may have told them some of his secrets, which could have prompted them to give him evil and mischievous advice. Please go to him and ask about whatever grave concern has tormented and overwhelmed him, and share your conversation with me afterward. I am not at liberty now to go in and visit with him unless summoned. Perhaps the Brahmins have inveigled him into some dangerous decision, or coaxed him into some ugly and harmful acts. Experience has taught me that when kings are angry, they do not seek advice—from anyone, or about anything."

Erakht replied, "I cannot go into the King's chamber now, for our relationship these days is not at its best."

Elath answered, "This is no time for hurt feelings or anger. There is no one else who can converse with him at this moment. I have heard him say many times, 'There has never been a time when Erakht visited me without washing away my worries.' Please forgive him whatever he has done to you, go in, and talk to him gently. Turn the conversation to some pleasant topic to dissipate his grief and to refresh his spirits. The peace and security of all his subjects rests upon the King."

She agreed, and went directly into the King's Chamber. She sat beside his head and said softly, "What is bothering our Most Gracious King? What have the Brahmins suggested to you? Why are you in such deep pain and unreachable grief? If we know, we may share it and offer you all the sympathy of which we are capable."

The King answered, "My Lady, do not ask me any further questions. The more you ask, the deeper my sorrow becomes. This is a matter you should raise no more."

She replied firmly, "Have my position and favour plunged so low with the King? What have I done to deserve such a rebuff? The King knows that the most intelligent of all the wise is the one who controls himself best in times of crisis. And that person is also the one most likely in those situations to seek advice from the experienced, and more diligently than others would. With that support he becomes the most adept at grappling with his problems through counsel, discussion, analysis, and planning. Regardless of the gravity of his crime, no criminal should be paralyzed by despair, but should always look for mercy. So the King should not grieve and disable himself with sorrow and distress, for they offer no protection from Destiny. Their outcome is self-destruction, which gives comfort to no one but the enemy."

The King answered, "Ask no further questions. My heart weeps for you. The matter you ask about promises no benefit for anyone. It involves my death as well as yours, and the deaths of those in my Kingdom whom I love as dearly as I love myself. The Brahmins have proposed that I kill you and many of my Companions, who are dearer to me than life itself. Could anyone in this world face that calmly and not be paralyzed with grief?"

When Erakht heard what the King said, she trembled with fear. But she prudently composed herself so the King would not notice her dismay. She said to him, "Have no fear, O King: we will all gladly sacrifice our lives for you. All of us, the royal wives and I, will always endeavour to please you. But I must ask you a favour, for the sake of nothing but my love and devotion to you. You must take it as my most straightforward and sincere form of support."

"What is it?" he inquired.

She said: "My request is that you will never again trust any of the Brahmins, nor seek their advice, until you are sure of yourself. Even then, you must discuss it more than once beforehand, with your trusted advisors. Murder is a grave and final deed. It is impossible to bring the dead back to life. It was said in the past that if one has a jewel and thinks it is no good, one should never throw it away before showing it to an expert.

"O King, you seem oblivious to who your enemies are. You should understand that the Brahmins have good reason to dislike you. You have killed twelve thousand of them in the recent past. These Brahmins are of the same stock as those who perished at your command. By my life, you should not have told them about your dream, or discussed it with them. They have advised you to take such drastic actions because they hate you, and harbour a deep and devastating grudge against you. They hope to liquidate you, together with your loved ones, including your minister, and thus assure their revenge. If you accept their advice and kill all those they have identified, they will then easily defeat you and seize your throne. Thus they will regain their reign of yesteryear.

"You, O King, should go without delay to Kabareon the Wise. He is a very intelligent scholar. You must tell Kabareon all that was seen in the dream, and ask for his interpretation and any other counsel you require."

The King was relieved. He called for his horse, which was promptly groomed and saddled. He mounted it and galloped off to visit with Kabareon the Wise. When he arrived, he dismounted and prostrated himself in his presence. Then he arose and stood before him, bowing deeply. Kabareon the Wise inquired, "What troubles you, O King? I see that you look uncommonly pale."

The King answered, "I have seen in my sleep the following eight dreams which I recounted to the Brahmins. I am afraid that their interpretation may unleash great evil upon me. I fear they will eventually defeat me, overthrow my rule, and usurp my throne."

The Wise Man replied, "If you wish to tell me your dreams, please do so."

The King then recounted to him all that he had seen in his dreams. The Wise Man then said, "You should not be afraid, O King, nor harbour any more sorrow.

"As for the two red fish on whose tails you dreamt of standing: they signify two messengers who will visit you from the King of Nahawan. They will be carrying a jewellery box containing two collars of glittering pearls and red rubies. Their value is four thousand pounds of pure gold.

"As for the two geese that flew up from behind and fell into your hands: they signify that you will receive two matchless horses from the King of Farasan.

"As for the serpent you saw crawling on your left leg: it signifies that you will receive from the King of Sinjeen a unique sword made of purest steel crafted as nowhere else in the world.

"As for the blood which bathed the King's body and made you red: it signifies that you will receive from the King of Kazarun a beautiful and wondrous purple cloak that emits light and shines in the dark.

"As for cleansing your body with water: it signifies that you will receive from the King of Rihzeen a cloak made of the finest linen fit only for monarchs.

"As for the White Mountain: it signifies that you will receive from the King of Kaidoor a white elephant that no thoroughbred horse can ever outrace.

"As for the fire above the King's head: it signifies that you will receive from the King of Arzan a crown set with precious pearls and rubies.

"But as for the bird that pecked the royal head: I will not consider its interpretation today. However, you ought not fret, for it does not represent any harm to you, though it implies anger, and abandoning someone you love dearly.

"Those, O King, are my interpretations of your dreams. You must rest assured that the envoys from these Kings will arrive seven days from now, and he shall receive them all."

When the King heard the interpretations from Kabareon, he prostrated himself once more in gratitude, and then returned home.

After exactly seven days, the herald announced the arrival of the royal messengers. The King prepared himself to receive them. He sat on his royal throne, and invited the nobility to be present. He received all the messengers bearing the gifts as described earlier by Kabareon the Wise.

When the King beheld all this, his appreciation for Kabareon and his knowledge was much increased and he said, "I must admit that I have exhibited a lapse of prudence by relaying my dreams to the Brahmins. This resulted in their wicked advice that I should perform all manner of savage acts. Had God not extended his mercy to me, I would have perished with all my loved ones. No one, therefore, should listen to the advice of others except for friends who enjoy sound and shrewd minds. Erakht has given me the correct advice which I have gratefully accepted, and thereby achieved the inspired outcome. Take all the gifts, set them before her, and let her choose whatever she likes."

Then he turned to Elath and said, "Take the crown, and the special royal robes, and follow me to the women's quarters." The King called for Erakht and Huraqnah. They were the most beloved of his wives. He directed Elath: "Display the crown and the robes before Erakht and let her have her choice." When this was done, Erakht chose the crown, and Huraqnah the finest of the robes.

It was customary for the King to spend alternate nights with Erakht and Huraqnah. It was also traditional that each would prepare a plate of rice with halva to offer him during his stay.

One night the King came to Erakht. She approached him, wearing the crown and carrying the tray of rice. Huraqnah took note, and prompted by pure jealousy she put on her gift of glittering clothes and intentionally passed by the King. The clothes were glowing and her face was glowing with the radiance of the sun. The King was stirred by her beauty. He turned to Erakht and admonished her, "You were foolish to choose the crown and leave the special garments, unique in our treasury, for Huraqnah to wear."

Erakht observed this admiration and praise for her rival, and was humiliated by his reproach and insinuation of stupidity. She was hurt and annoyed, lost her poise, flew into a jealous and violent rage, and struck the King with the tray, leaving the rice to drip down over his wounded face and dignity.

The King arose in high anger, summoned Elath, and said, "Have you seen how this ignorant woman treated me with such contempt? Look what she has done to me. Take her out and execute her without mercy or delay!"

Elath left the King and thought, I will not execute her before the King's anger abates. This woman has always been constant and she is gifted with acute understanding beyond any other woman or queen. This King will never discard her, particularly after she saved him from imminent death. She has done many good deeds and we all have great hope for her. I am sure he would blame and reproach me and say, "Why didn't you stay her execution until you discussed her Destiny once more with me?" Therefore I will not order her death until I see the King again. If I feel then that he is sad and repentant, I will bring her back alive to him. Thus I will save Erakht, and maintain the King's favour and the support of the people. But if I find out that he is indeed happy and at ease with his decision, executing her will not be an issue, and would not be further delayed.

Elath hurried home and delivered her to one of his trusted servants. He instructed him to guard and protect her until he found out the real intentions of the King. He then bathed his sword in blood, and hurried to the King pretending to be dismayed and sad. He addressed the King and said, "I have carried out the King's order regarding Erakht."

By that time the King's anger had abated. He remembered the beauty and comeliness of Erakht and became very disturbed. He tried to console himself, and pretended to be at peace, but he was clearly suffering and miserable. He tried to conceal his embarrassment by avoiding all mention of her. He was hoping that Elath, who enjoyed such good sense, had not really carried out the execution of Erakht. Elath had the good sense to know what was brewing in the King's mind. He said to him, "O King, you should not grieve or overwhelm himself with sorrow. That will do no good. On the contrary, the sorrow will only infect your body and eventually destroy it. You must be patient regarding matters over which you have no power. If you desire it, O King, I can divert you on any other subject you may desire."

The King replied, "Talk to me about any subject you please."

Elath began:

Once upon a time a pair of Pigeons managed to fill their nest with wheat and barley seeds. The Pigeon proposed to his partner, "If we find forage in the desert, we shall not touch the wheat and barley seeds that we have accumulated here in our nest. We shall store them instead for the winter. Then when we return to our nest we shall eat our fill."

They agreed on this. He then flew to the desert and left her behind. During the summer season, however, with its fierce heat, the seeds became dry and shrank. When the Male Pigeon returned he saw the seeds seemed much less than when he had left for the desert. He inquired angrily, "Did we not agree not to touch those seeds? Why have you ignored that and eaten from them?"

The Female Pigeon swore she never ate a single seed. She expressed regret, but in vain: he did not believe her. After heated and angry discussion, he pecked her so violently that she finally died of her wounds.

But when the rainy season commenced, and the raindrops fell on the seeds, the moisture caused them to expand and fill the nest as before. When the Pigeon observed this he realized his fatal mistake. Regret, sorrow and sharp remorse overcame him. He lay down by his companion and lamented with exquisite grief: "What use do I have now for the seeds, or even for life after your death. I call you but find you not, for I am unable to be with you ever again. Each time I think of the wrong I inflicted on you I am at a loss, since I can never reverse what I did." The Pigeon persisted in his unbearable grief, taking no food or drink, until he perished by her side.

A rational person will never rush into decisions that might carry a painful penalty—impulsive, hasty and irreversible outbursts which bring on the sort of guilt and pining that overwhelmed this Pigeon.

"I also heard the following:"

Once upon a time a man was carrying a heavy load of lentils in a sack on his head. He was homeward bound, and had to pass over a mountain. After a while he was terribly exhausted, so he put down the sack and lay down to rest. A Monkey clambered down from a nearby tree, took a handful of the lentils, and returned to his tree. But on his way up, one lentil fell down. He went after it but could not find it, and in the course of his search he lost the rest of the lentils as they slipped out of his hand.

The King may face the same situation. He has sixteen thousand other women he can enjoy at will and disport himself with whenever he pleases. But he seems to long for the only one that is no longer available.

When the King heard Elath, he dreaded that Erakht had indeed been executed. He berated his counsellor: "Why were you so inconsiderate? You purposely acted without delay. You should have acted with patience, particularly in the case of Erakht. Instead, you heard me give my order only once, and carried it out swiftly without investigating further or attempting to test my intentions."

Elath replied, "The King must know that only the words of God are final and do not change. They are the absolute truth. His words can never be replaced, nor challenged."

The King said, "You have destroyed my life and deepened my sorrow by executing Erakht."

Elath replied, "There are only two kinds of people who should grieve. The first are those who perform wicked deeds. The second are those who never performed any good deed. Their pleasure from this world and its amenities is meagre and short-lived. They will spend the longest time in regret and remorse as they face the manifold and measureless punishment later on."

The King said, "If only I could see Erakht alive, I would not grieve any more."

Elath replied, "There are only two kinds of people who should not grieve. The first are those who persist in performing daily good deeds. The second are those who never commit any wicked deed."

The King said, "It seems that I shall never see Erakht any more, after having her as my constant companion."

Elath replied, "There are only two kinds of people who cannot see. The first are the blind and the second are the mindless. The blind man cannot see the sky or its stars, the earth or its distances, the far or the near. The mindless man is the same, for he cannot tell the ugly from the beautiful, or vice from virtue."

The King said, "But if I could just see Erakht, I know I would be delighted."

Elath replied, "There are only two kinds of people that should be delighted. The first are those with strong eyesight and the second are those with an honest conscience. The first can discern things that come and go, or things far and near. The scholar can tell charitable deeds from evil ones, and thus realize what he should do to gain the rewards of the eternal home. He is able to seek his salvation and guide himself to the path of righteousness."

The King said, "We should keep our distance and be wary of you, Elath. It would seem that we must be on our guard with you."

Elath replied, "There are only two types of people from whom one should keep one's distance. The first type is a person who believes there are neither good nor sinful acts in this life, neither reward nor punishment in the eternal home, and no judgement on anyone's actions. The second is the person who pursues what is not his, listens to evil people, and follows the wicked passions of his heart."

The King said, "My hands after Erakht have become as empty as a zero.

Elath replied, "Three things only are empty like a zero: A river run dry, a kingdom with no king, and a woman without a husband.

The King said, "Your answers are very suggestive, Elath."

Elath replied, "There are only three kinds of people who can make inferences: the generous king who distributes gifts from his treasury, the woman who gives herself to the one she loves, and the scholar who pursues good deeds."

At this point Elath saw the excruciating grief that burdened the King and decided to tell him the truth. He said, "O King, you should know that Erakht is alive."

The King was overjoyed, and addressed him: "Elath, what restrained my anger was my trust in your sound advice and the honesty of your opinion. Your great knowledge prompted me to hope that you had spared the life of Erakht. Even though she committed a grave offence and spoke harshly to me, she never intended to be my enemy or to harm me. What she did was provoked by simple envy. I should not have provoked her, and should have endured what she did and said. I am very grateful to you. Please go now and quickly bring her back to me."

Elath left the King and went immediately to Erakht. He asked her to groom herself and be ready to meet the King. When she was prepared he took her directly to the King's chamber. The moment she saw him, she prostrated herself and said apologetically, "I thank God and the King for his overwhelming benevolence towards me. I am guilty of grave offence for which I do not deserve to stay alive. But my King has spared my life through his great forbearance and kindness, and his good nature and his care to fulfil his promises."

The King then replied to Elath: "Since you have given Erakht a new life by not executing her despite my orders, you shall be awarded the highest rank in the kingdom, recognized by me and with my subjects. Truly, you have given Erakht to me today as a supreme and invaluable gift. I have always been confident with your advice on all matters. But today, especially, your service deserves an increase in status and prestige. You are hereby given the authority to govern the realm in my name as you see fit, and you may pronounce judgement in any case. I hereby charge you with this absolute authority, for I have full confidence and trust in your judgement."

Elath answered, "May God prolong the King's happiness and reign! I do not deserve this for I am only his loyal servant. I ask only that the King should refrain from hasty decisions, lest he regret their impact when they draw him into grief and despair. The case of our Queen is of particular importance. She has been very sensitive to your welfare and always provided you with sound advice. She is unique in this world."

The King answered, "You have uttered the truth, Elath. I accept what you have said. From now on, I will never take hasty decisions: neither in grave matters, nor even in minor ones. I will always seek the advice and counsel of scholars and friends."

The King then rewarded Elath with numerous gifts, and gave him a free hand in dealing with the Brahmins who had advised him to kill all his loved ones. He went to battle against them and slew them by the sword. The King and his nobility were very pleased by this outcome.

They all thanked God, and then praised Kabareon for the depth of his knowledge. Through his wisdom and judicial faculties, he had provided the King with prudent advice and thus saved the King, his minister, and the King's good wife.

(The end of the Fable of Elath and Bilath and Erakht)

Chapter Eleven

Mihriz, King of the Rats

(Rational advisors are indispensable for sound governance)

The King addressed the Philosopher: "I understood your analogy about benevolent forbearance by rulers toward their aides and Companions. Now, however, I would like you to tell me now how one might recruit and employ a fine advisor, and what benefits wise advisors should offer."

The Philosopher replied, "That may be easily explained by the fable of the King of the Rats and his wise advisor, who saved him and his people and delivered them from grave predicaments."

The King asked, "How does the story go?"

The Philosopher began to recite ...

Once upon a time, a rat named Mihriz lived in the city of Badrur, which lay in the region called Dawrat, and occupied an area of a thousand parasangs in the Brahmin country. It was quite large and its population lived rather comfortably. Mihriz the Rat was the King of all the rats in that city and region. He had three Viziers whom he always consulted. One of them was called Rawthabad, who was very shrewd; the King greatly appreciated his reasoning and astute policy advice. The second was called Shirᶜa and the third, Baghdad. The King always conferred with the three of them on issues related to the welfare of his subjects.

One day they met and thrashed out many issues, until they came to this question: "Are we, or are we not, able to eradicate the instinctive fear of cats we inherited from our ancestors?"

The two Viziers Shirᶜa and Baghdad said, "The King is our sovereign, for he possesses the broadest vision and soundest judgment. It has been confirmed in the past that certain predicaments cannot be resolved except by wise folk who consistently define and pursue the people's goals. We rely on the benevolent forbearance of the King, on his wisdom and prudent planning, in this and all other issues. We derive a personal benefit from all the King's commands, for whatever the outcome, we stand to share in the King's great and enduring fame. All the rats, and the two of us in particular, can be depended upon to execute the King's bidding, especially as regards the cats, even at the risk of our lives."

When the two had finished their speech the King turned to the third Vizier. When he did not utter a word the King addressed him with impatience, "You there, you could have shared what you think on this issue rather than sitting there deaf and dumb, incapable of offering any answer!" When the Vizier heard the King's slight he answered, "The King should not have admonished me for my silence, for I have purposely waited to listen to all my colleagues had to say, so as to consider their judgement before offering mine."

The King answered, "Then now is the time to deliver your own thoughts."

He replied, "I have nothing more to add than this. If the King has in mind some means to this end, and has thought them through, then the King should proceed. If not, then he should neither engage the issue nor waste energy discussing it.

"It is a fact that children inherit from their fathers and forebears both general family characteristics and individual character traits. None of these hereditary traits can be altered: not even by an angel, let alone ordinary humans."

The King commented, "Neither hereditary personality traits nor any others, no matter how minor, can function beneficially without divine providence and intervention. Furthermore though everything must come to a specific end at a specific time, that finale is unknown to any human being. However, our lives under that providence and intervention require thorough foresight on our part, just as the eyesight requires the sunlight."

The Vizier replied, "What the King says is truly said. But when the chosen means to an end fail, and since resistance to hereditary personality traits is all in vain, then it is far better not to attempt any further initiatives. For whoever resists his hereditary makeup resembles someone who defaults on a contract. The result may then be even more disastrous than it might have been, with detrimental and irreversible consequences. What occurred to one of the well-known kings is a good example of this dilemma."

The King said, "How does the story go?"

Then Rawthabad the Vizier answered.

Once upon a time, a King lived in a palace close to the Nile. In his country there was an imposing mountain with plenty of trees, plants, fruits and springs. The wild beasts and the rest of the animals all foraged on that mountain. It also happened that on this mountain there was a tunnel from which poured forth one-seventh of all the winds from three-and-a-half regions of the world. It further happened that the King's very beautiful palace, which was exquisitely designed and without any match in the whole world, stood quite near that tunnel. The King lived there, as had his predecessors before him, and none of them imagined they would ever leave it or abandon the place.

One day the King consulted his most reliable Vizier and said, "You are aware that the gracious actions of our fathers have provided our abundant life here and now, and you know as well that all matters of state are now managed to our satisfaction. However, this house that we live in, ideal in every other respect, sits in a vortex of howling winds. If there were something we could do about that, it would provide the final satisfaction. It might then seem as if we had created Paradise in this present world, not to mention the glorious legacy that we would bequeath to posterity."

The Vizier answered, "I am your loyal servant and will execute your commands promptly."

The King replied, "This is not the answer I sought. I want you to tell me what you propose."

The Vizier replied, "At this moment, I have no other answer except this, for the King is more knowledgeable, wise and honourable than I. What you have proposed can never be accomplished except through divine providence. Such an awesome accomplishment is far beyond the power of ordinary people.

"It is improper for unimportant people to meddle in matters beyond them. Therefore it is the King's own responsibility to contemplate and choose a course of action himself. If he knows the means by which we can achieve our goal, and can correctly evaluate the good and the evil results that may ensue, then let him proceed. But if he does not, then it is only prudent to give this matter no further attention, and lose no more time on it.

"It is easy enough to talk about this issue now. But the possible consequences of chosen measures are always unknown to humans and quite difficult to anticipate. Therefore you must delve deeply in the issue and scrutinize it carefully; otherwise you may be hurt just like the donkey who set out to grow horns, but lost his ears instead.

The King asked, "What happened?"

Rawthabad the Vizier replied:

Once upon a time a man owned a Donkey. He continuously fed and fattened him well. Over time, the Donkey began to feel more frisky; he developed a raging appetite and lived in a prolonged state of excitement. One day, the owner drove the Donkey to a river to drink. There he saw a Jenny from afar. He was promptly aroused, brayed, and became agitated. Fearing that his Donkey might tear loose and run away, the owner tied

The Donkey and the Stag

him to a tree by the bank of the river. He then approached the owner of the Jenny and asked him to remove her, which he promptly did. Meanwhile, however, the Donkey kept circling the tree with increasing excitement and lust.

While his owner was watching and waiting for the Donkey to calm down, it happened that a Stag with great antlers also came with his owner to the river to drink. The Stag and the Donkey exchanged looks. The Donkey was immensely impressed by the many horns the Stag had. He knew immediately what was his real heart's desire. Deep in his mind he thought: "The Stag must have developed many horns because he had a lot of lances, bows and other arms. He must be a very skilful knight. If by any chance I could escape from my current position, I would definitely associate myself with this Stag, serve him loyally and execute all his commands. I would be ready even to become a horse. On the other hand, he may treat me generously and provide me with other arms the moment he assures himself of my loyalty and realizes the value of the advice I will render to him. If God had not willed that I should experience this unprecedented happiness, I am sure he would not have sent this Stag my way."

It also happened that when the Stag noticed the restlessness of the donkey he was fascinated and unable to drink. The Donkey then thought, "I see he is smitten by my handsome and intelligent looks."

When the owner of the Stag saw that his beast was not drinking, he drove him back home, which was quite close to the bank where the Donkey was tied. The Donkey carefully watched the Stag's path, and committed to memory a landmark that would allow him to find his way there in the future. The owner of the Donkey then took him home, tied him to his trough, and filled it with fodder. But alas the Donkey could neither eat nor drink, for his heart was busy with the thought of the Stag. He thought, "I must run off to him tonight." While his owner was busy that night eating and drinking at table with his friends, the Donkey exerted enough force to free himself from his halter, and ran off to the house of the Stag.

There the Donkey found the door firmly closed. When he looked through a crack in the door, he saw the Stag free from his halter too. Despite his excitement the Donkey did not want the people in the neighbourhood to see him, so he decided to hide just around the corner of the house until the next morning. Early the next day the Stag's owner drove him again to the river to drink, leading him by his halter. When the Donkey saw this he followed the Stag and found an opportunity to talk to him. But since the Stag did not understand the language of the Donkeys, he was violently startled and began attacking the Donkey. The owner looked back and realized what had happened. He promptly pulled out his stick and began beating the Donkey severely.

The Donkey quickly thought, "I am sure that this man is the only obstacle that stands between the Stag and me. He must be the only reason why I cannot talk to him, reassure him of my goodwill, enter his employment, and provide him with my services." Savagely, he then sprang on the man and bit his back so fiercely that the man could not free himself except after a tortured and painful struggle. The man then thought, " If I forgive the Donkey now, I may not be able to avoid his evil acts in the future. I must therefore mark him so I can avenge myself on his owner when I see him later." He pulled out his sharp knife, hacked off the Donkey's ear, and sent him home in torment. But upon his return the Donkey suffered worse from his owner's punishing rod than from the excruciating pain of his severed ear.

At that moment, the Donkey thought, "I must admit that my forefathers were more capable than I about such matters. They must have refrained from many pursuits when they realized the punishing consequences of failure."

The King then said, "I have listened to your fable, but you really should not worry about this issue. I am sure, God willing, that if we fail to achieve what we hope for, no harm should afflict either of us. I assure you that we are able to safeguard ourselves from all unwarranted results." When the Vizier noted that the King was adamant in pursuing his goal, he offered no further objection, and simply prayed for his success.

It came to pass that the King ordered his messengers to call on all his subjects, young and old, and requested that each of them bring a load of wood on a certain day in a certain month. All of the people complied. The King knew the exact time when the wind's intensity would be at its minimum. At that precise moment he commanded his people quickly to erect in the mouth of the tunnel a solid wall made of stone, wood and sand to block the wind, and the wind ceased blowing through the tunnel. Consequently all breeze and wind—even what was necessary— died out. The trees became desiccated and the lakes and rivers dried up. Six months later all the springs in the mountain had run dry, and the green plants and trees over an area of more than one hundred parasangs died. The cattle and the rest of the animals also faced a similar fate, resulting in the spread of illnesses and diseases that killed a great portion of the population.

As the catastrophe raged through the country, the survivors revolted, marched on the palace, and killed the King, and his Vizier along with his entire family. The mob then headed for the tunnel. They demolished the solid wall they had previously built, carried away the stones that blocked the mouth of the tunnel, and kindled the wood they had previously collected. The wind had been cooped up in the tunnel for six months, and it blustered forth so vehemently with such vehemence that it blew the fire from the burning wood over all the regions of the country. For two days and two nights fire devastated the towns, villages and forts that scattered all over the land.

"I have given you this fable to draw your attention to the fact that what is acquired through hereditary and natural factors is too difficult to eliminate. If anyone wishes nevertheless to embark on a certain means to achieve a specific end, it is advisable first to find a wise person to discuss it, and to consult with him at length. If such a person is not available, he should then consult with his people, and probe and investigate with them all kinds of evidence before taking any action. By taking this precaution one may become more knowledgeable about the results of his actions. He would then be more able to evaluate them intelligently— though only after thorough investigation and careful scrutiny ..."

When Mihriz the King heard all this he began consulting with his three Viziers in ascending order. He asked the youngest, "What is your opinion regarding the problem we now face, and what should we do about it?"

The Vizier answered, "I believe we should procure a lot of bells, and hang one on each of the cats' necks. Every time a cat goes back or forth we will hear the bell sounding, and thus be warned and not hurt."

The King nodded to the second Vizier and asked, "What do you think of your colleague's proposal?"

He replied: "I do not think I can support such an idea. Even if we find that many bells, who among us would have the courage and ability to approach any cat and hang the bell on its neck? Moreover, even assuming we succeed in hanging the bells on the cats' necks, we will still be unprotected from their harm, and thus fear will continue to immobilize us. Hence I believe we should all leave this city and live in the wild. Perhaps then the people of the city might realize that in our absence there is no need for the cats. Indeed, they may observe that they risk greater harm from the cats than from us. When they find out that not a single rat is living in town, they will surely turn against the cats and kill them all except the few who may find refuge far away. At that point we will return to the city and live normally as we did in the past."

The King turned to the third, Rawthabad, and asked, "What do you think of your colleague's idea?"

He replied: "I am not in favour of this idea. Our departure to the wilderness for a year will not ensure the demise of all the cats. Furthermore,

Hanging bells on the Cat's neck

we shall have to endure tremendous pain and suffering there, worse than our innate anxiety about the cats when it was our only form of hardship. Furthermore, even if we do return later to the city the situation may remain calm for only a very short while. People will surely bring back the cats after we return, for we will instinctively behave in the same corrupt manner as always. Consequently our environment of fear will be restored. Hence our endurance of all that hardship in a strange land will be all in vain."

The King then demanded, "Tell us then what you think!"

Rawthabad the Vizier replied: "I know of only one scheme that might succeed. The King must summon to his court all the rats living in the city and its vicinity. He should insist that each rat be assigned quarters in one of the local homes, large enough to lodge all the rats there at one time. Each rat would then store enough food in his quarters to feed all the rats for ten days. Every rat must open up seven holes in the walls of the house, and three into the man's wardrobe and bedroom.

"When this is accomplished, all the rats will move together into the house of a single family that owns only one cat. We shall keep careful watch at all seven holes to follow the movements of the cat so he cannot take us by surprise. I am sure that after we have his attention the houseowner will constantly be on the watch for us by one of the holes. At the opportune moment when he is thus distracted, we will slip *en masse* into his bedroom and wardrobe through the three holes, with the sole objective of messing his clothes and the bed, but without our usual aggressive thoroughness. No one will touch any food at all that might be found there.

"As soon as the owner of the house discovers this level of damage, he may think that one cat is not enough. Most likely he will acquire a second cat. We shall immediately intensify the destruction of his clothes and bed. As a result, the owner will surely observe the pattern and eventually draw this conclusion: 'With each additional increase in the number of cats the damage to my clothes and bed increases. I shall experiment now by disposing of one cat at a time to see how the situation changes, if at all.'

"As soon as he gets rid of the first cat, we shall reduce the intensity of our destruction somewhat. When he disposes of the second, we shall minimize our attack to the lowest level. When he gives the boot to the third, we shall promptly leave the house. We shall then move on to the second house and repeat this operation, and so on through all the houses in the city, until the people there begin to believe that it is the cats who are the cause of all great harm. At that moment they will exterminate all the cats in the city, and then throughout all the country round about."

The King and all the rats followed the advice of Rawthabad the Vizier. Within only six months all the cats that lived in the city and its vicinity were liquidated. A generation of people was succeeded by others who for an entire century throughout the entire country were bred in a culture of hatred for cats. As a result, the moment a mouse engaged in spoilage the people would exclaim: "Look,! A cat must have passed through town." If any contagious disease struck humans or their animals, people would take it as an omen: "A cat is about to pass through the city." By dint of this scheme the rats were able to rid themselves of their innate fear of cats, and settled into a pleasant tranquillity.

This despised and weak animal schemed successfully to rid himself of his enemy, and evaded all the harm he might have inflicted. Therefore we too should not despair nor lose hope for humans as they seek their own objectives. Humans are by far the shrewdest, the wisest and the most perfect of all animals. There is no doubt that they will ultimately overcome their enemies through sound planning and efficient management ...

(The end of the Fable of Mihriz, King of the Rats)

The Lioness, the Archer and the Jackal

Chapter Twelve

The Fable of
the Lioness, the Archer and the Jackal
(Harm inflicted on some people may soften their hearts)

Dabshalim the King addressed Baydaba the Philosopher: "Now that I have heard the last fable, tell me another which describes a person who willingly and rationally restrains himself from harming others when he realizes that he might be afflicted by a similar disaster. His fear of such a possible ordeal will serve as a warning to him and should be forceful enough to restrain him from aggressive and unjust treatment of others."

The Philosopher replied: "Only the insolent and the irrational pursue actions that injure and impair others. Such people misjudge the implications of their actions with respect to this world and the next. They may fail to perceive the gravity of their deeds, or the severe punishment they will have to face, or the ultimate consequences of their unwise and irrational actions. We may be aware that a few may have escaped the fatal consequences of their harmful deeds in this life. But that is only because their untimely and sudden death has postponed the wrathful retribution they have earned. Whoever does not evaluate the possible consequences of his action can never reasonably expect to avoid the catastrophe he provokes. An ignorant person, however, may possibly learn appropriate lessons from the harm that others inflict on him, and then restrain himself from further aggression or oppression towards others. Thus he may himself escape from similar and inevitable retribution.

"The fable of the Lioness, the Archer, and the Jackal is an example of what I have just proposed."

The King said, "How does the story go?

The Philosopher answered ...

Once upon a time a Lioness lived in a forest. She had two cubs of her own. One day she left them in their cave and went out hunting for food. Meanwhile an archer passed by and saw the cubs. He hunted them with his arrows and finally killed them both. He skinned them, put their pelts in his bag, and returned home, leaving their carcasses behind.

The Lioness returned to her cubs, but when she saw them dead she could not bear the calamity. Her body ached with severe and painful

225

tremors. She bellowed and roared with grief and agony. A Jackal happened to live close by and heard her anguished roar. He came running and asked, "What catastrophe has struck? Tell me."

The Lioness explained, "Both my cubs have been killed by an archer. He skinned them and left them dead on the bare ground."

The Jackal said, "Be fair to yourself and stop this wailing. You must understand that the archer has not inflicted any harm on you. Of course you grieve for your loss, but it is no different from what you have inflicted on many others. They lost their loved ones just as you now have lost yours, and now you are now feeling what you made them feel. It was said in the past, "You will be judged in the same way you judge others." Each action will beget a reaction of proportionate reward or punishment. You know that the quality and quantity of the harvest is usually related to the quality and quantity of the seeds."

The Lioness answered, "Please go on, and elaborate on what you have just said, and explain what is intended by it."

The Jackal replied, "Tell me first: how old are you now?"

The Lioness said, "One hundred years old."

The Jackal asked, "What has composed your diet?"

The Lioness answered, "The meat of beasts."

The Jackal asked, "Who fed you with it?"

The Lioness replied, "I hunted my own prey, and ate it."

The Jackal asked, "Did those beasts you used to eat have fathers and mothers?"

She said, "Yes they did."

The Jackal said, "Then why don't I hear the painful cries of those mothers and fathers similar to the miserable roaring I hear from you? You must know that the catastrophe that befell you followed from your lack of forethought about the results of your own actions. You have always acted without serious reflection about consequences, and an irresponsible thoughtlessness and lack of consideration for what your belligerent acts against others might provoke by way of retaliation."

When the Lioness heard the Jackal's explanation, she understood that she had simply reaped the fruits of her oppressive and unjust deeds to others. She repented, and decided to quit hunting other beasts and to abstain from meat altogether. She began to eat only fruit, and followed an ascetic and pious routine.

It happened that a Pigeon named Warshan, whose life depended on the fruit in that forest, nervously observed the Lioness' new lifestyle and novel eating habits. He pluckily approached her one day and said: "I was under the impression that the trees around us did not bear fruit this year due to drought. But when I saw you eating them, I understood what had become of the fruit. Why are you doing this? You are a carnivore, by nature. You have decided to turn away from meat, which had been your natural diet, and encroached on the main staple of others, thus reducing our supply to a minimum. I now realize that the trees did actually bear a harvest this year as they had in the past, and that you are the sole cause for the shortage. You have become a disaster for the trees, for the fruit, and for those creatures whose lives depend on them. They will quickly perish if others not normally destined to share their rations intrude into their lives and impose their will on them."

When the Lioness heard the words of Warshan the Pigeon, she abstained from eating the fruit and began to consume grass as her only food, and became an exceedingly devout ascetic ...

Baydaba concluded: "I have given you this example to show you that an ignorant person may hurt himself by simply refraining from harming others. The Lioness stopped eating flesh, which was her natural staple, as a result of the distressing death of her cubs. Then she abstained from eating fruit as a result of the complaint of Warshan the Pigeon. From start to finish she pursued an ascetical and pious way of life.

"These same issues should mean more to humans than to the lowly animals. This has been also corroborated by what the elders have said in the past, 'Do not do unto others what you do not want done unto yourself.' That calls for justice, and justice attracts both God's blessing and the people's approval.

(The end of the Fable of the Lioness, the Archer, and the Jackal)

The Ascetic and the Guest

Chapter Thirteen

The Fable of
the Ascetic and his Guest

(Performing duties beyond one's expertise is futile)

Dabshalim the King said to Baydaba the Philosopher, "Now that I have heard the previous fable, give me another which describes the person who does not focus on matters in which he is proficient. Instead, he concentrates on matters beyond his abilities, and loses himself in an awkward state of confusion and indecision."

The Philosopher replied ...

Once upon a time a pious and energetic Ascetic lived in the land of al-Karakh. One day a Guest came to visit him. To welcome his guest the Ascetic offered him some delicious dates, which they enjoyed together.

The Guest admired the dates and said, "These dates are very sweet and tasty. We have nothing like them where I live. I wish we had some there." Then he added, "I hope you could assist me in obtaining a few palm trees to plant in my home town. I have never studied the plants of your area nor their habitats."

The Ascetic replied, "Your proposition may be impractical, and your efforts all in vain. Our plants might not agree with your soil, even though your region may be hospitable to a wide range of other fruit-bearing trees. I also think that with the many types of fruit your area supports, you may not need another variety. Furthermore, the date palm is quite messy and might prove unhealthy to the people."

The Ascetic went further: "A person who seeks what may be unattainable is considered unwise. You will be very fortunate if you are content with what you have achieved already, and forego the pursuit of the unattainable."

The Ascetic had been communicating with his Guest in fluent Hebrew. That attracted the admiration of his Guest, who promptly decided to learn the language. He worked on it diligently for a few days.

One day, the Ascetic addressed him, "You are forsaking your own language in favour of Hebrew. I am afraid you may end up in an awkward situation similar to that of the Crow."

The Guest asked, "How does the story go?"

The Ascetic recounted: "Once upon a time a Crow saw and greatly admired the way a Quail pranced about. He wished to emulate her and adopt her gait. He exercised diligently but could not master it, and eventually lapsed into a depression.

"He decided then to resume his original gait, but to his dismay he could no longer walk gracefully as he had in the past. He became confused and began to regress. His eventual manner of walking became the ugliest among all living birds.

"I have given you this example because I observed that you left your original and natural language, and started to concentrate on Hebrew which does not suit you. I am sure you will never become proficient at it, and I fear that by the time you realized that you might have forgotten your own language. You would return to your family and countrymen one day, only to find you had the worst speech among them. I recall that it was said in the past, "Whoever attempts to acquire an ability which does not fit him, and was not handed on to him by his father and forefathers, and replaces rather than supplements his native abilities, is simply considered an irrational person.""

(The end of the Fable of the Ascetic and his Guest)

The Goldsmith, the Serpent, the Monkey, and the Tiger

Chapter Fourteen

The Fable of
the Traveller and the Goldsmith

(The ungrateful response to generosity)

Dabshalim the King said to Baydaba the Philosopher, "Now that I have heard the last fable, give me another describing a person who bestows his favour on the undeserving, and expects to receive their gratitude for his action.

The Philosopher answered, "You should appreciate, O King, that the characteristics of God's creatures differ from one family to the other. None of them, however—four-legged, two-legged, or winged—is nobler than human beings. Still, among humans you will always find the crass and the noble. Among the animals, however, domesticated or wild, and the birds, you will some find that are more sincere, more defensive, more grateful, or more even-handed than some human beings.

"Therefore it is imperative that prudent monarchs, as well as others, extend their benevolence to the deserving rather than the undeserving who will show their patron no appreciation or thanks. They should engage no one in their service without examining their character and behaviour. They must seek assurances of their loyalty, geniality, and gratefulness. They should not appoint a kinsman if he cannot acquit himself of the duties of the job. By the same token, they should not refrain from offering their patronage to any stranger who is willing to serve with highest efficiency, especially one who will sacrifice himself for them out of loyalty. Such a person appreciates the true responsibilities and duties assigned to him, and performs them with diligence and grace. His sound counsel will gain him appreciation, and he will be famed for his generosity. He will be known for his honesty and broad competence, and for his readiness to notice good deeds and amiable words.

"Those who manifest these tested and trusted characteristics are worthy of the generous appreciation of kings. They should be preferred among candidates for their service, on the strength of their qualifications.

"It is like the tasks performed by a caring and competent physician. He will not rashly try to heal a sick person without a thorough prior diagnosis. He will observe the patient, and thoroughly examine and probe his veins and arteries, to find out the nature and the cause of his illness. He will be able to prescribe the right medicine only after identifying all possible symptoms.

"Similarly, a prudent person will not employ anyone, or assign him powers and responsibilities, until he examines him thoroughly. Whoever attempts, then, capriciously or hastily to entrust someone with responsibility, may disgrace himself, harm others, and compound his original irresponsibility.

"On the other hand, a person may for good reason rely upon an untested novice whose ability and reliability are unknown. Surprisingly, such a nobody may prove grateful, and outperform his betters.

"On the other hand, a prudent official may follow a rigorous regimen of inquiry before appointing anyone, but still allow a weasel to run up one of his sleeves and out the other, naïvely trusting he will not be harmed. He could, instead, be like the person who carries his falcon on his wrist: only when the falcon seizes a prey, should it be fed on prey and praise together.

"It was said in the past, 'A person with a shrewd mind should not belittle great or small people or beasts. It is always wise to test them first and see how they fare'

"Our wise men and scholars have already given an appropriate example."

The King answered, "How does the story go?"

The Philosopher answered ...

Once upon a time a group of people dug a well. One day a Goldsmith, a Serpent, a Monkey, and a fearsome Tiger fell into the well. It happened that a Traveller was passing by, had a look into the well, and saw the four desperate creatures trapped deep below.

He thought, "There is nothing more likely to assure my happiness in the eternal home than rescuing a fellow man from his enemies."

He took his rope and let it down into the well. But the Monkey was the first to grab it because of his agility. So he climbed safely up and out of the well.

The Traveller returned the rope to the well, and the Serpent quickly coiled around it and saved herself.

He dropped it for the third time, and the fearsome Tiger clung to it and climbed to safety.

The three beasts thanked him, but pleaded with him not to save the man. "Do not pull this man out of the well and save him," they urged, "for the human being is least grateful of all creatures and this one especially so."

The Monkey introduced himself, "My home is in a mountain near the city known as Nawaderakht."

The Tiger said, "My home is in a forest close to the same city."

The Serpent added, "And I live in one of that city's walls. If you ever pass by and are in need of our assistance, just call us and we will reward you for the good deeds with which you have favoured us."

The Traveller disregarded the counsel of the three creatures, threw the rope to the man in the well, and pulled him out to safety. The man in his turn knelt before him in gratitude and said, "You have done me a great favour. If you ever pass through the city of Nawaderakht, ask for my home. I am a Goldsmith, and I would like to reward you for your generous act."

The Goldsmith then hurried home and the Traveller also went his way.

It happened one day that the Traveller did go to Nawaderakht on business. There the Monkey who had knelt in gratitude and kissed his feet, received him apologetically: "Monkeys, you know, do not own anything. But please sit down for a moment and wait for me." He hurried off and returned with some delicious fruit. The Traveller ate some of it and headed towards the gate of the city.

There the Tiger received him with gratitude. He knelt with deep respect and said, "You once bestowed on me a great and generous favour. Wait here until I return." He entered a very beautiful garden nearby, and found there the daughter of the King of that city. The Tiger killed her, took her jewellery, returned to the Traveller, and presented them to him. Unaware of their source, he gladly accepted them.

The Traveller thought to himself, "If those animals rewarded me this handsomely for what I did for them, I am sure the Goldsmith will be generous as well. Even if he has no money, he might agree to sell this jewellery for me. He may get a good price for it, since he is more knowledgeable of their real worth. We could then share the proceeds."

When he visited the Goldsmith, he was generously received and invited into his house. However, when the Goldsmith saw the jewellery he recognized it immediately. He was the very artisan who had cut and set the jewels for the daughter of the King. He said to the Traveller, "Rest in my house for a while until I get you better food from outside, for I am not satisfied with what I have to offer."

The Goldsmith was in great turmoil, and said to himself, "This is my opportunity to become wealthy. I will go to the King and tell him what I have seen. I am sure he will reward me generously, and I will then enjoy his high regard."

He hurried to the Court and sent the King the following message, "The person who killed your daughter and stole her jewellery is in my house."

The King sent his soldiers who brought the Traveller before him. When he saw the jewellery he did not spare a moment for reflection, but ordered him to be immediately tortured, paraded through the city streets, and crucified.

When the soldiers began torturing him, he wept and cried and repeatedly at the top of his voice, shouting, "Had I only listened to the advice of the Monkey, the Serpent and the fierce Tiger, and accepted what they told me about the absolute ingratitude of human beings, I would have then never fallen into this catastrophe!"

It happened that the Serpent overheard him and was agonized by what had befallen the Traveller. She decided to weave a scheme to save him. The Serpent promptly slithered away, approached the King's son, and bit him. The King called all his scholars to use all kinds of incantations and magic to cure him, but to no avail.

Meanwhile the Serpent went to one of her sisters from the Djinn, recounted how the Traveller had saved her life, and described the plight he had fallen into. The Djinn sympathized with the Traveller, and went straight to the King's son. She appeared to him and said, "You will not be cured unless the man you have unjustly punished performs the appropriate incantation and charms."

Meanwhile the Serpent had swiftly gone to visit the Traveller in prison and addressed him: "This is exactly what I meant when I tried to prevent you from performing good deeds to help your fellow human being. But alas, you ignored my request."

She then brought out some paper soaked with her poison, and told him, "If they ask you to perform any magical incantations and charms for the King's son, put this piece of paper in water and have him drink its solution. Be assured that he will be cured. If the King asks about your story tell him the truth, and, please God, you will be saved!"

The King's son reported to his father that he been told there would be no cure for him unless the Traveller, who was unjustly imprisoned, performed a magical incantation and charms. The King summoned the Traveller and ordered him to do what he could.

The Traveller said, "I know nothing about incantations, but I will ask the boy to drink the special potion from this paper, and I hope he will be cured by the Grace of God."

The boy drank, and was immediately cured.

The King was delighted, and asked him about his story. The Traveller described in detail what had happened to him. When he finished, the King gave him a rich reward. He then summoned the Goldsmith and had him forthwith crucified: for his lies, for his ingratitude, and for rewarding good deeds with evil ...

The Philosopher then concluded: "There is a great lesson to be learned, and a valuable example to contemplate, in reflecting upon the actions of the Goldsmith towards the Traveller: how the Goldsmith rewarded good deeds with ill; how he reneged on his sacred pledges of gratitude given to the Traveller when his own life was in severe danger and the Traveller saved him. Furthermore, one should learn from the gratitude of the animals that rewarded the Traveller by returning his favour and saving his life. These are lessons to be considered, and thoughts to benefit those who spend the time to reflect. They exemplify the ethical behaviour that encourages virtuous deeds in favour of gracious, honest, and loyal people only, whether or not they are kinsmen. For that truly mirrors a shrewd mind, merits blessed results, and wards off unwarranted harm.

(The end of the Fable of the Traveller and the Goldsmith)

The King's Son and his Companions

Chapter Fifteen

The Fable of
the King's Son and his Companions

(Destiny is a serious explanation of life)

Dabshalim the King said to Baydaba the Philosopher, "I have heard the last fable. I am sure that a person attains prosperity by virtue of his prudent judgement and the integrity and shrewdness of his decision. Yet I still wonder how an impudent and ignorant person can occasionally achieve success and recognition, while a wise and educated person may accomplish only disaster and harm."

Baydaba replied: "Just as a human being does not see except through his eyes, nor hear but through his ears, a person accomplishes nothing except by his industry. Achievement is attained through patient forbearance, the application of a shrewd mind, and constant verification of facts. Yet when all is said and done, it is still Destiny that will always override everything else.

"One can see that exemplified in the fable of the King's Son and His Companions."

The King asked, "How does the story go?"

The Philosopher began his narrative ...

Once upon a time four persons were travelling together on the same road. The first was the Son of a King; the second, the Son of a Merchant; the third, the very handsome Son of a Nobleman; and the fourth, the Son of a Ploughman. All of them were living at that time like paupers. They were lost in a foreign land, hurt, starving, exhausted, and possessed of nothing but the clothes they wore.

As they walked along, each one told of his past, and described the advantages and mode of life he had previously pursued and enjoyed.

The King's Son said, "You know, this life is determined by Destiny. Whatever is destined to happen to any human being will surely be fulfilled. The best and only thing one can do in the face of Destiny is to wait in placid patience."

The Merchant's Son said, "The shrewd mind is superior to everything else."

The handsome Nobleman's Son said, "Beauty is far more important than what both of you have suggested."

The Son of the Ploughman said, "Nothing in this world is worth more than hard work."

When these comrades arrived at the outskirts of a city called Matrun they rested for a while to discuss what they should do. The first to be addressed was the Ploughman's Son: "Why don't you go into the city and get us something to eat through your hard work?"

The Ploughman's Son agreed and went to the city. He asked the people he met to suggest a task that would allow him, through hard work, to earn enough food for four persons. Everyone suggested he work as a woodcutter. They said it was best for his purposes since wood was very valuable. The forest was located about a league from the city. He walked there, secured work as a woodcutter for one day, and diligently managed to cut a cord of wood. He then transported it to the city and sold it for one dirham. With that money he bought enough food for all of his comrades. Before he left the city, however, he wrote on its gate: "The value of hard labour is one dirham per day." Then he took the food and went to find his friends, who happily shared it.

The next morning they all said, "It is now the turn of the one who said nothing is better than beauty." The Son of the Nobleman muttered, "I am not good at anything. I have no idea what to do when I get to the city." But he was ashamed to think of returning to his friends without any food. So, after considering running off, he proceeded to the city. Unprepared to do anything, he sat down beneath a tree to rest, leaned back on the trunk, and fell asleep. To his good fortune, a very wealthy man of status happened to pass by. He admired the young man's beauty, which he took as a sign of nobility. He sympathized with him and gave him five hundred dirhams. Before he left the city, however, the handsome Nobleman's Son wrote on its gate: "The value of beauty is five hundred dirhams per day." Then he returned to his companions and shared with them the five hundred dirhams.

On the third morning, they said to the Merchant's Son, "It is your turn today to go to the city and try to get us something by using your shrewd mind." He went to the city and looked around. He noticed a merchant ship with a cargo of goods and commodities, which had just anchored at the shore. He also observed a few local traders approaching it with the intention of purchasing the entire cargo. They had gathered near the ship and were discussing the matter. He overheard them scheming: "Let us walk off without purchasing anything, despite the demand for such commodities. When the owners fear that no one plans to buy them they will sell at a reduced price." He recognized the opportunity and directly went to the owners of the ship without anyone noticing. He agreed with them on a futures contract at a value of one hundred thousand dinars.

He then let out that he was planning to ship the goods to another city. When the traders heard the news, they feared that they would lose all opportunity of buying the commodities, so they finally made a deal with him at double his cost. He was thus able to honour his first agreement with the shippers, and come away with a net profit of one hundred thousand dinars. Before returning to his companions with his money, the Merchant's Son wrote on the gate of the city, "The value of a shrewd mind for one day is one hundred thousand dinars."

On the fourth day the comrades told the King's Son, "It is now your turn. Let us see what benefits your Destiny can yield for us." He agreed, proceeded to the city, and sat by the gate with a feeling of uselessness. It happened that the childless King of that city died that day without issue to succeed him. The King's funeral cortège passed through the gate, and all the people exhibited deep grief for the death of their King, except for this young visitor. The people of the city resented his attitude, and the gatekeeper cursed and scolded him. He asked him angrily, "Who do you think you are, stranger? What business do you have sitting beside the gate of our city, and not exhibiting a respectable grief for the death of our King?" The gatekeeper then angrily chased him away.

The young man returned after all of them had passed, and sat down again in the same place. But after the burial the city notables and the rest of the people were returning from the cemetery and the gatekeeper espied him again. He flew into a wild rage and addressed him, "Didn't I order you not to sit here?"

He seized the young man and promptly threw him in jail. The next morning the city council conferred to decide on the future king. Rivalry between them was intense, however, and mutual suspicion, to the point where they were in a deadlock. Then the gatekeeper unexpectedly broke in to report: "I must inform you that yesterday I saw a young man sitting at the gate of our city. He did not seem to show any grief for the death of our King. He had nothing to say for himself, so I chased him away. When I came back from the cemetery, I saw him again sitting at the gate. Fearing he might be a spy, I threw him in jail."

The notables of the city decided to summon the young man. When he arrived, they asked him to identify himself and explain what he was doing in their city. He replied, "I am the son of the King of Fayrawan. When my father died, my brother usurped my right to succeed as King. I fled certain death and became a wanderer and eventually I came to this city."

After he had told his story he was recognized by a few who had visited Fayrawan in the past, and they spoke well of his father. The notables then agreed to select him as their future king. It was customary in that city for a new king to mount a white elephant and exhibit himself all through the city. When he did that he passed by the gate and saw what each of his companions had written. He instructed that the following be added to the inscriptions on the gate: the fact is that hard work, beauty, a shrewd mind, and all the good or evil achievements in this world are only the results of Destiny, and predestined by God the Almighty. I have been uplifted in status, prestige and welfare through His Design and His Will alone.

He then took his throne and forthwith despatched a messenger to summon his companions. He appointed the one with the shrewd mind to his council of ministers, and the hard worker as the agricultural overseer. As for the handsome young man, he made him a wealthy man and then exiled him, fearing he might have a bad influence on his subjects.

Later he gathered all the scholars and educated people of the land and addressed them:"My friends and companions are now established in their lives and fortunes by virtue of the Grace of God the Almighty. I wish all of you would also recognize and abide by the evidence of this truth. The good fortune and welfare that was provided to me was truly predestined. It was neither my beauty, nor my mind, nor my work that brought me to this high station. When I was driven away by my brother I never expected that I would manage to earn even my daily bread, let alone station or prestige. For I have met people in this land who enjoy far more beauty, prudence and diligence than I do. It was Destiny alone that guided me as God sustained me, and through His Will bestowed on me such a revered position."

It happened that a venerable scholar was there in the crowd. He stood up and said:"What you have said to us reflects a sound mind and deep wisdom. It is your shrewd intellect and honest intentions and sharp foresight that lifted you to this venerable position. You have gained our trust and justified our hope and expectations for you. We accept what you have told us, and believe in what you have claimed. You deserve the station and the nobility of the position that God has delivered to you, for it was He who bestowed on you your prudence and intellect.

"The happiest person on earth is the one whom God provides with a sound mind and a discerning judgment. God has graced us by guiding you to our city at the moment we lost our King, and in that way He has been generous to us."

Another scholar stood up and praised the Grace of God and said:"When I was a young boy, long before I travelled through the land, I was in the service of a man of high standing. Later I realized that I must reject the comforts and pleasures of this life and follow a way of abstinence from the leisure of this world. So I left his service. With only two dinars that he had previously given me, I decided to give one dinar in alms and keep the other for myself.

"That day I went to the market to shop. There I found a bird-catcher who wanted to sell a pair of hoopoes. I bargained with him, but he refused to sell the pair for less than two dinars. I bargained strenuously but he maintained his price. So I thought at first that I would purchase only one hoopoe and leave the other. Then I reflected again, and concluded that if they were a mated pair, it would be sad to separate them from one other. I sympathized with their situation and decided to rely on God's Will and purchase them both for two dinars. My intention was to let them go free, but I was afraid that if I released them they might end up in a place full of bird catchers and be caught again, particularly since they were too weak and hungry to fly. In their situation, they were helpless.

"So I decided to carry them to a wooded place with ample food, far away from the populated urban centres. There I released them to their freedom. Off they flew and landed on a fruit tree. When they had alighted atop the tree, they thanked me dearly. I heard one of the hoopoes telling the other: 'This wandering Traveller has saved us from imminent hardship and disaster. We must reward him for his good deed. We know that hidden near the roots of this tree is a jar full of dinars. Why not tell him about it and show him where it is, to let him benefit from it?'

"I told them, 'How could you show me a treasure that no one could see, when you yourselves failed to observe the net that caught you?'

"One of them answered me, 'You must know that when Destiny strikes, it will blind all eyes to what it does not wish them to notice. In our case, Destiny blinded us to the net, but not to the treasure.'

"I dug where they indicated, and pulled out the jar made of porcelain, which was full of dinars. I wished them health and safety and told them, 'I offer my thanks and gratitude to God, who taught you the unknown while you were flying in the skies, and revealed to you what is beneath the earth.'

"They replied to me, 'You are an educated and a knowledgeable person, yet don't you know by now that Destiny trumps all, and no one can ever transcend his Destiny?'

"Now that I have told the King what I experienced, I am ready if the King instructs me to bring the money I found, and deposit it in his treasury.

"The King answered, 'The money is yours to use as you please.'

(The end of the Fable of The King's Son and his Companions)

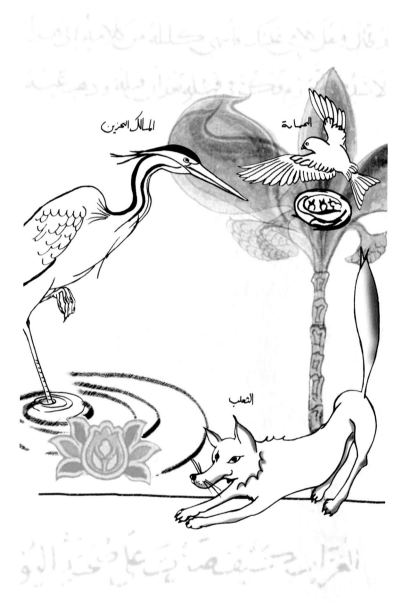

The Pigeon, the Fox and the Heron

Chapter Sixteen

The Fable of
the Pigeon, the Fox and the Heron
(Outstanding advisors to others may be failures to themselves)

The King said to the Philosopher, "Now that I have heard the last fable, offer me another that describes a situation wherein a person provides sound advice to others but not to himself."

The Philosopher replied, "The example is that of the Pigeon, the Fox and the Heron."

The King asked, "How does the story go?"

The Philosopher said ...

Once upon a time a Pigeon was in the habit of laying her eggs and raising her chicks on top of a great palm tree, which stretched high into the sky. She did so by dint of exhausting and painstaking effort, due to the distances she had to fly. After she completed the preparation of her nest, she laid her eggs and sat on them until the chicks hatched. An experienced Fox who knew the pattern of her reproductive cycle was in the habit of appearing below the palm tree. He would stand at the base and howl with all his might, and threaten the Pigeon that if she did not throw the chicks to him, he would have no choice but to climb the palm tree and devour them and her too. Terrified, she would comply and throw the chicks to the Fox.

One day a Heron flew by and landed atop the palm tree. At that time the Pigeon had two well-developed chicks. He noticed that the Pigeon was tense and distressed, so he asked her, "Pigeon, why do you look so pale and miserable?"

She answered, "My life has been ruined by a vicious Fox. He comes to the tree every time my chicks mature. He yells at me and threatens me, and I become so frightened I throw my chicks to him as he demands."

The Heron replied, "Next time he returns, just tell him, 'I am not going to throw you my chicks. If you wish, come up and find the surprise waiting for you. If you do succeed in devouring my chicks, I will fly away and save myself.' After he taught her the routine, the Heron flew away and landed on the bank of a nearby river. On schedule, the Fox came to the tree and shouted as he always did. The Pigeon replied as the

Heron had taught her.

The Fox then asked her, "Who taught you to say that?"

She answered, "The Heron"

The Fox then went down to the river, found the Heron standing there, and engaged him in conversation. "Heron, if the wind blows in from your right, where would you hide your head?"

The Heron said, "I would move it to my left."

The Fox asked, "And if it comes from your left side?"

The Heron replied, "I will move it to my right."

The Fox then asked, "But if the wind hits you from all sides?"

The Heron replied, "I would hide my head under my wing."

The Fox answered, "But how could you hide your head under your wing? I don't think you can do that!"

The Heron said, "Of course I can."

The Fox demanded, "Show me how. It seems that God has privileged you birds beyond other animals, for you seem to acquire more knowledge in one hour that we can accumulate in a whole year. You surpass anything we do. You are able to hide your heads under your wings and protect them from the cold and from the wind! Congratulations on such a gift! But show me how you do it."

The Heron complied, and hid his head under his wing. At that moment the Fox leapt upon the Heron and promptly broke his neck. He then said, "You are your own worst enemy. You successfully provide sound advice to the Pigeon, and teach her the right tricks to save herself. But when it comes to yourself, you fail to follow what you teach and advise others. Thus you fall an easy prey to your enemy."

The Fox then devoured the Heron.

(The end of the Fable of the Pigeon, the Fox, and the Heron)

Chapter Seventeen

Conclusion

By this time the King and the Philosopher had covered the full round of topics. The Philosopher then addressed the King: "I pray that the King lives a thousand years and reigns over all the seven regions of the world! May he also be provided with great wealth, and enjoy ample happiness and the love of his subjects! May Destiny assist him in all his endeavours!

"He now enjoys prodigious forbearance and knowledge, and has achieved the highest degree of thought, speech and foresight. There is no shortcoming in his shrewd mind, nor any fault or defect in his speech. He has mated resolve with compassion. He is no coward when challenged, nor impatient in distress.

"As a tribute I have collected in this book all the appropriate issues, and elaborated wholesome answers to all the King's queries. I have provided him with the best advice my judgement could devise, and the best interpretations and insights my experienced intellect could recall. This I have done to satisfy him, and to supply his good intentions with worthy ideas and sound insights for the acquittal of his responsibilities. Hence this book offers my most sage counsel and considered advice.

"Notwithstanding all that was said here, a person who summons others to perform acts of righteousness is not necessarily happier than the one who complies. Similarly, a person who provides good counsel and sound advice may not have better access to their desired outcome than those who receive the counsel and advice. By the same token, it does not follow that the person who teaches and guides others to perform beneficial deeds should be or will be happier than the pupils who follow his example.

"It is left to the King to understand what I have tried to set forth. But he should always remember that power and strength are not attained save through Almighty God, the Supreme, the Most High."